JEWISH HERITAGE TRAVEL

ALSO BY RUTH ELLEN GRUBER

Jewish Heritage Travel: A Guide to East-Central Europe

Upon the Doorposts of Thy House: Jewish Life in East-Central Europe, Yesterday and Today

Virtually Jewish: Reinventing Jewish Culture in Europe

JEWISH HERITAGE TRAVEL
A GUIDE TO EASTERN EUROPE

RUTH ELLEN GRUBER

NATIONAL GEOGRAPHIC
WASHINGTON, D.C.

For my family—then, now, and those to come

Photo credits: Cover, (Up) Omni Photo Communications, Inc./Index Stock; (Lo) Walter Bibikow/Getty Images.

All interior photographs by Ruth Ellen Gruber, except: p. 18, United States Holocaust Memorial Museum (USHMM), courtesy of Archiwum Panstwowe w Krakowie; p. 66, USHMM, courtesy of Shmuel Elhanan; p. 99, USHMM, courtesy of Amalie Petranker Salsitz; p. 139, USHMM, courtesy of Paula Kovacova; p. 183, USHMM, courtesy of Eva Halmos Kuhn; p. 213, USHMM, courtesy of George Pick; p. 251, USHMM, courtesy of Mitchell Eisen; p. 301, USHMM, courtesy of Flory Kabilio Jagoda; p. 319, USHMM, courtesy of Organization of Jews in Bulgaria.

ISBN-10: 1-4262-0046-3; ISBN-13: 978-1-4262-0046-5
Library of Congress Cataloging-in-Publication Data:
Gruber, Ruth Ellen
Jewish heritage travel: a guide to Eastern Europe / Ruth Ellen Gruber
p. cm.
Includes bibliographical references and index.
ISBN 978-1-4262-0046-5 (pbk.)
1. Jews--Europe, Eastern--History. 2. Holocaust survivors--Europe, Eastern--History 3. Europe, Eastern--Ethnic relations. 4. Jews--Travel--Europe, Eastern--Guidebooks. 5. Europe, Eastern--Guidebooks. I. Title

Founded in 1888, the National Geographic Society is one of the largest nonprofit scientific and educational organizations in the world. It reaches more than 285 million people worldwide each month through its official journal, NATIONAL GEOGRAPHIC, and its four other magazines; the National Geographic Channel; television documentaries; radio programs; films; books; videos and DVDs; maps; and interactive media. National Geographic has funded more than 8,000 scientific research projects and supports an education program combating geographic illiteracy.

For more information, please call 1-800-NGS LINE (647-5463) or write to the following address:

National Geographic Society
1145 17th Street N.W.
Washington, DC 20036-4688 U.S.A.

Visit us online at www.nationalgeographic.com/books.

For information about special discounts for bulk purchases, please contact National Geographic Books Special Sales: ngspecsales@ngs.org.

Printed in U.S.A.

Interior Design: Cameron Zotter

TABLE OF CONTENTS

DENMARK
SWEDEN
LATVIA
Baltic Sea
Telšiai
Plunge
Šiauliai
Vabalninkas
Panevėžys
LITHUANIA
Kėdainiai
Ukmergė
Jonava
Joniškis
Kaunas
KALININGRAD
Russia
Vilnius
Kalvarija
Eišiškės
Sejny
Tykocin
Krynki
Białystok
POLAND
Treblinka
WARSZAWA
(Warsaw)
Karczew
GERMANY
Łódź
Kock
Piotrków Trybunalski
Kazimierz Dolny
Włodawa
Łęczna
Mladá Boleslav
Wrocław
Szydłowiec
Lublin
Luboml
Kovel
Terezín
Úštěk
Roudnice nad Labem
Częstochowa
Kielce
Chmielnik
Bečov
Jičín
Rychnov nad Kněžnou
Chęciny
Sandomierz
Zamość
(Prague) PRAHA
Pińczów
Józefów
Luc'k
Osoblaha
Nowy Korczyn
Biłgorajski
Sokal
Kolín
Działoszyce
Plzeň
(Pilsen)
Heřmanův Městec
Bełżec
Belz
Kremenets
Golčův Jenikov
Kraków
Leżajsk
CZECH REPUBLIC
Oświęcim
(Auschwitz)
Tarnów
Łańcut
Zhovkva
Busk
Brody
Polná
Boskovice
Bobowa
Rzeszów
Velké Meziříčí
Grybów
L'viv
Zolochiv
Strážný
Lomnice
Třebíč
Brno
Holešov
Nowy Sącz
Rymanów
Drohobych
Rozdil
Ivančice
Dolní Kounice
Žilina
Bardejov
Lesko
Stryj
Mikulov
Trenčín
Stary Sambir
Šaštín-Stráže
Prešov
Bolekhiv
Rohožník
SLOVAKIA
Malacky
Trnava
Košice
Uzhhorod
Bratislava
Nitra
Olaszliszka
Sátoraljaújhely
Pezinok
Lučenec
Pribeník
Šamorín
Šahy
Mád
Sadhora
Nové Zámky
Miskolc
Tokaj
Sighetu Marmaţiei
Chernivtsi
Săpânţa
Sopron
Siret
AUSTRIA
Satu Mare
Kőszeg
Pápa
Szentendre
Rădăuţi
Szombathely
BUDAPEST
Debrecen
Gura Humorului
Murska Sobota
Abony
Szolnok
Şimleu Silvaniei
Kővagóörs
Vatra Dornei
Maribor
Lendava
Apostag
Kecskemét
Oradea
Bistriţa
Nova Gorica
SLOVENIA
Ptuj
Čakovec
HUNGARY
Varaždin
Cluj-Napoca
Ljubljana
Križevci
Koprivnica
Bonyhád
Stanjel
Szeged
Târgu Mureş
Baja
Piran
Koper
Zagreb
Bjelovar
Pécs
Subotica
Arad
Alba Iulia
Rijeka
Apatin
CROATIA
Osijek
ROMAN
Timişoara
Jasenovac
Braşov
Djakovo
Novi Sad
Rab
Doboj
Zemun
SAN MARINO
BOSNIA & HERZEGOVINA
BEOGRAD
(Belgrade)
BUCUREŞTI
(Bucharest)
Zenica
ITALY
Adriatic Sea
Split
Sarajevo
Vidin
SERBIA
Rousse
Mostar
Niš
Stolac
MONTENEGRO
BULGAR
Dubrovnik
Duklja
SOFIYA
(Sofia)
Podgorica
Samokov
kilometers
0
100
200
300
Ulcinj
Skopje
Plovdiv
0
100
200
300
MACEDONIA
Stobi
miles
ALBANIA
Present-day boundaries are shown.
Bitola
GREECE

Area Enlarged
EUROPE
ASIA
AFRICA
RUSSIA
ELARUS
UKRAINE
KYIV (Kiev)
Zhytomyr
Berdychiv
KHARKHIV
Sataniv
Medzhybizh
Uman
DNEPROPETROVSK
Sharhorod
MOLDOVA
Dorohoi
Botoşani
Suceava
Fălticeni
Iaşi
Roman
Piatra Neamţ
Băcau
IA
ODESSA
Sea of Azov
Kerch
Silistra
GEORGIA
Black Sea
Varna
IA
Karnobat
Burgas
TURKEY

FOREWORD

FOR YEARS I HAD NO INTEREST IN GOING TO EASTERN EUROPE. AS RECENTLY AS THE early 1990's, when my entire livelihood was already based on work done in or about Yiddish, the East European Jewish heritage language *par excellence*, my attitude toward heritage travel—if it was even called that at the time—was one that seemed to run in my family. Asked once if he'd like to go back to Poland, my father, who was born and raised in Warsaw, did nothing but snort with derision and say, "Poland? I don't want to see it, I don't want to hear about it, I don't want to know from it. On my map of the world, there's no such place as Poland." Had this been an isolated outburst, I don't think that he would have been so careful to deliver the tirade in Polish.

At the time, most so-called Jewish heritage travel in Eastern Europe involved hasidim going to graveyards. The original edition of this book played a major part in helping to broaden the face of Jewish travel in Eastern Europe, and the fact that we now take the notion of Jewish heritage travel for granted can serve as an index of just how influential it has been.

Ruth Ellen Gruber was one of the first writers to make people like me aware of the riches that we'd been so determined to ignore. I got a brief glimpse of her methodology at our first meeting, when she was in Toronto to promote the first edition of *Jewish Heritage Travel*. The next time I saw her was in Germany, in a castle not too far from Hamelin, home of the famous Pied Piper. The castle, which had been *renovated* in the 18th century, was the site of a week-long workshop devoted to klezmer music and Yiddish culture. Advertised throughout the European Union, the event attracted roughly 40 paying customers—a remarkable number of whom are now among the foremost klezmer musicians in Europe. A small and very select group. The first person I ran into on entering the castle was, of course, Ruth Gruber, who was busy filing a story with the Canadian Broadcasting Corporation about how the castellans of Jewish culture in Germany had seen fit to invite a Canadian—me—to their event.

I don't know how she does it, but Ruth Gruber seems to know everybody everywhere. When I ran into her in the castle, she already knew me, the rest of the predominantly American staff, the people sponsoring the event, and whom to contact at the CBC in Canada in order to sell a story about a Canadian Jew teaching Yiddish in a castle in Germany; I'd spent two weeks on a fruitless hunt for the same CBC person, and I live in Toronto. By the end of the event, Ruth also knew everyone who had paid to come to the workshop. And it's the same story in Chemnitz, Prague, Budapest, or Syracuse, New York—to mention only places where I have been. Ruth seems to know exactly what's going on in every city, and exactly where it's taking place.

This is the kind of knowledge that lies at the heart of *Jewish Heritage Travel*. The typical Jewish travel itinerary in Eastern Europe owes more to this book than many latter-day experts would care to admit. Fifteen years ago, there was no itinerary; this is the book that renewed and re-drew the map of Jewish Eastern Europe for the descendants of Eastern European Jews and anybody else interested in a culture that refuses to go away. It might change, but it isn't about to leave. And thanks to this book, we now know where to find it. Ruth Gruber has done more than fulfill her ambition "to put these places on the map"; she's shown us why we need to use that map and how much we stand to gain by doing so.

— MICHAEL WEX, AUTHOR OF *Born to Kvetch*

PREFACE

BEFORE WORLD WAR II, MORE THAN SIX MILLION JEWS LIVED IN THE REGION now composed by the 14 countries included in this book. Today, as many as several hundred thousand Jews still live in Ukraine, but the total Jewish population in all the other countries combined only amounts to about 150,000. *Jewish Heritage Travel* is a guide to the many traces of Jewish culture and civilization that remain, despite the destruction of World War II and postwar communism. It is designed as a practical guidebook, as well as a sourcebook for armchair travelers.

In 1992, when *Jewish Heritage Travel* first came out, there was little awareness of the rich Jewish heritage that still existed throughout the region. Historic synagogues or Jewish cemeteries were rarely included in mainstream travel books, and there were few initiatives aimed at conserving, preserving, or presenting Jewish heritage. Fifteen years ago, the countries included in this book were just emerging from communist rule; today, more than half of them are members of the European Union. Jewish-theme tourism has become a solid niche market. National and regional travel boards feature Jewish heritage itineraries, as do many travel agencies. Accurate inventories have been carried out, and various countries have placed Jewish heritage sites on their lists of national cultural monuments. In many places, local and state bodies, as well as individuals, volunteer groups, and Jewish communities, have restored ruined synagogues and cemeteries, erected new Holocaust memorials, opened new Jewish museums, programmed Jewish culture festivals, or revitalized former Jewish quarters.

Not only that, in all these countries the collapse of communism opened up broad new horizons for Jewish life. Jewish communities throughout the region have reconstituted themselves, and thousands of people have stepped forward to claim their Jewish roots. Jewish schools have opened; Jewish clubs, courses, summer camps, and cultural events proliferate; rabbis have taken up new posts, and there is an ever increasing number of kosher facilities.

This new edition provides updated and expanded information on hundreds of sites. I have also added many new places, including dozens of sites in two new countries, Lithuania and Ukraine. It is only possible to present a small minority of the thousands of Jewish heritage sites in the region, but I have provided resources, and in particular Web links, that will help you find more. The condition of Jewish heritage sites continues to change. I welcome on-site reports from readers—and I take this opportunity to thank the many people who have written to me with their own updates and observations over the years.

Many, many people have selflessly given me their time, advice, expertise, companionship, and encouragement in the preparation of this book. It is my pleasure to thank them here. My brother, Samuel D. Gruber, a world expert in Jewish heritage preservation, was in from the beginning in more ways than one and has provided constant advice and support; our parents and the rest of our extended family have been a source of joy and inspiration. Edward Serotta and John and Judith Macgregor have been stalwart friends, sounding boards and traveling companions. I am grateful to the U.S. Commission for the Preservation of America's Heritage Abroad for enabling me to carry out research on several countries and to the American Jewish Joint Distribution Committee for helping me in some of my travels. A special nod to the JDC's Herbert Block, Amir Shaviv, and Yechiel Bar Chaim, and to Andy Baker of the American Jewish Committee. Thanks, too, to Lubos Malina for taking me to Ustek, and to Lubos, Robert Krestan, and Druha Trava, whose music kept me going.

Jewish communities and institutions all over the region welcomed me and aided me in my work. Many individuals, including pioneers in the rediscovery and documentation of Jewish heritage sites, also provided invaluable assistance. In Poland, let me thank Lena Bergman, Krzysztof Czyzewski and the Borderland Foundation, Kostek Gebert, Henryk Halkowski, Jan Jagielski, Jack and Paz Lutz, Staszek and Monika Krajewski, Monika Krawczyk, Piotr Krawczyk, Wojtek and Malgosia Ornat, Rabbi Michael Schudrich, Chris

Schwarz, Michael Traison, and Tomasz Wisniewski. In the Czech Republic, Jiri Fiedler and Arno Parik of the Prague Jewish Museum, both true trailblazers in the documentation of Jewish heritage, took time to direct and advise me. Thanks, too, to Peter Gyori, Tomas Kraus, Lilly Pavlak, the Rexa-Zapotocky family, Dinah Spritzer, and Arthur, Claire, and Thomas. Maros Borsky provided invaluable help in Slovakia, and Fero Alexander was also there for me. In Hungary, I'm grateful to Rudi Klein, Lajos Lowy, Peter Wirth, Janos Gerle, Laszlo and Judit Rajk, Antonia Szenthe, Bob Cohen, Michael Miller, and the late, and much missed, Andras Roman. Becca Lazarova, Solomon Bali, and Sally Hindman provided insights and information on Bulgaria. In the Western Balkans, the indefatigable Ivan Ceresnjes kept me on track; thanks, too, to Jakob Finci, Vlasta Kovac, Ana Lebl and Goran Niksic, Sasa Lebl (who many years ago took me to visit my first Jewish cemetery), Zdravko Sami, and the Stanic family. Deep thanks go to Zvi Feine, Alex Sivan, Tania Grinberg, the Losneanu family, Christi Ezri, Felix Koppelman, Ladislau Gyemant, Mircea Moldovan, Hari Solomon, and Odette and Mirel Blumenfeld for their help in Romania. (Oh, and *tschiers* to Johanna Householder.) In Lithuania, Irena Veisaite, Ilya and Lara Lempertas, Simas Davidovicius, Chaim Bargman, and the staff at the Multicultural Center in Kedainiai literally showed me where to go. Deep thanks to Meylakh Sheykhat, Leonid Finberg, and my stalwart drivers Yuri and Vassily for all they did for me in Ukraine. I also want to express my gratitude to my agent, Carol Mann, and her staff, and to my editor, Larry Porges, and Cameron Zotter, the book's designer, at National Geographic Books.

I have used personal communications and unpublished material by several of the people named above, as well as locally published pamphlets and the books and websites listed in the text and bibliography, as source material for historical background and up-to-date information on some sites in this guide. Some of the material included in this book has appeared previously in articles I have written for the *New York Times*, the *International Herald Tribune*, www.centropa.org, the *Jewish Telegraphic Agency*, the London *Jewish Chronicle*, and *Distinguished Traveller* magazine, as well as in reports I prepared for the U.S. Commission for the Preservation of America's Heritage Abroad and the website www.jewish-heritage-europe.org. Some material has also been drawn from my book *Upon the Doorposts of Thy House: Jewish Life in East-Central Europe, Yesterday and Today.*

— Ruth Ellen Gruber

A TRIBE OF STONES

THE SEEDS FOR THIS GUIDEBOOK WERE SOWN MANY YEARS AGO, IN THE BITTER COLD of December 1978, when my brother Sam and I accompanied Romania's then chief rabbi, Moses Rosen, on his annual Hanukkah pilgrimage to Jewish communities scattered around Romania. Over the six days we traveled with him, we visited 19 Jewish communities. People huddled in heavy overcoats; youth choirs sang, puffs of steam coming from their mouths; candles flickered in the cold. We saw big, ornate synagogues and tiny prayer rooms; old-fashioned shuls painted with beautiful zodiac signs, and shabby meeting halls with no decoration. We experienced big-city Jewish life and marveled at small towns still reminiscent of the prewar shtetls we knew only from literature. We saw the mass graves of Holocaust victims and danced the hora with young Jewish students. We were warned about how to behave in a state then tightly ruled by the communist dictator, Nicolae Ceausescu—whisper, someone told us, they listen to everything.

One of the little towns we visited was Radauti, scarcely more than a village in the very north of Romania, a few miles from what was then the Soviet border—the town our paternal grandparents had come from. One old grizzled man recalled members of our family even though our grandparents had left for the United States before World War I. We picked our way through the centuries-old Jewish cemetery, and there we found the grave of our great-grandmother, Ettel, who survived the Holocaust and died in 1947. I was given my middle name, Ellen, in her honor. Later, in a dimly lit apartment in Bucharest, I visited the only member of our family who was still living in

Romania, the brother of our grandfather, Uncle Pinkas. Pinkas was then in his 90s, "the oldest man I ever saw," I told a friend at the time. He could scarcely remember his long-gone brother Frank, who had died in Ohio half a century before.

That trip in 1978 was not primarily a search for family roots; I was a journalist writing news stories. The stop in the ancestral village and visit with Uncle Pinkas were a bonus. Still, my experiences touched a chord. Nearly 30 years have passed since then, and 15 years have gone by since the first edition of *Jewish Heritage Travel* came out in 1992. This part of Europe has undergone dramatic changes, but the chord has continued to resonate. It is a chord that I am convinced resonates deep within any Jew whose ancestry lies in Eastern and Central Europe—and also a chord whose complex harmonies cannot fail to touch the non-Jewish world as well.

A Jewish guidebook to this part of the world takes a visitor into a multidimensional shadowland of *Then, Now,* and *What Might Have Been.* It is a journey particularly important now, as the Holocaust recedes into history and the new, postcommunist democracies—more than half of them now members of the European Union—continue their development in a world where religious, ethnic, and political extremism remain powerful and worrisome forces.

Then, in the Jewish context, means before the Holocaust; the time when the region was the world's Jewish heartland, home to millions of Jews—most living in abject poverty, many solidly prosperous in their near-total assimilation, some exerting the most important cultural, economic, and intellectual influence of the time. *Then* also means the horror; the story that must be told and retold: Auschwitz, Treblinka, Belzec, Terezin, Warsaw, Lodz, Iasi, Odessa, Jasenovac, Kaunas, on and on and on. The story of the Shoah can be told in these places on the spot; visitors can walk the streets where martyrs defended doomed ghettos, make pilgrimages to the camps where millions were slaughtered, pause for prayer or reflection at monuments and memorials, and above all, see, feel, and experience the places where Jews lived for so many centuries and now live no longer.

Now is the current state of affairs. Countries whose prewar Jewish population made up a considerable part of their inhabitants now have only a handful of Jews remaining. Yet, in all the countries included in this book, the end of communism enabled a reassertion of individual and collective Jewish identity and an extraordinary revival of Jewish communal life. For the most part, today's Jewish communities are miniscule, compared to what once existed. But they are alive—and lively.

In many places now—in Prague, Cracow, and Vilnius, to name but three—there are well-kept synagogues, Jewish cemeteries, and Jewish museums that present the rich history of Jewish society. Even in some provincial towns, such as Presov, Slovakia, or Szeged, Hungary, where today's Jewish communities may number only a few dozen, or at most a few hundred, souls, there are marvelous synagogues still in at least occasional use. Since the fall of communism, thanks to efforts by Jews and non-Jews, and public, private, and international sources, many synagogues have been repaired and restored even in places where no Jews live; new Jewish museums have been opened, and many desecrated or overgrown old Jewish cemeteries have been cleared, fenced, and set right. Also, as part of postcommunist reforms, most countries included in this book have instituted some sort of process to return prewar Jewish communal property to Jewish ownership (or compensate today's Jewish communities for property that was destroyed or seized by the state).

Nonetheless, thousands of Jewish cemeteries still lie abandoned and untended across the region. Hundreds of former synagogues also languish in disrepair or have been transformed for secular purposes, some still, however, marked by Hebrew inscriptions or rusting Stars of David. Each cemetery, or ruined cemetery, and each synagogue, or ruined or transformed synagogue, is a monument to the Shoah—the Holocaust—just as much or more so than are the many constructed memorials that now commemorate the dead. What's more, the cemeteries, synagogues, and surviving old Jewish neighborhoods commemorate not just Jewish death, but the Jewish life that flourished here for so many centuries.

What Might Have Been is, thus, a musing on past and present alike—and, also, on what is to come.

As Americans, many of our collective memories and intangible links as Jews were spawned over bowls of Bubbe's Eastern European borscht and blintzes, pastrami on rye, bagels, smoked carp, and chicken soup. Many of us who have little idea of our own forebears somehow identify with the ancestral legends and portrayals embodied in the stories of Isaac Bashevis Singer, I. L. Peretz, Sholom Aleichem, Sholom Asch, or the paintings of Marc Chagall—or even the stage-set Yiddish world of *Fiddler on the Roof*. But the fact that the names on countless overgrown gravestones in countless overgrown Jewish cemeteries in Central and Eastern Europe read like the membership list of any American temple is an especially poignant reminder of how close we all are both to what was destroyed and to what has been left. So, too, are the endless lists of names found on Holocaust memorials in the region.

In preparing the various editions of this book, I traveled thousands of miles to seek out, visit, and then revisit the physical remains of a vanished civilization. Over and over again, I felt like an archaeologist, or an explorer of Atlantis. I tried always to remain detached, to investigate, to inquire, to write up descriptions of synagogue buildings and ghettos and graveyards and to ignore the ghosts who clustered around the doorways or shimmered in the shadowy depths of forests grown up around the weathered tombs. Most of the time I was successful. After all, my father is an archaeologist, and artifacts were a part of my childhood. I have lived for years in Italy, where the ruins of the ancients are a part of the landscape altogether taken for granted.

But my travels have taught me that stones are not just pieces of rock.

"To every thing there is a season and a time to every purpose under heaven," we read in Ecclesiastes. "A time to mourn and a time to dance; a time to cast away stones and a time to gather stones together."

In 1983, my friend Monika Krajewska in Warsaw published *Time of Stones (Czas Kamieni),* a coffee-table book of photographs of Poland's Jewish cemeteries. Many similar photo books have been published since. But Monika's powerful images, interspersed with quotations from the Scriptures, from poetry, or from the tombstones themselves, make *Time of Stones* unique. In an introduction to the book, the late Polish writer Anna Kamienska described the weathered tombs as

> *a tribe of stones, a people of stones, an obstinate tribe which is ever marching and ever shouting and calling voicelessly. Against the background of native grasses, trees, nettles and blackberries, exotic Hebrew letters are still talking about those who lived here and passed away. About righteous men, just and charitable, about God-fearing and loving women who toiled for others.*

No, stones are not just stones, and Jews and non-Jews alike who visit the places described in this book may find themselves dealing with a maelstrom of emotions springing from this fact. Holocaust survivors will have special emotions. But even those of us whose links with these places are more distant also will feel their power. My own experience is a case in point. Even today, the voiceless cries described by Anna Kamienska can make themselves heard when I least expect it. I have visited hundreds and hundreds of Jewish heritage sites over the years, but even now, the dignity and melancholy power of a certain building or cemetery, the grandeur of a restored synagogue, or the lonely beauty of a tombstone can bring tears to my eyes, or a sudden shiver.

Other emotions are there, too, including pride, and even elation: It is uplifting to discover Jewish relics that stretch back hundreds of years, to witness their unique appeal. Buildings very different from those constructed by Christians; glorious frescoes of Jerusalem, of lions and stags and eagles and the mythical Leviathan. Tombstones whose beautiful Hebrew inscriptions and richly ornate carvings of unique Jewish symbols—the hands of the Cohens, the vessels of the Levites, the broken candles of Death—reach out with mystical significance across the centuries. There's anger, too, of course. At the destruction. At the waste. At the whitewashing of history. And at the fact that, until a decade or so ago, few people considered Jewish heritage of much interest or importance. That's why I wrote the book in the first place—to fill in this gap of perception; to put these places on the map.

When I first researched this book, I became absolutely mesmerized, even a little obsessed with what I was seeing. I wanted to visit, touch, see, feel as many places as I could. I almost felt it a duty. As I entered broken gates or climbed over broken walls into cemeteries where a Jew may not have set foot in years, I wanted to spread my arms and embrace them all, embrace all the tombstones, all the people buried there, all the memories. Back then, my trips were voyages of discovery. Everything was new; there was little literature on the subject, and few visitors had made their way to such sites. But even today, after scholars and genealogists and tour guides have studied and mapped and documented almost everything—I still feel the pull. And I hope others do, too.

WHAT YOU WILL SEE

Within the limited scope of a guidebook, it would be impossible to include all Jewish relics and sites of Jewish interest remaining in Eastern and Central Europe. Hundreds of synagogue buildings still stand, in one form or another, and thousands of Jewish cemeteries still exist. There are Jewish museums, Jewish exhibitions, old ghettos and shtetls, and hundreds of other historic sites, including Holocaust memorials. I have tried to describe in some detail a representative selection of these places, adding briefer descriptions of a number of other sites—the length of the entry, however, does not mean that certain sites are more or less interesting than others. In addition, I have provided Internet links to a variety of websites and portals where readers can find more information, including site descriptions, photographs, history, and lists. I have also provided contact numbers, addresses, or Web links for many of the Jewish communities and institutions that now function in the region.

Jewish Cemeteries

Often referred to in Hebrew as *Bet Hayyim* (house of the living), Jewish cemeteries are the most common remaining physical relics of Jewish civilization in Eastern and Central Europe. Several thousand of them still exist, most of them ruined to one extent or another and abandoned to the elements. Aside from a few tomb inscriptions dating from ancient Roman times and other archaeological finds, and a few isolated gravestones from the 11th or 12th century, the oldest Jewish cemeteries still in existence in the region date back to the late Middle Ages; others have tombstones dating from the 16th and 17th centuries. These are found primarily in the Czech Republic, with some in Poland, Romania, and Ukraine. Most remaining Jewish cemeteries in the region were established in the 18th and 19th centuries.

The physical appearance of gravestones, called *mazzevahs* (or *mazzevot*), varies somewhat from country to country and from era to era, depending on local cultural influences and, starting in the 19th century, on the degree of Orthodoxy or acculturation of the local Jewish community.

Orthodox Jews—with some regional variation, particularly in the Balkan areas, where Sephardic Jews predominated—tended to retain the traditional stelelike form and design of mazzevot, frequently adding symbolic carving and inscriptions in Hebrew. Often, particularly in Poland, Romania, Ukraine, and parts of the Czech Republic, these carvings are very elaborate. In many cases the designs refer to the name, lineage, profession, or personal attributes of the person commemorated. Among the more common carved symbols are two hands in the spread-fingered gesture of priestly blessing on the gravestones of a Cohen (priest), that is, a descendant of the biblical high priest Aaron, the brother of Moses. Another common symbol is a pitcher, or ewer, marking tombs of Levites, or descendants of the ancient tribe of Levi, priestly assistants who traditionally washed the hands of the priests. Books mark the graves of particularly learned people; hands placing coins into charity boxes denote those who were particularly generous or philanthropic. Candlesticks often mark the tombstones of women, since in Jewish ritual women bless the candles on the Sabbath; some carvings include hands blessing the flames. Numerous gravestones bear symbols referring to death, for example, broken candles or broken trees. In northern Romania there are vivid carvings of the hand of God breaking off a branch from the Tree of Life.

The images of a variety of animals decorate many tombs. Lions, symbolizing both the tribe of Judah and personal names such as Lev or Leib, meaning "lion," are frequent motifs. Carved stags indicate names such as Zvi or Hirsch. Birds often appear, including carved eagles, which may denote power. And mythical beasts, such as the winged griffin, are also common. There is often, too, a wealth of purely decorative carving—flowers, vines, geometric forms—and various folk designs derived from both Jewish and local folk traditions. Bunches of grapes are a frequent motif in winegrowing areas. In Poland, Romania, and Ukraine especially, gravestones were often painted in bright colors, and many stones still bear traces of this decoration.

A wide variety of carving styles can be seen; in some places carving styles are so distinctive that you can discern the work of individual, now anonymous, artists. Much care, too, was devoted to elaborating the Hebrew inscriptions. Often there is no other carving on the tombstone other than the epitaph, and the decorative script serves as ornamentation in itself. Old Hebrew epitaphs can be difficult to decipher, even for fluent Hebrew speakers, but many of them follow set formulas. Most Orthodox tombstones, for example, include an abbreviation for the phrase, "May his/her soul be bound up in the bond of life." (*A Field Guide to Visiting a Jewish Cemetery*, a recent book by Rabbi Joshua Segal, provides help in reading at least names and basic phrases.)

Famous rabbis, scholars, or other particularly revered people were sometimes buried in more elaborate tombs or mausoleums. These are often places of pilgrimage. Visitors place pebbles or candles on the tombs and often leave messages or prayers written on paper, known as *kvittels* (or *kvittleh*). Around the tombs of some of the great rabbis, and particularly those of revered Hasidic rebbes, or tzaddikim, modern followers have erected buildings or other protective shelters. These are know as *ohels,* from the Hebrew word meaning "tent" or "tabernacle."

In the 19th century, tomb inscriptions in local languages began appearing. Non-Orthodox Jews in particular eventually erected elaborate grave markers similar to those erected by the contemporary non-Jewish community. Some gravestones even incorporated portraits or laminated photographs of the deceased. Even these, however, often retained the traditional convention of writing the Hebrew letters *P N* or *P T*—the abbreviation for the words meaning "Here Lies"—above the epitaph.

Some Jewish cemeteries have a ceremonial hall near the entrance or on the grounds, where bodies were prepared for burial.

Synagogues

Hundreds of synagogue buildings still remain in the region, though most—including the dozens of extraordinary and often grandiose wooden synagogues erected in Poland, Lithuania, Belarus, and Ukraine between the 17th and the 20th century—were destroyed during or after World War II. The Nazis carried out a systematic program of defiling or destroying thousands of synagogues, beginning with the infamous Kristallnacht pogrom, or Night of Broken Glass, on November 9 to 10, 1938, when scores of synagogues in Germany and German-occupied territories were torched and ravaged. During the war years, local Jews were sometimes forced to help in the destruction; in some cases, such as in Bialystok, Poland, Jews were herded into a synagogue before it was set on fire. The destruction of synagogues continued under communist regimes. In some countries, more synagogues were destroyed after World War II than during the war.

The synagogues still standing range from several medieval synagogues to several big structures erected in the 1930s. Their conditions vary widely, from devastated shells or those used as warehouses and workshops, to those that have been totally rebuilt so that nothing remains to identify them as former synagogues, to some that have been beautifully restored and used as museums or for other cultural purposes. Only a small minority are still used as synagogues.

Architectural styles also span a broad spectrum, from medieval Gothic to the grandiose temples erected after Jewish emancipation in the mid-19th century. In parts of Ukraine and Poland, a number of monumental, fortress-style synagogues dating back to the 17th century or earlier remain standing, and a small number of very simple wooden synagogues survive in Lithuania. The one constant is that synagogues were almost always built in such a way as to never resemble or be mistaken for a Christian church. Indeed, under many Christian rulers, they were forbidden to do so. Sometimes synagogues were also forbidden to be taller than nearby churches, so some were built with foundations below ground level.

Elements found in synagogues:

- **Aron ha Kodesh,** or Holy Ark—This is the place where the Torah scrolls were (or are still) kept, built against or set into the eastern wall of the synagogue sanctuary. It often had rich decoration, and even in ruined buildings it is often possible to see where it was.

• **Bimah,** or place from which the Torah was read (similar to a pulpit)—In Conservative and Reform synagogues, the bimah tends to be in front, a platform beneath the Ark. In Orthodox synagogues, the bimah is characteristically in the center of the sanctuary, sometimes set off by an iron grille or other barrier. A typical Polish architectural style was to construct the synagogue around a central bimah whose four massive pillars rose to the ceiling and supported the vaulting. These four pillars are all that remains of the Old Synagogue in Tarnow, Poland.

• **Womens' gallery** or section—In Orthodox Jewish practice, women are separated from men in the synagogue. In some places, women prayed in side rooms or annexes. Others had an upper gallery reserved for women.

• **Fresco decoration**—Many old synagogues had beautiful wall and ceiling paintings that survive to some extent. Often these designs had biblical themes or encompassed religious texts. Ashkenazic (Central and Eastern European) Jewish tradition forbids the portrayal of the human figure, but elaborate plant and animal motifs are common. Among the most striking are the numerous representations of the animals mentioned in a Talmudic exhortation to be "as strong as a leopard, as light as an eagle, as fleet as a stag, and as brave as a lion to perform the will of thy father who is in heaven." (Sometimes the leopard is rendered as a tiger.) Imaginary scenes of the Holy Land and Jerusalem also form a fairly common motif.

We do not know who designed or built most synagogues, but in the 19th and 20th centuries, particularly in Central Europe, many were designed by leading architects. Among them were the Hungarian Lipot Baumhorn (1860–1932), modern Europe's most prolific synagogue designer, and the Vienna-based Wilhelm Stiassny (1842–1910), who designed several synagogues in the colorful Moorish style, which emerged in the mid-19th century and incorporated horseshoe arches, arabesques, spires that resembled minarets, and other vaguely Middle Eastern forms. Many felt that these elements reflected Judaism's origins and at the same time set synagogues off from Christian churches.

Shtetls, Ghettos, and Jewish Quarters

In many towns and villages, numerous buildings still survive in the old Jewish quarters or ghettos, where Jews either chose or were compelled to live in medieval times or later. These include not only buildings used by the Jewish community, such as schools, community offices, hospitals, the rabbi's house, or the mikvah (ritual bath), but also the homes and shops of ordinary people. Cracow's old Jewish quarter, Kazimierz, is the largest and most intact, and there are well-defined Jewish quarters in a number of towns in the Czech Republic. Likewise, in Lithuania and Ukraine, and to a lesser extent in Poland, there are still many localities that retain the look of the old shtetl, or predominantly Jewish small town, whose image forms such an important part of Eastern European Jewish literature and folklore. Sagging wooden houses line old market squares, people draw water from public wells, and chickens and geese wander at the sides of roads. You may even still see the place where mezuzahs were attached to doorways.

Museums, Monuments, and Memorials

Jewish museums and permanent exhibitions on Jewish history, culture, and traditions now exist in scores of places. Most have been opened since the fall of communism, and some are sited in newly restored synagogues. There are also hundreds of monuments and memorials commemorating the Holocaust. In addition to museums or memorials at the sites of major Nazi death camps, many local monuments commemorate victims. These range from huge sculptural memorials to plaques or stones marking mass graves or commemorating individual martyrs. Although the focus of this book is not Holocaust sites, I have noted major monuments and also some of the other memorials.

Jewish Culture Festivals

Hundreds of Jewish cultural events, including many festivals, take place in the region each year and make good focal points for trips. There are general Jewish culture festivals, Jewish film festivals, Jewish music festivals, and more. Some last a week or longer; others are one-day events—I list only a few here.

The annual **European Day of Jewish Culture** takes place in more than two dozen countries on the first Sunday in September. First held in 2000, it includes hundreds of performances, exhibits, workshops, and other offerings, and Jewish heritage sites are open to the public. Organizers are putting together a European Route of Jewish Heritage, which will highlight Jewish heritage sites across the continent *(www.jewishheritage.org)*.

The summer **Festival of Jewish Culture** in Cracow *(www.jewishfestival.pl)*, is the biggest and most famous Jewish festival in Europe. Founded in 1988, it takes place for nine days at the end of June and beginning of July, features more than 150 performances, lectures, workshops, and other events, and ends with a huge outdoor concert. Other festivals in Poland include **Bajit Hadash,** held each fall in Cracow *(www.judaica.pl)*; the **Warsaw of Singer Festival** *(www.shalom.org.pl),* a weeklong festival held each fall in Warsaw that concentrates on Yiddish culture; and two Jewish film festivals in Warsaw *(www.wjff.pl* and *www.warsawjff.ant.pl).*

Budapest is host each year to the **Budapest Summer Jewish Festival** *(www.jewishfestival.hu)* at the end of August. Several Jewish festivals take place each year in the Czech Republic. Among them are the **Nine Gates International Festival of Czech, German and Jewish Culture** *(www.9bran.cz)* and the **Amajim Jewish Festival** *(www.kviztrebic.cz/amajim* or *www.trebic.cz),* held at the end of July and beginning of August in Trebic, a small town in Moravia with an extensive old Jewish quarter.

BEFORE YOU GO

It is a good idea, particularly if you have not been to Eastern or Central Europe before, to do some pre-trip reading on both Jewish and general history in the region. Having some background on the tumultuous events over the centuries may help deal with the shock of seeing what remains today and the emotions that may come with it. Jewish visitors often experience sadness, grief, pain, anger, and other less easily defined feelings. The Jewish traveler to these areas should also be prepared to feel a sense of wonder and an inexplicable visceral identification or familiarity with the art and architecture—and even with the landscape. This, in turn, can lead to a broader sense of tranquillity or communion, particularly if visitors also choose to meet and mingle with members of today's emerging new Jewish communities.

Many books, fiction and nonfiction, deal with Jewish history in the region, and there is a vast and growing literature specifically on the Holocaust and the World War II period. A multitude of resources is also found on the Internet, including accounts by numerous travelers of their own journeys to Jewish sites in the region. The resources I list in the text and at the end of this book only skim the surface of what is available but will at least get you started.

GETTING AROUND

Major cities and towns can be reached by plane, train, or public bus, but in the countryside a car is the best means or transportation. Cemeteries, for example, can be a mile or more outside a town or village, sometimes down rutted dirt roads, in the middle or fields or forest, or on the top of a hill. Infrequent train and bus connections may make it impractical to visit more than one site a day; with a car one can see several related places in the space of a few hours—the cluster of interesting villages in northeastern Hungary near Tokaj, for example, or the group of shtetls near Cracow, Poland, or some of the fascinating towns around L'viv, Ukraine.

Cars, with or without drivers, can be rented in major cities. In most parts of the region, roads are generally good, though in remote country areas or in villages you may find stretches of dirt track. In parts of Romania and Ukraine, however, roads can be abysmal. The only country included in this book where I did not want to drive on my own was Ukraine; instead, I hired taxi drivers on a per-kilometer basis to take me where I wanted; on some days we drove for hundreds of miles. If you rent a car, make sure you get a good map, drawn to the largest scale possible. Service stations are now located at frequent intervals (though less so in Ukraine), and most have clean restrooms and well-stocked shops and snack bars. In most service stations you can pay with a credit card.

WHAT TO BRING

Most of the countries in this book are members of the European Union, and you can purchase just about anything you need, even in most small towns. (Kosher supplies can be hard to find, however, even in major cities.) English-language newspapers and periodicals are available in major cities, most good hotels have at least one English news channel on cable TV, and there is a growing network of Internet cafés, WiFi hot spots, and public Internet access points. Bring necessities such as prescription medicines with you. Also, make sure to carry your own soap and tissues that you can use for toilet paper.

Keep your clothes casual. Most Jewish cemeteries are totally overgrown or have sections that are overgrown with shrubs, trees, and weeds—including nettles; even cemeteries that are regularly maintained can become choked by weeds and high grass in the spring and summer. To reach many of them requires walking through fields or down country lanes. You may also have to clamber through weeds to reach some synagogues. In the countryside, mud is a constant factor at the slightest hint of rain. Therefore, wear athletic or other sturdy, comfortable shoes—not sandals. Women may find it more comfortable to wear trousers.

Also, wear a money belt for your valuables. Credit cards are widely accepted, and there are ATM machines everywhere, even in many villages, but it is also a good idea to bring some cash dollars or euros with you.

FINDING THE SITES

Ask, ask, and ask again after you get lost trying to follow the first person's directions. In this book, I use English spellings but also include local spellings in parentheses for each entry. (Ukrainian, Bulgarian, Macedonian, and, for the most part, Serbian, are all written in Cyrillic characters.) I include addresses for most sites, but they may not be much help; either there are no street signs, or it is easier (and often more effective) simply to ask for the synagogue or Jewish cemetery, rather than try to find a specific street. I also strongly suggest that you carry a notebook or pad on which local people can draw maps for you.

The word "synagogue" is pronounced more or less "SEEN-ah-goh-gah" all over the region. "Jewish cemetery" translates as the following:

Polish: Cmentarz Żydowski (SMEN-tazh Zhih-DOV-skee)
Lithuanian: Žydų kapinės (ZHEE-doo KAP-ee-nes)
Ukrainian: Cyrillic characters, pronounced: Yev-RAY-ski KLAH-do-vish-che or Yev-RAY-ski TSVIN-tar
Czech: Židovský Hřbitov (ZHIH-dov-skee ZHBIH-tawv)
Slovak: Židovsky Cintorín (ZHIH-dov-skee TSIN-tor-een)
Hungarian: Zsidó Temető (ZHEE-do TEM-eh-too)
Slovenian: Židovsko Pokopališče (ZHEE-dov-sko poh-koh-PAL-ish-che)
Serbian and Bosnian: Jevrejsko Groblje (Yev-RAY-sko GRO-blyeh)
Croatian: Židovsko Groblje (Zhee-DOV-sko GRO-blyeh)
Macedonian: Cyrillic characters, pronounced: EV-ray-skee GROH-beesh-ta
Romanian: Cimitir Evreiesc (Cheemi-TEER Yev-reh-YESK)
Bulgarian: Cyrillic characters, pronounced: Ev-REY-sko GROH-bi-shte
German: Jüdischer Friedhof (YOO-dish-er FREED-hawf)

I encourage you to contact the local Jewish communities in towns where they exist. Members of these communities have gone out of their way to show me places of Jewish interest, spend time chatting, and ply me with coffee and cake (or schnapps). Many older Jews speak German or Yiddish; many younger people now speak English. Thanks to the Internet, cell phones, and new Jewish community development projects, Jews in most countries are in close touch with each other, and people you meet in one town will most likely be able to connect you with friends or family in other places.

Detailed, locally published Jewish heritage guidebooks and other publications exist in some countries and regions, and I recommend you make use of them. In many places municipal tourist information offices can be extremely helpful. They may have maps or brochures on local Jewish sites, or, barring that, will explain to you how to reach them.

Many Jewish cemeteries and former synagogues are kept locked. In places where there is a Jewish community, the community office generally has the keys, or there may be a posted note telling where the key can be obtained. In many towns and villages, keys to the cemeteries or empty synagogues can be obtained from the local town hall or municipal museum. Many municipal tourist offices also keep keys or can contact someone for you who does. Synagogues used as art galleries and cultural centers generally post their opening hours. Workers or staff at synagogues that have been converted into warehouses, workshops, schools, and so on, usually have no objection to visitors taking a look.

If an elderly or obviously poor person, particularly in a village, has gone out of his or her way to help you, you may want to give him or her a tip. Use your judgment. It is not necessary, and some people will be offended if you offer them money. Also, beware of the hangers-on (Jewish or otherwise) at some major sites of Jewish interest who latch on to you, make a show of guiding you around, and then insist on a handout.

FINALLY, A WORD ABOUT ANTI-SEMITISM

Anti-Jewish prejudice has existed in this part of the world for as long as Jews have lived here. Under the communist regimes, anti-Semitism (also masquerading as anti-Zionism) was at times official policy. In Lithuania and Ukraine, which were part of the Soviet Union, Jews came under constant pressure and persecution for decades. The new postcommunist governments have taken stands against anti-Semitism, and it is no longer officially sanctioned. Still, popular anti-Semitism, on the right and on the left, has come out of the closet in some places, where newfound freedoms of speech, thought, and deed mean that anyone can say whatever he or she wants. At the same time, many people take a great interest in Jewish culture and demonstrate great sympathy for the Jewish people and causes.

Anti-Semitic incidents are reported from time to time in all countries included in this book, but the region has been little affected by the violent attacks on synagogues, Jewish institutions, and individuals that have taken place in Western Europe in the wake of the Israel-Palestinian conflict. Israel considers some countries in the region to be among its best friends. Be prepared, though, to see anti-Semitic slogans daubed on walls or even gravestones. And be prepared for the occasional shocking remarks by people you might meet. (You may be more shocked by prejudice expressed against Roma, or Gypsies, and other ethnicities; and don't forget that ethnic hatred helped spark the wars in former Yugoslavia that left hundreds of thousands dead.)

POLAND

CURRENT POPULATION: 38.5 MILLION
JEWISH POPULATION BEFORE WORLD WAR II: 3.3 MILLION
(PREWAR BORDERS)
JEWISH POPULATION TODAY: APPROX. 8,000–20,000

A LITTLE HISTORY

Over the past thousand years, Poland has been a harbor of refuge for Jews, as well as a grim scene of horror. Here, Jewish culture rose to some of its greatest glories; here, Jewish society suffered some of its most devastating defeats. Long a haven for Jews fleeing persecution elsewhere, Poland eventually became home to 3.3 million Jews—a vibrant, varied population embracing rich and poor, religious and secular, artists and fools, business tycoons and jobless *luftmenschen*. Polish territory was the heartland of the Jewish Diaspora, home to the largest Jewish community in Europe; as such it became Nazi Germany's main killing grounds.

Jews lived in (or at least visited) Polish lands as early as the tenth century. The first Jews to settle here came as merchants and peddlers fleeing persecution in the German states, particularly during the Crusades, and the earliest Jewish settlements were established in Silesia, in what is now southwest Poland. In the 13th century, after Tartar invaders laid waste to Christian and Jewish settlements alike, local rulers anxious to repopulate their towns welcomed new immigrants. Prince Boleslaw the Pious in 1264 issued a body of laws known as the Statute of Kalisz, which guaranteed Jews the right to live in the Kalisz region (in today's central Poland). In the 14th century, King Kazimierz (Casimir) the Great (whom legend credits with a Jewish lover named Esther, or Esterka) extended the statute to cover his entire domain. By the end of the 15th century between 20,000 and 30,000 Jews are believed to have lived in at least 60 Jewish communities across Poland and the Grand

Duchy of Lithuania, which formed a union with Poland in 1385. A formal Polish-Lithuanian Commonwealth, established in 1569, lasted until 1791 and at its peak extended far into what today is Ukraine, Belarus, and Latvia.

Living in tight communities under the protection of the king, usually near the marketplace or town fortifications, Jews were craftsmen, peddlers, moneylenders, and merchants. The burgeoning Jewish population did not go unopposed by the Roman Catholic Church or by local gentile merchants fearing competition. Anti-Jewish violence erupted on a number of occasions, and the first blood libel—the accusation that Jews kill Christians to use their blood for ritual purposes—was reported in 1347. Church leaders repeatedly tried to force Jews to wear a special badge and called for other restrictions, and Jews were barred from living in a number of towns. In the mid-15th century, Cardinal Zbigniew Olesnicki invited to Poland John of Capistrano, a Franciscan monk who had already won the nickname "Scourge of the Jews." Thanks to John's preaching, almost the entire Jewish community of Wroclaw was burned at the stake or expelled from the city for alleged blasphemy. Anti-Jewish riots linked to his preaching also broke out in Warsaw and Cracow.

In 1551, however, King Sigismund II Augustus granted Jewish community leaders wide-ranging judicial and administrative powers. Each community was to elect a council of elders called a Kahal, which would oversee tax collection and the administration of Jewish courts, schools, and other institutions. This laid the groundwork for the foundation, around 1580, of the Council of the Four Lands (Va'ad Arba Arazot), a supreme Jewish self-governing body that until 1764 ruled over virtually every aspect of secular and religious Jewish life. Headquartered in Lublin, the council joined rabbis and laymen representing the regions of Greater Poland, whose capital was Poznan; Little Poland, whose capital was Cracow; and Volhynia and Red Russia (Eastern Galicia and Podolia), both now in today's Ukraine. Lithuania originally was part of the council, but from 1623 had its own central organization. Among the council's duties were to collect taxes, regulate religious observances, sit as a court, and represent Polish Jewry to Polish officialdom.

Between 1500 and 1648, waves of immigration boosted the Jewish population of Poland and Lithuania to as many as half a million, making it the largest concentration of Jews in the world. Major centers of scholarship developed, Hebrew printing houses turned out splendid volumes, and magnificent synagogues were built. Then, in 1648 to 1649, a bloody uprising headed by the Cossack chieftain Bogdan Chmielnicki ushered in three decades of war, destruction, and chaos still referred to in Polish history as "The

Deluge." The Orthodox Christian Chmielnicki—who is regarded as a national hero in Ukraine—led hordes of fellow Cossacks, Ukrainian peasants, and Tartars in an orgy of plunder, pillage, and massacre. Their main targets were the Polish landlords who oppressed them, Roman Catholic clergy, and the Jews, many of whom served as tax collectors and stewards on Polish estates.

The Chmielnicki Uprising was followed by yet another Cossack rebellion and then by invasions by Sweden and Russia. The upheavals destroyed as many as 700 Jewish communities; estimates of the dead range into the hundreds of thousands. The destruction forced thousands to migrate west and south and pushed many Jews into mysticism, superstition, and self-isolation. Numerous self-proclaimed Messiahs drew followers. The most influential was the remarkable Shabbetai Zevi, born in Smyrna (today's Izmir, Turkey) in 1626, who proclaimed himself Messiah in 1665 and drew tens of thousands of followers all over Europe and the Middle East (see Ulcinj, Montenegro p. 315). Another popular false Messiah was Jacob Frank (1726–1791), who claimed to be the reincarnation of Shabbetai Zevi and gathered many followers into a sect whose beliefs mixed elements of Judaism, Catholicism, and Islam, and whose rituals were said to include sexual orgies.

Another important spiritual movement began at around the same time—Hasidism, which grew up as a revolutionary revival movement against the increasingly dogmatic and circumscribed Judaism preached and practiced by powerful rabbis. Its founder was Israel ben Eliezer, known to his followers as the Ba'al Shem Tov (Master of the Good Name), who was born around 1700 (see Medzhybizh, Ukraine pp. 128–29). After the Ba'al Shem Tov's death in 1760, his disciples spread his message. Eventually, Hasidism evolved into a system under which individual communities were led by a charismatic leader known as a tzaddik (or rebbe). In some places, Hasidism clashed sharply with mainstream Orthodoxy, but eventually it became the most powerful Jewish force in Eastern Europe in the 19th century. The Jewish Enlightenment movement, or Haskalah, emerged and grew at much the same time. It began in Germany in the late 18th century; bitterly opposed by both rabbinical Orthodoxy and Hasidism for introducing modern ideas and Western European cultural influence, it penetrated slowly and with difficulty into the east.

At the end of the 18th century, Poland disappeared as an entity, partitioned among Russia, Prussia, and Austria. Western Poland went to Prussia. Southern Poland and Galicia, including Cracow and much of what today is western Ukraine, went to Austria. The eastern and central regions, including Warsaw, went to Russia and became part of the so-called Pale of Settlement,

A group of young Jews in Kazimierz, the Jewish quarter of Cracow, just before World War II

a strip of territory along the empire's western border where the tsars forced Russian Jews to live. Poverty was widespread in the Pale, and the late 19th and early 20th centuries saw pogrom after pogrom. This persecution sparked the mass emigration of Jews to the west. Between 1880 and 1914 as many as 1.5 million Jews left the Pale; the vast majority went to America. The miserable conditions and persecution also sparked Jewish political activism. Labor unions and left-wing parties such as the Jewish Labor Bund, a militant Socialist Party founded in Vilnius in 1897, won widespread support, as did Zionism and also conservative parties such as the Orthodox Agudas Israel, founded in 1912. In Galicia, which was part of the Austro-Hungarian Empire, Jews were granted some measure of freedom in the 1780s through the Emperor Joseph II's Edicts of Tolerance, and they gained further rights over the years. Still, poverty and anti-Semitism prompted as many as 300,000 Galician Jews to immigrate to the United States between 1891 and 1913.

Poland was reconstituted as an independent state after World War I. Its eastern border stretched far into what today is now Lithuania, Belarus, and Ukraine, and much of what today is western Poland belonged to Germany. Anti-Semitism was a constant throughout the interwar period, and economic restrictions on Jews led to widespread poverty and unemployment. After the rise of Adolf Hitler in Germany and the death in 1935 of Poland's military dictator Marshal Jozef Pilsudski, anti-Semitism became an active part of government policy. Nonetheless, Poland's Jews formed a world that was full of spirituality, learning, culture, political activity, and other components of a rich and multifaceted life.

World War II began on September 1, 1939, when Nazi Germany invaded Poland. Out of the 3.3 million Jews living there at the outbreak of war, only 300,000 survived. Along with three million people, almost the entire physical infrastructure of a civilization was erased. Thousands of synagogues, prayer houses, and other Jewish buildings were razed to the ground; tens of thousands of books and ritual objects were destroyed. Tombstones were uprooted from ancient cemeteries and used to pave roads and build pigsties.

Tens of thousands of survivors emigrated—particularly after a 1946 pogrom in Kielce reminded them that anti-Semitism had not been killed along with Poland's Jews. Like most other communist countries, Poland broke relations with Israel after the Six Day War in 1967. The next year, the state launched a sweeping anti-Semitic campaign that forced 20,000 Jews out of the country. A few thousand Jews remained, but most regarded the Jewish experience in Poland as a closed chapter. That state of affairs began to change in the late 1970s and gained momentum after the rise of the anti-communist Solidarity movement in 1980. A number of young Jews began trying to pick up the threads that had been cut decades before. Young Jews and non-Jews alike, many affiliated with the anti-communist political opposition, also began caring for Jewish cemeteries and other sites of Jewish heritage. Numerous books on Jewish topics were published.

These trends have flourished since the ouster of the communists; there has been an explosion of Jewish cultural, educational, and commemorative activities, carried out by Jews as well as by interested members of the the non-Jewish community and state and local authorities. These efforts have been paralleled by an extraordinary revival of Jewish cultural and communal life. Though the numbers remain very small, Warsaw in particular boasts a full Jewish infrastructure including rabbis, synagogues, kosher facilities, and a Jewish school, as well as Jewish publications, cultural centers, clubs, and other institutions.

JEWISH HERITAGE IN POLAND

ABOUT 245 SYNAGOGUE BUILDINGS STILL EXIST, MOST OF THEM IN EASTERN AND southern Poland; but only a very few are still used for religious services.

Most have been converted into museums, libraries, warehouses, factories, cinemas, or even fire stations. Many stand empty or simply in ruins. There are about 1,400 Jewish cemeteries, but only about 400 still have tombstones. Most lie abandoned, but many have been fenced or cleared of undergrowth in recent years. A number of towns and villages, particularly in eastern Poland, still recall the look of the prewar shtetl—though this situation is changing fast. There are also several Jewish museums or permanent Jewish exhibitions and many monuments and museums commemorating the Holocaust.

Scores of cemeteries, synagogues, and other buildings have been returned to Jewish ownership under a 1997 law regulating the restitution of Jewish prewar communal property. In areas of the country where Jewish communities exist, the properties are returned to the Jewish community. Elsewhere, they are taken over and administered by the Foundation for the Preservation of Jewish Heritage in Poland, which was established by the Union of Jewish Communities and the World Jewish Restitution Organization. *(The foundation's website, http://fodz.pl, details restoration projects and other Jewish heritage news.)*

TIPS ON VISITING

Cracow's old Jewish quarter, Kazimierz, is the most important surviving Jewish complex in East-Central Europe and should not be missed. Easy day trips from Cracow can be made to Tarnow, Checiny, Szydlow, Chmielnik, and Dzialoszyce, as well as to Auschwitz. If you can, try to visit Zamosc and the new Holocaust memorial and museum at nearby Belzec. In the north, don't miss the synagogue museum in the onetime shtetl of Tykocin, located not far from the Treblinka death camp. From there, try to go all the way to Sejny and visit the Borderland Foundation.

WARSAW

(Polish: Warszawa)

Before the Holocaust, Poland's capital was the biggest and most important Jewish center in Europe. More than 350,000 Jews made up one-third of the city's population. More Jews lived in Warsaw than in all of today's British Isles; only New York had a bigger Jewish population. Today, only a few hundred Jews (or maybe a few thousand, as many Jews still do not identify themselves with the community) remain out of the city's 1.7 million people. Most of Warsaw's Jews today are elderly, but the city has witnessed a remarkable revival of Jewish life since the fall of communism. There are Orthodox and Reform religious congregations, a Jewish school, Jewish publications, and a wide roster of activities ranging from a kosher café to an annual Jewish book fair.

Jews settled in Warsaw in medieval times but were barred from living in the city from 1527 to 1768. During this period, they formed communities on the estates of Polish nobles outside the city limits. Once the residency ban was lifted, the Jewish population mushroomed. During the Polish partitions, Warsaw came under Russian rule, in the Pale of Settlement; more than 300,000 Jews lived in the city by 1910. Warsaw Jewry encompassed all facets and factions of Jewish life, all colors of the Jewish spectrum. Most Warsaw Jews remained Orthodox, and many were fervent Hasidim living highly traditional lives—mostly in poverty. But there were also Progressive Jews and widespread secular Jewish movements. Educational, scholarly, cultural, and intellectual life was extremely vibrant, with countless religious schools and yeshivahs, theaters, newspapers, libraries and bookshops, sports clubs, social clubs, and fraternal and civic organizations. Politically, too, Warsaw was fertile ground for many Jewish parties and movements, from leftist worker parties such as the Jewish Labor Bund to Orthodox ones like Agudas Israel.

Many Warsaw Jews lived in a district south and west of the picturesque Old Town, and it was here that the Nazis set up the Warsaw Ghetto in November 1940. About 450,000 Jews from the city and surrounding areas were crowded into two sections known as the Small Ghetto and the Large Ghetto. In less than a year, about 100,000 had succumbed to starvation or disease. Mass deportations began on June 22, 1942; hundreds of thousands of people were crammed into cattle cars and shipped to Treblinka. On April 19, 1943, some 300 Jews in the ghetto staged an uprising against the Nazis that ended in defeat after three weeks of bloody fighting. Cornered in their bunker at ul. Mila 18, most of the uprising leaders committed suicide rather than allow themselves to be captured. The ghetto was reduced to rubble. Only about 300 Jews were left alive in the city when it was liberated by the Soviet Army on January 17, 1945.

Most of Warsaw, not just the ghetto, was leveled in the war—the award-winning movie *The Pianist*, by Roman Polanski, vividly evokes the destruction. Warsaw's picture-perfect Old Town was painstakingly rebuilt, stone by stone, based on photographs and old paintings, but much of the city now consists of communist-era buildings and apartment blocks—foremost among them the Stalinist-style tower in the center of town built in the 1950s as a palace of culture. Thanks to a construction boom since the fall of communism, however, a forest of shiny new high-rises is rapidly changing the skyline.

Main Sites of Jewish Interest in Warsaw

The Holocaust annihilated all but a few traces of Jewish Warsaw; monuments and plaques denote the rest. Today's revived Jewish community is also making its mark, and ground is due to be broken in 2007 for a high-profile new Museum of the History of Polish Jews. The website http://jewish.sites.warszawa.u-m.gov.pl/wstep_a.htm, created by the Jewish Historical Institute and the City of Warsaw, provides a detailed guide to historical Jewish sites in Warsaw.

Synagogue and Jewish Community Complex: ul. Twarda—The neo-Romanesque Nozyk Synagogue, the only synagogue in Warsaw to survive World War II, was established in 1902 by the wealthy businessman Zalman Nozyk and his wife, Rywka, who presented it as a gift to the community. The Nazis turned it into a stable; it underwent a full restoration in the 1980s. Orthodox services are held here daily, under the leadership of Rabbi Michael Schudrich, the American-born Orthodox chief rabbi of Poland. There is a little kosher grocery store on the ground floor of an annex at the rear of the building.

The white building next door at Twarda 6 is a major hub of contemporary Jewish life. Here there are offices of Jewish organizations, an adult education center, and even a kosher café, Bakbuk, in its basement.

Jewish Theater: Plac Grzybowski 12/16—Warsaw's Jewish Theater, a few steps from the synagogue, gives regular performances of Yiddish classics as well as Polish works. The building also houses the offices of the Shalom Foundation, headed by the Yiddish singer and actress Golda Tencer; the foundation organizes cultural events including an annual autumn Jewish culture festival celebrating the Warsaw spiritually tied to the Yiddish writer Isaac Bashevis Singer. *(Additional information: www.shalom.org.pl)*

Prozna Street: One short block of buildings, off Plac Grzybowski, survived the destruction of the Warsaw Ghetto. The buildings are decayed, and some have to be propped up, but they are physical bridges to the past. For years plans have been discussed to reconstruct and preserve the block and turn it into a Jewish museum and monument.

Jewish Historical Institute: ul. Tlomackie 3/5—Housed in the dignified prewar building that once was Warsaw's Main Judaic Library, the Jewish Historical Institute comprises Poland's largest repository of Jewish-related archives, publications, and museum objects and also serves as a center for ongoing research. It has a genealogy center, and its bookshop is the best source of Jewish-themed publications in the city. Some of its rich trove of artifacts are kept on permanent display on the premises. Other material forms temporary exhibits that are featured in the new exhibition space in the modern skyscraper sited just next door across a narrow alleyway. This so-called Blue Tower stands on the site of Warsaw's domed Great Synagogue, built in 1878 and blown up by the Germans on May 16, 1943.

Old Jewish Cemetery: ul. Okopowa 49/51—Established in 1806, Warsaw's vast Jewish cemetery extends over 82 acres and contains the graves of about 250,000 people. Despite ongoing cleanup and restoration efforts by Jewish organizations and volunteer civic groups, much of it remains choked by shrubs, weeds, trees, and bushes. Tombstones range from intricately decorated mazzevahs to elaborate family tombs. Jewish luminaries from all walks of life are buried here. They include revered Hasidic rabbis, as well as the writers I. L. Peretz, S. Ansky, and Julian Styjkowski; the actress Rachel Kaminska; the historian Majer Balaban; and Lazarus Ludwik Zamenhof, the inventor of the artificial language Esperanto. A striking sculpted memorial honors Janusz Korczak (Henryk Goldszmit), who ran the orphans' home in the Warsaw Ghetto and went to his death at Treblinka along with the orphanage children. Another monument erected in 1993 commemorates all the 1.5 million children killed in the Holocaust.

One of the most impressive older tombs is that of wealthy merchant Ber Sonnenberg (1764–1826). Designed by the architect and artist David Friedlaender, the large, rectangular structure has two extremely elaborate sculptural relief panels. One shows the suburb of Praga, across the Vistula River, including its Jewish cemetery; the other is a remarkable vision of biblical Babylon.

Warsaw Ghetto Monuments and Site of Planned New Museum: Most of what was the Warsaw Ghetto and, earlier, the main Jewish neighborhood, was flattened during the war and today is the site of apartment blocks and new high-rises. A few old buildings do remain, however, as well as a few fragments of the former ghetto walls. Numerous plaques and other monuments mark ghetto sites. Many of these form a Route of Memory that was inaugurated on April 19, 1988, the 45th anniversary of the Warsaw Ghetto Uprising. Among the sites are:

- **Monument to Ghetto Heroes**: ul. Zamenhofa at Ghetto Heroes' Square. Sculpted by the artist Natan Rapaport, this imposing monument was erected on April 19, 1948, the fifth anniversary of the Warsaw Ghetto Uprising, and is the main site of Holocaust commemoration in the city. Its main face shows proud-looking Jewish fighters. On the rear is a bas-relief depicting Jewish martyrdom. The big field in front of the monument is where the new Museum of the History of Polish Jews will be constructed. The Finnish architects Ilmari Lahdelma and Rainer Mahlamaki designed the museum building as a "house of light" whose transparent walls will enclose a solidly curved inner shape representing a bridge between past and present. *(Museum website: www.jewishmuseum.org.pl)*
- **Site of the Jewish Resistance Bunker** at ul. Mila 18.
- **Buildings on Stawki Street** that were the headquarters of the SS and the Jewish hospital.
- The simple, stark monument marking **Umschlagplatz,** the staging area from which more than 300,000 Jews were deported to Treblinka.
- **A Monument to Janusz Korczak** stands at Jaktorowska 8, the site of the Ghetto orphanage that he directed. A new monument to Korczak stands in the middle of the city, near the Palace of Culture at the corner of Swietokrzyska street.

Praga District: Unlike downtown Warsaw, Praga, across the Vistula River, survived World War II practically intact, and most of its buildings date from prewar years. It has long been rundown and neglected and has a reputation for street crime—though the current process of gentrification may change this situation. Jews settled here in the 18th century, and many Jewish traces remain. The so-called Brodno Cemetery, at the corner of Odrowaza and Wincentego streets, was founded in 1780. It was destroyed in World War II, but the area was fenced off and some restoration work took place in the 1980s. An outbuilding in the yard of Targowa 52/53 was once a private prayer room that still bears traces of colorful decoration. The big building with the scalloped facade at Jagiellonska 8 was once a Jewish orphanage. Next door, where there is now a playground, was the site of the so-called Round Synagogue, built in 1835 and pulled down by the communists in the 1960s.

Addresses of Note in Warsaw

- Orthodox services at Nozyk Synagogue: ul. Twarda. Tel/fax: +48-22/652-2805. E-mail: varshe@jewish.org.pl. http://warszawa.jewish.org.pl. The kosher Café Bakbuk operates in the basement of the main Jewish community building at ul. Twarda 6. The center also has a kosher kitchen that serves lunches and can cater for groups.
- Beit Warszawa (Progressive): ul. Wiertnicza 113. Tel: +48-22/885-2638, fax: +48-22/885-8982. E-mail: office@beit-warszawa.org.pl. www.beit-warszawa.org.pl
- Chabad Center: ul. Slominskiego 19. Tel: +48-603/200-485. www.chabad.org.pl. The center has a glatt kosher restaurant, but you must call in advance to reserve.
- Jewish Historical Institute: ul. Tlomackie 3/5. www.jewishinstitute.org.pl. The bookstore specializes in Jewish topics and stocks many publications in English.
- Shalom Foundation: Plac Grzybowski 12/16. Tel: +48-22/620-3036. www.shalom.org.pl
- Union of Jewish Religious Communities in Poland: ul. Twarda 6. Tel: +48-22/620-4324, fax: +48-22/620-1037. E-mail: sekretariat@jewish.org.pl

Near Warsaw

GORA KALWARIA (GÓRA KALWARIA) (YIDDISH: GER OR GUR)—This town about 25 miles south of Warsaw was the seat of one of the most powerful Hasidic dynasties in Poland, founded by the tzaddik Isaac Meir Alter (1789–1866). Isaac Meir Alter's grandson escaped to the Holy Land in 1939, and the Ger dynasty carries on to this day. Long used as a warehouse, the town's redbrick synagogue is now a house of prayer and study for pilgrims. Located in a large courtyard entered from between Nos. 10 and 12 on the main street, Pijarska, it stands next to what was once the rebbe's house. The tombs of Isaac Meir Alter and his son, Arie Leib are in the Jewish cemetery, located between Zakalwaria and Wiejska streets.

KARCZEW—In Isaac Bashevis Singer's novel *The Family Moskat,* the female protagonist, Hadassah, is killed in the first days of World War II and is buried in the Jewish cemetery of this small town on the Vistula River about 15 miles southeast of Warsaw. For decades the cemetery lay forsaken, the three dozen or so gravestones broken or eroded, or tipped over and drifted over by low dunes of pale river sand. The carvings are poignant: a hand drops money into a charity box; candles flicker, waiting to be blessed. Bones (animal? human?) litter the sand; some years ago I watched Michael Schudrich, now the chief rabbi of Poland, gather and then, squatting down, rebury human bones we found on the surface.

Since then, the entire area of the cemetery has been surrounded by a fence. The gate is locked (the key is kept next door, at Otwocka 1). But the fence is low and does not seem to have stopped people from using the area as a shortcut. Shadowy footprints mark the sand, and the area is littered with empty bottles and broken glass; the entranceway seems to be used as a dump. Still, once inside, the power of time and place and memory are overwhelming; as the wind stirs puffs of sand, a hush hangs over the place, and even local noises—birdcalls, motors, children's voice, dogs—seem far, far away.

MSZCZONOW (MSZCZONÓW)–The cemetery in this village is situated at the edge of the main highway to Katowice, about 30 miles south of Warsaw near the Mszczonow exit. Clearly seen from the road, it dates back to the 18th century and has vigorously carved tombstones and the ohel of a local Hasidic rebbe, Rabbi Aron of Nadarzyn. The cemetery underwent extensive restoration and was fenced and cleared of undergrowth in 2004 and 2005.

PLOCK (PŁOCK)–A stately synagogue, built in the early 19th century, stands in this small town north of Warsaw, one of the few synagogues to have survived in this part of Poland. Located at Kwiatka 7, it long stood empty or was used as a warehouse. Plans were announced in 2006 to restore it fully and turn it into a Jewish museum dealing with the history and traditions of Jews from the Mazovia region.

TREBLINKA–In 1942 and 1943 as many as 800,000 Jews were killed in 13 gas chambers secluded in a forest near this village about 50 miles northeast of Warsaw. Their ashes were scattered on surrounding fields. The Nazis demolished the camp and eventually destroyed all traces of it; they went so far as to plow under the earth. A huge, somber monument now marks the site. Some 17,000 symbolic tombstones are ranged around a towering central pillar; each jagged stone represents a town whose Jews were killed in the camp. Only one stone commemorates a single person, Janusz

Korczak, who ran a Jewish orphanage in Warsaw and was shipped to Treblinka and murdered with the children in July 1942.

CRACOW

(Polish: Kraków)

POLAND'S HISTORIC ROYAL CAPITAL, CRACOW IS A SPLENDID CITY WHOSE FAIRY-TALE castle, centuries-old university, and many other historic monuments form a living museum around the vast and colorful main market square, or Rynek Glowny. There, every hour on the hour, a trumpeter climbs to the top of St. Mary's Basilica and plays a fanfare that is cut off abruptly in mid-note to recall a trumpeter who was killed by invading Tartars while playing the very same call to arms in 1241.

Unlike Warsaw, Cracow was scarcely damaged during World War II. Its old Jewish quarter, Kazimierz, forms one of Europe's richest and most important complexes of Jewish monuments. Jews lived in Cracow in the early 14th century. They were expelled from the city proper in 1495 and moved virtually en masse to Kazimierz, about a mile from the Rynek, which developed into a semi-autonomous Jewish town, protected by the king. Jewish culture and scholarship here reached high peaks in the mid-16th to mid-17th centuries, when great scholars such as Rabbi Moses Isserles Remuh (circa 1525–1572) flourished.

As part of Galicia, Cracow came under Austrian rule when Poland was partitioned. After obtaining full civil rights in the mid-19th century, Jews moved out to settle all over the city, though the core of Jewish life remained in Kazimierz—and here, too, the Orthodox part of the community, many of them living in poverty, remained. On the eve of World War II, about 65,000 Jews lived in Cracow. The Germans occupied the city on September 6, 1939, and imposed stringent anti-Jewish measures. They set up a ghetto in March 1941; mass deportations began in June 1942. Only about 2,000 Cracow Jews survived the Holocaust. Today, about 200 Jews live in the city.

MAIN SITES OF JEWISH INTEREST IN CRACOW

Kazimierz District: Kazimierz was left a ghost town after the Holocaust. Under communism, it became a rundown slum. Since the fall of communism, however, the district has undergone a remarkable transformation. A vibrant tourist, cultural, and educational industry has grown up based on its Jewish character. Many buildings, including several historic synagogues, have

The entrance to the 16th-century Remuh synagogue in Cracow's former Jewish quarter, Kazimierz, which is still used for religious services.

been restored; information plaques and other tourist-friendly infrastructure have been put in place; and chic new "Jewish style" restaurants, cafés, bookstores, and galleries draw a growing number of patrons. There's a heavy element of kitsch, but that, too is part of life. My favorite Jewish-style restaurants include Klezmer Hois *(ul. Szeroka 6. Tel/fax: +48-12/411-1245. www.klezmerhois.pl)*, located in a former mikvah, and Alef *(ul. Szeroka 17. Tel: +48-12/421-3870. www.alef.pl)*.

Institutions include the Center for Jewish Culture, located in a renovated former prayer house, and the Galicia Jewish Museum, both of which feature series of lectures, concerts, and exhibits on Jewish themes. And every summer, the annual Festival of Jewish Culture draws thousands of fans. Founded in 1988, the nine-day festival is a rich mix of more than 150 separate concerts, workshops, performances, exhibitions, lectures, and more ending with a huge outdoor concert, "Shalom on Szeroka." The tiny Jewish community, too, is active, with a resident rabbi and lively youth group.

Most of the Jewish sites in Kazimierz are grouped around two squares, elongated Szeroka street, where several synagogues are located, and Plac Nowy, once the Jewish marketplace. Sites in or on the edge of the district include:

• **Old Synagogue:** ul. Szeroka 24—Erected in the 15th century and remodeled many times since then, this was the first synagogue to be constructed in Kazimierz. It is a fortresslike building with a distinctive facade marked by slim corner towers. Ruined during World War II, it was rebuilt in the 1950s as the Museum of Jewish History and Culture—a branch of the Cracow History Museum. There is a permanent exhibition of Judaica and other objects, but the main exhibition is the synagogue itself, with its elaborate wrought-iron bimah and vaulted ceilings.

• **Remuh Synagogue and Old Jewish Cemetery:** ul. Szeroka 40—Built in the mid-16th century and remodeled several times over the centuries, the synagogue is still the center of religious life in Cracow. Regular services are held in the tiny vaulted sanctuary, which preserves the original 16th-century Ark. Entered through a courtyard with an elegant, arched gate, the synagogue was founded by Israel Isserles, the father of the scholar Moses Isserles, or Remuh, whose fenced-off tomb in the Old Jewish Cemetery next to the synagogue is still a place of pilgrimage.

Used from 1551 to 1800, the Old Jewish Cemetery was already in poor condition in the 1930s, and was totally devastated by the Nazis. In 1959, however, excavations unearthed more than 700 beautifully carved tombstones dating back to the 16th century, which had been buried under the surface. These were re-erected in neat rows, providing what is more of a museum of cemetery art than a real cemetery. Broken fragments, meanwhile, were used to create a very moving mosaic memorial wall.

• **Kupa Synagogue:** ul. Miodowa 27—Originally built in the 1640s, the synagogue was severely damaged during and after World War II. A recent full restoration by the National Fund for the Restoration of Cracow's Monuments conserved its brilliantly colored murals from the 1920s and 1930s—the only examples of this type of 20th-century Jewish art to have survived in Cracow.

• **High Synagogue:** ul. Jozefa 38—Built around 1560, the synagogue occupies the upper floor of a building whose facade features four buttresses and three arched windows. Recently restored, it now serves as an exhibition hall. The Austeria Jewish bookstore is on the ground floor.

• **Izaak Synagogue:** ul. Kupa 16—The wealthy community elder Izaak Jakubowicz financed the building of the synagogue in 1638. It was restored in the 1990s, revealing beautiful, if fragmentary, frescoes and richly decorative stuccowork and other architectural detail under a lofty vaulted ceiling. The upstairs women's gallery has a wonderfully graceful arcade. Today, the sanctuary hosts an exhibition that includes life-size cutout figures of prewar Jews, material on the Holocaust, and a film on prewar Jewish life. The Jewish youth group Czulent uses the annex next door.

• **Popper Synagogue:** ul. Szeroka 16—Also known as the Bocian Synagogue, the Popper Synagogue is at the end of a deep shady courtyard used in summer by the Alef café-restaurant. Built in 1620, its heavily buttressed structure remains intact, but all interior decoration has been lost, and the synagogue has long been used as a cultural center.

• **Tempel Synagogue:** ul. Miodowa 24—A magnificent synagogue with gorgeous, Moorish-style interior decoration, the Tempel was built in the 1860s for the local Progressive (Reform) community and is the only 19th-century synagogue to have survived the Holocaust in Poland intact. It was fully restored in the 1990s and is now used for services by visiting groups and also serves as a concert hall.

• **Galicia Jewish Museum:** ul. Dajwor 18—Established by the British photographer Chris Schwarz in 2004, the museum houses a permanent exhibition of Schwarz's photographs of Jewish heritage sites in southeastern Poland. Located in a converted factory, it also hosts a wide range of cultural and educational events and has a café and well-stocked bookstore.

• **Plac Nowy:** The former Jewish market is dominated by a circular building dating from 1900 that was used from 1927 as a kosher slaughterhouse for poultry. The square still functions as an open-air marketplace and is also a popular hub for youth-oriented cafés, pubs, and music clubs. The pale green building on the corner of Meiselsa street is a former prayer house, now the Centrum Judaicum, a Jewish culture center that hosts lectures, exhibitions, and many other programs.

• **New Jewish Cemetery:** ul. Miodowa 55—Still in use today, this vast cemetery was founded in 1800, after the old cemetery was closed. It encompasses thousands of tombstones representing the whole range of Jewish symbolism and design. Many prominent Cracow Jews are buried here, among them the painter Maurycy Gottlieb (1856–1879) and the prewar Reform rabbi Ozjasz Thon, who was a member of the Polish Parliament and who died in 1936.

World War II Ghetto: The Nazis set up the Cracow Ghetto in March 1941 in the Podgorze District, just across the Vistula River from Kazimierz. Plac Bohaterow Getta (Ghetto Heroes Square), now ringed with modern buildings, was in its heart, the place from which Jews were deported to death camps, mainly Auschwitz, Belzec, and nearby Plaszow. Here, at No. 18, a museum contains exhibits on the ghetto and the Nazi occupation. It is housed in what during the war was the Sign of the Eagle Pharmacy. A new ghetto memorial in the form of empty chairs was dedicated in 2006, and a fragment of the ghetto walls can be seen on Lwowska street. The onetime enamelware factory run by the German industrialist Oskar Schindler still stands at Lipowa 4.

Plaszow: off ul. Kamienskiego—The infamous Plaszow concentration camp, located southeast of the ghetto, was built on the site of a Jewish cemetery. It was here that Oskar Schindler managed to save some 700 or more Jews by putting them on a "list" to work in a planned munitions factory. There are monuments here to Jews and others murdered in the camp.

Addresses of Note in Cracow

- Jewish Community: ul. Skawinska 2. Tel/fax: +48-12/429-5735
- Chabad: ul. Jozefa Dietla 35/9. Tel: +48-669/977-992
- Centrum Judaicum, Center for Jewish Culture: ul. Meiselsa 17. Tel: +48-12/430-6449. www.judaica.pl
- Galicia Jewish Museum: ul. Dajwor 18. Tel: +48-12/421-6842. www.galiciajewishmuseum.org
- Czulent Jewish youth organization: www.czulent.pl
- Festival of Jewish Culture: ul. Jozefa 36. Tel: +48-12/431-1517, fax: +48-12/431-2427. www.jewishfestival.pl
- Kosher hotel: Hotel Eden, ul. Ciemna 15. Tel: +48-12/430-6565; fax: +48-12/430-6767. www.hoteleden.pl. A fully kosher hotel, which also has a private mikvah and kosher dining facilities.

Several bookstores in Cracow specialize in Jewish topics and stock many publications in English:

- Austeria: ul. Jozefa 38
- Galicia Museum bookshop: ul. Dajwor 18
- Jarden Bookshop and Tourist Agency: ul. Szeroka 2. www.jarden.pl
- Massolit Books and Café: ul. Felicjanek 4. Tel: +48-12/432-4150. American-run; probably the best English-language bookstore in East-Central Europe.

Near Cracow

AUSCHWITZ-BIRKENAU AND OSWIECIM (OŚWIĘCIM)–The biggest and most notorious complex of Nazi extermination camps is situated outside Oswiecim, about 40 miles west of Cracow. Auschwitz (the German name for Oswiecim) has become synonymous with the Holocaust, and the notorious "*Arbeit Macht Frei*—Work Makes You Free" slogan over the camp's main gate is one of the most potent Holocaust images. At least 1.5 million people, the overwhelming majority of them Jews from all over Europe, were murdered here, mainly at the so-called Auschwitz II camp at Birkenau, about two miles away from the main facility. The camps form a complex that each year draws more than half a million visitors ranging from heads of state to school groups to pilgrims paying homage to the dead.

Auschwitz and Birkenau were declared national monuments and designated as museum memorials in 1947. At the Auschwitz I camp, exhibits were set up in barracks and administration buildings. So-called national pavilions were created to display exhibitions on how citizens of various countries suffered under the Nazis. Many of these, however, were pure communist propaganda. Throughout the museum complex, the fact that 90 percent of the victims were Jews—and killed only because they were Jews—was scarcely mentioned. This misrepresentation changed radically after the fall of communism. Exhibitions, publications, and other on-site informational material were revamped and expanded to illustrate the true history of the camp and its victims.

Before World War II, Oswiecim was a shtetl known in Yiddish as Oshpitsin. Well over half of its population was Jewish. In the town of Oswiecim itself there is now a Jewish study and prayer center, the Auschwitz Jewish Center, which conducts cultural and educational programs. The center opened in 2000 in a complex including the Chevra Lomdei Mishnayot Synagogue, the only surviving synagogue in town, which had been used for years as a warehouse. The synagogue has been restored for religious use, and an adjacent building includes an exhibition about Jewish life in Oswiecim before the Holocaust. In September 2006, the center merged with the Museum of Jewish Heritage—A Living Memorial to the Holocaust in New York. Oswiecim also has a restored Jewish cemetery. *(Museum Memorial: www.auschwitz.org.pl; Auschwitz Jewish Center: Plac Ks. Jana Skarbka 3/5. Tel: +48-33/844-7002. www.ajcf.org)*

BOBOWA—This small village in the rolling farmland of southern Poland was a major Hasidic center, home to the court of Shlomo Halberstamm (1847–1906), known as the Bobover rebbe. His successor, the rebbe Ben Zion Halberstamm, was killed by the Nazis in 1941, but Ben Zion's son survived the Holocaust and moved the headquarters of the Bobover Hasidim to New York. Even during communist times, pilgrims came to pay their respects at the tombs in the Jewish cemetery, located high on a hill overlooking the village. Much of the town center retains the look of an old shtetl. The 18th-century synagogue, with a wooden-galleried front, a steeply sloping peaked roof and a wonderfully carved wooden Ark, was long used as a weaving workshop. Returned to Jewish ownership in 1993, it was refurbished by Bobover Hasidism and is again used as a place of prayer.

CHECINY (CHĘCINY)—Quaint houses and shops still cluster around the market square in this former shtetl 55 miles north of Cracow. The stone synagogue, built in 1638, is located at Dluga 19. Now a culture center, it retains a two-tiered mansard roof and other original features, including vaulted ceilings, a stone portal with a Hebrew inscription, and the frame of the Aron ha Kodesh. An overgrown Jewish cemetery with early 17th-century tombstones lies on a forested hilltop above town near the castle.

CHMIELNIK—Before World War II, about 12,000 people—as many as 10,000 of them Jews—lived in this small town near Kielce. Today, the population numbers only 4,000. Local historian Piotr Krawczyk summed it up succinctly: "No Jews here; no people." For the past few years, Krawczyk, Chmielnik's mayor, and other local activists have worked to restore the memory of Jewish presence. Chmielnik sponsors a Jewish culture festival each summer (usually in June), and local authorities are seeking funds to restore the synagogue and complete a Holocaust memorial at the site of one of the Jewish cemeteries.

The synagogue, a large masonry structure with barrel vaulting, was originally built in the 1630s. The Nazis turned it into a warehouse, but the interior still retains traces of lovely decoration, including 18th-century stuccowork and frescoes of lions, geometric forms, and the signs of the zodiac. Chmielnik had two Jewish cemeteries, both destroyed by the Nazis. New houses stand on the site of one of them (but not, I was told, in any area where there were actual graves). Piotr Krawczyk led me over the site of the other cemetery, just across the street, where the town had begun fencing off the area in preparation to build a large memorial there to the town's Jews. It was an open, sloping field, and walking was difficult; the lumpy surface hid toppled and buried gravestones.

DABROWA TARNOWSKA (DĄBROWA TARNOWSKA)–A large synagogue stands empty on Berka Joselewicza street in this town near Tarnow. Designed by Abraham Goldstein and built in 1865, it has a multistory arcaded facade added in 1937. Inside, there are traces of delicate frescoes of animals, plants, zodiac symbols, birds, texts, and curtains. Across the street is a Jewish cemetery. Here, in June 1942, according to an eyewitness quoted by Martin Gilbert in his book *The Holocaust,* the local rabbi and a group of his followers went to their deaths in a remarkable display of bravery. Somehow they managed to bring a bottle of vodka when the Nazis herded them to the graveyard. They toasted each other with the traditional wish *l'chaim*—to life—then joined hands and began to dance. The Nazis shot them down as they were dancing.

DEBICA (DĘBICA)–The fine synagogue in this small town near Tarnow was built in the 18th century. It stands right on the main road and has been used for years as a sort of department store. Some of the architectural elements, such as columns and arched ceilings, remain. The Jewish cemetery, restored in the 1990s, has a Holocaust memorial. There is also a memorial in the forest where 600 Jews were killed and buried in a mass grave.

DZIALOSZYCE (DZIAŁOSZYCE)–The roofless wreck of a neoclassic synagogue dominates a plaza near the main square of this dusty village about 30 miles north of Cracow. Designed by the architect Felicjan Frankowski, it was built in 1852. Only the outer walls remain, punctuated by tall, round-topped windows and sculpted ornamentation; adult birch trees somehow grow right out of the stone, and one Hebrew inscription remains above one empty, circular window.

In 1939, 70 percent of the town was Jewish. In the first few days of September 1942, the Nazis shot as many as 2,000 Jews and tossed their bodies into mass graves near the Jewish cemetery. They deported 8,000 more to the death camp at Belzec. The cemetery was destroyed, and a memorial now stands on Skalbmierska street, at the foot of the hill where it was located.

When I first visited Dzialoszyce in 1990, a wrinkled old woman approached my companions and me and mumbled some Yiddish words at us.

The roofless ruins of the 19th-century synagogue in Dzialoszyce, north of Cracow

She apologized that it had been such a long time since she had spoken the language and told us she had worked for the local rabbi. "I will never forget what he told me," she said. "He said that when the birds go away from here, the Jews will go away, too. One year there was a hard winter; there were no birds. And after that…" *(Additional information: www.dzialoszyce.org)*

GRYBOW (GRYBÓW)–I find something particularly moving about the abandoned, scallop-roofed synagogue in this pretty little town southeast of Cracow, almost next door to the soaring redbrick Catholic church. According to locals, during the war the Jews gave some of the synagogue items to the Catholic priest, who buried them for safekeeping. These mementoes are now displayed in the church—some candlesticks, a menorah, prayer books, and Torah fragments.

On my latest visit, in 2006, a woman emerged from the house next door when she saw me taking pictures of the synagogue. Gray-haired and elegant, she spoke with emotion about the building. "The structure is still sound, but each year it gets worse and worse," she told me. "Bricks fall, one after the other; the roof begins to collapse. Even five years ago it was a different story." I asked her about the Jewish cemetery, which I remembered as a site of overgrown desolation set high on a hilltop on a dirt road past the Catholic cemetery. "Oh, it's beautiful!" she exclaimed. She began to give me directions, but decided to get her coat and show me the way herself. Much had changed. What I remembered as a dirt track was now a paved road lined with new houses. The cemetery, I found, had recently been cleared of major brush and saplings and enclosed by an iron rail fence. We walked around the entire perimeter, circling the cemetery and looking out at the spectacular views of rolling farmland and rich pastures dotted by yellow spring flowers.

NOWY KORCZYN—The synagogue near the main square of this run-down village 40 miles from Cracow was built in the 18th century. Today it is a majestic wreck, with a ruined, colonnaded porch. I went inside, worrying the whole time that the roof might crash down on my head. There, on the eastern wall, two proud lions with exuberant tails stood rampant above the delicate pillars of the ruined Ark, supporting a crown. The crown represented the Torah, and, bizarrely, a trick of lighting, or a trick of my own imagination, made it seem as if the exposed brickwork inside the empty niche was actually a scroll.

In the summer of 2006, Olaf Wajs, a bearded young man wearing a *kippah,* was introduced to me as the last Jew in the village. "Growing up, I knew I was Jewish; both my parents are Jewish," he told me. "But it was something we never spoke about: My father and my grandfather had both lost their jobs during the 1968 persecution." Olaf told me that the Jewish cemetery in Nowy Korczyn had been totally destroyed and the tombstones had been used to pave local roads. "I'm trying to find them and recover them," he said. He already had organized the construction of a fence around the cemetery site on Grotniki Duze street. He also had recently affixed a mezuzah to the doorpost of his house. "I want to cultivate the traditions of my ancestors," he told me. "I am left here as the only guardian, the only memory of the Nowy Korczyn Jewish community." *(Contact: Olaf Wajs, ul. Stopnicka 10. E-mail: olaf_wajs@op.pl)*

NOWY SACZ (NOWY SĄCZ)—Nowy Sacz, 45 miles southeast of Cracow, was a Hasidic center, home to the tzaddik Chaim Halberstamm (1793–1876), who founded a noted dynasty. Halberstamm's tomb is in the Jewish cemetery on Rybacka street, and there is a private Hasidic prayer room at Jagiellonska 12. The 18th-century Great Synagogue at Berka Joselewicza 12 is well preserved as a district museum and art gallery, with a permanent exhibition on local Jewish history. A plaque commemorates the 25,000 local Jews killed in the Holocaust. The former Jewish community building, hospital, and yeshivah also still stand.

PINCZOW (PIŃCZÓW)–Jews lived in this town between Cracow and Kielce as early as the 16th century and eventually made up such a large percentage of the population that their presence gave rise to a popular saying: to be "as crowded as the Jews in Pinczow." The cube-shaped Old Synagogue on Klasztorna street, just off the main square, dates back to the early 17th century and is the town's only remaining Jewish relic; a newer synagogue and the three Jewish cemeteries were destroyed during and after the war. The Old Synagogue was desecrated by the Nazis and later used to store fertilizer. Starting in the 1990s, it underwent a slow but sensitive restoration and now represents one of the best preserved Renaissance synagogues in Poland. It features beautifully restored fragments of 18th-century frescoes attributed to the Jewish painter Jehudah Leib. (Leib's son decorated the interior of the synagogue in Boskovice, Czech Republic.) Painted wall inscriptions of texts came to light during the restoration, and the carved Aron ha Kodesh—a fine example of local stonework—has been preserved and restored. Administered as a branch of the Regional Museum in Pinczow, the synagogue houses an exhibit of photographs and other material on local Jewish history. The surrounding wall now forms a memorial mosaic built from thousands of fragments of shattered tombstones.

SZYDLOW (SZYDŁÓW)–A tiny but exceptionally interesting walled village between Kielce and Tarnow, Szydlow is a fine example of a Gothic urban architectural complex. Its three main buildings are the castle, the synagogue, and a Gothic church, all massive stone structures that would have anchored the town defenses. Built in the 16th century, the synagogue is one of the oldest in Poland. It is large and blocklike, with heavy buttresses on all sides and a crenellated roof. Legend has it that it was founded by King Kazimierz (Casimir) the Great's Jewish lover, Esterka. It was converted into a culture center in the 1960s; the arched-and-vaulted sanctuary was painted white, but the frame of the Aron ha Kodesh was left intact.

TARNOW (TARNÓW) (YIDDISH: TORNE OR TARNE)–Located about 45 miles east of Cracow, Tarnow has one of Poland's loveliest

Old Town districts, centered on a market square, or Rynek, edged by pastel-colored buildings. Its town hall was originally built in the 14th century, and the late Gothic cathedral dates from around 1400. The regional museum at Rynek 21/22 has a fine collection of Judaica items and other material on local Jewish history and traditions, including a document dating from 1667 granting Jews privileges to live and trade in Tarnow.

Jews first settled here in the mid-15th century, and the old Jewish section grew up off the Rynek, along winding Zydowska (Jewish) street, where the haunting remains of the 17th-century Old Synagogue can be seen. The Nazis torched the building in 1939 and blew up the ruins a few years later. All that's left are the four pillars of the central bimah, now covered by a protective canopy and marked with a memorial plaque. About 25,000 Jews lived in Tarnow in 1939, nearly half the town's population—elderly people remember the streets crowded with Jews in black coats and beards. On June 13, 1940, more than 700 Tarnow men, including some Jews, were dragged to the Moorish-style mikvah (which still stands). The next morning, they were shipped by train to Auschwitz. This was the first transport to Auschwitz, which at that time was a concentration camp for political prisoners and others. A monument across from the mikvah, on Plac Wiezniow Oswiecimia (Auschwitz Prisoners' Square) commemorates these first deportees. About a block away, at the corner of Nowa and Warynskiego streets, a plaque marks the site where the domed New Synagogue stood until the Nazis blew it up. Thousands of Jews were executed in the main square in June 1942—a plaque at the corner of Zydowska street commemorates them. Almost all the rest were deported to their deaths in Belzec, Auschwitz, or Plaszow.

Tarnow's Jewish cemetery, at the intersection of Szpitalna and Sloneczna streets, is one of the most impressive in Poland, with thousands of distinctively carved tombstones dating back to the 17th century. The animal and plant motifs, as well as the style of Hebrew lettering, have close links to naïve folk art traditions. A Holocaust memorial there is constructed from one broken pillar that survived the destruction of the New Synagogue. *(Additional information: www.muzeum.tarnow.pl/judaica/przewodnik/english.htm)*

WODZISLAW (WODZISŁAW)–The hulking ruin of a late 16th- to early 17th-century synagogue crouches in a slight hollow near the center of this village on the main road between Kielce and Cracow. It is a magnificent, battered, and very evocative wreck. A Holocaust monument stands in the fenced-in remains of the destroyed Jewish cemetery, right on the road, just outside of town. Wodzislaw was the birthplace of Simcha Bunam (circa 1765–1827), a lumber merchant and trained pharmacist who opened himself to Western culture and learning but eventually turned inward and became an influential Hasidic master in Przysucha.

LUBLIN

A BEAUTIFUL (IF STILL SOMEWHAT RUNDOWN) CITY IN EASTERN POLAND, HOME to a renowned Roman Catholic university, Lublin was long a major center of Jewish life, commerce, culture, and scholarship. Jews settled here as early as the 14th century, eventually forming a separate Jewish town at the foot of the castle hill. For nearly two centuries, Lublin was the main seat of the Council of Four Lands, the ruling body of Jews in Poland that was established around 1580.

The Hasidic master Yakov Yitzhak ha-Levi Horovitz (1745–1815), a charismatic figure known as ha-Hozeh, or the Seer, of Lublin, had his court here. Nearly blind, he was said instead to have the ability to see into people's souls. He and two fellow Hasidic masters, Menachem Mendel of Rymanow and the Maggid of Kozhenets (Kozienice), became convinced that the Napoleonic Wars heralded the end of the world. The Messiah would come and redeem the Jews, they believed, if Napoleon conquered the world and turned it over to the Redeemer. All three prayed fervently for such a victory; all three died in 1815, the year of Napoleon's final defeat at Waterloo.

Before World War II, the Jewish community numbered 40,000, or nearly 40 percent of the city. The Jewish quarter was a labyrinth of streets, squares, and alleyways, with numerous synagogues and study houses. The Nazis razed almost all of it. They deported most Lublin Jews to the Majdanek death camp, just outside Lublin, or to Belzec, in the south. Still, more than 4,500 Jews remained in the city at the war's end.

A few important Jewish sites have survived, but, for the most part, commemorative plaques and monuments tell the story. The local tourism board has put together a Jewish heritage itinerary, which can be walked in a few hours. *(A pamphlet is available at the tourist information office at Jezuicka 1/3 or at www.um.lublin.pl/lang/en/szlaki/2.pdf.)* A plaque in the parking area at the base of the castle steps commemorates the old Jewish town that once spread out around the spot. Another plaque, on Tysiaclecia avenue, marks where the magnificent Maharshal and Maharam Synagogues stood. The Maharshal Synagogue, built in 1567, is believed to have been the first synagogue to employ the distinctive four-pillar central bimah plan, which became typical for many Polish synagogues. The Grodzka Gate once formed the entrance to the Old Town from the Jewish quarter. Just inside, the Grodzka Gate–Theater NN Center maintains a multimedia exhibition on prewar Lublin, which features a scale model of the city, including the Jewish quarter, as it was in 1939. A few doors away, at Grodzka 11, a plaque marks the former Jewish orphanage and memorializes Jewish children murdered here by the Nazis on March 24, 1942.

Several Jewish-style restaurants have recently opened in the Old Town. Among them are the Mandragora Jewish Pub *(ul. Rynek 9. Tel: +48-81/536-2020. www.mandragora.lublin.pl)* and Szeroka 28 *(ul. Grodzka 21. Tel: +48-81/534-6109)*.

Main Sites of Jewish Interest in Lublin

Old Jewish Cemetery: entrance from ul. Kalinowszczynza, just past the church—Founded in the early 1500s, this is believed to be Poland's oldest existing Jewish cemetery. It was desecrated many times over the centuries, and the Nazis tore it up and used its stones for paving. Still, precious graves remain, including that of the Seer of Lublin and the great Talmudic scholar Shalom Shachna, who died in 1558. The oldest tombstone—believed to be the oldest Jewish gravestone in Poland in situ—is that of the scholar Jakob Kopelman ha Levi, who died in 1541.

New Jewish Cemetery: ul. Walecznych—Founded in 1829, the cemetery was totally devastated during World War II but underwent extensive renovation in the 1980s and 1990s. A modernistic memorial center housing the symbolic tomb of Rabbi Yehuda Meir Shapiro, an influential Jewish scholar who died in 1933, now stands at the entrance. There are also many memorials to Holocaust victims.

Former Yeshivaht Chachmei Lublin: corner of ul. Unicka and ul. Lubartowska—Founded by Rabbi Yehuda Meir Shapiro in 1930, this yeshivah was an influential bastion of traditional Orthodoxy, even though it was shut down in 1939. In 1923, Shapiro inaugurated what is known as the Daf Yomi cycle of studying one page a day of the Talmud. All over the world, hundreds of thousands of Jews follow this program, and celebrations are held at the completion of the full seven-year cycle. In

2005, such celebrations took place in the former yeshivah building for the first time since 1938.

After the war, the huge building became part of Lublin's medical school. It returned to Jewish ownership in 2004, and in 2006 a suite of rooms, including a new little synagogue, was inaugurated as the new headquarters of the tiny Lublin Jewish community. Plans were under way to create a Jewish museum there, too. The former premises of the Jewish community, at Lubartowska 8, just outside the Old Town, also has a small prayer room and a small commemorative display of ritual and historical materials. A sculptural Holocaust monument has stood since 1963 in a little plaza a few steps away, just off Lubartowska. As of this writing there were plans to move it, probably to a site near the former Yeshivaht Chachmei Lublin.

Majdanek: The site of the death camp where the Nazis murdered more than 350,000 people, including more than 100,000 Jews from the Warsaw and Lublin Ghettos, is located on the outskirts of the city. It includes a museum with chilling exhibitions. There is a memorial incorporating an immense mound of human ashes, as well as a huge monument shaped like a menorah. *(Additional information: www.majdanek.pl)*

ADDRESSES OF NOTE IN LUBLIN

- Jewish community: ul. Lubartowska 85
- Grodzka Gate-NN Theater Center: ul. Grodzka 21. Tel: +48-81/532-58-67 www.tnn.lublin.pl

---

NEAR LUBLIN

KAZIMIERZ DOLNY—Picturesquely situated on the Vistula River 25 miles west of Lublin, Kazimierz Dolny is one of the loveliest towns in Poland and has long been a favorite summer resort and artists' retreat. Jews settled here in medieval times. Eventually many were merchants, using the river to float timber, grain, and other goods to Gdansk. Before World War II Jews made up nearly two-thirds of the town's population; Jewish names can be found among the graffiti scratched in prewar years by visitors to the ruined hilltop castle.

The town is centered on a large market square, or Rynek, lined with Renaissance buildings. The stone synagogue, originally built in the second

The Holocaust memorial in Kazimierz Dolny, built of broken tombstones, was erected in the 1980s on the site of a Jewish cemetery.

half of the 18th century, stands in what is called the Maly (small) Rynek. Devastated by the Nazis, it was rebuilt to its original outer appearance in the 1950s and used until the mid-1990s as a cinema. A plaque there memorializes the 3,000 or so local Jews killed in the Holocaust. The synagogue has been returned to Jewish ownership and can now be visited—entry is through the flower shop built into one side. The Goldsmith Museum *(ul. Senatorska 11)* exhibits some Jewish silver ritual objects.

Both of Kazimierz Dolny's Jewish cemeteries—the old one dating to the 16th century and the new one established in 1851—were wrecked by the Nazis. Today, a striking Holocaust monument stands at the site of the New Cemetery, on a hill just outside town on the road to Opole Lubelskie. In the mid-1980s, hundreds of recovered gravestones and fragments were built into an immense, mosaiclike wall, split by a jagged vertical crack symbolizing the sudden extinction of the Jewish community. Stepping through the crack, you find yourself in a dense, peaceful forest, where the remnants of the New Cemetery stand amid the trees that have grown up over the past 60 years. The physical (and symbolic) transition from sunlight to deep shadow makes you catch your breath.

The Jewish-style restaurant U Fryzjera *(ul. Witkiewicza 2. Tel: +48-81/881-0426. www.ufryzjera.pl)*, unlike some Jewish-style places, serves pork; its menu marks "Jewish" and "not Jewish" dishes.

KOCK–This little town's slumbering present belies a colorful past. Located between Warsaw and Lublin, Kock is famous in Hasidic lore as having been the seat of the 19th-century tzaddik Menachem Mendel Morgenstern. Born in nearby Goraj in 1787 and trained as a pharmacist, Menachem Mendel arrived in Kock in 1829 and soon drew a huge following—the Yiddish writer Joseph Opatashu vividly described the atmosphere in his novel *In Poilishe Velder* (*In Polish Woods*). In 1839, a mysterious incident prompted Menachem Mendel to go into seclusion, and he spent the last 20 years of his life locked in his room, following prayer services through holes drilled in his door. This behavior spawned a wealth of mystic tales and legends. Nothing was ever explained, however, and before his death Menachem Mendel ordered all his writings destroyed.

Today, a monument formed from tombstones marks the tzaddik's burial place in the Jewish cemetery. The cemetery lies just outside town, down a dirt road—follow Hanki Sawickiej street from the main square to a roadside shrine to John the Baptist and turn right. Ruined during the war, it is now a huge fenced forest with few markers other than the tzaddik's tomb. (The farmer in the house just beyond the cemetery has the key.) In the village itself, a number of quaint wooden houses recall prewar times. One, at the corner of Wojska Polskiego and Polna streets, has a little wooden tower and was the residence of a 20th-century tzaddik.

Outside town, on Berek Joselewicz street, two irregular boulders in a small fenced area under a pair of trees mark the grave of Berek Joselewicz, a Jewish Polish Army colonel and cavalry chief who led a 500-member Jewish regiment that fought for Polish independence with Tadeusz Kosciuszko's forces against the Russian and Prussian Armies in 1794. Born in 1760, Joselewicz died in the Battle of Kock in 1809, fighting against the Austrians during the Napoleonic Wars.

KRASNIK (KRAŚNIK)–Two synagogues stand side by side on Boznicza (Synagogue) street in the middle of this town south of Lublin. The

A horse and cart drive past the distinctive wooden house in Kock where a rabbi once lived.

main synagogue, built in the mid-17th century, retains colorful frescoes and other interior decoration. Both are supposed to be open to visitors, but it is not always possible to gain entrance. A handful of tombstones and a weathered Holocaust memorial remain in the ruined Jewish cemetery. Israeli soldiers cleaned up the site in 2006.

LECZNA (ŁĘCZNA)–The thick-walled, 17th-century synagogue on Boznicza (Synagogue) street in this small town east of Lublin was rebuilt after World War II and houses the Leczna Regional Museum. The restoration preserved the central four-pillar bimah and decorated Ark. There is a large exhibition on local Jewish history and traditions in the sanctuary and a wonderful exhibit of colorful Jewish paper-cuts by the Cracow-based artist Marta Golab in the foyer. The town library next door was once a Jewish prayer house. Prewar houses near the synagogue and the nearby small marketplace (Rynek II) retain the look of an old shtetl. A group of tombstones salvaged from the destroyed Jewish cemetery has been set in the synagogue yard as a monument.

WLODAWA (WŁODAWA) (YIDDISH: VLODAVA)–Wlodawa, on the border with Belarus and Ukraine, has an important complex of beautifully restored synagogues, now housing the Leczna-Wlodawa Lake District

Museum. The stately Great Synagogue, built between 1764 and 1774, was severely damaged by the Nazis and then used for decades as a warehouse. It was opened to the public in 1986 after a full reconstruction. The large central section, housing the sanctuary, has tall arched windows and a high-peaked, multisloped mansard roof. This central block is flanked by two smaller side elements with ground-floor arcades. Inside, four columns support the vaulted ceiling, denoting where the central bimah once stood. The walls and ceiling vaults contain original frescoes and stuccowork from the 18th century. An extremely elaborate Aron ha Kodesh fills the eastern wall. It was constructed in the 1930s in brightly painted stuccowork to replace the original wooden Ark that had been destroyed in a fire. Lacy decoration frames a big, gilded menorah, surrounded by twisted columns and other symbolic imagery, including musical instruments, fruit, and hands extended in blessing. At the top, two winged griffins support the tablets of the Ten Commandments.

The sanctuary houses a valuable exhibition on local Jewish history and traditions, and in the former women's prayer room a permanent installation re-creates a Jewish schoolroom. Shelves are full of books, a table stands ready for students, clothes hang on pegs. Next door, the Small Synagogue, built in 1786, has wonderful original decoration including wall frescoes and inscriptions. The third synagogue in the complex, a prayer house built in 1928, is used as the museum's offices and storerooms.

Jews settled in Wlodawa in the late 16th or early 17th century. The community was virtually wiped out during the Chmielnicki Uprising in 1648 but quickly recovered; on the eve of World War II, 5,600 Jews made up more than 60 percent of the population. They were all taken to Sobibor, a Nazi death camp a few miles to the south, where about 250,000 people were killed between 1942 and 1943; about 300 managed to escape during a prisoners' revolt in October 1943. A monument to the victims stands on the site, and the Leczna-Wlodawa Lake District Museum operates a small branch at Czerwonego Krzyza 7.

LODZ

(Polish: Łódź)

Today a struggling industrial city of more than 800,000 people, Lodz was home to Poland's second largest Jewish community before World War II, a dynamic mix of wealthy capitalists, a comfortable middle class, and a proletariat underclass who often lived in squalor. During World War II it was the site of one of the Nazis' most infamous Jewish ghettos; today it has a tiny but increasingly active reborn Jewish community.

Lodz was a small, insignificant town until the mid-19th century, when, largely thanks to Jewish (and German) input, it began to develop into a major textile center. Jews began settling here in the late 18th century and played important roles as factory owners, bankers, merchants, and professionals, as well as members of the proletariat. By the beginning of the 20th century, an enormous gap existed between the elite Jewish upper class and the poorer workers and artisans who maintained traditional lifestyles—or else were secular Socialists. The Yiddish writer Israel Joshua Singer brilliantly evoked this tapestry in his novel *The Brothers Ashkenazi*.

Before World War II, more than 200,000 Jews lived in Lodz—about one-third of the city's total population. In the spring of 1940, the Nazis forced them all, rich and poor alike, into a ghetto. Conditions were terrible; those who did not die of illness and starvation were deported to death camps. Fewer than 900 Jews remained in the ghetto at the war's end.

Main Sites of Jewish Interest in Lodz

Jewish Communal Complex: ul. Pomorska 18—Only a few hundred Jews live in Lodz, but the community is remarkably active. Its gregarious leader, Cantor Simcha Keller, has played a particularly important role in reviving Jewish life in the city. The downtown communal compound includes a prayer room, offices, a guesthouse, and a pleasant kosher café and restaurant, Café Tuwim. The Jewish community maintains a library and archives, including community records from the wartime ghetto, and can help with genealogy research and arrange local Jewish-interest tours.

Synagogue: ul. Poludniowa 28—Lodz's splendid main synagogues were all destroyed in November 1939, soon after the Nazis marched in. The Great Synagogue, one of the largest and most magnificent in Poland, stood at the corner of Zachodnia and Zielona streets. One small synagogue still stands. It was built at the end of the 19th century as a private prayer house for the businessman Wolf Reicher and his family; Reicher starved to death in the Lodz Ghetto in 1941, at the age of 83.

Piotrkowska Street: Lodz's main artery, its Fifth Avenue or Champs Elysées, stretches straight as a ruler for miles, lined by elegant mansions that housed banks, businesses, and the homes of the upper crust. Sculptures and

A life-size statue of the pianist Artur Rubinstein, a native son, is one of the attractions of Piotrkowska street in Lodz.

monuments dot the sidewalks, including life-size bronze figures of the Lodz-born pianist Artur Rubinstein (1887–1982) and poet Julian Tuwim (1894–1953). The beautifully ornamented former bank of Wilhelm Landau is at Piotrkowska 29, and the former mansion and bank of Maksymilian Goldfelder is at Piotrkowska 77. No. 242/248 was a textile factory built by the industrialist Markus Silberstein.

Poznanski Palace: The stupendous domed mansion built by the textile magnate I. K. Poznanski stands on Ogrodowa street, near where Piotrkowska street begins, right next to Poznanski's sprawling redbrick factory. Poznanski (1833–1900) was Lodz's richest tycoon, a sort of Polish Great Gatsby. His mansion now houses the Lodz History Museum. The opulence of the furniture and fittings, many of them original, is astonishing. The museum includes considerable material of Jewish interest, including a gallery dedicated to Artur Rubinstein and exhibitions on Julian Tuwim and Lodz-born Jerzy Kosinski, the author of *The Painted Bird.* Two other mansions owned by the Poznanski family house the Music Academy, at Gdanska 32, and the Museum of Art, at Wieckowskiego 36.

New Jewish Cemetery: ul. Zmienna—The New Jewish Cemetery, founded in 1892 to replace an earlier cemetery that no longer exists, is one of the most important Jewish monuments in Poland. Extending over 104 acres, it encompasses some 180,000 tombs of all sorts and styles—including traditional-style gravestones, sarcophagi, and elaborate mausoleums. The most impressive mausoleum is I. K. Poznanski's towering family tomb: a huge domed ediface as big as a house. About 40,000 people who died in the Lodz Ghetto were buried here; outside the main gate there is a large Holocaust memorial. *(Additional information: www.jewishlodzcemetery.org/cmentarz.html)*

Ghetto: The Nazis herded some 230,000 Jews into the Lodz Ghetto, which they set up in the Baluty District, north of the city center, around Rynek Balucki. This was the original place of Jewish settlement in Lodz, and the poor neighborhood where most of the city's working class lived before World War II. A plaque at Limanowskiego 1 commemorates the ghetto victims, and other plaques throughout the area mark ghetto landmarks. The building at Lagiewnicka 36 housed the ghetto hospital. (For a compelling evocation of the Lodz Ghetto, listen to the 2005 CD *Song of the Lodz Ghetto,* by the Jewish music group Brave Old World. It includes songs that were sung on ghetto streets and decades later collected from survivors by the Israel musicologist Gila Flam.)

Addresses of Note in Lodz

- Jewish Community: ul. Pomorska 18. Tel: +48-42/632-0427, tel/fax: +48-42/633-5156. E-mail: jewishcommunitylodz@neostrada.pl
- Kosher restaurant: Café Tuwim, ul. Pomorska 18
- Kosher hotel: Linat Orchim, ul. Pomorska 18. Tel: +48-42/632-4661, fax: +48-42/632-3722. E-mail: linatorchim@poczta.internetdsl.pl. www.linatorchim-lodz.internetdsl.pl

At the impressive Holocaust memorial at the Belzec death camp, a path cuts through a symbolic field of ashes.

ELSEWHERE IN POLAND

BELZEC (BEŁZEC)–"This whole Jewish universe of Galicia was wiped off the map and buried in this grave." So stated Poland's then president, Aleksander Kwasniewski, at the inauguration in 2004 of a devastating new Holocaust memorial complex at Belzec, the site of one of the Nazis' most lethal death camps.

Belzec is located on the Ukrainian border, in the southeast corner of Poland. Here, between March and December 1942, the Nazis murdered more than half a million Jews, most from what is now southeast Poland and western Ukraine. The victims were shipped in by train and taken almost directly to gas chambers where they were killed with exhaust fumes. Later, the Nazis tried to erase all traces of the slaughter. They dug up and burned the corpses, demolished the gas chambers and other buildings, and plowed under the fields. The Polish government erected a small monument in the 1960s, but for the most part, the site—just beyond the Belzec train station—was ignored and abandoned.

The new monument, designed by Polish artists Andrzej Solyga, Zdzislaw Pidek, and Marcin Roszcyk and carried out as a joint project of the Polish government and the American Jewish Committee, is breathtaking. Industrial slag covers the entire area, creating what looks like a field of ashes. Iron letters around the perimeter spell out the names of every shtetl and city whose Jews were killed here. The iron has rusted; red stains spread out like bloody tears. A long corridor cuts through this deathscape, penetrating deeper and deeper as it approaches a granite memorial wall. You may start in sunlight, but by the time you reach the end, rough stone towers high above your head, and the twists of rusty iron that mark the upper edges cast unsettling shadows.

There are no crowds at Belzec; no concession stands; few facilities other than an excellent little museum attached to the monument site. I was alone when I entered the pathway into the memorial. Ahead of me, though, something flitted in the air and caught the light—one white butterfly; I followed it all the way to the end. Later, I saw another white butterfly, or maybe it was the same one, flitting and fluttering low across the gray field of slag. I watched it as it went; there was only one. It zigged and zagged above the surface. Then up it flew, over the wall, into the forest. *(Additional information: www.belzec.org.pl)*

BIALA (BIAŁA)–Located in southwest Poland near the border with the Czech Republic, Biala has a large and extremely picturesque cemetery on a forested hillside. It features typical Polish-Silesian–style gravestones that have elongated oval upper sections framing exceptionally fine carving (see Osoblaha, Czech Republic pp. 172–73). There are about 800 gravestones, the oldest from the 17th century.

BIALYSTOK (BIAŁYSTOK)–Before World War II, some 40,000 Jews lived in this city in northeastern Poland. There were scores of synagogues and prayer houses, and Jews ran most shops and businesses. In the 19th century, Jews played a major role in making Bialystok an industrial center; the city was a focus of Jewish labor union activity and the Bund Party, as well as the Haskalah. Zionism, too, had a big following. Today, little is left but plaques, monuments, street names, and a few old houses.

Only three synagogue buildings survive. A small prayer house from the 1930s, at Warynskiego 24a, is used as an art gallery. Another, totally remodeled, stands at Branickiego 3. A third, on Piekna street, has been rebuilt to house a foundation named for Lazarus Ludwik Zamenhof, the Bialystok-born optician who created the Esperanto language. Zamenhof, born in 1859, was convinced that language barriers only intensified prejudice and hatred. His new international language, he thought, could help bring peace: Esperanto means "the hoping one." A plaque at the corner of Biala and Zamenhofa streets marks his birthplace.

The big Jewish cemetery on Wschodnia street, in the northern Bagnowka District of town, is the only one of Bialystok's prewar Jewish cemeteries to have survived. Once it comprised more than 40,000 tombstones; fewer than a fifth of that number remain. For decades the whole area was totally overgrown by a jungle of trees, bushes, and weeds. Much has been newly cleared, exposing the tombstones for the first time in many years. Many are toppled and broken; the ones that stand—some of them shaped like tree trunks—seem like the scorched survivors of a forest fire. One tall black memorial commemorates a pogrom in 1906, when 70 people were killed. I visited the cemetery with Tomasz Wisniewski, a non-Jew who has devoted the past 25 years to researching and recording Jewish heritage in the Bialystok region. "This whole area," he once told me, "is one big cemetery. Its history is only wars, invasions, pogroms. There is nowhere else like it."

Several monuments and plaques commemorate the Holocaust. A monument off Legionowa street now marks the spot where in 1941 the Germans herded as many as 2,000 Jews into the 18th-century Great Synagogue and set it on fire; its shape recalls the synagogue's dome twisted by flames. A memorial in a park just off Proletariacka street commemorates the 3,500 Jews killed there in August 1943. Another monument honors the hundreds of resistance fighters in the Bialystok Ghetto killed in an uprising against the Nazis in 1943.

CHELMNO (CHEŁMNO)–Chelmno, 50 miles northwest of Lodz, was the site of the first Nazi death camp in Poland; between 170,000 and 360,000 Jews were killed here, mainly stuffed into vans and gassed with carbon monoxide fumes. There is a large, decaying monument here, as well as a tiny museum and a memory wall, but the site is well off most commemoration routes and gets few visitors.

CZESTOCHOWA (CZĘSTOCHOWA)–The site of Jasna Gora Monastery, Polish Catholicism's holiest shrine, Czestochowa in south-central Poland had a vibrant Jewish community. The large Jewish cemetery underwent extensive renovation work in 2004 in conjunction with a big commemorative exhibition on Czestochowa Jews. Monuments there honor Jewish resistance fighters and mark the mass graves of Holocaust victims. The city's philharmonic hall was built on the site of the synagogue and has a memorial plaque to the Jewish community. *(Additional information: www.czestochowajews.org)*

DUKLA—Located north of the Dukla mountain pass between Slovakia and Poland, Dukla was once a prosperous wine-trading center. The pass was the scene of bloody fighting in World War II. The ruins of a massive brick synagogue, built in 1758, stand behind a fence on Cergowa street, near the town's main square. It still has an impressive stone portal. The ruined Jewish cemetery at the southern edge of town long lay abandoned, but some restoration work has been carried out in recent years.

JOZEFOW BILGORAJSKI (JÓZEFÓW BIŁGORAJSKI)—Located in southeast Poland near Zamosc, Jozefow was founded in 1725 as a private town owned by the Zamoyski family. Jews settled in the area soon afterward. An important Hebrew publishing house was established here in the mid-19th century. By 1921 nearly 80 percent of the 1,350 inhabitants were Jewish. The Nazis set up a ghetto here for local Jews and Jews from nearby villages; on July 13, 1942, they marched as many as 1,500 of them into the forest at Winniarczykowa Hill, shot them dead, and buried them in a mass grave. A memorial stone now marks the spot, about a mile from town on the road to Bilgoraj.

Today, Jozefow Bilgorajski is a sleepy little town whose center exhibits a mix of shabby modern construction and prewar wooden buildings. The baroque-style synagogue, built in the late 18th or early 19th century, now serves as the town library. The librarian was very helpful and had information on hand about local Jewish history; she gave me explicit directions to the Jewish cemetery, located near quarries on a hill just outside town. Access is via a dirt road off Kamienna street. The oldest gravestones date from the 1760s, and some bear fine carving and even traces of polychrome decoration. Some parts of the cemetery are very overgrown and difficult to reach, but I found other sections fairly clear, even during high weed season.

KIELCE—Halfway between Warsaw and Cracow, Kielce is infamous as the site of the last pogrom in Poland, a massacre of 42 Jews by a Polish mob who attacked the Jewish community house on July 4, 1946. Sparked by rumors that Jews had killed a Christian child to use his blood for ritual purposes, the

Some of the tombstones in the Jewish cemetery in Jozefow Bilgorajski date back to the 1760s.

pogrom was the worst of a series of Polish attacks on Jewish survivors returning to their homes after the Holocaust. Some 25,000 Jews had lived in Kielce in 1939; most were killed in Treblinka. After the pogrom, nine people were hastily tried and executed for the murders, but the attack remained a divisive memory for decades. Many Poles blamed it on provocation by Soviet-backed secret police, but during the communist era public discussion of the affair was virtually taboo.

At a ceremony in 1996 marking the 50th anniversary of the pogrom, a memorial plaque was dedicated at the house at Planty 7 where the attack took place, and Poland's prime minister formally asked forgiveness. Nobel laureate Elie Wiesel, however, bluntly raised uncomfortable questions.

"What happened in this place showed that 'normal' citizens could be as cruel as the killers of any death camp," he told the crowd. "Auschwitz, Majdanek, Treblinka, Belzec, Chelmno... were German inventions; Kielce was not. Kielce's murderers were Poles. Their language was Polish. Their hatred was Polish." On July 4, 2006, the first major, public memorial to the pogrom was dedicated as part of ceremonies marking the 60th anniversary of the attack. A sculpture by the American artist Jack Sal, it represents a huge number 7 (recalling both the Planty address and the month the pogrom took place) lying on its side. It is located near Planty street within sight of the former synagogue, which, situated at a major city traffic circle on Warszawska street, was reconstructed after the war and now serves as the district archives. Small monuments there commemorate victims of the Holocaust and also commemorate Poles who rescued Jews. There is also a Holocaust memorial in the ruined Jewish cemetery.

KRYNKI—Before the outbreak of World War II, Krynki was a thriving commercial and industrial town near the center of Poland. Today it is an isolated farming village only a mile or two from the Belarus border. Jews settled here in the 16th century, and Krynki grew to be an overwhelmingly Jewish town, the center of a thriving leather industry. It became a hotbed of Jewish political activity and the site of one of the first Jewish labor unions in Russia. During the war, Jews actively fought back when the Germans began liquidating the Krynki Ghetto, but the revolt was futile; most of Krynki's Jews were killed on the spot or deported to the Grodno Ghetto or straight to Auschwitz.

Traces of three synagogues and the Jewish cemetery survive. All are clearly marked on a big town map set up on the main square. One synagogue, a two-story brick structure on Czysta street, was long used as a warehouse but today is boarded up and appears to be empty. The Great Synagogue, built in 1754, is just a huge pile of rubble on Garbarska street; nothing is left but its foundations. The third synagogue, a faded pink building from 1850 with low eaves and a sloping roof, was turned into the town cinema, the Krokus. The first time I visited, in 1990, a villager, his face as brown and wrinkled as a walnut, came out of the rickety wooden house next door, holding out a book. "Take this," he said. "I don't understand anything about it." It was a Hebrew book, the Psalms, published in 1845. Its leather binding was cracked and falling apart. The old man had come from the part of Poland that became Soviet territory after the war. He fled across the new border in 1948, ending up in one of the houses left by Krynki's slaughtered Jews. He found the book of Psalms stuffed into the attic.

Krynki's Jewish cemetery, surrounded by a broken wall, lies behind some derelict wooden farm buildings off Legionowa street. It has about 3,000 tombstones, many of them badly eroded. Vines and weeds make it difficult to approach—or even to see—them in some seasons. Some tombstones were used as building material. "Look," a local farmer said to me to get my attention—and then he pried away a stone from the foundations of a shed to reveal a once polished surface and Hebrew inscription.

LANCUT (ŁAŃCUT)–Located in southeastern Poland east of Rzeszow, Lancut is noted for its magnificent 17th-century palace, once the seat of the noble Lubomirski and Potocki families. Jews settled here in the 16th century. Hasidism became a powerful force, and local tzaddikim are buried in the ruined Jewish cemetery on Moniuszko street.

The Lancut synagogue, built in 1761, is one of the treasures of Jewish heritage in Poland. Located just outside the gates of the palace, it was beautifully restored as a Jewish museum in the 1980s and 1990s. The outwardly simple structure conceals a sanctuary alive with colorful decorations including wall prayers, stucco bas-reliefs, frescoes, and false marble. There are lions, unicorns, monkeys, grapes, birds, deer, flowers, landscapes, zodiac signs, and more in rich shades of green, blue, orange, and yellow. The gorgeously decorated central bimah is particularly striking. Frescoes on it depict biblical tales—the sacrifice of Isaac, Adam and Eve, the Flood—but human figures are shown only by their hands and feet, in accordance with the stricture against human imagery. Curled around the inner part of its cupola is a fresco of the mythical Leviathan devouring its tail, a motif that symbolizes the time of the Messiah. The synagogue also includes displays of Jewish ritual items and other material relating to Jewish religious life and local Jewish history. (At present, the synagogue is only open during summer months.)

LESKO–The synagogue and Jewish cemetery are two of the leading attractions in this small town in the far southeastern corner of Poland, where Jews settled in the 16th century. The striking-looking synagogue, just off the main square, probably dates to the mid-17th century. Seriously damaged during World War II, it was totally rebuilt in the 1960s for use as a museum. The exterior features a curving gable, bas-relief Hebrew inscriptions, the tablets of Moses, and a tall, round tower that was added during reconstruction. It now serves as a local arts and crafts gallery. On a sleepy summer Sunday I was the only customer; I couldn't resist purchasing a painted folk carving of the late Pope John Paul II, with bright blue eyes, red shoes, and a swarm of angels around his head.

The Jewish cemetery lies a short walk down the street, on a slope near a forest. One of the oldest and most picturesque of Poland's Jewish cemeteries, it includes perhaps 2,000 richly decorated, well-preserved tombstones dating back to the 16th century, spread out under shady saplings.

LEZAJSK (LEŻAJSK) (YIDDISH: LIZHENSK)–One of the greatest of the early Hasidic masters, Elimelekh, lived in this small town in southeast Poland from 1777 to his death in 1788. Born in 1717, Elimelekh was a mystic who helped develop the concept of the Hasidic tzaddik as a holy man who could serve as a mediator between his followers and God. His tomb in the Jewish cemetery on Gorna street draws thousands of pilgrims.

OLESNICA (OLEŚNICA)–The first sizable Jewish settlements in what is today Poland were established in the early Middle Ages in Silesia, and Olesnica is one of two towns where synagogue buildings from that period remain. The redbrick building on Luzycka street near the market square was built in the 15th century but already in the 16th century was transformed into a church. It has a steep peaked roof, one squat tower, and traces of tall Gothic windows. (The other synagogue from this period, also a beautifully compact little church with a tower, is found in Strzegom, west of Wroclaw.)

ORLA–The beautiful 18th-century synagogue in this town in eastern Poland was devastated by the Nazis, who used it as a field hospital and then a warehouse for chemical fertilizer. Traces of polychrome decoration, including floral wall motifs, survive, however, as does the central four-pillar bimah. The synagogue has been undergoing restoration for years for use as a cultural center, but lack of funds has slowed the process.

PIOTRKOW TRYBUNALSKI (PIOTRKÓW TRYBUNALSKI)–The large Jewish cemetery in this town just off the Warsaw-Katowice highway is located on Spacerowa street, near the Catholic cemetery. The oldest stones date from the late 18th century, and many have very fine carved decoration incorporating Jewish symbolism and imaginary beasts. There are Holocaust memorials and mass graves. The 19th-century Great

Synagogue on Wojska Polskiego street was turned into the town library, and a smaller synagogue is a children's library.

POZNAN (POZNAŃ)—The huge and ornate synagogue built in 1910 was once the pride of this city in western Poland. The Nazis stripped it of all its Jewish character and turned it into a swimming pool. It still serves as a municipal swimming pool, but it has a commemorative plaque outside. Special events, including artistic installations, are sometimes held there, and there are ongoing, so far unresolved, debates about whether and how to restore the building for cultural use.

PRZEMYSL (PRZEMYŚL)—Two synagogues still stand in this gracious but somewhat rundown city on the border with Ukraine in the southeast corner of Poland. One, the Scheinbach Synagogue at Slowackiego 15, built for the Reform community from 1886 to 1890 and designed by Marceli Pilecki, was reconstructed as a library in the 1960s. The other, built in 1909, stands abandoned and falling ever more into ruin on Unii Brzeskiej Square, in the Zasanie District across the river. There is a large Jewish cemetery next to the main municipal cemetery, with tombs from the 19th and 20th centuries.

PRZYSUCHA—The grandiose synagogue in this town in central Poland, built in 1750, today stands empty. One of the largest of Poland's surviving synagogues, it conserves traces of structural and decorative detail, including the central bimah, the women's gallery, a few faded frescoes and much of the Aron ha Kodesh. Attached to the outside wall is a rare example of a *kune*, or pillory, where Jews sentenced by the Jewish community court would be locked in punishment. Przysucha was the seat of the influential Hasidic master Jacob Isaac ben Asher Przysucha (1766–1814), known in lore simply as "The Jew." His tomb is in the cemetery near the synagogue.

RADOMSKO—There's a very interesting Jewish cemetery in this town in central Poland, just off the main Warsaw-Katowice highway. Enclosed by a tall, redbrick wall, it has about a thousand tombstones, many carved with fantastic renditions of lions, deer, birds, and mythical beasts such as griffins and the Leviathan. Some of the grave markers are made of iron, and there is a monument to the 8,000 Jews from Radomsko killed during the Holocaust.

RYMANOW (RYMANÓW)–Jews in this little spa town in southeastern Poland once specialized in importing Hungarian wine into Poland. Rymanow also was the seat of Menachem Mendel, the Hasidic master who, along with the Seer of Lublin and the Maggid of Kozhenets, believed that the Napoleonic Wars foretold the coming of the Messiah. According to one story, during the battles in which he was victorious, Napoleon always saw the vision of a red-haired Jew praying for him. As he went into his last great battle at Waterloo, he did not see the vision. Waterloo, in 1815, spelled a crushing defeat for Napoleon. The red-haired Menachem Mendel and his two friends all died that year.

The hulking wreck of Rymanow's synagogue long represented to me a powerful evocation of Jewish life and loss. Fragments of beautiful frescoes, including biblical animals and a scene of the Western Wall in Jerusalem, remained on its walls despite shattered windows and a collapsed roof. In 2005–06, the synagogue returned to Jewish ownership and Hasidic followers of Menachem Mendel restored it enough to pray there again. The building has a new metal roof, and clear glass has been put in the windows. When I saw it, scaffolding still surrounded the building, and it was not clear what the next step would be, or what was being done to preserve or restore the frescoes.

RZESZOW (RZESZÓW)–Two austere 17th-century synagogues stand next to each other off the market square in this historic city in southeast Poland. Destroyed during World War II, they were rebuilt for cultural use and bear commemorative plaques. The Old Town, or Small, Synagogue is a compact building with a small tower that today houses a Jewish Research Center, part of the district archives. The New Town, or Great, Synagogue, a rectangular building with arched windows and brick buttresses, is now an art gallery and cultural center. There is a Holocaust memorial in the park across the street, the site of the Old Jewish Cemetery. Rzeszow's District Museum, at 3-Maja 19, has a large collection of Judaica.

SANDOMIERZ–Originally built in the mid-18th century, the synagogue in this beautiful medieval walled city south of Lublin stands on Zydowska (Jewish) street. Rebuilt after World War II, it has a distinctive double mansard roof and retains rich interior decoration. Today it is used as the state archives. Some Judaica items are displayed in the town museum. There is a ruined Jewish cemetery with a Holocaust memorial built of gravestones located near the bus station. Inside the cathedral a painting from 1710 depicts a blood libel. (In the summer of 2006, the painting was covered up, at least temporarily.)

SEJNY—The two most prominent buildings in this little town near the Lithuanian border in the far northeast corner of Poland are the Roman Catholic church and the big, white former synagogue, which was built in 1857 when about 70 percent of the town was Jewish. There are no Jews in Sejny today, but the synagogue and other onetime Jewish buildings now house the Fundacija Pogranicze, or Borderland Foundation, a remarkable institution dedicated to keeping the memory of Jewish and other local minority cultures alive. Established in 1990, it sponsors publications, conferences, exhibits, concerts, workshops, and other exchanges; it runs a theater program and has its own klezmer band. The restored synagogue, with its spacious interior and scalloped facade, is used as a concert and exhibition hall. The former yeshivah houses a gallery and art workshops, and the former Hebrew high school has been transformed into the Borderland House, with offices, exhibition space, and an extensive research library. The foundation also recovered many of the Jewish tombstones uprooted by the Nazis and used as paving; in 2002 it helped organize the dedication of a memorial at the site of the Jewish cemetery, on a hill just north of town. *(Borderland Foundation: ul. J. Pilsudskiego 37. www.pogranicze.sejny.pl)*

SUWALKI (SUWAŁKI)—The Jewish cemetery in this town in northeast Poland is a haunting sight. Fenced and well-maintained, it is almost totally empty. Nearly all the tombstones were uprooted by the Nazis. A few stand in small isolated clumps; one bears the photograph of the person interred. Recovered stones and fragments form a commemorative mosaic wall in the center of the space. The cemetery is located near the cemeteries of other religions, those of Christian denominations but also an old graveyard used by a Muslim Tartar community, testifying to the area's historic religious and ethnic mix.

SZCZEBRZESZYN—The 17th-century synagogue in this little town near Zamosc was left a total ruin by the Nazis but was reconstructed in the 1960s and is used as a local cultural center. The exterior looks much as it did before the war, with a tall, double-mansard roof. The sanctuary preserves fragments of the original decoration, including the Ark, flanked by two fluted columns. The Jewish cemetery is up the lane—a sign points the way.

Though partly ruined and partly overgrown, it has many fine tombstones, some showing traces of polychrome decoration.

SZYDLOWIEC (SZYDŁOWIEC)–A sleepy little town in central Poland, Szydlowiec has a grand town hall, a picturesque church, and a small castle. It also has one of the most impressive remaining Jewish cemeteries in Poland, with 3,000 or more gravestones dating back to the early 19th century. Jews settled here in the 16th or 17th century, and before World War II comprised about 80 percent of the local inhabitants. The cemetery is sited at the edge of a modern apartment and shopping development just off the main road into town from Radom (turn left on a short, unnamed street just past a bank and small shopping center). Elaborately carved tombstones crowd up against the main fence and locked main gate, like people pressing their faces to a window. You can wander for hours here. The stones are in generally good condition, and their decorative carving represents a textbook of Jewish symbolism: lions, stags, birds, and other animals; the raised hands of the Cohens; the pitcher of the Levites; books; broken candles symbolizing lives snuffed out. Some still bear faint traces of polychrome decoration.

The cemetery is used as a public space by local people. Entry is at the rear, where there is a big breach in the perimeter wall. There are tramped paths through the stones and weedy undergrowth, and a few signs of vandalism. A sadly derelict Holocaust memorial stands at the center; when I visited last, I noted that someone had spray-painted a green swastika on its face.

TARNOGROD–The towering baroque synagogue in this little town near Zamosc was built in 1686. Devastated during World War II, it was later used as a warehouse. Renovated now, it serves as a public library and bears commemorative plaques on an outer wall. Some interior decoration remains. The Jewish cemetery, on Stroma street, was destroyed during the war, then restored in 1990. Some tombstones were reerected, but many beautifully carved stones and fragments were used to form a memorial wall.

TYKOCIN (YIDDISH: TIKTIN)–In 1522, the noble family that owned this quaint village near Bialystok invited ten Jewish families to settle here. By the 19th century, there was a Jewish majority in the village; on the eve of World War II Jews made up just under half the local population.

The grand, early baroque synagogue is one of Poland's best known sites of Jewish heritage. Built in 1642, it was ravaged by the Nazis, but it was beautifully restored in the 1970s and is used as a Jewish museum. As many as 70,000 people visit here each year—tour buses arrive as soon as the doors open at 10 a.m. Inside, brilliantly colored frescoes, including texts in Hebrew and Aramaic, decorate the walls of the vaulted sanctuary. The richly ornate Aron ha Kodesh and the four-pillared central bimah, with its two rows of arches, dominate the space. Glass cases display precious items of Judaica. Exhibitions in the synagogue's tower (used in centuries past as a prison) include a room arranged as if it were the study of a rabbi and another with a table set for the Passover seder. There is also a fascinating scale model of Tykocin, showing its spatial relationship grouped around two poles: the grand synagogue at one end, and the grand Catholic church at the other. Not much has changed: In the wooden window frames of a house on Kaczorowska street near the synagogue you can still see a decorative Star of David.

Tykocin's Jewish cemetery, partially enclosed by a broken wall, lies on Pilsudskiego street, heading out of town beyond the synagogue. There are said to be as many as 500 tombstones, but most are toppled or illegible, or simply eroded stumps pushing up through a field. About 2,000 Jews lived in Tykocin on the eve of World War II. The Nazis shot 1,400 of them dead on August 25, 1941, and deported the rest to the Bialystok Ghetto. A monument on the road to Lopuchowo marks the spot of the mass execution.

WROCLAW (WROCŁAW) (GERMAN: BRESLAU)–An industrial city in Lower Silesia, Wroclaw has a splendid historic center rebuilt after its World War II destruction. The city was long part of Germany; in 1920, its Jewish population of more than 23,000 made it the third largest Jewish city in Germany. Jews are known to have settled here in the 12th century. In 1453, after riots instigated by the anti-Semitic preaching of John of Capistrano, Jews were expelled from the city and not permitted to return officially for nearly 200 years. In the 19th and 20th centuries, Wroclaw became a center of the Reform movement. Abraham Geiger, one of the founding fathers of Reform Judaism, served as rabbi here from 1838 to 1863. The famous Jewish Theological Seminary was established here in 1854 and functioned until the Nazis closed it down in 1938. Most of Wroclaw's synagogues, including a magnificent domed Reform temple, were destroyed during the Kristallnacht pogrom, November 9 to 10, 1938. By that time, many Jews had managed to leave Wroclaw and only about 4,000 lived in the city.

Today, several hundred Jews live in Wroclaw, forming the second largest Jewish community in Poland. Jewish life centers around the complex on

Wlodkowica street, where the only surviving synagogue stands. This is the White Stork Synagogue, built from 1827 to 1829 and designed by Karl Ferdinand Langhans. The neoclassic facade, marked by tall arched windows, still looks ruined, but inside, thanks to a German grant, it has undergone considerable restoration. Wroclaw's Old Jewish Cemetery, founded in 1856, is now maintained as a municipal Museum of Cemetery Art. The earliest known Jewish gravestone in Poland, that of a David ben Shalom, who died in 1203, is conserved here. Located on Slezna street, the cemetery has about 12,000 graves, including 300 elaborate monuments ranged around the walls. Notable people buried here include the German Social Democratic leader Ferdinand LaSalle (1825–1864) and the parents of Edith Stein, a Jewish intellectual and convert to Catholicism who became a nun, was killed at Auschwitz, and was canonized by Pope John Paul II. Another large Jewish cemetery is located on Lotnicza street on the other side of town. Long-ruined and totally overgrown, it has undergone some clearance and restoration work in recent years. *(Jewish community and synagogue: ul. Wlodkowica 7/9. Tel: +48-71/343-6401. E-mail: wroclaw@jewish.org.pl. http://wroclaw.jewish.org.pl)*

ZAMOSC (ZAMOŚĆ)–Zamosc, in southeastern Poland, was founded in 1580 by the Polish chancellor Jan Zamoyski, who consciously designed it as an ideal Renaissance city. Its regular urban plan, centered on a lovely, arcaded market square, was laid out by the Italian architect Bernardo Morando, whom Zamoyski brought in from Venice. Zamoyski invited Sephardic Jews to settle in 1588, and within a few years there was a well-established Jewish quarter on what is now Zamenhofa street. Ashkenazic Jews began arriving in the 17th century and eventually became the dominant, and then the only, Jewish community. Zamosc became a center of Jewish scholarship and in the 19th century was a focus of the Haskalah. The Yiddish writer I. L. Peretz (1851–1915), one of the fathers of Jewish literature, was born and brought up here. The socialist leader Rosa Luxemburg (1870–1919) also came from Zamosc.

On the eve of World War II, some 12,000 Jews made up just under half of the population. The Nazis renamed the town Himmlerstadt and began to deport the entire local population to make way for planned colonization by German settlers. About 5,000 Jews managed to escape to the Soviet Union. The Nazis confined the rest in a ghetto and in 1942 deported them all to the death camp at nearby Belzec.

Today, the massive synagogue, looking like a fortress with big side arches and a flat roof with pointed crenellations, stands at the corner of Zamenhofa and Bazylianska streets. Originally built in the early 17th century, it was rebuilt and remodeled many times, including after World War II, when the partially ruined building was turned into the town library. Much of the interior decoration was preserved, including fine stuccowork on walls and vaulted ceiling, a stone Aron ha Kodesh, and some traces of frescoes. The synagogue was recently returned to Jewish ownership, and the library was moved out; a full-scale restoration is planned, but meanwhile the empty sanctuary is open to visitors. The 17th-century building next door housed the community offices and Jewish school, while Zamenhofa 3 (now the site of a jazz club) once housed a mikvah. Around the corner on Rynek Solny (Salt Market) stand several fine mansions that once belonged to Jewish merchants. A few steps away, a row of shops whose porch is supported by slim columns was built a century ago to house kosher butcher shops.

RESOURCES ON POLAND

A WEALTH OF MATERIAL ON JEWISH HERITAGE AND JEWISH HERITAGE SITES IS readily available at tourist offices and bookstores. These publications include at least two maps of Jewish heritage around the country and a very useful illustrated guidebook by Adam Dylewski, published in several languages:

Dylewski, Adam. *When the Tailor Was a Poet . . . Polish Jews and Their Culture: An Illustrated Guide.* Bielsko-Biala: Pascal, 2002. *(The entries from this guide can be found—in English—at the website www.diapozytyw.pl/en/site.)*

WEBSITES:

- www.bagnowka.com — Database on Jewish heritage sites in eastern Poland
- www.diapozytyw.pl/en/site/ — Comprehensive website on Polish Jewish history and heritage. The entire text of the guidebook *When the Tailor Was a Poet* is posted here.
- http://fodz.pl — Foundation for the Preservation of Jewish Heritage in Poland
- http://fzp.jewish.org.pl/english/index.php — English-language portal to contemporary Polish Jewish life.
- http://jewish.sites.warszawa.um.gov.pl/wstep_a.htm — Online guide to Jewish sites in Warsaw
- www.heritageabroad.gov — U.S. Commission for the Preservation of America's Heritage Abroad. Includes a detailed survey of Jewish monuments in Poland
- www.jewish.org.pl — Portal to the Polish Jewish community website
- www.jewishgen.org/cemetery/e-europe/poland.html — Jewish cemeteries in Poland

- www.jewishtravel.pl — Database on Jewish heritage sites in Poland
- www.kirkuty.xip.pl — Jewish cemeteries in Poland
- www.lodzjews.org — Jewish history and heritage in Lodz, Poland
- www.polishjews.org — Genealogy site, with history and photos

ADDITIONAL PUBLICATIONS:

- Bartosz, Adam. *Tarnowskie Judaica.* Warsaw: Wydawnictwo PTTK Kraj, 1992
- Bergman, Eleonora, and Jan Jagielski. *Zachowane Synagogi i domy modltwy w Polsce: Katalog.* Warsaw: Jewish Historical Institute, 1996
- Dobroszycki, Lucjan, and Barbara Kirshenblatt-Gimblett. *Image before My Eyes.* New York: Schocken Books, 1977
- Gross, Jan T. *Fear: Anti-Semitism in Poland after Auschwitz.* New York: Random House, 2006
- ———. *Neighbors: The Destruction of the Jewish Community in Jedwabne, Poland.* New York: Penguin, 2002
- Hoffman, Eva. *Shtetl: The Life and Death of a Small Town and the World of Polish Jews.* New York: Houghton Mifflin, 1997
- Krajewska, Monika. *A Tribe of Stones: Jewish Cemeteries in Poland.* Warsaw: Polish Scientific Publishers, 1993
- Kugelmass, Jack, and Jonathan Boyarin. *From a Ruined Garden: The Memorial Books of Polish Jewry.* New York: Schocken, 1983 (Reprint, New York: Columbia University Press, 1997)
- Piechotka, Maria and Kazimierz. *Heaven's Gates: Wooden Synagogues in the Territories of the Former Polish-Lithuanian Commonwealth.* Warsaw: Krupski I S-ka, 2004
- Podolska, Joanna. *Traces of the Litzmannstadt-Getto: A Guide to the Past.* Lodz: Piatek Trzynastego, 2004. A guidebook to the Lodz Ghetto
- Polin. *Studies in Polish Jewry.* Oxford: Littman Library of Jewish Civilization. 1986-present. (Annual volumes of articles)
- Powers, Charles. *In the Memory of the Forest.* New York: Penguin, 1997
- Richmond, Theo. *Konin, a Quest.* London: Jonathan Cape, 1996
- Samuel, Maurice. *Prince of the Ghetto.* Philadelphia: Jewish Publication Society, 1959
- Steinlauf, Michael C. *Bondage to the Dead: Poland and the Memory of the Holocaust.* Syracuse: Syracuse University Press, 1997
- Tencer, Golda. *And I Still See Their Faces: Images of Polish Jews.* Warsaw: Fundacja Shalom, 1996
- Weiner, Miriam. *Jewish Roots in Poland: Pages from the Past and Archival Inventories.* New York: YIVO/Routes to Roots Foundation, 1998. (See also *www.rtrfoundation.org*)
- Wisniewski, Tomasz. *Jewish Bialystok and Surroundings in Eastern Poland: A Guide for Yesterday and Today.* Ipswich, MA: Ipswich Press, 1998

LITHUANIA

CURRENT POPULATION: 3.6 MILLION
JEWISH POPULATION BEFORE WORLD WAR II: 240,000
JEWISH POPULATION TODAY: APPROX. 4,000

A LITTLE HISTORY

FAMED FOR ITS RICH CULTURE, REVERED SCHOLARS, AND INTENSE SPIRITUAL ENERGY, Lithuania holds a special place in Jewish collective consciousness. For centuries until the eve of the Holocaust, Vilnius, "the Jerusalem of Lithuania," was recognized as one of the major Jewish centers in the world, home not just to learned rabbis, but to potent social, political, and cultural movements that had an impact far beyond Lithuania's borders.

Historically, Lithuania extended much farther than it does today, and some Jews lived on Lithuanian territory as early as the eighth century. Major settlement began in the early Middle Ages. The Grand Duke Gediminas, who founded the first Lithuanian state in the 14th century, encouraged Jews to move north from Kievan Rus and other lands he conquered. By the 15th century, the grand duchy extended from the Baltics to the Black Sea, encompassing much of today's Belarus and Ukraine. The grand duchy formed a union with Poland in the 14th century, and in 1388 the Grand Duke Witold issued a charter modeled on the Polish Statute of Kalisz that granted Jews extensive rights and privileges.

Lithuania and Poland remained united for four centuries, until Poland was partitioned at the end of the 1700s. Jews were expelled briefly from Lithuania at the end of the 15th century. They suffered badly from the Cossack uprising led by Bogdan Chmielnicki in 1648–49 and also faced various restrictions on trade and residency. Still, this period was generally a time of steady development. About 250,000 Jews lived in Lithuanian lands by the 1790s. Great

Students at the Schwabes Hebrew gymnasium in Kaunas strike a boisterous pose in a late-1930s picture.

yeshivahs grew up, and Lithuania became a center of rabbinical Judaism and Talmudic study. In the 18th century, Elijah ben Solomon Zalman, the Gaon (Eminence) of Vilna, took the stage as one of the towering figures of modern Judaism. He and other Lithuanian religious leaders embraced a studious, intellectual approach to Judaism that made them bitterly antagonistic to the emotional appeal of Hasidism. Thanks to their influence, Lithuanian Jews, known as Litvaks, won the reputation of being more austere and intellectual than Jews from the southern part of Eastern Europe.

With the partition of Poland, Lithuania came under the Russian tsars and formed part of the Pale of Settlement imposed in the 1790s. In the latter part of the 19th century, tens of thousands of Jews emigrated, many to the United States and to South Africa. Lithuanian Jews, meanwhile, built up a highly developed system of education and publishing in both Hebrew and Yiddish. The Haskalah movement, or Jewish Enlightenment, was influential, and Vilnius became a hotbed of political activity; the Jewish Labor Bund, the first Jewish workers' social democratic organization, was founded there in 1897. Zionism also gained ground as a popular force, and Jewish writers, artists, musicians, and other creative personalities blossomed amid an exhilarating and fertile cultural environment.

World War I, the ensuing Russian Revolution, and resultant border changes hit Lithuanian Jewry hard. Early in World War I, the tsarist government expelled thousands of Jews from the Kaunas region into the interior of Russia. At war's end, Lithuania Jews found themselves in three new countries: an independent Lithuania, an independent Poland (which occupied Vilnius), and the Soviet Union.

About 160,000 Jews lived in independent Lithuania before World War II. Another 60,000 or so lived in and around Vilnius. The Germans occupied the country in 1941 and, aided by many local Lithuanian collaborators, annihilated as much as 95 percent of the Jewish population. Rather than deport Jews en masse to death camps, the pattern was to take them to remote areas outside their towns, shoot them dead on the spot, and bury them in mass graves. Lithuania became a Soviet republic after World War II; borders were redrawn and Vilnius again became its capital. The Soviet clampdown stifled most Jewish practice and expression. Restrictions relaxed to some extent at the end of the 1980s, and Lithuanian independence in 1991 enabled the reemergence of an active Jewish community. About 4,000 Jews live in the country today, most of them in Vilnius.

JEWISH HERITAGE IN LITHUANIA

Many villages and small towns around Lithuania still look like old shtetls, with shops and wooden houses clustered on market squares and narrow lanes. Only about three dozen synagogue buildings or prayer houses still stand, though. Importantly, these include as many as a dozen wooden synagogues, all in small towns or remote villages.

There are about 200 Jewish cemeteries around the country; most are overgrown or desecrated and a number no longer have any tombstones. In addition, there are about 200 sites where Jews were massacred during the Holocaust and buried in mass graves. Most of these have monuments and are well maintained, but they are generally located in hard-to-find forested areas. Some have large signposts pointing the way, and thanks to an initiative started in 2001 by Britain's Lord Greville Janner, the chairman of the

Holocaust Educational Trust, most are also now marked by black roadside directional pillars.

In addition to the Vilna Gaon Jewish State Museum in Vilnius, a number of other museums around the country include Jewish material in their collections. *(Online photo database of these objects: www.jewishstudies.lt)*

TIPS ON VISITING

Lithuania is a small country and you can see a lot in a few days. Try to go out in the countryside and visit the various wooden synagogues. If you get to the west of the country, look up Jakov Bunka and see his Holocaust memorial outside Plunge.

Given the poor signage and lack of detailed guidebooks and informational material, most visitors prefer to hire guides, particularly when they venture into the countryside. There are a dozen or more expert guides specializing in Jewish heritage; arrangements can be made through the Jewish museums, tourist offices, or Jewish communities. Three whom I have used are Simonas Davidavicius, the director of Sugihara House in Kaunas *(tel/fax: +370-37/423-277, e-mail: sugiharahouse@yahoo.com)*; historian Ilya Lempertas in Vilnius *(tel/fax: +370-5/244-8935, e-mail: lempertas@gmail.com)*; and Kaunas-based Chaim Bargman, with whom I traveled in the provinces *(tel: +370-37/779-948 or +370-681/77166)*.

VILNIUS

(Yiddish: Vilne)

Long renowned as the Jerusalem of Lithuania, Vilnius for centuries was a legendary focus of Jewish life and learning. Today it is the bustling modern capital of a European Union member state, centered on a beautiful Old Town rich with centuries-old historic monuments. Jews settled here in the 16th century and by 1568 had established an organized community. In the following decades, thanks to newcomers from Prague, Germany, and Poland, the Jewish population grew, and Vilnius—better known to generations of Jews by its Yiddish name, Vilne, or Hebrew, Vilna—developed into a leading center of Jewish scholarship and rabbinical study. All this took place against wars, upheavals, and rocky relations with both local rulers and local Christian townspeople. Russian occupiers expelled Jews from the city briefly in the

1650s, and attempts to restrict Jewish residency and economic activity persisted through the 18th century.

The 18th century, however, produced one of modern Judaism's most influential intellectual and spiritual leaders, Elijah ben Solomon Zalman, famed as the Gaon (Genius or Eminence) of Vilna, who lived from 1720 to 1797. Recognized as a prodigy as a child, the Vilna Gaon delved deeply into the Talmud, the Kabbalah, the Hebrew language, and even subjects such as mathematics and science, which he deemed necessary for achieving a true understanding of the Torah. He wrote widely on a vast number of topics, and his teachings influenced generations of scholars. In the 1770s, the gaon became the leader of the *mitnagdim*, or traditionalist opponents to Hasidism, and ordered the excommunication of what he termed the heretical new sect. Followers of Hasidism, he declared, "have sin in their hearts and are like a sore on the body of Israel."

Vilnius maintained its position as a center of Orthodox Jewish scholarship throughout the 19th century, but the Haskalah also found fertile ground. Vilnius became a magnet for secular writers and intellectuals and, partly in response to anti-Semitic violence, a hotbed of Zionism and other Jewish political activity. The city hosted the founding meeting of the socialist Jewish Labor Bund in 1897, and when Theodore Herzl visited in 1903, he was greeted by eager throngs as "the king of the Jews." Under Polish rule during the interwar period, the city became Europe's foremost center for Yiddish language and learning. YIVO, the research institute for Yiddish language and culture (now headquartered in New York City), was established here in 1925.

Nonetheless, anti-Semitism grew steadily. At the outbreak of World War II, Vilnius was annexed by Lithuania, which in turn was annexed by the Soviet Union in 1940. Many Jews were deported into Russia, but about 60,000 were in the city when the Germans, cheered on by local Lithuanians, marched in on June 24, 1941. By the time the Red Army liberated the city on July 12, 1944, only about 6,000 Jews remained alive.

As elsewhere in the Soviet Union, Jewish life was stifled under Soviet rule. After Lithuania became independent in 1990, a Jewish community was reconstituted, and today about 2,500 Jews live in the city. There are new Jewish clubs, schools, media outlets, and other institutions. The Vilnius Yiddish Institute, founded in 2001 as the first Yiddish center of higher learning to be established in post-Holocaust Eastern Europe, runs a wide variety of projects and has helped Vilnius recapture its role as a center of Yiddish studies; each summer, students from all over the world take part in the institute's intensive, month-long Yiddish study program. Dozens of plaques, meanwhile, commemorate events, mark prewar Jewish buildings, or honor Jews who once lived here—from the violinist Jascha Heifetz, who was born in Vilnius in 1901, to the French novelist and diplomat Romain Gary, who wrote about his childhood on Basanaviciaus street in his novel *Promise of Dawn.* The booklet "Vilnius: 100 Memorable Sites of Jewish History and Culture" includes a map that locates most of them.

Main Sites of Jewish Interest in Vilnius

Old Jewish Quarter: For more than 300 years, the magnificent Great Synagogue towered over Vilnius's historic Jewish quarter. Built in the early 1630s, the synagogue stood surrounded by the gated *shul-hoyf,* or synagogue courtyard, a teeming warren of narrow alleys and arched passageways where at least a dozen other prayer houses were clustered. Before World War II, there were more than a hundred synagogues and prayer houses in the city. On streets nearby were found schools, yeshivahs, printing houses, theaters, and other Jewish institutions, including the renowned Strashun Library. Today, evocative street names and commemorative plaques are almost all that is left. Only a small part of Zydu, or Jewish, street remains, cutting through the heart of the city's Old Town; the Jewish quarter, undergoing restoration, has become a fashionable area of restaurants, cafés, and boutiques. The Great Synagogue stood between Zydu street and today's Vokieciu street. Dynamited by the Nazis, it survived the war a gutted shell that the Soviets demolished in 1957. A kindergarten was built on the spot. Today, a monument to the Gaon of Vilna—a huge, stylized, and rather bizarre portrait bust—marks the site of the house next door where the gaon lived. A big information panel, in English and other languages, posts old pictures of a lost world totally different from what is here now.

Vilna Gaon Jewish State Museum: Established in 1989, the museum is the city's main Jewish cultural institution. Vilnius had two prior Jewish museums. The first opened in 1913, but its collections were mostly destroyed in World War II. Holocaust survivors established a new Jewish museum in 1944, but this institution was closed down five years later by the Soviet authorities. Today's museum includes thousands of objects, documents, and works of art, displayed in several separate branches, three in the city center, one a Holocaust museum at the Paneriai Forest outside town, and one dedicated to the sculptor Jacques Lipchitz in the southern town of Druskininkai. *(Additional information: www.jmuseum.lt. E-mail: jewishmuseum@jmuseum.lt)*

• **Tolerance Center:** Naugarduko g. 10/2. Tel: +370-5/231-2357—Located in a restored prewar Jewish theater and adjacent Jewish soup kitchen, this is the Jewish museum's main venue. Its permanent exhibition includes ritual objects, documents, and other material on Lithuanian Jewish life and history. Among the most important artifacts are precious fragments from the Vilnius Great Synagogue's Aron ha Kodesh. There is also a collection of paintings by 20th-century Jewish artists. For me, the most fascinating exhibit is a surviving fragment of "The Throne of King Solomon," a huge and extraordinary sculptural installation incorporating dozens of puppets, animal figures, architectural carvings, and a 15-branched candelabra, that was created in the early 1900s by Aaron Chait, a Jewish folk artist in the village of Kelme.
• **Tarbut Gymnasium:** Pylimo g. 4. Tel: +370-5/261-7917—Material on local Jewish personalities, such as the violinist Jascha Heifetz, and on other topics, including Jewish resistance to the Holocaust, are exhibited here, in the former Jewish school building that also houses the offices of the Vilnius Jewish community.
• **"Green House" Holocaust Museum:** Pamenkalnio g. 12. Tel: +370-5/262-0730—The exhibition here, in a small wooden house, details the history of the Shoah in Lithuania.

Choral Synagogue: Pylimo g. 39—As noted, before the Holocaust there were a hundred or more synagogues and prayer houses in Vilnius alone. Today, the Choral Synagogue is one of only two synagogues in all Lithuania that survived World War II and are still in use as Jewish houses of worship; the other is in Kaunas. A grand building with a Moorish-Romanesque striped facade and big central arch topped by the tablets of the Ten Commandments, it was designed by the architect David Rosenhaus and built in 1903 for a congregation largely made up of *maskilim,* or followers of the Jewish Enlightenment movement—intellectuals, cultural figures, professionals, businessmen, and industrialists.

Geliu Street Synagogue: Geliu g. 6—Built in the early 19th century and rebuilt and expanded many times, this synagogue survived World War II, but was used as a metal workshop during Soviet times. Today it belongs to the Jewish community but stands empty and dilapidated, awaiting restoration.

Old Jewish Cemetery: Vilnius's oldest cemetery was founded in the 15th century on the right bank of the Neris River, in an area called Snipiskes. It was closed in 1830 and demolished by communist authorities in the late 1940's; a big sports center was built on the site. A monument commemorating the cemetery now stands on the grounds of the complex on Olimpieciu street.

Uzupis Cemetery: Between 1828 and the 1940s, as many as 70,000 Vilnius Jews were buried in what was a huge, hillside cemetery. It was demolished under the Soviets in the 1960s. Tombstones were taken away and used as building material, many of them to construct an imposing staircase, the 380 steps leading up to the palatial headquarters of the state trade union. In the 1990s, these stairs were removed and the tombstones returned to the Jewish community. Some of them (along with other tombstones) have been used to create a striking new monument that now stands at the site of the cemetery on Olandu street.

Seskine Jewish Cemetery: Suderves g. 28—Currently used by the Jewish community, this cemetery was established just before World War II. The first people buried here died in the Vilnius Ghetto. The cemetery includes a number of Holocaust memorials, as well as the imposing mausoleum of the Gaon of Vilna, whose remains were moved here when the Old Jewish Cemetery was demolished. Also moved from the cemetery and conserved in the mausoleum are the remains of Count Valentin Potocki, known as Ger Tsedek—a Polish nobleman who was burned at the stake in 1749 for converting to Judaism.

World War II Vilnius Ghetto: The Nazis occupied Vilnius on June 24, 1941. Little more than two months later, in early September, they herded Vilnius's Jews into two ghettos, separated by Vokieciu street. One was in the medieval Jewish quarter around Zydu and Stikliu streets, and the other, larger ghetto extended from Vokieciu to Pylimo street. (A plaque at the corner of Rudninku and Ligonines streets shows a map of the two ghettos.) About 10,000 Jews were confined in the smaller ghetto and 30,000 in the larger one; as many as 10,000 of the city's Jews had already been killed. By October 24, all the Jews in the smaller ghetto had been killed, and the ghetto was, as the phrase goes, liquidated. The larger ghetto remained in operation until the end of September 1943. Conditions were horrendous, but a measure of life went on. One of the most detailed descriptions can be found in the diary kept by Herman Kruk, a cultural and political activist who headed the ghetto's library.

Signs in Vilnius for a pre-war shop that sold salt and naphtha are written in Polish and Yiddish.

Kruk hid the diary before he was deported to the concentration camp in Klooga, Estonia, where he was killed in September 1944. "I know I am condemned and awaiting my turn, although deep inside me burrows a hope for a miracle," he wrote at one point. "Drunk on the pen trembling in my hand, I record everything for future generations."

The library where Kruk worked was in the building at Zemaitijos 4 (formerly Strashuna 6), which also housed various other ghetto institutions. Most importantly, it was the center for resistance activities, with hidden areas for secret meetings, firearms practice, and more. Down the street, the building facades at Zemaitijos 7 and 9 bear prewar Yiddish shop signs that were uncovered during restoration work. One advertises "colonial goods"—spices—and the other salt and naphtha. High up on a building directly across the street is a Star of David etched on a partially ruined wall.

Outside the ghetto area, a monument at a building complex at the intersection of Maironio and Subaciaus streets marks the site of a labor camp for about 1,250 Jews that was set up when the ghetto was liquidated. The camp, whose inmates worked in German Army garages, functioned until July 1944.

The camp buildings originally were a housing complex for Jewish poor erected in the early 1900s.

Paneriai (Ponary Forest) Memorial Museum: Agrastu g. 17—The peaceful Paneriai Forest, about 6 miles southwest of downtown Vilnius, conceals the killing grounds where the Nazis and their Lithuanian collaborators massacred tens of thousands of people, most of them Jews, between July 1941 and July 1944. The site is now a memorial park. A Soviet monument erected here in 1985 spoke of 100,000 victims, without specifying the number of Jews; a black granite plaque added in 1990—and a big separate memorial unveiled in 1991—state that 70,000 of the victims were Jewish. Some scholars, however, now put the total number of people killed here at 50,000 to 55,000. "We'll never know the real total," said Ilya Lempertas, an old friend and Jewish historian who took me around the site. "After the war, only ashes were found, and there were only a few witnesses."

Executions took place at the edges of several stone-lined pits, originally intended as oil cisterns but never completed. Here, aided by special Lithuanian police units, the Germans lined up Jews (and others, including several thousand Soviet and Polish prisoners of war and Polish intellectuals), machine-gunned them, and let the bodies fall. Between 200 and 4,000 were killed at a time. As many as 35,000 Jews had been killed in this fashion by the end of 1941. Beginning in December 1943, the Nazis tried to cover the traces of the massacres, bringing more Jews to the site to exhume the bodies and burn them. In April 1944, a group of these Jews managed to escape through a tunnel they dug from the bottom of one of the pits.

A small museum, a branch of the Vilna Gaon Jewish State Museum, tells the chilling story of the massacres. It displays photographs of some of the known victims and poignant artifacts found on the site: broken dishes, watches, keys, Soviet Army dog tags, tefillin, coins, scissors, rosary beads, belt buckles, spectacles, shoes, a doll.... On one wall hangs a tattered scarf; a woman wrapped her baby in it and threw the bundle into a passing cart.

Today, paths meander through the forest to the memorials and to the edges of the pits. "Unfortunately, we are walking on ashes," Ilya remarked. He told me that the ashes in the soil meant that in summertime, the forest here was carpeted with wonderful fresh strawberries. "I brought a visitor here once, and his driver gathered a lot of the berries," he told me. "She offered us some, and we had to find excuses to tell her why we wouldn't eat them."

Addresses of Note in Vilnius

- Jewish community: Pylimo g. 4. Tel: +370-5/261-3003, fax: +370-5/212-7915. E-mail: office@litjews.org. www.litjews.org
- Chabad house: Saltiniu g. 12. Tel: +370-5/215-0387
- Kosher restaurant: Kineret Restoranas, Rauglyklos g. 4A
- Vilnius Yiddish Institute: History Department, Vilnius University, Universiteto g. 7. Tel: +370-5/268-7293. www.judaicvilnius.com
- Center for Studies of the Culture and History of East European Jews: Sv. Ignoto g. 5. Tel: +370-5/262-3707. www.jewishstudies.lt

Near Vilnius

EISISKES (EIŠIŠKĖS) (YIDDISH: EISHYSHOK)–Millions of people know the onetime shtetl of Eishyshok through the stunning "Tower of Life" exhibition at the Holocaust Memorial Museum in Washington, D.C. Here, some 1,600 photographs of prewar Eishyshok Jews are displayed in a space that soars upward three stories. Collected by the Israeli scholar Yaffa Eliach, who was born in Eishyshok, the photographs (like those in the Polish book *And I Still See Their Faces*) bring the murdered Jewish community to life. They show the townspeople in formal portraits and candid snapshots, at weddings and bar mitzvahs and in everyday moments. Eliach's book, *There Was Once a World: A 900-Year Chronicle of the Shtetl of Eishyshok,* details the history and Jewish life of the town in intimate detail. Some 3,500 Jews lived in Eishyshok before World War II; Eliach was one of only 29 who survived the Holocaust. Today, about 4,000 people live in Eisiskes; few remember their town's Yiddish name.

Eisiskes is located about 50 miles due south of Vilnius, only a few miles from the border with Belarus. I drove into town late on a summer afternoon. The sky was clouding up, and I spent some time simply driving around, seeing if I could discern anything that might hint of the town's former Jewish character. I got little sense of the place. It felt, in fact, empty; the Jewish soul was now in Washington, D.C. The main square had been destroyed and rebuilt; side streets were lined by neat wooden houses and log cabins, some of them painted bright colors. Tall crosses and other personal shrines stood in some front gardens. I stopped and had a bite to eat and asked the waitress if there was a Jewish cemetery—like many if not most people in Eisiskes she spoke Polish. Yes, she said, and she gave me directions how to get there. I followed her instructions but could not find the place. After some more aimless driving, I asked other people, and still I could not find the cemetery. It began to rain, and I found myself on a lonely stretch of gravel road, leading out of town, heading straight into a glorious rainbow.

This vision may have been an omen. The next person I asked was a woman in her 50s, playing in front of her house with her daughter and young grandchildren. She offered to lead me to the cemetery if I would bring her back home afterward, and climbed into the car. How did I, a foreigner, know about Eisiskes, she wanted to know, and my Polish was inadequate to tell her why, in the Jewish world, her town was famous. She directed me through some narrow lanes more or less to the spot that the waitress had indicated. There I saw a "Lord Janner pillar," pointing to a dirt road. We followed this route and ended up at an isolated clump of trees, a half mile or so out of town, where a memorial stone stood amid an overgrown clearing, marking the site where Jewish men from the village had been shot and killed.

"There is a second cemetery, on the other side of town," the woman told me. "Shall we go there?" She directed me to the Catholic cemetery, where I turned through a redbrick arch and pulled up at another memorial of mass execution, this one well maintained. The inscription on the stone was in Yiddish, Lithuanian, and English. In this place, on September 25 and 26, 1941, it said, "the Nazi assassins and their local collaborationists murdered ferociously" about 2,500 Jewish women and children.

Every year on November 1, the Catholic All Saints' Day, the woman told me, the grassy areas in front of both memorials are filled with flowers and candles. Is there a synagogue building in town? I asked her. "No," she replied. "We have a Catholic church."

TRAKAI—The early medieval capital of Lithuania, Trakai is a popular tourist spot near Vilnius, with a medieval castle set on a picturesque lake. Historically it was a center of the Karaites, an ancient Jewish sect originating in Baghdad whose members believe in the Torah but reject the Talmud and rabbinical authority. The Grand Duke Vytautas brought them here from the Crimea in the 14th century. There is a wooden Karaite prayer house, or kenassa, dating from around 1800, as well a small Karaite Ethnographic Museum and typical Karaite houses—all are on Karaimu street.

UKMERGE (UKMERGĖ) (YIDDISH: VILKOMIR)—Jews settled in this town in central Lithuania in the 17th century and prospered as tradespeople and craftsmen. They were particularly active in the leather industry, and there was a school here for Jewish shoemakers. At its peak in the late 19th century, the Jewish community numbered 10,000. Jews were expelled into Russia in 1915 but returned after World War I and by the 1930s made up 40 percent or more of the local population.

The former synagogue, totally reconstructed and used now as a sports center, stands at the corner of Vasario and Vienuolyno streets in the heart of what was once a Jewish neighborhood. Vienuolyno street is still lined with evocative examples of typical prewar wooden houses, and an ornate yellow building on Vasario street once served as a Jewish school. The site of the Jewish cemetery, on Vilniaus street, is now a big public park with one boulder standing in the center as a monument.

On September 18, 1941, the Jews from Ukmerge and several neighboring towns were marched to their deaths at a site in the nearby Pivonija Forest. The mass graves of nearly 10,400 people—a number roughly double that of the entire Jewish community in Lithuania today—are now marked with a solemn and dignified monument. Follow Vilniaus street outside town and turn left at a narrow asphalt road marked with a striking wooden monument showing an eagle—symbol of the German Reich—pecking at a human figure. The road winds through more than a mile of dense pine forest. A tall arch, with an inscription reading, in Lithuanian, "For Eternal Memory," marks the memorial site. I found it a profoundly moving and rather eerie place; the constant wind in the trees sounded like voices.

KAUNAS

(Yiddish: Kovno)

Founded as a fortress in the early Middle Ages, Kaunas is Lithuania's second largest city and served as the capital of independent Lithuania between the two World Wars, when Poland occupied Vilnius. Located at the confluence of the Neris and Nemunas Rivers, it has a small but charming medieval Old Town, which is now undergoing restoration.

Jewish traders and merchants settled in Kaunas in the 17th and 18th centuries, but until the mid-19th century, life was precarious and they were expelled several times. A separate, much older, Jewish community also existed on the opposite bank of the Neris, in the suburb of Slobodka (now a city district called Vilijampole). After residency restrictions were lifted in 1858,

Jewish life blossomed. By 1900, Jews made up 40 percent of the local population, and Kaunas had become a center of Jewish culture, with a celebrated yeshivah in Slobodka. The tsarist regime exiled Jews from Kaunas to the interior of Russia in 1915, but thousands returned, and the community grew and prospered in the interwar years. There were about 40 synagogues, and a vast network of public and private Jewish schools and other institutions; the city supported at least five daily Jewish newspapers. Anti-Semitism was on the rise, however, and Zionism became popular.

About 37,000 Jews lived in Kaunas on the eve of World War II—between a quarter and a third of the local population. The Soviets occupied the city in June 1940, then the Germans marched in on June 24, 1941. The Nazis set up a ghetto in Slobodka, and began the systematic murder of Kaunas Jews. Most were taken for execution at several of the tsarist forts that had formed the city's 19th-century defenses. The Ninth Fort in particular became the main killing site. By February 1942, half of Kaunas's Jewish population had been annihilated; only about 2,500 survived the war. Today, several hundred Jews live in Kaunas.

Main Sites of Jewish Interest in Kaunas

Choral Synagogue: Ozeskienes g. 13—Before World War II, Kaunas had more than three dozen synagogues. The Choral Synagogue was built in 1871 and, along with the synagogue in Vilnius, is one of only two prewar synagogues still used in Lithuania for prayers. Its towering facade, topped by a dome, is a landmark on a major downtown artery. A pillar-like memorial in the yard behind commemorates the 1,600 to 1,800 children killed at the Ninth Fort. It incorporates representations of children's drawings and a rising field of stars; at the top, two giant hands symbolize hands that can help but also hands that can kill. *(Jewish community: Gedimino g. 26b. Tel: +370-7/203-717, fax: +370-7/201-135. E-mail: kzb@pub.vdu.lt)*

Old Town Area: Several former Jewish buildings stand in or near the Old Town. A former synagogue on Puodziu street is used now as an auto repair shop. Another, a small building with arched windows at Zamenhofo 7, has recently been restored by private owners. At the edge of the Old Town, a large, empty synagogue overlooks the intersection of Jonavos and Gertrudos streets. A redbrick corner building next to the Best Western hotel on Gruodzio street was a Jewish orphanage and still bears a faded inscription in Yiddish and Russian. Around the corner, the building at Poskos 21 was a

Jewish old-age home. A plaque at Nemuno 11 marks the site of a former Jewish high school, the Schwabes Hebrew gymnasium.

Old Jewish Cemetery: Radvilenu Plentas between Basanaviciaus and Baranausko—Though enclosed by a fence, the Old Jewish Cemetery is in terrible condition, desecrated and vandalized. When I visited, my companion, a local Jew, was reluctant to venture too far into it: He said it has the reputation as a meeting place for drunks and young toughs.

World War II Ghetto: In July and August 1941, the Nazis and Lithuanian police crammed 30,000 Jews into two ghettos set up in Slobodka, today known as Vilijampole. Before the war, Slobodka was a poor district, almost entirely Jewish, that was noted for its yeshivah but also infamous for its muddy streets, poor sanitation, and ramshackle wooden houses. Even before the ghettos were established, pro-Nazi Lithuanian thugs staged violent pogroms here that left more than a thousand dead. The two ghettos were closed off from each other and separated by Paneriu street; the smaller ghetto was destroyed on October 4, 1941. Conditions were overcrowded and wretched. Thousands were taken away to be executed, but thousands also died from disease and malnutrition. At the same time, a Jewish underground resistance group operated, and more than 250 managed to escape and join partisan units outside.

Today, a simple monument at the corner of Ariogalos and Linkuvos streets, so small that it is easily overlooked, commemorates the ghetto. Aside from one or two other plaques in the area, little else is left to tell the tale; as Soviet forces neared Kaunas in July 1944, the Germans blew up most buildings and sent about 8,000 remaining Jews to the Dachau and Stutthof camps in Germany. A few old houses on Naujaulio, Linkuvos, and Jurbarko streets still remain from prewar days.

Ninth Fort: Zemaiciu Plentas 73—The Ninth Fort was the main killing grounds for Kaunas Jews. Located in the northwest of the city, the sprawling, redbrick complex was the ninth to be built in a ring of tsarist-era fortresses. Jews were also executed at others, including the Fourth and Seventh Forts, but the Ninth Fort was the scene of most of the slaughter. Tens of thousands were imprisoned here and then shot to death in the moats; on one day alone, October 29, 1941, 9,200 men, women, and children were massacred. Jews from France, Austria, and elsewhere were killed

The grandiose, Soviet-era monument at the Ninth Fort in Kaunas was erected in 1984 and originally bore no reference to Jews.

here, too. A transport of Jews from France was brought to the fort in May 1944; one of them scrawled a haunting last message on the wall of the holding cell: "We are 900 Frenchmen."

The fort anchors a large museum and memorial complex. A huge, Soviet-era sculptural monument depicting human faces disappearing into flames looms over grassy fields where the ashes of burned bodies were scattered. Erected in 1984, it originally bore no reference to Jews, but a new monument nearby now presents a more accurate account of Ninth Fort victims. A museum, also opened in 1984, has a spectacular stained-glass installation, but, like the monument, it, too, scarcely mentioned that Jews made up most of the Ninth Fort victims. Today, revamped exhibitions in the museum and in exhibition rooms in the fort itself chronicle the suffering of Lithuanians under Soviet and German occupation but also provide meticulous information on the annihilation of Kaunas's Jews. They include a trove of photographs taken surreptitiously in the Kaunas Ghetto and material on the dramatic escape of 64 prisoners from the fort in 1944. One room is dedicated to diplomats and others who rescued Jews in the city.

Sugihara House and Foundation: Vaizganto g. 30—Chiune Sugihara served as Japanese consul in Kaunas in 1939 and 1940. The house where he lived has been turned into a little museum and study center. When the Soviet occupation forces ordered diplomats to leave Kaunas in July 1940, Sugihara and his Dutch colleague Jan Zwartendijk managed to stay on for a few more weeks. From July 31 until August 28, Sugihara issued Japanese visas to thousands of Jewish refugees who had fled to Kaunas from Poland. Most of them, traveling by train, managed to reach Japan and eventually found safety in Shanghai, China.

Near Kaunas

JONAVA–A small town northeast of Kaunas, Jonava was founded in 1775, and Jews were invited to settle there at that time. The town stood on important trade routes, and the Jewish community grew quickly—by around 1900, 80 percent of the town was Jewish. About 3,000 Jews—60 percent of the local population—lived here on the eve of World War II. A memorial marks the site at the edge of a forest where 2,100 Jewish men, women, and children were massacred in July and August 1941 by the Nazis and their local collaborators. (A sign marks the turnoff from the road to Ukmerge.)

Two synagogue buildings remain in Jonava—both somewhat derelict and transformed out of recognition, but both bearing plaques that identify them as former synagogues. One is a simple concrete structure at Klaipedos 28. The other is a much larger building with a peaked roof, set back from the pavement on Sodu street, opposite a bank. Nearby Kauno street still has the air of a shtetl, with peak-roofed little houses and an outdoor public well. The Jewish cemetery is on a hill, at the top of a long flight of steps at the end of Sodu street. Several dozen stones are spread out in neat rows over a field; many seem to have been reerected, though there is evidence of vandalism. Most of the stones are small and simple, with little or no decoration other than the epitaph.

KEDAINIAI (KĖDAINIAI) (YIDDISH: KEIDAN)–A historic market town in central Lithuania, Kedainiai preserves a charming old center that includes a number of important sites of Jewish heritage, including three former synagogues. The town was founded in the 14th century. In the 17th century, it became a center of the Reformation and attracted Protestants from Germany and elsewhere, particularly Scotland; many of them were fleeing persecution at home. Jews and members of other religious denominations also found a home here, each creating their own communal space. Jews established a synagogue, hospital, and other institutions on and around the Old Market Square (Senosios rinkos). Though a series of wars and natural disasters wreaked havoc on the town, the Jewish community grew. As a boy, Elijah ben Solomon Zalman—later to become known as the Gaon of Vilna—came here to study Talmud. By the late 19th century, Jews made up half the local population. They were active in trade and industry, and Jewish market gardeners are credited with helping make Kedainiai Lithuania's cucumber capital—a status it still enjoys today.

Two of Kedainiai's surviving synagogues stand side by side on the Old Market Square. Used as warehouses after the war, the two peaked-roof buildings were restored after 2000 and now form a fine cultural complex. The so-called Winter Synagogue, which was built in 1837 and used in cold months, as it was heated, houses a branch of the Kedainiai Regional Museum that opened in 2002 as a multicultural center whose programs focus on the contribution of Jews and other minorities to local history. Its sanctuary is now used for concerts, lectures, and exhibitions; upstairs, in the former women's gallery, is a small display of Judaica and a map and model that locate Jewish buildings in the town. The staff includes English speakers who are very accommodating in helping visitors find sites and learn about local Jewish history. Next door stands the so-called Summer Synagogue, which was used only in warm weather because it was unheated. Built in the 17th century and remodeled in the late 18th century, it now houses an art school.

A third synagogue is now a warehouse-workshop. It stands on Smilgos street and bears a plaque commemorating the Gaon of Vilna's days in Kedainiai as a young student. Nearby, a few sagging wooden houses still stand (though it's unclear how much longer they will resist gentrification and urban renewal). One has a unique example of an attached shed whose roof could be opened so that it could be used as a sukkah—the booth used by Jews during the Sukkoth holiday.

Kedainiai has two Jewish cemeteries, just outside town. The old one, founded in the 18th century, was destroyed and has no tombstones—it is a fenced field, with a commemorative monument. A few hundred yards away, however, a later cemetery preserves several hundred tombstones and is well maintained by municipal authorities. There is also a monument, at the end of a long dirt road, at the forest site where more than 2,000 local

Visitors stand inside the gate of the only Jewish cemetery in Kedainiai that still has tombstones.

Jews were shot to death by the Nazis on August 28, 1941. (Ask at the multicultural center for directions.) A plaque commemorating Kedainiai's destroyed Jewish community was dedicated at the Old Market Square in 2006. *(Memory and genealogy website: www.keidan.net)*

MARIJAMPOLE (MARIJAMPOLĖ) (YIDDISH: MARIAMPOL)–The lovely synagogue in this town near the Polish border in southern Lithuania has been reconstructed for use as a teachers' training college. It stands flush on the pavement at P. Butlerienes 5. The Jewish cemetery is also in fairly good condition.

VILKIJA–There is an interesting and well-maintained Jewish cemetery in this former shtetl in central Lithuania about 12 miles northwest of Kaunas. Located just east of the town, across the street from the Christian cemetery, it has about 80 tombstones. The oldest date back to the 1860s, but most are from 1890 to 1920.

ELSEWHERE IN LITHUANIA

DRUSKININKAI—A historic spa near the border with Poland, Druskininkai was the hometown of the sculptor Jacques Lipchitz. Born here in 1891, he left to study in Paris in 1909 and immigrated to the United States in 1941. He died in 1973. A museum at Sv. Jokubo 17 *(open May–October)*, a branch of the Vilna Gaon Jewish State Museum in Vilnius, is dedicated to his life and work.

JONISKIS (JONIŠKIS) (YIDDISH: YANISHOK)—Two large, beautifully proportioned 19th-century synagogues stand next to each other near the center of this town just south of Lithuania's border with Latvia. The scalloped-roofed White Synagogue (so-called because it outer walls are plastered white) was built in 1823 and turned into a Jewish school and function hall when the neo-Gothic Red Synagogue, with walls of unplastered brick, was constructed in 1865. Both are listed as historic monuments. The Red Synagogue has a big Star of David worked into its facade. Much of its interior decoration remains intact, including its Aron ha Kodesh—believed to be one of only two Arks that survived World War II in provincial Lithuania. After World War II, the Red Synagogue was used as a warehouse and dwelling, and the White Synagogue was turned into a sports hall. Both synagogues have been undergoing a fitful process of renovation, slowed and halted at times because of lack of funds. In the meantime, the Red Synagogue is used on occasion for concerts and other events, and the town museum has set up a small exhibition there on local Jewish history, which can sometimes be visited. *(Tel: +370-426/52492 or ask at the Town Hall)*

Jews settled in Joniskis in the latter part of the 18th century and by 1880 made up about three-quarters of the town; on the eve of World War II, there were 1,200 Jews out of a local population of just over 5,000. On August 29, 1941, hundreds of Joniskis Jews were taken to the Vilkiausis Forest, about three miles south of town, and killed. A monument marks the spot, and there is also a semiruined Jewish cemetery just north of town, reached by a dirt road turning right off the main road toward the Latvian border.

KALVARIJA—Kalvarija is little more than a sleepy village in southern Lithuania near the border with Poland. But it is the site of one of Lithuania's most important surviving complexes of Jewish heritage—and it's important for me personally as the hometown of my great-grandfather, Pesach Susnitsky. Pesach left Kalvarija around 1880, when Jews made up more than 80 percent of Kalvarija's population, and ended up in the small town of Brenham, Texas—where "Pesach" became "Philip." He was the patriarch of a huge family of children, including my grandmother, and the little wooden synagogue he helped found there in 1894 still stands. Pesach Susnitsky died in 1939 at the age of 83, and his grave is in the Brenham Jewish cemetery.

In Kalvarija, two synagogues face each other across a fenced compound on Sodu street, a few steps from the town's big white church. One, the so-called Summer Synagogue, a baroque building dating from the second half of the 18th century, is a ruin. Its roof has fallen in, and through the gaping windows you can see grand broken arches and other architectural detail. The Winter Synagogue opposite, believed to have been built in the early 19th century, has been undergoing full renovation for use as a cultural venue and music school; by the end of the summer 2006, the exterior had been almost completely rebuilt, although the interior was not finished. A redbrick rabbi's house, decorated with a big Star of David, stands between them.

The Jewish cemetery is located on the other side of the little Sheshupa River that winds through the town. The Germans destroyed most of it, and many stones were stolen. A small, fenced-in, triangular plot with several dozen simple tombstones remains, right in front of a huge electric grid. Ugly, barrack-like housing has been built on the area, with common privies, apparently built right atop the graves.

The first time I visited Kalvarija, I tripped and fell over a half-buried brick as I took pictures of the synagogues, twisting my ankle so badly that I could hardly walk. The injury took weeks to heal, but everyone told me that my spill was *bashert*—fated—and maybe it was. Since I couldn't walk, the friend I was with and I decided to drive straight to the Jewish cemetery after my fall. Hobbling, I starting photographing the site. Just then an old man came by, wheeling a bicycle. "I know everything, everything," he smiled. All his teeth were capped in gold. "I remember everything how it was." He propped up his bike and began to talk. He described how the cemetery had once extended much farther, stone after stone, all the way down to the river. Pigs and dogs frolicked around us as he spoke, and a man went by leading a cow.

We asked the old man if he remembered the Susnitsky family—and he did. "Of course! There were a lot of Susnitskys here, a lot!" In particular, he recalled two Susnitsky brothers, Alter and Yankel. "Alter was a big, tall man," he said. "Yankel was small, curved over, and had a hunch back." He demonstrated, curving over his own body. The brothers lived together in a big house on a hill, he said, and then he led us there to see it. Indeed, it was one of the most imposing wooden houses in the village. Both brothers were killed when the Germans deported the Jews to nearby Marijampole during World War II, he told us.

The old man said Jews had lived all over town. "So many, so many!" He gestured forlornly. He was clearly nostalgic for past times, and the disappearance of the Jewish community represented for him a change for the worse. Nonetheless, in describing the Jews in town, he used the Polish term "Zydek" or "little Jew"—a term Jews regard as pejorative. The Jews in Kalvarija were "good people," and "wealthy," he said. They took care of each other, and everyone got on with everyone. "They were called Yankele, Alterke, Menashe, Meyshke," he said. "They would say, 'Oy vey, oy vey.'"

KUPISKIS (KUPIŠKIS) (YIDDISH: KUPISHOK)–Jews may have settled in this town in northeastern Lithuania as early as the 14th century. A large synagogue stands on Lauryno Stuokos-Guceviciaus Square. Still one of the most impressive buildings in town, it has been restored for use as a library and culture center. A Holocaust Wall of Memory was dedicated there in 2004. The Jewish cemetery was almost totally destroyed.

PANEVEZYS (PANEVĖŽYS) (YIDDISH: PONEVEZH)–Panevezys is located in north-central Lithuania, on the Nevezys River, from which it derives its name. Jews settled here at the beginning of the 18th century. By the end of the 19th century, they made up half of the local population; poverty was widespread, however, and many emigrated to South Africa. Still, there were ten synagogues, dozens of prayer houses, and a number of Jewish schools. The Bund labor movement was also active. Local Jews were exiled to Russia during World War I, but most returned, and a yeshivah established after World War I drew talented students.

A few dozen Jews live in Panevezys today, and the Jewish community office occupies two rooms in the redbrick building at Ramygalos 18 that once housed a Jewish high school for girls. The yeshivah building is now a big bakery on Savanoriu Square, and the destroyed Jewish cemetery on Sietyno street is now a park with a monument. One old house on Ukmerges street, just off the modernized main square, conserves its prewar facade with an upper-story arrangement of stuccowork that incorporates the tablets of the Ten Commandments and resembles a Hanukkah menorah.

The Germans occupied Panevezys in 1941 and set up a ghetto. Little more than a month later, 8,000 Jews, mostly women and children, were taken into the dense Pajuoste Forest between the villages of Kaimiskis and Trakiskis, shot dead, and buried in four mass graves. A monument in a big fenced clearing marks the spot. About 3,500 men were taken miles away into the Green Forest (Zalioji Giria), on the way to Vabalninkas, and killed. Signs from the main road indicate the way to both memorial sites.

A monument on Klaipedos street marks the site of the wartime ghetto. As I took some pictures of it, my glance fell on a house next door, whose white wall was defaced by graffiti. The first thing I noticed was a swastika. Then I looked closer. Above the swastika, someone else had drawn a Star of David—and above that, in Hebrew, the words "*Am Yisrael Chai*—The people of Israel live."

PLUNGE (YIDDISH: PLUNGYAN)–"I'm just one man," Jakov Bunka told me. "But I do the work of a minyan, of ten." Bunka, now in his 80s, is the Jewish conscience of Plunge, the last Jew in a town where once more than half the population was Jewish. For decades he has striven to keep alive the memory of the rich Jewish history here. He speaks to school groups and shows visitors around; he rescued tombstones from the destroyed Jewish cemetery and built a monument with them; he wrote a history of Plunge Jews *(posted online in English at www.jewishgen.org/yizkor/plunge/plunge.html);* and put together an exhibition on local Jewish life and traditions. Besides all that, he has created one of the most extraordinary memorials to the Holocaust I have even seen.

Bunka and his family, along with several hundred other local Jews, escaped to the Soviet Union at the beginning of World War II. He joined the Soviet Army, fought valiantly against the Nazis, and became a highly decorated officer. When he returned home, he found little trace of the 2,500 Jews who had lived in Plunge and surrounding villages before the war. The Germans had entered Plunge on June 25, 1941; in July, helped by Lithuanian collaborators, they marched more than 1,800 Jews into the forest near the village of Kausenai, shot them dead, and buried them in mass graves. Hundreds more were massacred at other sites in the area.

Bunka is a wood-carver, a noted folk artist in a country famous for its wood-carving traditions (today, he specializes in Jewish scenes, which have

The towering image of a chained man, by the artist Saulius Ambraska, forms part of the Holocaust memorial created near Plunge by the Jewish sculptor Jakov Bunka.

been exhibited internationally). Starting in the mid-1970s, he began carving huge sculptures out of thick tree trunks to memorialize the Holocaust dead. He crafted the first one, a 13-foot-tall figure with tightly bound hands, out of cedar wood in 1976 and erected it at the mass-grave site near the village of Sateikiai. The former mayor of the town had asked him to do it—and the operation had to be kept secret, as in those hard-line communist days, such commemorative work was virtually taboo. "No one knew what we were doing; I worked on it in a wood-carvers' camp deep in the forest," Bunka told me. "We didn't tell anyone."

A decade later, in the waning days of communist rule, Bunka started work on the memorial for Plunge Jews near Kausenai. He crafted the first towering sculpture from the trunk of an oak tree, in 1986. It shows a mother and father, with four small children and a newborn baby, grouped together under a vigorous crown of leaves. Bunka called it "Born to Live." "This symbolizes how it is impossible to exterminate a people," he wrote in a memoir. "The roots remain. And from those roots grow new branches covered with leaves." Over the years, he enlisted several Lithuanian artist friends to contribute their own huge wood carvings to the growing complex. City authorities, meanwhile, added paths, fences, stairs, and a parking area, and private individuals also contributed to the upkeep. By now, nine remarkable sculptures, each vividly representing a separate theme, are situated around the hilly forested site. Bunka himself carved four: the "Born to Live" piece; the sculpture at the entrance to the site, which represents a mother and child; one depicting the tragedy of the Jewish family; and one a memorial to his brother and father, who had also joined the Soviet Army but died in combat. The other sculptures, each by an individual artist, bear carvings depicting a chained man, a Jewish sage, Nazism as a savage beast, despair, and a group of young women. The site also commemorates Lithuanians who saved Jews. "When I came back after the war, I felt it was my mission to make a memorial for the destroyed Jews of my town," Bunka told me. He has also erected memorial sculptures at mass-grave sites near Salantai and Plateliai and hopes to be able to create at least one more—at the massacre site in Skaudvile, where his sister, an aunt, and his grandparents were killed.

Before the war, there were six synagogues in Plunge, as well as a yeshivah, Jewish schools, and other infrastructure. In the 1930s, there was even a Jewish mayor. Bunka took me around the town, pointing out what was left. Three former synagogues remain. Two were reconstructed out of recognition after the war and transformed for commercial use. Returned a few years ago to Jewish ownership, they now stand empty. Across the road, a small wooden prayer house, built in 1931 and used most recently as a dwelling, seems almost at the point of collapse. It is here that Bunka would like to establish a Jewish museum to house the collection of documents, photographs, memorabilia, and other material that he has amassed over the years. Currently, it is displayed in an annex of the local art museum, but visitors must contact Bunka in order to gain access.

The Soviet authorities destroyed Plunge's already desecrated Jewish cemetery in 1972. They built a school on the site, and local people took away tombstones to use as building material. In 1995, Bunka set out to gather as many of the stones as he could. He recovered nearly 90 of them and reerected them as a memorial, shoulder to shoulder, on the part of the cemetery next to the school that had not been built on. "We got one stone in 1998," he recalled. "Someone called me to say that he had found a stone in his vegetable garden. He was digging, and saw the Hebrew letters." *(Contact: Jakov Bunka, V. Macernio g. 6-16. Tel: +370-448/52156. www.shtetlinks.jewishgen.org/plunge/plunge.html)*

RIETAVAS (YIDDISH: RITOVE)–A big, empty synagogue stands in the middle of this town near Plunge, where Jews settled in the 17th century. In Soviet times, it was used as a movie theater. The Jewish cemetery is still fairly intact, and a monument marks the spot in the forest near Viesvenai where Jews were massacred in 1941.

SIAULIAI (ŠIAULIAI) (YIDDISH: SHAVL)–Jews settled in this city in northern Lithuania in the 17th century. Thanks in part to good railway connections, they prospered as merchants and also built factories—one of the most important was the big leatherworks founded by the industrialist Chaim Frenkel in 1879. In the interwar years, when Lithuania was independent, Siauliai was the country's second largest city, and the Jewish community, also the second largest, had far-reaching economic, cultural, and even political interests. About 8,500 Jews lived here on the eve of World War II. About 5,000 were enclosed in a ghetto; a small monument stands on Traku street. Many Siauliai Jews were deported to German concentration camps in 1944, but thousands were killed in the Kuziai Forest—a monument on the road to Grudziai marks the site. The Jewish community was reestablished in 1992 and now numbers about 200 people.

Chaim Frenkel's sprawling redbrick leatherworks still stands. Next to it, at Vilniaus 74, his sumptuous mansion, built in 1908 and probably designed by his son, Jacob, serves as a branch of the town's Ausra Museum and includes a new section dealing with local Jewish history. The museum includes a collection of fascinating drawings by the artist Gerardas Bagdonavicius, who depicted synagogues and Jewish scenes in the 1930s. (These drawings were kept at the Ausra Museum branch at Vytauto 89; it was not clear if they would be included in the new Jewish exhibit. Copies of them are on display at the Vilna Gaon Jewish State Museum in Vilnius; see pp. 70–71) The only surviving synagogue in town is a small, redbrick prayer house down the street from the Frenkel factory, which Frenkel built for Jewish workers at his factory. It is now a church. *(Jewish community: Visinskio g. 24. Tel: +370-41/426-796, fax: +370-41/426-678)*

TELSIAI (TELŠIAI) (YIDDISH: TELZ)—Telsiai is the capital of northwestern Lithuania's Samogitian region, an area whose people are renowned for their stubbornness. Jews settled here in the 17th century, and by 1900 they made up more than half the local population. A yeshivah established in 1875 became one of the most influential centers of Orthodox learning in the country—and beyond. It anchored a complete Orthodox educational system for boys and girls, from kindergarten through college. The yeshivah functioned until 1941, when the Germans marched in and, with the help of local Lithuanian collaborators, annihilated the Jewish community.

During the war a ghetto was set up, right off the town's main square. About 14,000 Jews from Telsiai and surrounding towns and villages were confined here. Today, small stone memorial pillars mark the ghetto borders. There are still a number of old wooden buildings in the area; one sagging house with a corrugated iron roof has upper windows shaped like the tablets of the Ten Commandments. A freestanding wooden building at the end of Elektrines street, now an appliance store, was once a synagogue. The Jews from the ghetto were massacred in half a dozen places in the surrounding forest, all of which have monuments. *(The tourist information office on the main square, at Turgaus a. 21, is very helpful in providing information and directions.)*

The building of the famous yeshivah, used as a workshop and warehouse after the war, still stands on Izdines street. It has lost the distinctive decorative gable that once defined its facade, and its windows have long been boarded up, but there is a plaque on the facade describing the building's original function. As it happened, when the war broke out, two of the yeshivah's main rabbis were in the United States on a fund-raising trip. They reestablished the school in Cleveland, Ohio, where it remains a leading center of traditional Orthodox study to this day. Around the corner stands a brown wooden building that was once a Jewish girls' school, and the site of the destroyed main synagogue of the town is now commemorated as Sinagogos street. The Alka Museum, at Muziejaus 31, includes documents, everyday objects, and other material on local Jewish life and history in its collections.

The Soviet authorities began demolishing the town's Jewish cemetery in the mid-1980s but halted before they finished the job. Located on Stoties street, most of the cemetery area is now a park. A few dozen stones remain, in a partially fenced section. One of the surviving tombs is the simple ohel of Rabbi Joseph Leib Bloch, a prominent head of the yeshivah, who died in 1930.

VABALNINKAS (YIDDISH: VABOLNIK)–An out-of-the way village in northeast Lithuania, Vabalninkas preserves the atmosphere of a prewar shtetl and also has a fascinating and well-maintained Old Jewish Cemetery. The main square of the village, dominated by a big, white church with two steeples, is lined by low wooden houses where Jews once lived and maintained their shops. Several side streets also retain evocative old buildings. Two former synagogues stand next to each other just off the square—both were converted long ago for storage or commercial use. One has arched windows, but otherwise they look like big houses. A road separates them, but originally they stood in one yard.

The Jewish cemetery is on a dirt road just outside town amid fields dotted by grazing milk cows. The turnoff is clearly marked with a big road sign reading "Senosios Zydu Kapines—Old Jewish Cemetery." The large, fenced area has an unlocked gate and includes hundreds of tombstones shaded by dozens of big trees. Most stones are fairly small; some are irregular chunks with one smoothed face where the epitaph is written, and only a very few have carved decoration other than the inscription. Few, if any, are believed to date from after World War I. A monument formed by a boulder stands at the entrance.

A memorial site in the Zadeikiai Forest, clearly indicated from the road, marks the spot where the Jews from Vabalninkas were killed by the Nazis and their local helpers.

ZAGARE (ŽAGARĖ) (YIDDISH: ZAGER)–Zagare, on the border with Latvia, has two sections, Old Zagare and New Zagare, and long had two separate Jewish communities. Jews settled here in the 18th century, and more than 2,000 lived here before World War II. Three synagogue buildings still stand. One is a fire station and one is a warehouse. There are two Jewish cemeteries, both of which still have tombstones. The extensive Old Jewish Cemetery, established in the mid-18th century, is particularly valuable. Monuments mark World War II massacre sites in the Naryshkin town park and the Jewish cemetery in New Zagare.

WOODEN SYNAGOGUES

LITHUANIA'S SURVIVING WOODEN SYNAGOGUES REPRESENT A UNIQUE PATRIMONY and some of the most precious sites of Jewish heritage in Eastern Europe. Unfortunately, little has been done to preserve them. For the most part very simple buildings, these gems only hint at the magnificence of the dozens of grand wooden synagogues destroyed during World War II. In a sense, their simplicity was their salvation. I have grouped examples of them here, as they form a whole and can be the basis for an itinerary around the country. In addition to the wonderful sites listed below, and the two mentioned elsewhere in Plunge (see pp. 87–90) and Telsiai (see pp. 91–92), wooden synagogues can be found in the villages of Alanta, Kaltinenai, Laukuva, Veisiejai, Seda, and Tirksliai.

KURKLIAI (YIDDISH: KURKLI)–The lovely wooden synagogue in this hamlet about 60 miles north of Vilnius stands isolated amid a timeless scene of quaint wooden cottages, lush greenery, roadside wells, and outdoor plumbing. It was immediately recognizable as I drove around looking for it: a square, gray-plank building, with a low-peaked roof and squat square tower, standing beside a small stream at the intersection of two dirt roads. It looks blind, its doors and windows boarded up. The walls bear remnants of decorative vertical ribbing, and some of the windows are tall and narrow, with pointed tops; a birdhouse is attached below the tower. The synagogue, believed to have been built in 1935, was apparently used as a barn after the war; today the interior is empty. The dirt road leading to it is a turnoff from the main road, just opposite the Soviet war memorial and lovely wooden church and bell tower.

PAKRUOJIS (YIDDISH: POKROI)–A beautiful, graceful, and unutterably doleful wooden synagogue stands at the rim of a little river valley, at the edge of the evocative remnants of a shtetl. Believed to have been built in 1801 and the oldest surviving wooden synagogue in Lithuania, it is recognizable by the double-mansard roof. Used as a movie theater and sports hall in the 1950s, it stands abandoned today. The whole building is sagging. Windows are boarded up, and the weathered outer planking has buckled. Old pictures show that it once had a beautifully ornate interior, with a richly carved Ark and central bimah. The walls and ceiling bore intricate—and sometimes surprising—naïve paintings. One showed a big, smiling lion, another a locomotive pulling a train. On the ceiling was a tangle of painted fruit trees, storks, and flowers. One painting vividly depicted the messianic image of the Leviathan swallowing its tail; its curved body surrounded a homey drawing of a two-story house with potted shrubs out front and three smoking chimneys.

The Jewish cemetery is located on the road to the hamlet of Linksmuciai, amid rich pastureland and lowing cattle. There are couple dozen stones, shaded by big birch trees and enclosed by a bright blue wooden fence and gate. A local priest helped clean and restore the cemetery after the depredations of World War II and the Soviet period. In the middle stands a monument to Jewish community, its base made from fragments of broken tombstones. It bears inscriptions in Yiddish and Lithuanian. Perhaps because of the priest's Catholic sensibilities, the Lithuanian text describes the Jews of Pakruojis waiting for resurrection. *(Additional information: www.shtetlinks.jewishgen.org/pakruojis/)*

ROZALIMAS—Centered around a mustard-colored wooden church, the beautiful little village of Rozalimas, a few miles south of Pakruojis, vividly evokes the feel of an old shtetl. Most of the houses in its center are made of wood. Jews settled here in the early 19th century and made up about half the town's population until 1915, when the tsarist government deported them deep into the Russian interior. Some returned after the Bolshevik Revolution, but many remaining Jews left Rozalimas following a fire that destroyed much of the village in 1930; on the eve of World War II, only a few dozen Jews lived here. Only three survived the Holocaust.

The synagogue, built in the late 19th century, is a ramshackle building of weathered gray planks with a corrugated iron roof. It looks like a big, abandoned house, forgotten somehow at the intersection of two apparently nameless dirt roads near the main square. For years after the war it was used as a barn for a collective farm and then as a pigsty for the hospital in Pakruojis. After Lithuania became independent in 1991, the hospital sold it—to the owners of a chain of folk-style restaurants in Kaunas who wanted to dismantle the building and use the weathered wood as part of their restaurant decor. "The mayor stepped in to prevent this," Birute Maiksteniene, a Rozalimas school teacher who has interested herself in local Jewish history, told me as we sipped coffee around her dining room table. "There were no Jews here to take care—there was no one to take care. But I don't think it will be destroyed

The simple wooden synagogue in Rozalimas is one of only about a dozen wooden synagogues that still remain in Lithuania.

now. It will live until it falls down." Mrs. Maiksteniene helped a Dutch friend, Dora Boom, research the Jewish history of Rozalimas *(posted on the Internet: www.shtetlinks.jewishgen.org/Rozalimas/)*. They and other friends also cleaned up the little Jewish cemetery, a few eroding tombstones on a bluff outside town, partly surrounded by pine trees and wild cherries. *(Contact: Birute Maiksteniene, Kanapines g. 6. Tel: +370-8/421-43308. E-mail: bgm@omni.lt)*

ZIEZMARIAI (ŽIEŽMARIAI) (YIDDISH: ZHEZMIR)–Ziezmariai lies just off the main highway between Vilnius and Kaunas and, given its location, has probably the most easily visited of Lithuania's wooden synagogues. Believed to have been built in the mid-19th century, the synagogue is recognized as a heritage site and bears a plaque, dedicated in 2005, that identifies it as part of the planned European Route of Jewish Heritage. It is a large building, with remnants of a decorative portal. The windows, some of them tall and arched, are boarded up. Inside, heavy wooden pillars still support the ceiling, and there are remains of the women's gallery. During Soviet times, it was used as a barn. The key is kept by Agrippina Semenkova, a Russian woman in her 80s, who lives next door. She is an Old Believer—a member of a Russian Orthodox sect that still follows the liturgy as it existed before reforms in the 17th century.

RESOURCES ON LITHUANIA

Ample material in English is available locally on Jewish heritage sites in Vilnius, but otherwise little exists. (An English-language guidebook to Jewish sites around the country was to be published in late 2006 or early 2007, but as of this writing it was not available.) English-language publications found in bookstores include:

- Agranovski, Genrich, and Irina Guzenberg. *Vilnius: 100 Memorable Sites of Jewish History and Culture.* Vilnius: Vilna Gaon Jewish State Museum, 2006
- Bubnys, Arunas. *The Holocaust in Lithuania.* Vilnius: Genocide and Resistance Research Center of Lithuania, 2005
- Katz, David. *Lithuanian Jewish Culture.* Vilnius: Baltos lankos, 2004
- Lempertas, Izraelis. *Litvakes.* Vilnius: Versus Aureus, 2005
- Levinson, Yosif. *Skausmo Knyga/The Book of Sorrow.* Vilnius: Vaga, 1997. Locations and photographs of monuments marking World War II mass graves throughout Lithuania.

Websites:

- www.hum.huji.ac.il/cja/Architecture/Wooden-synagogues-Lithuania.htm — Photo documentation of surviving wooden synagogues in Lithuania
- www.jewishgen.org/cemetery/e-europe/lithuania.html — Jewish cemeteries in Lithuania
- www.jewishstudies.lt — Center for Studies of the Culture and History of East European Jews. Website includes a searchable photo database of Jewish material in provincial museums.
- www.jmuseum.lt — Vilna Gaon Jewish State Museum
- www.litjews.org — Lithuanian Jewish community
- www.ncsj.org — Advocates on behalf of Jews in Russia, Ukraine, the Baltic States and Eurasia

Additional Publications:

- Alexander, Naomi. *Once upon a Time in Lithuania.* London: David Paul, 2006
- Dawidowicz, Lucy. *From That Time and Place: A Memoir 1938–1947.* New York: Norton, 1989
- Eliach, Yaffa. *There Was Once a World: A 900-Year Chronicle of the Shtetl of Eishyshok.* New York: Little, Brown & Co., 1998
- Gitelman, Zvi. *A Century of Ambivalence: The Jews of Russia and the Soviet Union 1881 to the Present.* New York: Schocken, 1988
- Kruk, Herman. *The Last Days of the Jerusalem of Lithuania: Chronicles from the Vilna Ghetto and the Camps, 1939–1944.* Edited by Benjamin Harshav. Translated by Barbara Harshav. New Haven: Yale University Press, 2002

UKRAINE

CURRENT POPULATION: 46.5 MILLION
JEWISH POPULATION BEFORE WORLD WAR II: 2 MILLION
JEWISH POPULATION TODAY: APPROX. 100,000–300,000

A LITTLE HISTORY

UKRAINE IS A VAST COUNTRY WITH A COMPLEX HISTORY. STRETCHING FROM THE borders of the European Union across the top of the Black Sea toward the Caucasus, it came under the domination of many tribes and rulers over the centuries and has been a cradle of some of the Jewish world's most influential movements. Home to the shtetl—the typical, mainly Jewish small town that was a bastion of traditional life—as well as to the big-city universe of high-powered capitalism and radical secular culture, it gave birth to Hasidism and also formed a hotbed of revolutionary politics.

Jews lived on the Black Sea coast in ancient times, and in the eighth century, the rulers of the powerful Khazar tribe in the Crimea converted to Judaism, prompting many of their subjects to do the same. Ancient sources relate that at the end of the tenth century, when Prince Volodymyr of Kiev, who ruled the proto-Russian state of Kievan Rus, decided to abandon paganism and embrace a monotheistic religion, he consulted Khazar Jews along with Christians and Muslims before he made his choice—Orthodox Christianity. Evidence shows that Jews were already living in central Ukraine at that time, and Jews are known to have migrated eastward into Ukraine in the 12th century, fleeing persecution in western Europe.

In the mid-14th century, much of Ukraine came under the Grand Duchy of Lithuania, and when Poland and Lithuania formalized their union as a commonwealth in 1569, most Ukrainian territory became part of Poland. It was in this period that the Jewish population began to blossom, as the Polish nobility invited Jews to settle in their private towns and manage their vast estates. These settlements developed into the characteristic shtetls that became the hallmark of Jewish life in Eastern Europe. By the end of the 1500s, about 45,000 Jews are believed to have lived in this region. (See also Poland pp. 15–19.)

Jews suffered tremendously during the 1648–1649 uprising led by Bogdan Chmielnicki (Bohdan Khmelnytsky) to free Ukraine from Polish domination. Chmielnicki's main targets were Roman Catholic priests, Polish noblemen, and the "accursed Jews," who served the Poles as stewards and tax collectors. As many as 100,000 or more Jews were brutally slain and hundreds of communities destroyed. In Ukraine, Chmielnicki is revered as a freedom fighter and national hero. Streets and squares all over the country are named for him, and there are monuments to him in many towns. In 1667, Ukraine was divided; the part east of the Dnieper River was incorporated into Russia, while Poland kept the west.

Hasidism was born in the 18th century in western Ukraine; where the movement's founder, Israel ben Eliezar, known as the Ba'al Shem Tov (Master of the Good Name), lived and preached. Hasidism eventually became the region's dominant Jewish stream, and Hasidic masters, or tzaddikim, drew followers to courts in many towns.

Life in the region changed radically again at the end of the 18th century, when Poland was partitioned among Austria, tsarist Russia, and Prussia. In 1791, the Russian empress Catherine the Great restricted Jewish residence to the Pale of Settlement—a strip of territory along Russia's western border. In 1817, another law stated that Jews could only live in shtetls—though certain wealthy Jews could obtain permits to live in some big cities. Much of today's Ukraine was found in the Pale. (Galicia, which encompasses the westernmost part of Ukraine and also southeastern Poland, came under Austrian rule.) Still, large parts of eastern Ukraine were also barred to Jews. Conditions in the Pale were often miserable; poverty was widespread. Economic conditions and persecution, including brutal pogroms in 1881 and 1882 and in the early 1900s forced hundreds of thousands to emigrate.

The Pale remained in force until the Bolshevik Revolution in 1917. But World War I, the revolution, and the ensuring civil wars that raged between 1918 and 1921 wreaked enormous destruction. All factions attacked the Jews, in what was the most deadly anti-Jewish violence in Ukraine since the 17th century. As many as 35,000 or more Jews were killed. As result of these conflicts, western Ukraine became incorporated into a reestablished independent

A Jewish couple and their grandchildren at their home in Stanislawow (today Ivano Frankivsk) in 1929

Poland, and eastern Ukraine was taken over by the Soviet Union. This reallocation determined the fate of Jews (and Jewish heritage sites) in the 20th century. Jewish communities remained numerous and active in Poland. But the hundreds of thousands of Jews in the Soviet sector were subject to the regime's ruthless campaign of militant atheism. Synagogues were closed, demolished, or converted for secular use, and religious life was crushed. For a decade or so, the regime promoted a secular Yiddish culture, but this, too, was eliminated by the end of the 1930s.

In World War II, German armies occupied most of today's Ukraine. Hundreds of flourishing Jewish communities in the Polish areas were annihilated, synagogues were destroyed, and cemeteries uprooted. As many as 1.4 million of the 2 million Jews estimated to have lived in the territory of today's Ukraine were killed. Many were shipped to death camps, but the Germans, aided by local Ukrainian collaborators, shot tens of thousands dead on streets or in forests. At the war's end, Soviet borders shifted west, taking over the western part of Ukraine. Survivors returned to some cities, but the Soviet anti-Jewish campaign, joined by traditional Ukrainian anti-Semitism, remained intense. Memory of hundreds of years of Jewish history in Ukraine was suppressed; specific Jewish suffering in the Holocaust was ignored or became a footnote to overall casualties in what the Soviets called the Great Patriotic War.

With the collapse of the Soviet Union, Ukraine became independent in 1991. Since then, tens of thousands of Jews left the country for Israel. The 100,000 to 300,000 who remain make up one of Europe's biggest Jewish populations. Jewish congregations of various sorts have been revitalized or newly established in scores of towns and cities throughout the country. More than 120 rabbis lead congregations, and there are more than 60 Jewish community centers. Dozens of other Jewish organizations, institutions, schools, clubs, media outlets, and programs of all sorts now exist, including welfare operations that serve tens of thousands of needy, elderly Jews. A number of synagogues and other communal properties have reverted to Jewish ownership, and dozens of memorials to Holocaust victims have been erected.

JEWISH HERITAGE IN UKRAINE

There are at least 300 synagogue buildings, more than 700 Jewish cemeteries (or sites of Jewish cemeteries) and about 500 sites of World War II mass graves in Ukraine—probably more exist. This guide concentrates primarily on sites in western Ukraine, that is, the section of the country that was part of Poland between the two World Wars and became incorporated into the Soviet Union after 1945. In tsarist times, it had Ukraine's densest Jewish population, and as part of prewar Poland, active Jewish communities flourished until the Holocaust. Until the Bolshevik Revolution, Jewish settlement was barred in parts of what is today eastern Ukraine; under Soviet rule, Jewish practice was suppressed.

Most people looking for Jewish heritage sites in Ukraine are on "roots trips" and concentrate on the town where their ancestors came from. Others are primarily interested in praying at the tombs of the Ba'al Shem Tov and other great Hasidic personalities. But the country has some of the most important and exciting sites of Jewish heritage in Europe, sites that could easily form part of mainstream tourist itineraries. In addition, the fast-developing Jewish revival means that there are active synagogues and kosher facilities all around the country.

Ukraine's large Jewish population is mostly secular; on religious, cultural, and political fronts it is fragmented and sometimes fractious. At this writing, Ukraine has three chief rabbis and four umbrella groups for Jewish organizations and communities. Chabad Lubavitch is very active, and there are also mainstream Orthodox synagogues and Reform and Conservative congregations. The American Jewish Joint Distribution Committee runs a network of "Hesed" welfare and Jewish community centers. *(A full list of Chabad institutions can be found at www.fjc.ru.)*

TIPS ON VISITING

THE SURVIVING FORTRESS SYNAGOGUES SUCH AS THOSE IN ZHOVKVA, BRODY, AND Sataniv, and centuries-old Jewish cemeteries such as those in Busk, Bolekhiv, Sataniv, and Kremenets are outstanding examples of art and architecture. Quite a few villages, such as Sharhorod, retain the look of the old shtetl, and important Jewish urban centers, such as L'viv, Kiev, and Drohobych, still have much to show. L'viv and Kiev make good hubs for day trips.

As anyone who read Jonathan Safran Foer's 2002 novel *Everything Is Illuminated* will know, tourist infrastructure in Ukraine is limited, and traveling can be an adventure. Roads can be terrible, too—not to mention blocked by flocks of farm animals—particularly in the countryside. Ukraine, in fact, is the only country where I did not want to do the driving myself. Instead, I hired taxi drivers on a per-kilometer basis. Jewish communities and institutions, as well as travel agencies, can help you find English-speaking guides.

The Ukrainian language is similar to Russian, and both are written in Cyrillic characters. Until Ukrainian independence, most towns were known widely by their Russian names. Given the many border changes, some also are well known by their Polish (or Hungarian) names. And many are best known in the Jewish world by their names in Yiddish or German. Towns are listed here by the transliteration of their Ukrainian names; some are also accompanied by their names in the alternative languages noted above.

KIEV

(Ukrainian: Kyiv)

SPREAD OUT ON A RIDGE ABOVE THE DNIEPER RIVER, THE UKRAINIAN CAPITAL is a vibrant, modern city of broad, tree-lined boulevards, shady parks, and wide plazas. Known as the "mother of Russian cities," it is studded with historic monuments ranging from ancient golden-domed churches to fine examples of art nouveau. Founded in the eighth century, Kiev in the early Middle Ages became the fabled capital of the Kievan Rus, the cradle of ancient Russia; it was conquered and reconquered over the centuries.

Jewish merchants and traders settled in Kiev from its earliest days. A tenth-century letter from the Kiev Jewish community, written in Hebrew on parchment, was among the tens of thousands of manuscripts discovered in a genizah, or cache of documents, found in the ninth-century Ben Ezra Synagogue in Cairo, Egypt. An appeal to help ransom a Jew named Jacob ben Hanukke from his creditors, it is the oldest known document that mentions Kiev by name. By the 13th century Kiev had developed into a Jewish cultural and religious center, but the end of the 1400s ushered in centuries of persecution, upheaval, expulsions, and other restrictions. Many Jews died during the Cossack uprising led by Bogdan Chmielnicki in the mid-17th century. (A huge 1888 statue of Chmielnicki on horseback dominates Kiev's central Sofiyskaya Square. Its original design was to have shown him trampling his defeated enemies: a Jesuit priest, a Polish nobleman, and a Jew.)

After tsarist Russia annexed Kiev in 1667, Jews were barred from the city for more than a century. The community began to revive at the end of the 18th century, but, even though Kiev was in the Pale of Settlement, Jews were soon banished again under Tsar Nicholas I, who took the imperial throne in 1825. Only in 1861, under reforms introduced by Alexander II, were two districts, Lybid and Podil, opened up to some—mainly wealthy—Jewish residents. The convolutions that other Jews, barred from the city, had to negotiate in order to do business or spend the night there formed a running motif in some of the stories by the great Yiddish writer Sholom Aleichem. Nonetheless, the community grew and prospered. By 1872, there were nearly 14,000 Jews in Kiev; by 1917 there were more than 87,000. Life was precarious, however. A government-backed pogrom in 1881 destroyed Jewish homes and shops; residency and other restrictions remained in force. In 1911, an infamous blood libel case erupted after a 12-year-old boy was found murdered. Police identified a gang of thieves as the probable killers, but right-wing forces claimed the boy had been killed by Jews to use his blood for ritual purposes. Amid anti-Semitic frenzy, the district attorney had a Jew, Mendel Beilis, arrested and jailed. The affair grabbed international headlines and sparked a storm of protest across Europe and the United States. At a trial in 1913, the charges collapsed and Beilis was acquitted. Despite the difficulties and a restive anti-Semitic climate, Jewish businessmen, industrialists, professionals, writers, and other cultural figures played prominent roles in the life of the city. Among the most notable were the Brodsky brothers, Lazar and Lev, sugar-industry tycoons who financed the building of synagogues and other general philanthropic endeavors and who were the local equivalent of the Rothschilds. (Their mansions still stand; Lazar and his wife Sarah lived at Institutska 12, and Lev at Lypska 9.) Kiev also became a center of the Zionist movement.

World War I, followed by the Bolshevik Revolution and ensuing civil war, were years of turmoil and violent upheaval. Refugees swelled the Jewish population to 120,000 by 1923. In World War II, the Germans took Kiev on September 19, 1941. Many of the 175,000 Jews who had lived there before the war managed to escape, but the vast majority were doomed, most of them machine-gunned at the Babyn Yar ravine at the edge of town. Under postwar Soviet rule, Kiev again developed a Jewish population, as refugees flowed in to the city. By 1959 as many as 200,000 or more Jews lived there. But Jewish religious life, culture, and education were stifled by state anti-Semitism, and there were few possibilities for overt Jewish affiliation. Tens of thousands left when barriers to emigration were lifted in 1990, but as many as 60,000 to 70,000 Jews still live in Kiev. Most are secular or unaffiliated, but active Orthodox congregations occupy two recently renovated synagogues, and there are also small Reform and Conservative congregations. The city is the seat of numerous Jewish institutions including the central offices of four national Jewish umbrella organizations. There are Jewish schools, cultural centers, media outlets, kosher restaurants, and a respected Judaica Institute that carries out research and academic work.

MAIN SITES OF JEWISH INTEREST IN KIEV

Synagogue of the Jewish Community of Kiev: vul. Schekavytska 29— The splendid main synagogue of Kiev's Jewish community stands in the evocative Podil District, the lower part of town along the Dnieper. Built in 1894, the redbrick building with white-trimmed arched windows was Kiev's first permanent Jewish house of worship and has survived more than a century of pogroms, persecution, war, and upheaval. The Germans turned it into a stable during World War II, and the Soviet regime kept it, and the few

Jews who came here to pray, under tight surveillance. Today the synagogue anchors a Jewish compound that also includes a mikvah, kosher kitchen, and matzo bakery. Inside, it features a gilded wooden Ark with fine carving and filagree-like detail and striking new stained-glass windows. "Our synagogue is unique, and not only for its architectural beauty," Rabbi Ya'akov David Bleich, one of Ukraine's three chief rabbis, said in 2003 at the ceremony rededicating the building after a multimillion dollar renovation. "First of all for being a significant source of vitality for the Jews of Ukraine, and for being the only operating synagogue in the capital during 50 postwar years."

Central Synagogue: vul. Shota Rustaveli 13—Located in downtown Kiev near the colorful Bessarabian Market, the Central Synagogue is also known as the Brodsky Synagogue, in honor of the brothers Lazar and Lev Brodsky, the superrich sugar magnates who helped finance its construction in 1897–98. The two-story brick building, with a tall arched facade and deep portico, takes up an entire corner block and recalls the Renaissance fortress synagogues that once were the pride of many Ukrainian cities. The Soviet regime closed it down in 1926, and in the 1950s it was turned into a puppet theater. Returned to Jewish ownership in the 1990s, it underwent a full renovation and now serves as the center of Kiev's Chabad-oriented congregation. Crystal chandeliers hang from the vaulted ceiling above a stately wooden Ark that is topped by gilded lions. There is a Jewish bookstore in the lobby. (Just down the street, what is now the Kinopanorama movie theater was once the so-called Merchants's Synagogue, built in 1898–1899.)

Galytzky Synagogue: vul. Zhilanska 97—Built in 1909–1910, this spacious brick synagogue with a decorative, neo-Romantic facade stands in an area still known today as the Yevbaz—an abbreviation for Yevreyski Bazaar, or Jewish Market. Soviet authorities closed it down in 1929 and turned it first into a canteen and then into a factory. The building was returned to Jewish ownership in 2001 and underwent top to bottom reconstruction that brought it back to a semblance of its original appearance. It now serves as an educational center called Midrasha Tzionit, run by the Jewish Agency for Israel. The sanctuary is used as a conference hall, with a permanent multimedia exhibition on Jewish history, culture, and traditions stationed around its sides.

Karaite Kenassa: vul. Yaroslavov Val 7—The lavishly ornate, Moorish-style building, now the premises of an actors' organization, was constructed in

The Sholom Aleichem monument in downtown Kiev portrays the great Yiddish writer tipping his hat to passersby.

1898–1902 as a kenassa, or prayer house, for the Karaite community that flourished here before the Bolshevik Revolution. An ethnic Turkish people, Karaites follow a breakaway Jewish sect that originated in eighth-century Iraq. They recognize the Torah and celebrate major Jewish holidays but have modified other Jewish traditions and reject the Talmud and rabbinical Judaism.

Sholom Aleichem Monument: vul. Rognidynskaya—In the late 19th and early 20th centuries, many writers and other Jewish cultural personalities made Kiev their home. Most prominent among them was the celebrated Yiddish author Sholom Aleichem. His evocation of the shtetl and its characters, such as his famous Tevye the milkman, has colored the way much of the world thinks about Jews and Jewish life in prewar Eastern Europe. Among other things, his stories served as the inspiration for the musical *Fiddler on the Roof.* Born Sholom Rabinowitz in 1859 in the small town of Pereslayev, Sholom Aleichem took as his pen name the Yiddish expression meaning "peace be with you." In his stories, he gave Kiev the name "Yehupetz" and described it as a "crazy commercial city." A statue of him, looking dapper in an overcoat and scarf and raising his hat in greeting, stands just around the corner from the Brodsky Synagogue. Plaques mark the buildings where he lived, at Saksagansky 27 and at Bolshaya-Vassilikovska 5; the Kiev History Museum at Khreschatyk 2 has a collection of materials on him and his work. Sholom Aleichem left Kiev following a bloody pogrom in 1905. He died of tuberculosis in New York in 1916; more than 150,000 people attended his funeral.

Golda Meir Monument: vul. Baseyna 5a—A plaque bearing a portrait of the late Israeli prime minister marks the site where she was born in 1898.

Babyn Yar (Babi Yar) Memorial: vul. Melnikova—On September 28, 1941, just days after they occupied Kiev, the Germans ordered all Jews in town to assemble on Melnikova street, in the northern part of the city near the Jewish and other cemeteries. Announcements plastered on walls ordered them to bring their documents, money, valuables, warm clothing, and underwear. "Any Jew not carrying out this instruction and who is found elsewhere will be shot," they warned. More than 30,000 Jews complied, assuming that they were to be deported. Instead, German soldiers and local Ukrainian police herded them into Babyn Yar, or Grandmother's Ravine. Here, they were beaten, stripped naked, lined up at the edge of the ravine, and, group after group, mown down by machine-gun fire. The Nazis kept meticulous records; according to their count, on September 29 and 30, a total of 33,771 Jews were murdered. In all, more than 100,000 people were killed at Babyn Yar, including at least 80,000 Jews, as well as Roma (Gypsies), members of the underground, and Soviet prisoners of war. For decades after the war, the area remained a wasteland; the Soviets suppressed memory of the carnage. In 1961, the Russian poet Yevgeny Yevtushenko protested the silence with an angry and eloquent poem that began, "No monument stands over Babi Yar. . . ." The composer Dmitri Shostakovich set the powerful words to music in his Symphony No. 13, which premiered in 1962.

Erected in 1991, a giant menorah commemorates the 80,000 or more Jewish victims killed at Babyn Yar during the Holocaust.

The forested ravines of Babyn Yar still exist; today they are skirted by parks where children play and people jog or sun themselves on benches. New apartments and high-rises dot the area. Three monuments, though, now commemorate the slaughter. One is a huge Soviet memorial erected in 1976 in a grassy sunken bowl off Dorogozhitska street. It is an immense heroic sculpture of writhing bodies poised at the edge of an abyss. The inscription ignores the fact that most of the victims were Jewish. A new Jewish monument, a giant menorah, was dedicated in 1991 a few hundred yards from the place where the Babyn Yar victims were actually killed; a path through the woods leads to the ravines themselves. The monument is in a paved plaza at the end of a long path off Melnikova street, by the television station. In 2001 a third monument, formed of giant bronze sculptures of broken toys, was erected in a park near the other monuments specifically to honor the children murdered in Babyn Yar.

Addresses of Note in Kiev

- Jewish community: vul. Schekavytska 29. Tel: +380-44/463-7085
- Jewish community (Chabad): vul. Shota Rustaveli 13. Tel: +380-44/235-9082. www.greatsynagogue.kiev.ua
- Kosher restaurants: King David (sit-down, upscale). Tel: +380-44/235-7418;

Makkabi (snack bar)—both attached to the Central Synagogue at vul. Shota Rustaveli 13.

- Ha Tikva Progressive Jewish community: vul. Pyrogova 10-B. Tel: +380-44/265-3890
- Judaica Institute of Kiev: vul. Kurska 6. Tel/fax: +380-44/248-8917. www.judaica.kiev.ua or www.judaicamuseum.kiev.ua
- Center for the Study of the Culture and History of East European Jews: vul. Voloska 8/5. Tel/fax: +380-44/463-5789. E-mail: judaicacenter@ukma.kiev.ua. www.judaicacenter.kiev.ua

---

Near Kiev

BERDYCHIV (BERDICHEV)–Now a rather run-down town 120 miles southwest of Kiev, Berdychiv looms large in Jewish life and legend. Jews settled here in the early 18th century, and the town developed into an archetypical shtetl. The vast majority of its population was Jewish; in 1897, Jews made up 80 percent of the town. There were said to be at least 80 synagogues and prayer rooms, but the town was also a hotbed of the Jewish Labor Bund. Great Yiddish writers set stories in Berdychiv or used it as models for fictional towns.

Charismatic rabbis made their home in Berdychiv. The most famous was Levi Yitzhak, one of the most influential early Hasidic masters. Born around 1740, he was a disciple of the tzaddikim Shmuel Shmelke of Nikolsburg (see Mikulov, Czech Republic pp. 162–63) and the Maggid of Mezhirech. He became rabbi of Berdychiv in 1785 and served here until his death in 1810. Levi Yitzhak believed in the innate goodness of human beings, and his optimism and good cheer imbued his teachings. He believed that people could serve God in their daily actions as well as through prayer, and even prayed and wrote in Yiddish so that ordinary Jews could understand his words.

About 30,000 Jews lived in Berdychiv on the eve of World War II—about half the town's population. The Germans marched in on July 7, 1941. By October, they had massacred almost all of them. One of the victims was the mother of the Berdychiv-born Soviet Jewish writer and journalist Vasily Grossman (1905–1964). As a war correspondent with Soviet forces, Grossman covered World War II battles and was one of the first to document Holocaust atrocities in the Soviet Union and Poland. After the war, Moscow silenced him for writing about Soviet and Ukrainian complicity in the slaughter of Russian Jews.

Today, a few hundred Jews live in Berdychiv, and one synagogue has been restored for worship. The huge Jewish cemetery is located on the main road out of town toward Zhytomyr. Rabbi Levi Yitzhak's tomb, protected by a newly refurbished ohel as big as a small house, stands surrounded by thousands of tombstones. Inside, his grave is covered by a simple slab, flanked by racks to hold candles. The sea of tombstones is an astonishing sight. Most are strangely shaped—they remind some of giant boots or a crowd of crouching animals, each with a long body and alertly raised head, sniffing the air. Extensive work in recent years has cleared the cemetery of trees, shrubs, and other vegetation, but when I visited, in the summertime, the area was choked with grass and weeds; most of the tombstones were buried, only their noses peeking up above the green. A few people were at work, keeping the area immediately around the ohel clear. *(Genealogy and Jewish history website: www.berdichev.org. Synagogue: vul. Svetlova 8. Tel: +380-41/432-0222)*

ZHYTOMYR—This city west of Kiev has one of the liveliest and most active Jewish communities in western Ukraine, thanks in large part to the energetic Chabad rabbi, Shlomo Wilhelm. The synagogue at Malaya Berdichevskaya 7 is a one-story building with big arched windows. There is a wide range of programs, including a soup kitchen at the synagogue complex. The Jewish cemetery has been restored, and there is a new monument to Holocaust victims. *(Synagogue: vul. Malaya Berdichevskaya 7. Tel: +380-41/ 237-6494, fax: +380-41/222-6608)*

L'VIV

L'VIV, THE HISTORIC CAPITAL OF GALICIA, HAS GONE BY MANY NAMES OVER THE centuries. It was Lwow under Polish rule, Lvov under the Russians, and Lemberg under the Austrians. Italians know it as Leopoli. All mean "lion" and derive from the name of the Galician Prince Leo, during whose reign it was founded in the 13th century. Today L'viv is a graceful and gracious city of faded grandeur, filled with ancient churches, grand baroque mansions, and other important monuments that trace its rich, convoluted, and multiethnic history. Its quaint squares, broad boulevards, and decorative street facades, meanwhile, exude a heady Central European charm. The city will be a real gem when restoration work, already under way, is more complete.

Jews have lived in L'viv since its earliest days. Poland's King Kazimierz the Great, who conquered the city in 1340, granted Jews equal rights and formally allowed them to set up two communities, one within the city walls, near the main market square, or Rynok, and another outside the walls in what was then the Cracow suburb, today a downtown district behind the

Opera House. The outer community became the larger of the two, and a magnificent synagogue was built there in the 1630s. Two decades later, L'viv withstood sieges mounted by Bogdan Chmielnicki's Cossacks and, later, by Russian forces; Jews took active part in the defense of the city.

When Poland was partitioned at the end of the 18th century, L'viv came under Austrian rule. The city became a center of both Hasidism and the Haskalah. There was a strong trend toward assimilation, and an immense, domed synagogue was built on the Stary Rynok square in the 1840s for the Progressive, or Reform, congregation. The Jewish community expanded rapidly, particularly after achieving full civil rights in 1867, and Jews moved out of their old neighborhoods to other parts of the city. A Jewish neighborhood, with many Jewish institutions, developed near the Old Jewish Cemetery, off today's Horodets'ka street. By 1910, more than 50,000 Jews made up 28 percent of the local population. Thousands of Jewish refugees poured into the city during World War I. But as German, Ukrainian, and Polish ethnic factions fought for control of the city, Jews came under attack from all sides. In the interwar period, when L'viv was part of Poland, Jews formed one-third of the local population and the third largest Jewish community in Poland. Despite growing anti-Semitism, the community led a lively and multifaceted life, with a multitude of institutions, organizations, and movements that spanned the political and religious spectrum.

At the outbreak of World War II, the city first came under Soviet rule; the Germans, welcomed by many Ukrainians, took the city in July 1941. At the time, about 150,000 Jews lived in L'viv, including thousands of refugees. The Nazis, aided by Ukrainian collaborators, initiated a reign of anti-Jewish terror. Thousands of Jews were shot dead and most of the city's synagogues and Jewish cemeteries were destroyed. Jews were forced into labor camps and, in November, more than 120,000 were herded into a ghetto in the northern part of town. Over the next two years, most were deported to their deaths at the Belzec extermination camp. Thousands, too, were shot dead at a mass execution site outside town. When the Soviet Army liberated L'viv on July 26, 1944, only a few hundred Jews were still alive in the city.

Today there are about 5,000 Jews in L'viv. As in its heyday, the community is fragmented into numerous religious, political, and cultural streams.

Main Sites of Jewish Interest in L'viv

Tsori Gilad Synagogue: vul. Brativ Mikhnovski 4—Located near the railway station, this is the only synagogue functioning in L'viv out of the dozens that operated here before World War II and is the seat of the established Orthodox congregation. Regular services are held here, led by American-born Rabbi Mordechai Bold, a member of the Karliner-Stolin Hasidim who came to L'viv in 1993. Built in 1924, the synagogue has a design that recalls that of Galicia's Renaissance fortress synagogues. Inside it has wonderful decoration, including brilliantly colored wall paintings from the 1930s—rare surviving examples of 20th-century synagogue art that feature lions, griffins, puffy clouds, and landscape scenes.

Golden Rose Synagogue and Inner Jewish Quarter: L'viv's historic inner Jewish district includes Rus'ka, Fedorova, and Staroyevreys'ka (Old Jewish) streets, a few steps from the main market square, or Rynok. Many of the buildings are in poor condition, but restoration work is under way. The ruins of the Zolota Roza, or Golden Rose, Synagogue (also called the Turei Zakhav, or Golden Gate, Synagogue), stand here. The synagogue was built in about 1580 as a private family synagogue for Isaac Nachmanovych, the head of the Jewish community, who lived at Fedorova 27. The Nazis blew it up in 1941, and today, only part of a wall and a couple of arches at the edge of an empty space remain. Local advocates want to rebuild the synagogue and create a Jewish museum and culture center here.

A few steps away, the History of Religions Museum, in the former Dominican Church and Monastery at Na Muzeyna 1, includes a valuable collection of Jewish ritual objects and other material. Exhibits include a matzo-making machine, ritual objects, paintings, and old phonograph records from the 1920s with illustrations of praying Jews printed on the records themselves. (There are plans to open a full-scale Jewish museum in the old Jewish quarter and to move this collection into the new premises. L'viv's Ethnographic Museum also has a large collection of Jewish material, but it is currently not on view.)

Outside the old Jewish quarter, on the other side of the Rynok, the L'viv Art Gallery, at Stefanyk 3, includes a number of works on Jewish themes and by Jewish artists including Maurycy Gottleib and Bruno Schulz.

Holocaust Memorials: A tall statue of an anguished figure reaching toward heaven forms the centerpiece of a gated Holocaust memorial garden on the other side of the railroad bridge behind L'viv's grand opera house, where the L'viv Ghetto began. A big menorah stands at the entrance to the memorial, and plaques bearing the names of victims line the pathway.

Elsewhere, a big wall plaque at the Klepariv train station commemorates the hundreds of thousands of Jews who were shipped off from there to the Belzec death camp in 1942 and 1943. Nearby, off Shevchenka street, there is a monument at the site of the Janovska forced labor and concentration camp, from which thousands of Jews were deported to Belzec or executed at the nearby Piaski ravine.

Elsewhere in L'viv: A small monument on the Stary Rynok square marks the place where the huge, domed Progressive (Reform) synagogue stood until it was demolished in 1941, but otherwise few traces remain of the original "outside the walls" Jewish quarter. Around the corner, a former 19th-century Hasidic synagogue on Vulgilna street, just off St. Theodore Square, houses a Jewish culture center.

The sprawling Krakovski Market, a boisterous warren of booths and stands selling everything you can imagine, stands on the site of L'viv's medieval Jewish cemetery, which was destroyed after World War II. The authorities toppled the tombstones, laid them flat, and covered them with gravel and then concrete. Some of the stones were used as building material. The large New Jewish Cemetery on Yeroshenko street opened in 1855 (after the old cemetery was closed). It now forms part of the huge municipal cemetery. It was devastated by the Nazis; the elegant domed ceremonial hall was blown up and tombstones uprooted for use as paving stones. The cemetery still functions, however, although the Jewish section is now also the site of Christian burials.

The neighborhood near the Krakovski Market has a number of sites of Jewish interest. A big portrait wall plaque at the corner of Kotlarska and Shpitalna streets honors the Yiddish writer Sholom Aleichem, who lived there in 1906. The former Jewish hospital, now a maternity hospital, is a monumental, Moorish-style brick building located on Jacob Rappoport street (named after the 19th-century doctor and philanthropist). Completed in 1901, it looks like a cross between a factory and a synagogue, with a slim tower and narrow dome featuring decorative tile designs. Stars of David were incorporated into the striped and crenellated facade. A Hesed social welfare center, run by the American Jewish Joint Distribution Committee at Kotlarevski 30 includes a library, a small exhibition, and a little theater.

A grand building at Sholom Aleichem 12 houses a Jewish culture center, a Holocaust center, the premises of the L'viv chapter of B'nai Brith and the offices and meeting place of L'viv's small Progressive Jewish congregation. The building originally was the headquarters of the Jewish community and housed a Jewish court, or Beth Din; in the interwar period it also had a Jewish museum—an old display case lies empty in a corridor. Under the Soviet regime, it formed part of the city's medical school. Around the corner, on Nalyvaika street, faded traces of Yiddish and Polish shop signs remain on the walls of some of the buildings. The ghostly Hebrew and Latin letters, carefully preserved now, make a striking contrast to the bold Cyrillic splashed across the windows of local boutiques.

ADDRESSES OF NOTE IN L'VIV

- Synagogue: vul. Brativ Mikhnovski 4. Tel: +380-32/233-3535
- Jewish Culture Center, Holocaust and Progressive Jewish community offices: vul. Sholom Aleichem 12
- Jewish Culture Center: vul. Vulgilna 3
- Hesed Arieh Center: vul. Kotlarevski 30. Tel: +380-32/238-9860 www.hesed.lviv.ua
- Jewish Revival in Galicia Center: vul. Fedorova 29

NEAR L'VIV

BELZ—"*Belz, mayn shtetele Belz*," begins one of the most famous of all Yiddish songs. Belz, my shtetl Belz . . . "*mayn heimele*—my little home." The song, written by Jacob Jacobs and Alexander Olshanetsky in 1932 is a nostalgic evocation of idyllic life in the prewar world of East European Jewry. Once, I sat with a Holocaust survivor in Hungary, and tears trickled down her face as we listened to a scratchy tape of the song sung by another survivor.

Belz today is a small, dusty town northwest of L'viv, a few miles from the Polish border, where roosters crow and geese roam the roadsides and swarm into the street. Jews settled here in the early 16th century, but Belz only came to Jewish prominence after Shalom Rokeach (1779–1855), a disciple of the Hasidic master known as the Seer of Lublin, became rabbi there and founded the important Belz Hasidic dynasty. Rokeach, called the Sar Shalom, was a charismatic figure and attracted thousands of followers. He built a magnificent synagogue and spoke out for tradition against the encroachment of the Jewish Enlightenment, or Haskalah. Many legends grew up around him, and Belz became the leading center of Hasidism in Galicia.

Jews numbered more than half the Belz population before World War II. The Nazis deported more than 2,500 to death camps in 1942. The Belz rebbe of the time managed to escape before the deportations. He survived the war in a number of ghettos and in 1944 reached the Holy Land, where he reestablished the seat of the dynasty in Tel Aviv. Today, little is left physically of Jewish Belz other than the cemetery at the end of Mickiewicz street and a few old wooden houses. The cemetery was ruined in the war but its remnants are lovingly preserved *(cemetery caretaker Olga Prokopek: Tel: +380-32/575-2417)*. The tombs of the tzaddikim remain a powerful focus of pilgrimage by Hasidic Jews—so much so that a big, new hotel and hospitality center, with kosher dining facilities and a ritual bath, opened here in 2006, just opposite the graveyard.

In addition, representatives of the Belz Hasidim and local authorities have begun work to create a Jewish museum and culture center at the site where the fortress-style Great Synagogue, study house, and the other buildings of the rebbe's court once stood. The area, now an empty field just off the town's main square, where a school was built in the 1950s, has already been designated a historical and cultural reserve. Test excavations have located the synagogue's foundations.

BOLEKHIV (BOLECHÓW)–If I felt like a pilgrim anywhere in Ukraine, Bolekhiv may be the place. I have no family connections there, and, as far as I am aware, no famous rabbis are buried in its Jewish cemetery. Bolekhiv, though, near Stryj south of L'viv, was the home of a man I consider a Jewish hero—Dov Ber Birkenthal, an 18th-century wine merchant and Jewish community leader who was also known simply as Ber of Bolechow. Ber was born in 1723 and spent much of his adult life traveling to and fro between Galicia and northern Hungary, on frequent wine-purchasing missions to the Tokaj region. Several years before his death in 1805, he wrote a fascinating memoir that provides illuminating insights into conditions for Jews—and non-Jews—of the period in Polish Galicia and Hungary. He described how he sought out and drove hard bargains on wine, and he dwelled at length on the perils of the road—everything from complicated currency exchanges and customs duties to drunken wagon drivers; icy, unfordable rivers; double-dealing business partners; flea-ridden inns; and even occasional attacks by roving bandits. Ber met the great Hungarian Hasidic master Isaac Taub when the future tzaddik of Nagykallo (or Kallo) was little more than a boy. He became particularly friendly with the Jews in the wine-producing village Tarcal, near Tokaj and Mad, and in 1765 brought them a magnificent set of gold and silver ritual objects, which he had ordered specially made by craftsmen in L'viv.

Jews settled in Bolekhiv in the 16th century, and, in addition to the wine trade, they became active as craftsmen and merchants dealing in livestock, salt, and other goods. In the 19th century, they established several factories. By 1900, Jews made up more than three-quarters of the town. Nearly 3,000 Jews lived in Bolekhiv before World War II. All but a few dozen were deported to their deaths at the Belzec death camp or shot and killed in mass executions by German units and Ukrainian police. American author Daniel Mendelsohn details the experience of his relatives in his 2006 book, *The Lost: A Search for Six of the Six Million.*

Bolekhiv today is poor and run-down. A former synagogue, built a century after Ber's death, stands on broad Petrushevich street, just opposite a newly remodeled Orthodox church. After the war, it was used as a workers' club, but it now stands vacant, in dilapidated condition. I ventured rather nervously inside to take a look at the colorful landscape frescoes that decorate the vaulted ceiling, though it was not clear whether these dated from the days when the building was used as a synagogue or from its postwar years as a club.

Ber of Bolechow lies in the extraordinary Jewish cemetery situated on a slight hill just outside of town. Shaded by ancient trees, hundreds of tombstones are arrayed here, the oldest dating from 1648. Most are richly carved with opulent decorative calligraphy, flowers, animals, and arabesques. The stones tilt at odd angles, and many lie toppled; walking among them can be tricky. Paths cut through the area, and people and real live animals pass by. On my visit I walked slowly among the tombstones. Carved stags, birds, and lions leaped out at me. Then one stone caught my eye. Its decoration grabbed my attention first— a bear and a bunch of grapes. Could it be the tombstone of Ber of Bolechow, I wondered? The imagery certainly fit. Looking closer, I could make out that the name of the person buried here was, indeed, Dov Ber. Excited, I photographed the stone, and eventually got a friend to help with a translation of the epitaph. The date was illegible, and the full name was Dov Ber, the son of Israel Isser. Alas—this did not seem to be Ber of Bolechow's tomb; Ber's father was named Yehudah. Ber's "plain and short" epitaph, I read later, described him as "the learned, the renowned leader, the open-handed, the aged." *(Additional information: www.jewishgen.org/yizkor/bolekhov/bolekhov.html)*

BRODY—The ruins of the Great Synagogue, built in 1742, loom next to a playground and apartment development on Shkolna street, near the main square of this quiet town east of L'viv. One of Ukraine's so-called fortress synagogues, the building, even in ruins, is bigger and more magnificent than almost anything else in town.

Jews lived in Brody in the 16th century. By 1826 the more than 16,000 Jews made up nearly 90 percent of the local population. The Jewish journalist and author Joseph Roth was born here in 1894 and eloquently evoked life in Galicia in works such as his 1932 novel, *The Radetzky March*. Brody's Jewish population dwindled over the 19th century; still, about 10,000 Jews lived here on the eve of World War II. The town was occupied first by the Soviets and then, from July 1941, by the Germans, who forced local Jews into a ghetto. Some Jews were able to escape to join resistance units or the Soviet Army, but by May 1943 most had been deported to the Belzec and Majdanek death camps.

Brody has a vast Jewish cemetery, whose earliest tombstone dates from 1802. Thousands and thousands of exceptionally tall, massive, carved slabs stand like sentinels, row after row, in a flat field at the edge of a forest just outside town. The area is fenced, but you can squeeze through the gap between two fence posts at the right-hand corner of the enclosure—I have to admit that the number and density of the stones made me feel a little claustrophobic, as if I were in the middle of a huge crowd of people. Heroic efforts have been under way in recent years to protect and preserve the cemetery, which had become totally overgrown by brush and more than 2,000 trees. At its edge, there is a monument commemorating the Jews killed in the Holocaust.

BUSK—The power and beauty of the ancient Jewish cemetery in Busk provides a telling contrast to the rather charmless, depressed-looking village itself, located east of L'viv on the road to Brody. Jews settled here more than 500 years ago, and in the 18th century the town became a center of the messianic followers of Shabbetai Zevi and Jacob Frank. Nearly 2,000 Jews lived here before World War II.

The cemetery is located on Shevchenka street, just outside town near a picturesque wooden church. Hundreds of massive tombstones—the oldest believed to date from 1520 or even earlier—spread out over a hill, many of them tilted at impossible angles and some fallen to the ground. Many bear exceptionally rich and well-preserved carving. Parts of the cemetery were destroyed, and stumps of broken tombstones poke up through the grass. The area is used for grazing, and this keeps the weeds down. Flocks of geese waddle honking among the stones. Deeply worn paths run through the cemetery—local people, as well as cows and sheep, walk through, paying no heed to the history. On a rise, in the middle of the cemetery, a black marble plinth stands as a memorial to Holocaust victims.

In the town itself, there is a large, late 19th-century synagogue just off the main square. It was long used as a warehouse, but the front part has been converted into a dwelling; lace curtains hang in the windows, and a cactus plant sits on one windowsill.

DROHOBYCH (POLISH: DROHOBYCZ)–Located near the Polish border, about 60 miles south of L'viv, Drohobych was the birthplace of two extraordinary Jewish cultural figures who have left a lasting mark on how Jews and the Jewish experience are perceived—the painter Maurycy Gottlieb and the writer and artist Bruno Schulz. Gottlieb, born in Drohobych in 1856, died at just 23 years of age in Cracow in 1879. In his brief but prolific life, he created some of the most iconic Jewish works of art of the 19th century. Though part of the Jewish Enlightenment movement and an ardent Polish patriot, Gottlieb was deeply influenced by Romanticism and fascinated by the traditional world of Jewish Orthodoxy. His most famous works on Jewish themes, including the 1878 painting "Jews at Prayer on the Day of Atonement," are imbued with both awe and nostalgia. The portraits he painted of himself are sensitive portrayals of a young man who was just coming into his own when he passed away.

Bruno Schulz was born in 1892 and lived most of his life in Drohobych, where he worked as a high-school art teacher and wrote and painted in his free time. His life, too, was cut short: A Gestapo officer gunned him down on a Drohobych street on November 19, 1942. Schulz gained fame in the 1930s with luminous, expressionistic short stories set in a town modeled on Drohobych. Critics consider him one of the most important 20th-century Polish writers; he is sometimes called the Polish Kafka. Schulz's sexually charged drawings, published around 1920 as *The Book of Idolatry*, also won him admirers. When the Nazis marched into Drohobych on July 1, 1941, Schulz came under the protection of the Gestapo chief, Felix Landau, who had been impressed by Schulz's artwork. Landau brought Schulz to his villa and ordered him to decorate his son's bedroom with wall paintings of fairy tales. The fate of these paintings—Schulz's last works—erupted into an international scandal in 2001. A German filmmaker discovered the faded murals, which had been painted over, but soon after, Yad Vashem, the Holocaust memorial and museum in Jerusalem, managed to have them cut out of the walls, smuggled out of the country, and transported to Israel.

Drohobych today is something of a ghost town. The uneasy ethnic mix of Poles, Jews, and Ukrainians that colored the prewar atmosphere no longer exists. Jews were the largest of these three groups; some 15,000 Jews made up about 40 percent of the local population in 1939. Most of them were deported to the Belzec death camp or shot on city streets or in the Bronica Forest outside town; a monument there marks the spot. In the city today, the crumbling facade of the Choral Synagogue rears above a downtown marketplace on Orlik street. Built in the 1860s, it was once the pride of the city, one of the biggest synagogues in Galicia; after World War II it was used as a furniture store. Reconstruction of the building began in 2005, with the aim of turning it into a Jewish cultural, prayer, study, and welfare center, but the process is slow, and in the meantime broken windows still gape, patches of stucco have fallen away, and bushes and weeds grow from the roof like strange tufts of hair. The former Progressive synagogue, a squat, square building with tall arched windows and four stumpy towers, still stands at the corner of Mazepa and Sholom Aleichem streets, but today it is used as a sports hall. The ruined Jewish cemetery is a jumble of desecrated tombstones.

The places where Bruno Schulz led his life and the places he described in his stories still exist, though, and Drohobych draws a stream of literary pilgrims. A plaque with a portrait of Schulz marks the house at Jurij Drohobych 12, where he lived. The high school where he taught is now the main hall of a pedagogical college and has a plaque to Schulz's memory. Today's Stryjska street is the road that Schulz, in his stories, called the Street of Crocodiles.

ROZDIL—The evocative, fenced-in remains of the ruined Jewish cemetery in this town south of L'viv stand near a brick synagogue, now used as a warehouse. The cemetery key is kept by the gold-toothed family who live across the dirt road. Most of the space is bare; a few clumps of weathered but richly decorated stones bristle from the earth at impossible angles. Horses and cows graze under trees. Many stones lie toppled or face down; tossed, it seems, like straws—how, I wondered, could such massive stones have been so disarranged? A local resident once told a visiting Jew whose family came from Rozdil that after the war, a man who had taken tombstones to line his cellar died the next day, so nobody else dared to try.

STARY SAMBIR—The old Jewish cemetery in this town near the Polish border southwest of L'viv is on a hill just outside the city limits on the main road to Uzhhorod. A big sign in English and Ukrainian marks the spot. The

An intricately carved tombstone in the Jewish cemetery at Stary Sambir depicts a candelabra flanked by cornucopias full of fruit and flowers.

cemetery, it states, was established in the 16th century. Devastated during and after World War II, it was restored in 2001 thanks to the efforts of an American, Jack Gardner, who was born in Stary Sambir. Gardner (who has since passed away) also saw to the erection of a Holocaust memorial commemorating the destroyed community. The cemetery's hundreds of tombstones stand in rows and straggle up the hill behind. Some are weathered and illegible, but many feature beautiful examples of carving.

One synagogue remains standing in Stary Sambir, in an area just outside the town center that retains something of the air of a prewar shtetl. The red-brick building is closed, and the arched windows on its dignified facade are bricked up. Little slim pointed turrets decorate the corners of the roof. The synagogue stands on a little plaza—ironically named after the Cossack leader Bogdan Chmielnicki, who wreaked such havoc on Jews in the mid-17th century. A narrow gravel road curves behind it, past sagging old houses and chickens wandering in the grass.

STRYJ—About 45 miles south of L'viv, Stryj was home to Jews for centuries. Today it exudes a pastel air of faded elegance and has a pleasant main square still lined with shops and small houses. Jews were invited to settle here at the beginning of the 16th century by the local governor, and King Stefan Batory issued an order in 1576 that gave Jews the same rights as other citizens. About 12,000 Jews lived in Stryj before World War II, making up about 40 percent of the population. The Polish author Julian Stryjkowski (1905–1996) was born here and wrote a series of novels describing prewar life in shtetls such as Stryj. In his most famous novel, *Austeria,* people seek refuge in a Jewish-run inn as Cossacks advance on the eve of World War I.

Stryj's Renaissance fortress synagogue was built in 1660. Today its hulking ruins stand in the center of the city on Yuri Lypi street not far from the main square. Only the outer walls survive—a massive shell of crumbling brick, pierced by tall, arched windows. The great, arched doorway is closed by an iron gate decorated with a menorah and Stars of David.

ZHOVKVA (YIDDISH: ZHOLKVA, POLISH: ŻOŁKIEW)—Just 12 miles northwest of L'viv, Zhovkva is a treasure house of stunning Renaissance architecture, including a mighty, 17th-century synagogue. Established in 1594, the town was laid out as a harmonious urban whole by the architect Paulus Szczesliwy. Jews settled here from the start. In the mid-17th century, thousands of Jews sought refuge here from the Chmielnicki Uprising and helped defend the city. In the following decades, Zhovkva prospered under the protection of the King John III Sobieski, who maintained a residence here. It became a center of Hebrew printing and also the Haskalah. More than 5,000 Jews, about half the local population, lived here before World War II.

Zhovkva's synagogue was built in 1687 and is a wonderful example of the monumental, fortress-style synagogue that was common in this part of Eastern Europe. Today a grimy dusty pink, it has a flat roofline with the

The fortress-style synagogue in Zhovkva was built in 1687. There are plans to turn it into a Jewish museum.

crenellations and blind arcaded tracery typical of the style and period. The Germans tried to dynamite the building in 1941 but only partially succeeded. The interior was gutted, but the outer walls survived. Despite partial restoration in the 1950s and 1990s, the grand building has remained empty and derelict on the edge of an open market, a sentinel from the past. Zhovkva's old center was declared a state historical and architectural reserve in 1994, and, with help from international donors, a slow process is now under way to restore the synagogue fully and turn it into a museum of Galician Jewry.

ELSEWHERE IN UKRAINE

CHERNIVTSI (GERMAN: CZERNOWITZ, ROMANIAN: CERNAUŢI)–Chernivtsi today is a provincial town in southwest Ukraine, just north of the Romanian border. For nearly 150 years, though, it was the cosmopolitan capital of the Austro-Hungarian Bucovina region, a "little Vienna," the saying goes, where even street sweepers could speak five languages, including Yiddish. It preserves a beautiful, if run-down, town center, full of ornate Hapsburg architecture, including an important university campus.

Jews settled here as early as the 15th century, but the main flowering of Jewish life came in the 19th century. From mid-century in particular, the city became a vibrant center of Jewish secular and Progressive intellectual activity. Jews flourished in all walks of life amid an atmosphere famed for its multicultural tolerance. Many upper-class Jews spoke German, rather than Yiddish, and were deeply assimilated into mainstream Austrian society. A sumptuous Reform Temple was inaugurated in 1877, and the university, founded in 1875, attracted many Jewish students. Zionists, Hasids, and Orthodox Jews were active, too, and there was also a poverty-stricken underclass. Jews took part in mainstream local politics, and socialist parties and the Jewish Labor Bund had strong followings.

As part of these trends, Chernivtsi became a focus of Yiddish language and literature. In 1908, it hosted the first international conference on the role of Yiddish in Jewish life. The meeting drew 70 delegates representing many political and religious factions. They included the authors I. L. Peretz and Sholem Asch, along with other prominent scholars, writers and activists. The most heated debates centered on whether Hebrew, which was then being revived and modernized after centuries of disuse, or Yiddish, which was spoken by millions of Jews, could, or should, be considered the Jewish national language. In the end, delegates adopted a resolution declaring Yiddish "a" national language of the Jewish people, along with Hebrew. *(The website www.ibiblio.org/yiddish/Tshernovits/ includes documents and photographs from the conference.)*

With the defeat of the Austro-Hungarian Empire in World War I, Chernivtsi became part of Romania. About 28,000 Jews lived there at the time, nearly half the local population. By the eve of World War II, refugees had swollen the Jewish population to 50,000. The Soviets occupied the city first. Then, on July 1, 1940, German and Romanian forces moved in and immediately launched waves of anti-Jewish violence that left thousands dead. Most other Jews were deported to ghettos and labor camps in Transnistria, a part of Ukraine occupied by German and Romanian forces. Chernivtsi and northern Bucovina were annexed by the Soviet Union after the war, while southern Bucovina remained part of Romania. Survivors reconstituted a large Jewish community, but the authorities soon clamped down on religious practice and closed the synagogues.

About 1,500 Jews live in Chernivtsi today, and only one synagogue functions. A small building dating from the 1920s, it has detailed wall paintings showing biblical animals, the signs of the zodiac, and other images. Some of its fittings came from other synagogues that were destroyed or converted for other use. Rabbi Noikh Kofmansky leads services and runs a kosher kitchen here, and there is also a mikvah. Kofmansky, a trained physicist and Vizhnitzer Hasid, was born in Chernivtsi but lived in Israel for two decades before he returned as a rabbi in the mid-1990s. "When I came back, the synagogue was broken down, there was no kitchen, no mikvah," he told me. "It's good if you have lovely work and think you are doing the right things in the right place."

The once magnificent Tempel Synagogue is now a movie theater, the Kino Theater Chernivtsi. Stripped of its decoration, its plain white facade dominates a major downtown intersection. Elsewhere, the former Choral Synagogue, on Mickiewicz street, is now a boxing gym. The imposing Jewish National House on downtown Theater Square is home to various Jewish offices, a Jewish library, and a Jewish culture center. Built in 1908—a time when all major minorities in the city erected cultural headquarters, it has an ornate facade featuring tall Ionic columns beneath an arch and supported by sculpted Atlas figures.

Chernivtsi was home to many prominent Jewish cultural figures, and dotted around the city are commemorative plaques to some of them, including Joseph Schmidt, who served as cantor of the Tempel Synagogue and also won international fame as an operatic tenor—he played Carnegie Hall during a U.S. tour in 1937. Schmidt died in a Swiss refugee camp in 1942, aged 38. Writers who were born here included the Israel novelist Aharon Appelfeld. A larger-than-life-size bust of the poet Paul Celan stands in a little park at the corner of Paul Celan and Holovna streets. Celan is renowned worldwide for his wrenching poem on the Shoah, "Todesfuge," or "Death Fugue," and its insistent line, repeated over and over: "Death is a Master from Germany." Born Paul Antschel in Chernivtsi in 1920, he committed suicide in Paris in 1970.

The enormous Jewish cemetery lies on Zelena street, across from a big Christian cemetery. It is a vast space, most of which is heavily overgrown. Beautifully carved gravestones and imposing family tombs are immersed in a dense jungle of trees, shrubs, vines, and weeds. Paths cut through the area, but most of the monuments are totally shrouded and inaccessible, history and memory all but obscured. Near the entrance, a ruined, but still elegant, domed Ceremonial Hall still stands, with a memorial wall of broken tombstones set beside it. As I left the cemetery, I couldn't help noticing that on the Ceremonial Hall's crumbling brick, someone had spray-painted a Star of David hanging from a gallows, and the German words "Death to Jews."

Addresses of Note in Chernivtsi

- Jewish community: vul. Shevchenko 48/8. Tel: +380-372/52-6697 or +380-503/38-0498
- Synagogue: vul. Kobilitsa 53
- Jewish Center, Jewish National House: Theater Square 5. Tel: +380-372/52-2757. www.bukjew.iatp.org.ua
- Hesed Shushana Center: vul. O. Kobilyansky 53. Tel: +380-372/55-2728. http://shushana.h1.ru/ENG/eng_index.html

• **Sadhora** (Sadagora, Sadgura): Now a suburb of Chernivtsi, Sadhora was home to one of Hasidism's most flamboyant dynasties. It was founded by the rebbe Israel Friedmann (1797–1850), the great-grandson of the Maggid of Mezhirech, one of the Ba'al Shem Tov's main disciples. Friedmann first set up a court in the Russian-ruled town of Ruzhin, where he drew thousands of followers. Hugely wealthy, he lived in a palatial mansion, with guard dogs, an elegant horse-drawn carriage, and court musicians. He served his guests off gold and silver plates and traveled with an entourage of servants. Friedmann fled Russia and moved to Austrian-ruled Sadhora in 1842, after serving jail time for alleged complicity in the death of two Jews. Here he built another opulent palace and resumed his luxurious lifestyle—drawing fire from other Hasidic groups. Israel's son, Rabbi Abraham Jacob Friedmann, succeeded his father as tzaddik and continued the opulent court. He built a huge, Moorish-style synagogue that looked like a castle, with turrets, towers, and big arched windows. Pictures of the "Wonder Rabbi's Palace" appeared on souvenir postcards of the day. The big synagogue still stands, but for decades under the Soviets it housed a machine shop for collective farms. It is empty now, and rapidly deteriorating. Nothing is left of the once luxurious fittings, but the sheer size of the place still hints of its original splendor.

The Sadhora tzaddikim are buried at one end of Sadhora's vast Jewish cemetery; their tombs are protected by a modern ohel, where I found prayer books waiting for the faithful and piles of paper *kvittleh* with written prayers and supplications. (I got the key from the rabbi in Chernivtsi.) The cemetery is fenced, and I entered through an unlocked gate on Nalepky street. As many as 4,000 or 5,000 tall tombstones are spread out over a flat field. Most are very weathered, but many still bear beautiful, vigorously carved decoration. The grass and weeds were almost waist high: I swam through them and had considerable trouble picking my way; hundreds of tombstones have been toppled, and, hidden by the weeds, they made walking difficult. *(Additional information: www.shtetlinks.jewishgen.org/sadgura/sadgura.html)*

DNEPROPETROVSK—This city in eastern Ukraine has one of the largest and most active Jewish communities in Eastern Europe, with a wide range of cultural, social, and religious programs. The Golden Rose Choral Synagogue, built in 1852, was returned to the Jewish community in 1994 and fully restored. It retains its graceful colonnaded portico; the interior was modernized. Today it forms a complex with a full-service Jewish community center and the Tkuma Holocaust Museum and study center. *(Jewish Center and Golden Rose Synagogue: vul. Sholom Aleichem 4. Tel: +380-562/36-2983. www.jcc.dp.ua. http://jew.dp.ua/sinagogi.htm)*

KERCH—The synagogue in this Crimean town now serves a thousand-strong Jewish community. With a big Star of David on its facade, it also houses the Jewish Museum, whose collections include some 600 ritual objects and everyday items. It also houses a collection of Jewish tombstones, dating from the 18th to the 20th century, many of them rescued from places where they were used as paving or building material after World War II. A monument at Bagerov Yar, outside town, marks the spot where local Jews were massacred during the Shoah. *(Jewish Communty: vul. Tsiolkovskoho 6. Tel: +380-656/12-5592)*

KHARKHIV (KHARKOV)—The domed, redbrick Choral Synagogue, located on Pushkinskaya street in this industrial center in eastern Ukraine—the country's second largest city—was returned to the Jewish community in

1990. Built in 1913, it was closed by the Soviets in the 1920s and turned into a sports club. Today, as many as 50,000 Jews live in Kharkhiv. There are Chabad, a mainstream Orthodox, and small Reform congregations, as well as a Holocaust Museum and an array of Jewish schools, organizations, welfare programs, and a full-service Jewish community center. In 2002, at a ceremony attended by then president Leonid Kuchma, a large Holocaust memorial incorporating a huge Menorah was dedicated at Drobitsky Yar outside town, where thousands of Jews were massacred in World War II. *(Synagogue: vul. Sumskaya 45)*

KOVEL—The grand synagogue in this town north of L'viv is now used as a clothing factory. It took lengthy discussion with a woman at the gate to allow me to enter the factory yard and look at—and then photograph—the imposing red facade, but eventually she also let me go inside. Downstairs, phalanxes of jeans were hanging, waiting to be finished. Upstairs, under the partially blocked dome, dozens of seamstresses were sewing some sort of army green outfits. As soon as I pulled out my camera, the floor manager strode over and, invoking the authority of the absent director, told me I was not allowed to photograph and should not be up there in the first place. So I left.

KREMENETS—Kremenets is a pretty town east of Brody, surrounded by wooded hills and dominated by the ruins of a medieval castle. Jews settled here in the 15th century. The community prospered in the 16th and 17th centuries. One of its rabbis was the brother of Prague's Rabbi Judah Loew ben Bezalel. The spectacular Jewish cemetery includes more than 2,000 massive tombstones, some dating back to the early 17th century and most bearing rich decoration. They spill down a steep slope just outside of town, abandoned to the elements. It can be a breathtaking sight, but on a rainy day in mid-July, I found grass, weeds, wildflowers, and other vegetation so tall and thick that they hid most of the stones in a waving sea of green.

About 9,000 Jews lived in Kremenets on the eve of World War II. The vast majority were shot and buried in mass graves. A monument marks the spot: a black marble plaque on a cylindrical plinth made of stones, set in a little clearing by a clump of trees surrounded by vegetable plots and modern apartment blocks. Etched into the marble is the anguished face of a woman trying to ward off her fate.

Both the cemetery and the Holocaust monument are on roads that appear to have no names; the cemetery is near a bright blue church off a steep cobbled lane that deteriorates into a dirt track. Finding them, thus, takes a little asking around. This situation may change soon. A major project is under way to clean and restore the cemetery. It will document the tombstones and translate their epitaphs, shore up the eroding hillside, repair the fencing, and pave the local access roads. *(Additional information: www.jewishgen.org/Ukraine/KremenetsNewsletters.htm)*

LUBOML (YIDDISH: LIBIVNE)–Luboml feels empty. The little market town, about a hundred miles north of L'viv, was once dominated by a huge fortress synagogue built in the 17th century. Some 5,000 people lived here, 90 percent of them Jews. Old pictures show the marketplace bursting with people wheeling and dealing and buying and selling everything you can imagine: horses, cattle, pigs, shoes, hats, furniture, clothing. In other old pictures shoemakers pose proudly in front of elegant high heels of their handiwork; school boys grin in their flat winter caps; little girls named Roza and Rivka stand coyly on a street in short skirts and heavy stockings. Luboml was a typical shtetl, famous for nothing. People lived here, worked here, played here, studied here, and that was that. Today, thanks to a documentation project and exhibition called "Remembering Luboml: Images of a Jewish Community," millions have seen these pictures and heard stories of people from the town. Initiated by Aaron Ziegelman, who emigrated to New York from Luboml as a child in 1938, the Luboml Exhibition Project has collected about 2,000 photographs and other material and includes a traveling exhibit, a film, a book, and a website.

So, Luboml itself feels empty. Before World War II it was part of Poland. The Soviets occupied it from 1939 to 1941, and then the Germans marched in. Aided by local Ukrainians and Poles, they massacred all but about 50 Jews then living in the town. Luboml's center today is a drab mix of communist-era buildings and a few prewar houses. "Here is where the synagogue stood," says local historian Mikola Dzei, pointing to a gap between two buildings. "It was demolished in 1947; the Bolsheviks destroyed it for building material."

I met Dzei in the town museum, which has a small room dedicated to Luboml Jews. Dzei is obsessed by the history of his town. "Not just Jewish history," he said, "but, after all, 90 percent of the population here was Jewish." He has spent more than a decade collecting photographs, documents, postcards, and other material, some of which is included in the American Luboml exhibit. At his home, he pulled out box after box, binder after binder, to show me. "Here," he said, and presented me with some colorful tattered labels from vodka produced by a prewar, Jewish-owned local distillery. Later, he took me to the field outside town where Luboml Jews were shot to death on October 1, 1942. "This way, from town, was the road of death," he said. "There were a lot of clay pits here; people were shot and their bodies were thrown into them." The site is lonely; Dzei is one of the few people who visits. A monument in the middle of an overgrown field says 5,000 people were killed here. *(Additional information: www.luboml.org. Local historian: Mikola Dzei, e-mail: kolya@mail.ru)*

LUC'K—Luc'k, northeast of L'viv, has important historic monuments including a fortress castle. The Great Synagogue, built in 1626–28, was also monumental and resembled the crenellated towers of the fortress. Today, it houses the Dynama sports complex. The shape of the building is much as it was, a massive cube with a tower. Flaking stucco on the outer walls reveals the centuries-old brick, but inside, there is no trace of the building's original function. "Total conversion," a heavy-set woman in skin-tight leggings said as she took me around and showed me the facility.

MEDZHYBIZH (MEDZHIBOZH)–Picturesquely situated under a large medieval fortress near the confluence of two rivers, Medzhybizh, about halfway between L'viv and Kiev, is celebrated in Jewish lore as the birthplace of Hasidism. The founder of the Hasidic movement, Israel ben Eliezer, better known as the Ba'al Shem Tov (Master of the Good Name), or the Besht, lived here from 1740 until his death in 1760. His tomb in the Old Jewish Cemetery is a place of pilgrimage and veneration.

The Ba'al Shem Tov's life is shrouded in mystery. He left no writings and the stories passed down by his disciples are the stuff of legends. Believed to have been born around 1700 in a village called Okop, he wandered throughout the region preaching joyous communion with God through faith and love—rather than through book learning and scholarship—and became revered as a particularly powerful, wonder-working holy man, a mystic healer able to perform miracles. In Medzhybizh, he added rich spiritual teachings to his healing. Thousands flocked to be near him; by the time he died, he had gathered around him as many as 100,000 followers, and Hasidism stood poised to become one of Eastern Europe's most influential Jewish streams.

I visited Medzhybizh on an unseasonably chilly and blustery summer's day. It was not a time of pilgrimage or celebration; the area of town around the Ba'al Shem Tov's tomb was eerily empty, dormant without the pilgrims but waiting for the crowds. The street leading to the cemetery is called Ba'al Shem Tov Boulevard, and its street sign, like most other signage in the neighborhood, is written in Hebrew. The newly built ohel protecting the Ba'al Shem Tov's tomb stands alone, as big as a house, in the cemetery. Elaborately carved old tombstones, the oldest dating from the 1550s, dot the rest of the enclosure. Outside the perimeter looms a big, new synagogue complex, built in the same white brick as the ohel. I paused in the cemetery for a few minutes, listening to the wind whooshing in the tall weeds and wildflowers, admiring a long pastoral vista that could have been a scene from 100 or even 200 years ago. Inside the ohel, I found one solitary person seated in front of the Besht's white marble tombstone, a young woman in a headscarf and long black dress, bent over a prayer book, a pair of crutches propped behind her chair.

In addition to the old cemetery, there is also a large newer cemetery, founded in 1845, that functioned until World War II. And near forest ravines north of town a monument marks the spot where, on September 22, 1941, the Germans gunned down 3,000 Jews and buried them in a mass grave.

ODESSA—The "Pearl of the Black Sea," Odessa is a stunning port city whose rich Jewish history goes back more than 200 years. Some of modern Judaism's most famous figures lived here, and the city was celebrated in literature and song.

Jews settled here in the late 1700s. By the end of the 19th century, the Jewish population topped 140,000, and by the eve of World War II, some 180,000 Jews lived in the city, about 30 percent of the total population. Odessa's Jewry spanned the full religious, social, and political spectrum, and Jews played an active role in all walks of life. The city's status as an international trade center drew Jews from all over Russia and beyond. By the beginning of the 20th century, more than two-thirds of the city's banks were under Jewish administration; more than half the city's lawyers, and about 70 percent of its medical practitioners, were Jewish. At the same time, thousands of factory workers and other laborers formed a restive proletariat underclass.

Religious life, too, ran the gamut. The imposing Brodsky Synagogue, built in 1863, was the first Reform temple built in tsarist Russia, its four domed towers making it a city landmark. Crowds of non-Jews as well as Jews flocked there to hear its famous cantors and choir.

Jewish success, however, took place against the background of anti-Jewish agitation. Violent pogroms rocked the city in 1821, 1859, 1871, 1881, and 1905. They spurred thousands to emigrate but also sparked the growth of

Zionism and other revolutionary movements. Odessa became the main port—the "Gateway to Zion"—from which Russian Jews left for Palestine. Some of the Zionist movement's leading figures lived here, including Leon Pinkser, Ahad Ha'am, Meir Dizengoff (who helped found Tel Aviv and became its first mayor), and the secular Zionist Ze'ev Jabotinsky. Jabotinsky's grandson took part in a ceremony in 1997 unveiling a plaque on the house at Yevreyskaya 1, where Jabotinsky lived.

Odessa was a magnet for Jewish intellectuals, artists, and writers, many of them steeped in Western-oriented, secular Jewish cultural expression. There were Jewish theaters, Jewish literary salons, Jewish libraries. Fierce polemics erupted among authors who wrote in Yiddish, Hebrew, and Russian. Sholom Aleichem lived here from 1891 to 1893 and evoked the city in a number of his stories. The Hebrew poet Chaim Nachman Bialik, famous for his wrenching evocation of the 1903 pogrom in Kishinev, "In the City of Slaughter," lived in Odessa for two decades. Isaac Babel (1894–1940) was born in Odessa and, writing in Russian, set many of his stories in the city.

The Bolshevik Revolution clamped down hard, and by the end of the 1920s, the Soviet regime had shut down the city's dozens of synagogues. At the outbreak of World War II, tens of thousands of Odessa Jews managed to flee or were drafted into the Soviet Army, but as many as 80,000 still lived there when the Romanian Army, aided by German forces, occupied the city on October 16, 1941. On October 23–25, Romanian troops massacred as many as 30,000 Jews in reprisal for a bomb at the Romanian headquarters on October 21st that had killed the Romanian commander and several dozen soldiers. Monuments mark the massacre sites, at a former artillery dump outside town and at the main square of the harbor. At the end of the war, a few thousand Jews remained in the city, many saved by Christian neighbors. A monument to these rescuers was established in 1996 in Prohorovsky Square.

Many survivors returned to Odessa after World War II, and the Jewish population again grew to more than 100,000. Tens of thousands left when the Iron Curtain fell. Today the city has about 30,000 Jews. Most remain secular and unaffiliated, but there are ample options for Jewish involvement.

The imposing Great Synagogue, built in the 1860s in a combination of Moorish and neo-Romantic styles, stands at Yevreyskaya 25. It was used for half a century as a sports center, its lofty, barrel-vaulted sanctuary cut in half horizontally. After the building was returned to Jewish ownership in 1997, the ground floor was partially renovated with international help, and religious services once more take place. There are plans to restore the entire building and restore it to its original splendor.

A charming, late 19th-century synagogue at Osipova 21 now belongs to Odessa's Chabad community. Used for decades as a warehouse, it was beautifully refurbished and now anchors a complex that includes a kosher kitchen. The historic Brodsky Synagogue, long used as a state archive, is also slated for restoration.

Another 19th-century synagogue, once used by the kosher slaughterers and butchers, stands at Malaya Anautskaya 46a. A Moorish-style building with a tripartite facade and decorative arched windows, it now houses the lively Migdal Jewish Community Center, whose activities include a Jewish theater group, various clubs, holiday celebrations, and social and educational programs. It also houses a library, a Jewish museum, and a kosher restaurant.

Addresses of Note in Odessa

- www.moria.farlep.net/vjodessa/en/ — a virtual tour of Jewish Odessa, with photographs
- Great Synagogue: vul. Yevreyskaya 25. Tel: +380-48/234-7850
- Jewish community (Chabad): vul. Osipova 21. Tel: +380-48/221-8736
- Migdal Jewish Community Center: vul. Malaya Anautskaya 46a. Tel: +380-48/237-2128. www.migdal.ru
- Kosher restaurant: Rozmarin, vul. Malaya Arnautskaya 46a. Tel: +380-48/234-4644 (located in the Jewish community center)

SATANIV (SATANOV)–A legend about the Jewish cemetery in Sataniv goes like this: The Ba'al Shem Tov came to town, after local Jews begged him to pray to God to stop a terrible plague. He told them the plague would end once a mortal sin that was hiding away somewhere was dealt with. The villagers searched everywhere but found nothing. The Ba'al Shem Tov then suggested they search the cemetery. Here, amid the hundreds of tombstones, they found one old, forgotten *mazzevah,* covered in moss and illegible. The Ba'al Shem Tov had the grave opened; lying there was a body that looked as if it had just been buried. The dead man complained that he was angry, that he was furious. When burying a body next to him, he said, drunken

The fortress synagogue in Sataniv is a ruin but still preserves traces of its interior decoration.

gravediggers had disturbed his own grave, injured his corpse, and broken one of his teeth. The Ba'al Shem Tov calmed the dead man and told him to intercede with God to end the plague. He took the broken tooth, promising to return it in the world to come. The dead man reentered his grave, local people tidied his gravestone, and, sure enough, the plague ended. Years later, just before he died, the Ba'al Shem Tov ordered that the broken tooth be buried in his own grave along with him.

Sataniv lies between L'viv and Chernivtsi. Its Jewish cemetery, whose oldest stone dates from 1554, is one of the most beautiful and artistically important in Eastern Europe. Hundreds of tombstones spread out on a hilltop, affording a spectacular view of the Zbruch River and surrounding countryside. Many bear particularly elaborate ornamentation, employing a unique range of iconographic motifs—including some of the rarest and most mysterious carvings to be found on Jewish tombstones. Three stones feature a rendering of the so-called three-hare motif, which depicts three hares, chasing each other in a circle, joined by their ears. It is an optical illusion—each hare appears to have two ears, but among them only three ears can be counted. This motif has been found in medieval carvings and artwork from China to the British Isles, but Sataniv is one of the few places where it appears in a Jewish context. One of these stones is easily found. It stands right next to a protected tomb at the top of the hill. The date of death is illegible, but the person buried here was a woman, Rivka, the daughter of Eliezer Sussman.

From the cemetery, there is a wonderful view of the town's ruined fortress synagogue, one of the oldest surviving synagogues in Ukraine. Built in the 16th or early 17th century, it actually was a fortress, forming part of the city's defenses. Today a ruined hulk, it towers over the low houses around it. I crawled in through a low opening. On the eastern wall of the cavernous sanctuary, the Aron ha Kodesh still stands, an elegant, ravaged Gothic alcove flanked by pillars and topped by wonderful rearing lions holding aloft a crown. The space directly above the niche for the Torah is still painted bright blue, and two golden griffins extend their wings and paw the air, forming a frame for priestly hands raised in blessing.

SHARHOROD (SHARGOROD)–The little town of Sharhorod, about 200 miles southwest of Kiev, is one of the best preserved Jewish shtetls in Ukraine. Many old Jewish houses—most of them abandoned now and in poor condition—cluster in the streets around a 16th-century fortress synagogue, and the Jewish cemeteries have wonderfully carved and decorated tombstones.

Founded in the late 16th century, Sharhorod was built by the Polish chancellor Jan Zamoyski at around the same time he established Zamosc, in Poland. Jews lived here from the start. The synagogue was built in 1589 and formed part of Sharhorod's defenses. These were put to the test in the following centuries. Cossacks, Poles, Russians, and invading Ottoman Turks all fought over the region. During Turkish occupation from 1672 to 1699, the synagogue was used as a mosque. Jews in Sharhorod prospered in the 19th century. But World War I, the Bolshevik Revolution, and subsequent civil war brought disaster. All factions attacked the Jews. During World War II, Sharhorod was in the part of Romanian- and German-occupied Ukraine known as Transnistria. Jews from Romania were herded into a ghetto here along with local Jews. Hundreds died from disease and harsh conditions, but they were not deported to death camps.

Under Soviet rule, the Sharhorod synagogue was turned into a fruit juice and wine factory. The sanctuary was cut in two horizontally, but the exterior retained intact. Today, the synagogue is listed as a historic monument, and a big mezuzah is now prominently displayed on the door. The factory is no longer in operation, but huge vats still crowd the former sanctuary around the surviving four pillars of the central bimah.

Sharhorod's Jewish cemeteries are remarkable. One is a small plot, near the old part of town, that contains just a few, richly ornamented old stones, half sunken into the earth. The other two are right next to each other, on a hill off the Muravskoe Road, across a little bridge from town. A small Jewish community lives in Sharhorod, and I found the new section of the cemetery, still in use, astonishing. Many of the monuments are shaped like trees with their boughs lopped off, some are topped with Stars of David and some are painted shades of brown or red or blue. Other tombstones, too, are painted bright colors—one, the grave of a Cohen, is sky blue with the traditional priestly hands painted bright yellow. Other tombs bear detailed, lifelike portraits of the deceased etched into the stone. The old part of the cemetery stretches out beyond the new section, part of it enclosed by a crumbling wall and much of it overgrown. Hundreds and hundreds and hundreds of gravestones, some dating to the 17th or even 16th century, and many with intricate carving, extend on and on, as far as the eye can see. *(Additional information: www.shargorod.org. Jewish community: vul. R. Lyuksemburg 1. Tel: +380-43/442-2205)*

SOKAL—The raw shell of an 18th-century fortress synagogue stands in this little town north of L'viv off a lane behind the hot pink Bar Eden. Jews settled here in the 16th century. Before World War II they made up nearly half the local population. The synagogue still retains a few elements of decorative detail—slim columns flanking the interior of its arched windows, stuccowork, and fanciful crenellations along the top of the outer walls. One Hebrew inscription also remains, high on the upper facade in one of the crenellations. Bushes and saplings have grown up inside the roofless ruin of the sanctuary. When I visited, the entrance was used as a dump and, frankly, apparently as a toilet.

UMAN—One hundred twenty-five miles due south of Kiev, Uman is the site of one of the most revered places in Hasidic Judaism—the tomb of Rabbi Nachman of Bratslav, the great-grandson of the Ba'al Shem Tov, the legendary founder of Hasidism. Nachman died in Uman of tuberculosis at the age of 38 in 1810. He had moved there shortly before his death, after nearly a decade as tzaddik in Bratslav, wanting to be buried a town where thousands of Jews had been massacred in 1768 by Haidamak Cossacks. A charismatic, contentious figure who sometimes claimed he was the Messiah—or at least that he was the only authentic tzaddik, Nachman was famous for his allegorical stories, which were recorded by his faithful disciple and friend, Nathan of Nemirov.

Nachman attracted a huge number of followers, receiving them at his court at Rosh Hashanah, the Jewish New Year, at Hanukkah, and at the springtime holiday of Shavuoth. The Rosh Hashanah pilgrimage was the most important—Nachman, in fact, told his followers that they were obliged to be with him on that Holy Day. For more than a century after Nachman's death, Bratslaver Hasidim flocked there by the thousands every Rosh Hashanah. Under the Soviets, Uman was a closed city; foreigners were barred entry, and mass pilgrimages were banned. Restrictions were lifted in the late 1980s. By now, thousands and thousands of Nachman's followers converge on Uman each year—in 2006, the Rosh Hashanah crowd was estimated at 20,000 people from about 20 different countries. Singing, chanting, and dancing in the streets, men in beards, sidelocks, and prayer shawls turn the town into a festive—and very crowded—Jewish city. An enormous new synagogue, hotels and guesthouses, kosher shops, souvenir and prayer book stalls, a mikvah, and other infrastructure have sprouted up to meet the needs of the annual crowd. *(Additional information: www.breslov.com)*

UZHHOROD (HUNGARIAN: UNGVÁR)–The former synagogue in this town on the Hungarian border is now used at a concert hall. It is a beautiful, Moorish-style building from the late 19th century, whose reddish pink facade is dominated by a huge, fretted horseshoe arch. Inside, it has rich ornamentation and a stained-glass dome. Jews settled here in the 17th century or earlier, and the town, long part of Hungary, developed into a major Hasidic center. About 12,000 Jews lived here before World War II, roughly 40 percent of the local population. There is a large Jewish cemetery, dating back to the 18th century. Today there is also a small but active Jewish community. *(Hesed Shpira Jewish Center: vul. Podgornaya 8. Tel: +380-31/261-9201. www.hesed-shpira.com.ua)*

ZOLOCHIV (ZOLOCHEV)–A striking new Holocaust memorial stands on the main road, at the site of the destroyed Jewish cemetery in this town east of L'viv. Dedicated in 2006, it comprises a symbolic gravestone backed by pillars recalling the candles of a menorah and commemorates the 14,000 local Jews killed in the Shoah. New plaques in the town's castle commemorate 2,000 Jews killed and buried there in a mass grave and also non-Jewish people killed by Soviet secret police before the Nazi occupation.

RESOURCES ON UKRAINE

FEW ENGLISH-LANGUAGE RESOURCES ABOUT UKRAINIAN JEWISH HERITAGE ARE available locally. A map and guide to Jewish heritage in Kiev, published by the Judaica Institute of Kiev, can generally be purchased at the bookshop in the city's Central Synagogue. In L'viv, look for Yuriy Biryulyov's 2002 brochure, "Jewish Heritage in L'viv." There is a wealth of other material on the Internet.

WEBSITES:

- www.fjc.ru — Federation of Jewish Communities in the former Soviet Union. Jewish institutions linked to Chabad.
- www.heritageabroad.gov — Full text of the U.S. Commission for the Preservation of America's Heritage Abroad survey of synagogues, Jewish cemeteries, and sites of mass burials. The most comprehensive listing of Jewish heritage sites in Ukraine
- www.jewishgen.org/cemetery/e-europe/ukraine.html — Jewish cemeteries in Ukraine
- www.judaica.kiev.ua — Kiev Jewish Studies Institute
- www.ncsj.org — Advocates on behalf of Jews in Russia, Ukraine, the Baltic States, and Eurasia
- www.shtetlinks.jewishgen.org/sadgura/ReischToronto.html — Links to resources on the Bucovina region in northern Romania and western Ukraine

ADDITIONAL PUBLICATIONS:

- Beizer, Michael. *Our Legacy: The CIS Synagogues, Past and Present.* Jerusalem: Gesharim, 2002. (Also see www.jafi.org.il/education/worldwide/synagogues/)
- Ber of Bolechow. *The Memoirs of Ber of Bolechow (1723–1805).* Translated by M. Vishnitzer. New York: Arno Press, 1973 (Reprint of 1922 Oxford University Press ed.)
- Biryulyov, Yuriy, ed. *L'viv Sightseeing Guide.* Lviv: Centre d'Europe Publishing House, 2004
- Frank, Ben G. *A Travel Guide to Jewish Russia & Ukraine.* Gretna: Pelican Publishing Company, 2000
- Gitelman, Zvi. *A Century of Ambivalence: The Jews of Russia and the Soviet Union 1881 to the Present.* New York: Schocken, 1988
- Mendelsohn, Daniel. *The Lost: A Search for Six of the Six Million.* New York: HarperCollins, 2006
- Polec, Andrzej. *Zapomniani: My Zydzi Krezowi.* Olazanica: Bosz, 2006
- Strolia, Virginijus, and Mikhail Kal'nitsky. *Touring Kyiv.* Kiev: Baltija Dryk, 2003
- Weiner, Miriam. *Jewish Roots in Ukraine and Moldova: Pages from the Past and Archival Inventories.* New York: YIVO Institute for Jewish Research, 1999. (Also see www.rtrfoundation.org)

CZECH REPUBLIC

CURRENT POPULATION: 10.2 MILLION
JEWISH POPULATION BEFORE WORLD WAR II: 118,000
JEWISH POPULATION TODAY: APPROX. 3,000

A LITTLE HISTORY

THE CZECH REPUBLIC GAINED INDEPENDENCE ON JANUARY 1, 1993, WHEN Czechoslovakia, which had wrested itself from Soviet domination in the so-called Velvet Revolution of 1989, split peacefully into two independent states: the Czech Republic and Slovakia. Czechoslovakia had been created in 1918, joining the historic Czech lands of Bohemia and Moravia with Slovakia and part of Silesia following the breakup of the Austro-Hungarian Empire in World War I.

Today's Czech Republic comprises Bohemia, Moravia, and part of Silesia. Jewish traders journeyed to Czech lands as early as the ninth century, and by the 13th century Jewish life had taken root in Prague, Brno, Mikulov, and elsewhere. These medieval Jewish communities counted on royal protection for their security—in return for high taxes and other services. Conditions deteriorated in the late 14th and early 15th centuries as local rulers imposed restrictions, and persecutions and pogroms took place. In the early 15th century the Czech lands were wracked by civil war when Hussite reformers rebelled against the ruling Catholic hierarchy. In the aftermath, the king lost his protective role over Jews. In the middle of the 15th century, local rulers expelled the Jews from most royal towns.

Bohemia, Moravia, and Hungary (which then included Slovakia) became part of the Hapsburg domains in 1526. Under Emperor Maximilian II, who ruled from 1564 to 1576—and even more so under his successor, Rudolf II—the Jews of Bohemia and Moravia enjoyed a golden age. Maximilian issued an imperial charter canceling expulsion orders, granting Jews freedom of trade and commerce, and promising them a permanent home in Prague. Along with his wife and courtiers, he even paid a formal visit to Prague's Jewish Town, the ghetto area where Jews had been confined since medieval times. Outstanding Jewish personalities emerged in all fields during this period, and the partial economic freedom, combined with better social conditions, led to a rapid expansion of the Jewish population.

The pendulum swung back somewhat in the 17th century. New restrictions on Jews culminated in 1726 and 1727 with the so-called Familiants Law issued by Charles VI, which limited the number of Jewish families allowed to live in Bohemia and Moravia. It also stipulated that only one son from any Jewish household could legally marry and start a family. Although not scrupulously enforced, these restrictions remained in effect until 1849 and prompted tens of thousands of Jews to emigrate. The Empress Maria Theresa, who came to power in 1740, held virulently anti-Jewish views and imposed a steep "toleration tax" on Jews for the privilege of being allowed to live in Bohemia. The ascension to the throne of her son, Joseph II, in 1780 spelled dramatic changes. Joseph's Edicts of Tolerance, issued over the next decade, removed most restrictions on Jewish economic activity and also included provisions that forcefully encouraged Jewish assimilation. Among these were the 1787 order for all Jews to adopt German surnames. Nonetheless, Jews in the Czech lands were not officially granted full civil equality until the mid-19th century, and it wasn't until the creation of the dual Austro-Hungarian monarchy in 1867 that Jews achieved full emancipation. Freed from residential restrictions, Jews began an exodus from small towns and villages into larger cities. Many rural Jewish communities disappeared altogether; a law passed in 1890 formally abolished Jewish community organizations in many towns where only a few Jews remained. As the 19th century advanced, Jews in Bohemia and Moravia tended to become more secular and assimilated into the mainstream population. There was much intermarriage and conversion to Christianity. At the same time, Jews also found themselves embroiled in a growing clash between the German-speaking and Czech-speaking population. Czech-Jewish and German-Jewish movements sprang up, with the Czech-Jewish allegiance eventually becoming dominant.

The Czechoslovak Republic, founded on October 28, 1918, was a rare experiment in democracy in East-Central Europe. Jews contributed greatly to its economic and cultural development. Tomas G. Masaryk, its founder

A Jewish couple celebrates their 1938 wedding in what is today the Czech Republic.

and first president, supported Zionism and fought anti-Semitism—he lashed out publicly against Christian superstition during a notorious blood libel case in the town of Polna in 1899 and in 1927 visited Jewish settlements in Palestine. The Munich Pact of September 30, 1938, sacrificed Czechoslovakia to Adolf Hitler, forcing the country to cede its frontier regions to Nazi Germany in a move that was supposed to forestall war. Dozens of synagogues and Jewish cemeteries in this territory were destroyed by the Nazis less than two months later, in the so-called

Kristallnacht pogroms of November 9–10. On March 15, 1939, one day after Slovakia declared itself an independent state, Nazi troops occupied the rest of Czechoslovakia and declared the formation of the Protectorate of Bohemia and Moravia. The protectorate was home to more than 90,000 Jews, more than 77,000 of whom were killed in the Holocaust. (More than 26,000 Czech Jews managed to flee the country before the war broke out).

Bohemia, Moravia, and Slovakia were reunited as one country again after the end of the war, but postwar Czechoslovakia fell under communist control in 1948, and Jews, along with members of other religious groups, continued to suffer persecution. The immediate postwar communist leadership included many Jews (or people of Jewish background)—party secretary Rudolf Slansky among them. This boosted anti-Semitism among the people. But when anti-Semitism became part of the official communist line in the early 1950s, Slansky and 13 other senior officials were put on a show trial. Eleven of the 14 defendants were Jewish—eight Jews, including Slansky, were executed. Hundreds of other Jews were arrested, dismissed from their jobs, or sentenced to hard labor. Anti-Zionism gained ground, and, like almost all other communist states, Czechoslovakia broke relations with Israel after the Six Day War in 1967. After the Soviet-led invasion crushed the short-lived Prague Spring reform movement in 1968, the Czechoslovak communist regime remained one of the most oppressive in the Soviet Bloc.

The years since the Velvet Revolution and the subsequent Velvet Divorce from Slovakia have witnessed a vivid revival of Jewish life in the Czech Republic, as well as a growing recognition that Jewish heritage and culture are an important part of the local Czech experience. Although only a few thousand Jews live in the country, there are active Jewish communities in Prague and nine other cities.

JEWISH HERITAGE IN THE CZECH REPUBLIC

Under communism, independent researchers, as well as staff researchers at the Jewish Museum in Prague, pioneered the systematic documentation of Jewish heritage sites. This process has continued since the fall of communism, accompanied by an exemplary policy of recovery, repair, and restoration of many sites. Following the property restitution process, most cemeteries and many synagogues fall under the jurisdiction of the Jewish community, which has set up special bodies in Prague and

Brno to administer and maintain them. But state and local authorities and even private citizens have also taken an active part in preservation. Jewish heritage sites by now are firmly ensconced on tourist—and educational—itineraries, and infrastructure has been expanded and improved. The Czech Republic, in fact, is the country where, in researching this edition of *Jewish Heritage Travel,* I found the most changes—for the better.

About 200 out of the country's estimated 360 prewar synagogues remain standing in one form or another. More than 50 were destroyed by the Nazis, and another 100 were demolished under the communist regime. Many surviving synagogues have been converted into museums or other cultural centers, or into Christian churches (mostly of the local Czech Hussite denomination). A number that stood empty or in ruins, or were used as warehouses during the communist period, have been restored in recent years; a score of Jewish museums or permanent exhibitions have been opened, revamped, or expanded.

More than 300 out of the estimated prewar 430 Jewish cemeteries still exist. Here, too, important efforts to fence, clear, repair, and preserve these sites have taken place. Remnants of several dozen old Jewish quarters also remain. These range from extensive ghetto complexes, to individual streets with a few remaining Jewish houses, to small-town or village Jewish quarters. Notable efforts have been undertaken in several of these places to restore and develop them as town attractions.

The Czech Republic has an extensive network of extremely helpful municipal tourist information centers. Most have English-speaking personnel, and many have brochures and other information in English on local Jewish heritage sites. The keys to Jewish cemeteries are often kept at these centers, too. Historically, many Czech towns also had German names, and I have included some of these here. *(Additional information: www.chaiworks.org)*

TIPS ON VISITING

PRAGUE, OF COURSE, HAS THE BIGGEST AND MOST IMPORTANT CONCENTRATION of Jewish sites. Many places, such as Kolin, can be easily reached from Prague and make excellent day trips. If you go to Terezin, also make sure to visit the beautifully restored synagogue in Ustek and restored cemeteries in Roudnice and Libochovice. The cluster of fascinating old Jewish quarters in Moravia—among them in Mikulov, Trebic, Boskovice, Lomnice, and Dolni Kounice—are easily reachable from Brno.

PRAGUE

(Czech: Praha)

THE "GOLDEN CITY," CAPITAL OF ANCIENT BOHEMIA AND TODAY'S INDEPENDENT Czech Republic, Prague is a city of lore and legendry and historically one of Europe's most important Jewish centers. Numerous exceptional Jewish relics are here, and the Prague Jewish Museum has perhaps the greatest collection of Judaica in all Europe—a collection that was put together, with cruel irony, by the Nazis, who gathered material from 153 destroyed Jewish communities throughout Bohemia and Moravia.

Jews lived in Prague in the 11th century, forming a community in the Mala Strana District, below the castle. Eventually the main Jewish quarter, or Jewish Town, was established across the Vltava (Moldau) River, not far from the historic Old Town Square. On the whole, Jews flourished in Prague, but their fortunes were also marked by waves of persecution. At Easter in 1389, almost all Jews in the city—more than 3,000 people—were massacred in an attack spurred on by local priests who claimed that the Host had been desecrated. One of the few survivors was Avigdor Kara, a poet, scholar, and Kabbalist who lived on until 1439 and whose tomb is the oldest preserved gravestone in the Old Jewish Cemetery. Kara described the bloody attack and wrote a moving elegy on it that is still recited in Prague on Yom Kippur.

For centuries, conditions for Jews depended on the whim of the Hapsburg monarchs. Maximilian II (*R.*1564–1576) and Rudolf II (*R.*1576–1612), permitted Jews a large measure of economic freedom, and Jewish culture flourished as never before. Towering Jewish personalities emerged and became the stuff of legend. The best known was Rabbi Judah Loew ben Bezalel (circa 1525–1609), a scholar and educator known as the Maharal ("most venerated teacher and rabbi"). Centuries after his death he became celebrated in folk tales as a mystic miracle worker who dabbled in magic and alchemy. He is said to have halted a plague that killed only Jewish children; rocks thrown at him by a mob were said to have turned to flowers. Most famously, legend has it that he created the Golem—an artificial man made of clay and magically brought to life to protect the Jews. So deeply rooted in Prague culture did the figure of Rabbi Loew become that a statue of him was erected as part of the decoration of the New Town Hall that was built in 1910. It shows the aged rabbi recoiling from Death, who approaches him in the guise of a naked young woman.

Other prominent personalities from that period included the mathematician, historian, and astronomer David Gans (1541–1613), the dynamic financier Jacob Bashevi (1580–1634), and Mordechai Maisel (1528–1601), a remarkable figure who served as mayor of Jewish Town and sponsored numerous Jewish organizations, activities, and construction projects. Maisel paved the streets of the Jewish quarter and donated Torah scrolls to Jewish communities as far away as Jerusalem; he supplied food, clothing, and loans to the needy and even provided dowries for poor young women.

The pendulum swung back against the Jews in the 18th century. Persecutions culminated when the Empress Maria Theresa expelled Jews from the city between 1745 and 1748. Under Joseph II, conditions improved to such an extent that the Jewish Town quarter officially took the name Josefov in his honor—a name it keeps to this day. The 19th century saw a process of gradual emancipation. Forced residency in the Jewish Town ghetto was abolished in 1852, and by 1867 Jews enjoyed full equality. Many soon moved out to other districts, and Jews became prominent in the Prague business, cultural, and intellectual scene. Among the most famous were the writers Franz Kafka, Max Brod, and Franz Werfel.

More than 55,000 Jews lived in Prague at the outbreak of World War II. At least two-thirds of them were killed. Half of the survivors emigrated by 1950, but the hard-line communist regime barred emigration between 1950 and 1964, and Jewish life was stifled by official communist anti-Semitism. A new wave of emigration followed the Soviet invasion in 1968 that crushed the Prague Spring reforms.

The fall of communism sparked a vivid Jewish revival. Today, about 1,500 people are affiliated with Prague's Jewish community—though thousands more people with at least some Jewish ancestry may live in the city. The community runs an old-age home, a kindergarten, and a school, and there are Jewish events of all types throughout the year. The Prague Jewish Museum in particular anchors a rich cultural and educational program. Synagogues have come alive again, too, with regular Orthodox, Reform, and Conservative religious services held in venues including the Old-New Synagogue, the High Synagogue, the Spanish Synagogue, the Chabad House synagogue, the Jubilee Synagogue, and the premises of the Bejt Simcha congregation.

MAIN SITES OF JEWISH INTEREST IN PRAGUE

Josefov, Prague's Jewish Town: A rich mix of contemporary Jewish life and celebrated Jewish heritage makes Prague's historic Jewish quarter one of the most popular tourist attractions in the city—so much so that during peak season it can be difficult to walk for all the crowds and attendant kitsch. Lying between the Vltava River and the Old Town Square, the district is steeped in ancient Jewish lore, but it actually bears very little resemblance to the way it looked to generations of Jews who lived there over the past 800 years. After emancipation in the mid-19th century, wealthier and upwardly mobile families moved out, and Josefov became something of a slum, where the poor (Jews and non-Jews) lived amid a welter of dank, narrow streets, tiny squares, dark passageways, and crowded courtyards. It was romantic perhaps, but insalubrious. The city swept almost all of it away a century ago in an urban renewal project that saw the demolition of almost every old building except a handful of synagogues and a few other sites, including the Jewish Town Hall. The historic old ghetto was replaced by the handsome complex of buildings we see today. At Maiselova 12, across from the Old-New Synagogue, notice the Jews symbolized by the Star of David, money, and stereotype profiles in the decoration of the facade of the building.

The author Franz Kafka was born on the edge of the Jewish quarter on July 3, 1883, and spent much of his short life in and around the district. (He died in 1924 and, along with his parents, is buried in Prague's New Jewish Cemetery.) A monument to Kafka, erected in 2004, stands next to the Spanish Synagogue, a few steps from where the Kafka family once lived. The 12-foot sculpture, by the Czech artist Jaroslav Rona, shows a small figure of Kafka perched atop an empty suit of men's clothing that seems to be walking. Rona has said he was inspired by one of Kafka's stories, "Description of a Struggle," in which a character rides on another person's shoulders "into the interior of a vast but as yet unfinished landscape." On the spot where Kafka was born, at U Radnice 5 (also called namesti Franze Kafky 3), there is a museum devoted to Kafka and his times, and a life-size bust of the writer gazes quizzically from the corner of U Radnice and Maiselova. Another museum on Kafka is located in the Mala Strana District *(Hergetova Cihelna 2b. Tel: +420/257-535-507. www.kafkamuseum.cz)*.

• **Jewish Town Hall:** ul. Maiselova 18—With its distinctive tower and big clock with Hebrew letters instead of numbers, the Jewish Town Hall is one of the landmarks of the old Jewish Town. Located across a narrow alleyway from the Old-New Synagogue, the building was constructed in the 1560s, partly financed by Mordechai Maisel. Today it houses the offices of the Federation of Jewish Communities, as well as the offices and function rooms of the Prague Jewish community and the seat of the Orthodox chief rabbi. There is a kosher restaurant, Shalom, on the ground floor.

The Old-New Synagogue in Prague was built in the 13th century and is the oldest synagogue in continuous use in Europe.

Security is tight, so make sure you bring identification with you if you wish to enter or eat there.

• **Old-New Synagogue:** Cervena ulice—The Old-New Synagogue (or Altneu Shul) is the oldest synagogue still in use in Europe. Built around 1270—and then known as the New Synagogue, as it was the second synagogue to be built in the Jewish quarter—it got its present name years later, when a still newer synagogue was erected. Regular religious services are held here.

The compact Gothic building, with its high peaked roof and distinctive brick gables (added in the 15th century), stands slightly below street level in a space that once served as a Jewish marketplace. Inside, striking Gothic vaulting soars over the twin naves. The central support pillars define space for the bimah, which is enclosed by a late Gothic iron grille. Carvings of grapevines surround the Ark.

Over the centuries, many legends have grown up about the Old-New Synagogue. The best known, perhaps, is that Rabbi Loew hid the body of the Golem in its attic after removing the breath of life from the artificial man, and that the inert form remains up there to this day. Legend tells us that Rabbi Loew created the Golem to defend the Jews. But if it is in the attic of the synagogue, why wasn't it brought to life again during later hardships? The answer, the story goes, is that the magic word used to do so had been forgotten. (The Old-New Synagogue is owned and administered by the Jewish community, which charges an entrance fee outside the hours of prayer.)

• **High Synagogue:** ul. Cervena 5—Located in an upper floor of the building across the alley from the Old-New Synagogue, the High Synagogue was built around 1568 by Mordechai Maisel, to a design by the master builder Pankratius Roder. The square sanctuary, under a decorated vaulted ceiling, formed part of the Prague Jewish Museum during the communist period but today is used again as a house of prayer and study.

• **Prague Jewish Museum:** One of Europe's most noted Jewish institutions, the Prague Jewish Museum contains what is probably the continent's largest collection of Judaica—some 40,000 objects and 100,000 books. The museum was founded in 1906 to preserve items from the synagogues destroyed in the clearance of the old ghetto. Most of the material, however, comes from the 153 provincial Jewish communities destroyed by the Nazis. Run by the communist state after World War II, the museum returned to Jewish administration in 1994. Its director and curators embarked on a continuing process of updating and revamping exhibitions and exhibition space, so that the museum now uses its collections to document and detail local Jewish history and traditions as well as to showcase objects. In addition to the permanent exhibitions, it stages temporary shows throughout the year and also runs educational programs. The museum celebrated its centenary in 2006 with a full "Year of Jewish Culture" that included special events all over the country.

The museum collections are displayed thematically in some of the historic synagogues that survived the demolition of the ghetto, and the buildings themselves form an important part of the exhibitions, as do two cemeteries: the Old Jewish Cemetery and the Cemetery in Zizkov. *(Prague Jewish Museum offices: ul. U Stare Skoly 1/3. Tel: +420/221-711-511. E-mail: office@jewishmuseum.cz. www.jewishmuseum.cz)*

Maisel Synagogue: ul. Maiselova 10—Built in the 1590s by Mordechai Maisel as a private prayer house, the Maisel Synagogue was the most opulent building in the Jewish Town. The original synagogue burned down in 1689, and the baroque reconstruction was much less elaborate. Extensive rebuilding from 1893 to 1905 gave it a pseudo-Gothic appearance. The synagogue today houses a sweeping exhibition on Czech Jewish history, tracing the story of Jewish life in Prague and surroundings from medieval times until the end of the 18th century. Among its displays are stunning silver ritual objects.

Spanish Synagogue: ul. Dusni 12 (entrance only from Vezenska ulice)—Built in 1868 on the site of Prague's oldest synagogue, the Spanish Synagogue was designed by the architect Ignatz Ullmann and constructed in extravagant Moorish style. The overwhelming interior decoration, installed in the late 1880s, covers every inch of wall and ceiling space with gilded arabesques, fretwork, and colorful geometric designs. The synagogue underwent a full restoration in the 1990s and now houses the second part of the Prague Jewish Museum's historical exhibition, detailing the Jewish experience in Prague from the late 18th century to the present. Next door, the Robert Guttman Gallery serves as a venue for temporary exhibitions, particularly those by modern artists.

Pinkas Synagogue: ul. Siroka 3—Situated at the edge of the Old Jewish Cemetery, the Pinkas Synagogue was built in 1535 as a private prayer house for the wealthy Horowitz family. It was rebuilt several times, partly because of repeated flooding and water damage due to its low-lying position near the river. After World War II, the synagogue became a memorial to the Jews from Bohemia and Moravia who were killed in the Holocaust. The names and dates of birth and death of all 77,297 victims were carefully inscribed, one by one, on the walls of the sanctuary.

The inscriptions were removed during restoration work begun in the late 1960s—in part because of the communist regime's anti-Semitic policy. Excavation during this project revealed an ancient mikvah and well in dank subterranean rooms. The communist government deliberately prolonged the restoration process, keeping the synagogue closed to the public. Only in 1991 was it reopened. The names of Holocaust victims were then carefully reinscribed, and the synagogue again serves as a memorial. Its upper floor houses a poignant exhibit of materials from the Holocaust period, in particular from the Terezin Ghetto. These include drawings and poems by the children there, who were educated in secret and used their creativity to express their fears, hopes, and broken dreams. Few of these children survived the war. Their drawings were saved and hidden by their teacher, the artist Friedl Dicker-Brandeis, shortly before she herself was deported to her death in 1944.

Old Jewish Cemetery: entrance from Pinkas Synagogue courtyard—No single Jewish relic captures the imagination the way Prague's Old Jewish Cemetery does. Here, 12,000 tombstones crowd together in a small, irregular plot of land. Tilted over in crazy patterns, eroded, sunk into the earth, they make an unforgettable sight. Founded at the beginning of the 15th century, the cemetery was in use until 1787. The oldest identified gravestone is that of Avigdor Kara from 1439. Lack of space caused graves to be placed on top of each other, layer after layer, over the centuries. This caused the irregular hilliness, marked by bristling clumps and clusters of tombstones. The unique appearance has exerted a special appeal on generations of artists. Already in the 18th and 19th centuries, painters loved to portray the haunting contrasts between the tumbled stones and the lush vegetation that then grew among them.

Many of the gravestones are superb examples of carving and craftsmanship, both of epitaph inscriptions and symbols—animals, the Cohen's hands, the Levite pitcher, objects relating to names or professions. Many famous Prague Jews are buried here, including Mordechai Maisel, David Gans, and noted rabbis—including the legendary Rabbi Loew himself. Visitors literally by the busload place pebbles on the tombs in remembrance and, particularly at Rabbi Loew's impressive mausoleum, leave written messages in many languages asking him to intercede to bring them good luck and blessing.

Klausen Synagogue: ul. U Stareho Hrbitova 1—The baroque Klausen Synagogue, the biggest in the ghetto, was built in the late 17th century to replace three smaller buildings. It stands at the exit of the Old Jewish Cemetery. Its spacious, oblong sanctuary has a high, barrel-vaulted ceiling, and tall arched windows flank the Aron ha Kodesh. The museum's "Jewish Customs and Traditions" exhibition is housed here.

Ceremonial Hall: ul. U Stareho Hrbitova 3—Built next to the Old Jewish Cemetery in 1911–12, this pseudo-Romanesque hall houses an exhibition on Jewish funeral practices. Among the key exhibits is a fascinating cycle of paintings from the Prague Jewish Burial Society, dating from the 1880s.

Jewish Cemetery in Zizkov: Fibichova ulice, in eastern Prague—The fascinating Jewish cemetery here was opened in 1680 as a graveyard for Jewish victims of the plague and was the main Jewish burial ground in Prague between the closure of the old cemetery in 1787 and the opening of the new cemetery in 1890. Most of the cemetery was demolished in the 1950s to make way for a park, where a huge, futuristic-looking television tower was erected in the 1980s. The surviving section, however, includes the imposing tombs of important personalities, including the influential Prague chief rabbi Ezekiel Landau (1713–1793).

Elsewhere in Prague

Jubilee Synagogue: ul. Jeruzalemska 7, near Wenceslas Square—Designed by the architect Wilhelm Stiassny, the Jubilee Synagogue replaced three synagogues destroyed in the clearance of the old ghetto. It was formally named the Emperor Franz Joseph Jubilee Synagogue in honor of the Hapsburg ruler. The decision to build it was made in 1898, the 50th anniversary of Franz Joseph's ascension to the throne. It was constructed in 1905 to 1906 and formally dedicated in 1908—the 60th anniversary of his reign. A gorgeous building that incorporates Moorish, Byzantine, and art nouveau elements, it is still used for regular religious services. With its striped facade, towers, arches, and a rose window incorporating a Star of David, it is a monument to the assimilationist dreams of Prague Jews of the era. An inscription over the door reads: "Do we not have one father? Were we not created by the same God?"

Charles Bridge: The Hebrew words *Kadosh, Kadosh, Kadosh Adonai Tzvaot* (Holy, Holy, Holy Is the Lord of Hosts) are affixed in gold letters above a big figure of the crucified Jesus, one of the sculptures lining the famous Charles Bridge across the Vltava River. The story has it that in the 17th century the Jewish community was forced to pay for these words (which appear to refer to Jesus) to be placed on the cross in punishment for the alleged desecration of the crucifix by a Jew.

New Jewish Cemetery: Izraelska ulice, near the Zelivskeho metro station—Founded in 1890 next to the main Olsany Cemetery complex, the New Jewish Cemetery is still in use by the local Jewish community. Laid out initially to encompass 100,000 graves, it was founded during one of the most prosperous and optimistic periods of Jewish life in Prague and makes a very moving contrast to the Old Jewish Cemetery in Josefov. The wealth and importance of the community can be seen in the many large and elaborate family tombs and other monuments in styles ranging from neo-Gothic to art nouveau. The names on the tombs read like the membership list of any U.S. temple: Bacher, Beck, Ehrenfeld, Epstein, Katz, Kraus, Roth, Singer.... According to the epitaphs, they were doctors, businessmen, lawyers, teachers.... A white, crystal-shaped stone marks the grave of Franz Kafka and his family; a plaque there commemorates Kafka's three sisters, who were killed in the Holocaust.

Other Cemeteries and Synagogues: A number of Jewish cemeteries and synagogue buildings still stand in various districts of the city well away from the main tourist trail. Some are relics of Jewish communities that lay outside of today's Prague. Others reflect the fact that many Jews moved out of Josefov after obtaining civic equality in the mid-19th century.

• **Synagogue in Smichov District:** Corner of Plzenska ulice and Stroupeznickeho ulice—Jews established a community in this suburb (now a fairly central district) at the end of the 18th century. A neo-Romanesque synagogue built here in 1863 was totally reconstructed in a modern functionalist style by the architect Leopold Ehrmann in 1931. Long-empty, it was reconstructed and reopened in 2004 as the archive of the Prague Jewish Museum.

• **Smichov/Radlice Cemetery:** U Stareho Zidovskeho Hrbitova ulice in southwest Prague—Founded in 1759, this cemetery has many graves from the 18th century but has been abandoned and vandalized over the years.

• **Synagogue in Karlin District:** ul. Vitkova 13—The synagogue here was built in 1861 and is now used as a church.

• **Liben Synagogue:** Zenklova ulice at Palmovka metro station—Jews lived in Liben, a suburb now well within the city limits, in the 16th century, and the first synagogue was built here as early as 1592. It was replaced around 1860 by the current large neo-Romanesque building, set in a small park. Long used as warehouse, it was restored in the 1990s and now serves as a venue for concerts and exhibitions.

• **Liben Jewish Cemetery:** Between Na Malem Klinu ulice and Strelnicni ulice—Used between 1893 and 1975, this cemetery is a sort of secret Jewish garden behind a tall wall. There are about 300 tombstones amid trees and ivy.

• **Synagogue in Michle District:** U Michelskeho Mlyna ulice—The synagogue, now used as a church, is a neo-Gothic reconstruction of a building possibly built in the 18th century or even earlier.

• **Synagogue and Jewish Cemetery in Uhrineves:** Jews settled in this outlying suburb in southeast Prague in the 17th century, and the cemetery, at the end of Vachkova street, dates from the early 18th century. Long-abandoned and overgrown, it has many fine carved gravestones. The mid-19th century synagogue, at Pratelstvi 79, was long used as a laundry but is now a shop and dwelling.

Addresses of Note in Prague

- Federation of Jewish Communities in the Czech Republic: ul. Maiselova 18. Tel: +420/224-800-824, fax: +420/224-810-912. E-mail: fedzid@vol.cz. www.fzo.cz
- Jewish Community of Prague: ul. Maiselova 18. Tel: +420/224-800-812, fax: +420/222-318-664. E-mail: sekretariat@kehilaprag.cz. www.kehilaprag.cz
- Jewish Liberal Union in the Czech Republic: E-mail:zlu@volny.cz. www.volny.cz/zlu
- Bejt Praha (Conservative/Reform): Tel/fax: +420/222-310-199. E-mail: office@bejt-praha.cz. www.bejt-praha.cz
- Bejt Simcha (Reform): ul. Manesova 8. Tel/fax: +420/222-252-472. E-mail: chevra@bejtsimcha.cz. www.bejtsimcha.cz
- Masorti (Conservative): Tel: +420/608-176-579. E-mail: masorti-en@masorti.cz. www.masorti.cz
- Chabad: ul. Parizska 3. Tel/fax: +420/222-320-200. E-mail: chabadprague@mbox.vol.cz. www.chabadprague.cz

Kosher restaurants:

- King Solomon, ul. Siroka 8. Tel: +420/248-18752. Upscale.
- Shalom Restaurant, ul. Maiselova 18. Tel: +420/223-21049. In Jewish Town Hall.
- Shelanu Cafe & Deli, ul. Brehova 8. Tel: +420/221-665-141. www.shelanu.cz. Chabad-run, casual kosher dining and takeout.

Jewish tour/travel agencies:

- Precious Legacy Tours: ul. Kaprova 13. Tel: +420/222-321-951, fax: +420/222-321-954. www.legacytours.net
- Wittmann Tours: ul. Manesova 8. Tel/fax: +420/222-252-472. www.wittmann-tours.com

Near Prague

BRANDYS NAD LABEM (BRANDÝS NAD LABEM) (GERMAN: BRANDEIS)–Jews settled in this ancient town on the Elbe River north of Prague in the 16th century. The large Jewish cemetery, located on the road to Kostelec nad Labem, was founded in 1568 and has some of the oldest tombstones in the Czech Republic still in situ. Some have unusually vivid carving. Entry is through an imposing cemetery house, which houses an exhibition on local Jewish history. The town's early 19th-century synagogue at Na Potoce 140 is used as storage space for the Prague Jewish Museum.

BUDYNE (BUDYNĚ)–The Jewish cemetery in this town near Terezin dates from the 18th century and sits like a walled, secret garden in the middle of farmland a mile or so outside town, just past a Christian cemetery. In 1990, I climbed over a partially ruined wall and hacked my way through a jungle of brush engulfing desecrated tombstones. On a recent visit, I found the wall repaired and intact; it towered well above my head; only the tops of trees showed above its rim. The heavy new gate was locked tight, but it had a keyhole big enough to peer through. I peered through into another world. The cemetery was now an open, grassy space, clear of brush; an alley of tall trees led toward the rear, where I could see the stones standing distinct. Under one of the trees stood a metal park bench.

KOLIN (KOLÍN)–A historic (and now industrial) town about 35 miles due east of Prague, Kolin has one of the country's most important complexes of Jewish relics, most of them centered near the attractive main market square and soaring early Gothic St. Bartholomew's Church. Kolin was founded in the 13th century, and Jews were already living here by the early part of the 14th century. In medieval Bohemia, the Jewish community was second only to that of Prague in size and importance. (To get a good orientation, stop in at the Regional Museum, whose branch at Brandlova 27 has a collection of local Judaica and a scale model of the town as it appeared in 15th century, clearly showing the Jewish quarter.) At its height, in the mid-19th century, the Jewish population numbered about 1,700; only 500 or fewer lived here on the eve of World War II.

The former Jewish quarter is just off the main square, on Na Hradbach and Karoliny Svetle streets. During the communist period, the neighborhood became a slum, but there has been a constant process of gentrification since the early 1990s, and there are now a number of quaint shops and restaurants. The baroque synagogue, built in the second half of the 17th century, stands in the courtyard of the house at Na Hradbach 157/12. The highly decorated building next door was once the Jewish school. The synagogue has been nicely restored, with much of the ornate baroque interior decor intact. There are delicate frescoes of grapevines and bunches of grapes on the walls and vaulted ceiling and an ornate Aron ha Kodesh, donated in 1696 by the Vienna financier Samuel Oppenheimer, whose nephew, David, was at the time Bohemia's provincial rabbi. Across the street, the former Jewish Town Hall, with its overhanging upper story, is now a shop.

The helpful Kolin Municipal Information Office is conveniently located right here, at the entrance to the synagogue. It stocks a lot of material in English about local Jewish sights and history and holds the keys to the two Jewish cemeteries.

Kolin's Old Jewish Cemetery is one of the most historically and artistically important in the Czech Republic. Entry is through a heavy door on Kmochova street. There are more than 2,600 tombstones; the earliest that survive date from the late 15th century and constitute the oldest Jewish gravestones in situ in Bohemia outside the Old Jewish Cemetery in Prague. Trees shade the tombs; trailing ivy creates a sense of timelessness. Many local rabbis and other prominent personalities are buried here. Among them is Bezalel Jehudah ben Liva-Loew, who died in 1599. He was a son of Prague's famous 16th-century rabbi Judah Loew ben Bezalel, the legendary creator of the Golem.

The New Jewish Cemetery, opened in 1888 after the old cemetery closed, is located on Veltrubska street in the northern part of town, near the Christian cemeteries. It was hit by bombs during World War II, and part of it was sold off and demolished. Vandalism has also taken a toll. Still, it is worth it to visit and see the grand tombs of the upper and middle classes, businessmen, community leaders, professionals, even an opera singer. There is also a large memorial, erected in 1950, listing the names of the 487 Holocaust victims from Kolin. Inside it, a chamber holds soil brought from six places where Jews suffered in World War II: the Terezin Ghetto, the Terezin Small Fortress, Auschwitz, Majdanek, Warsaw, and Lodz.

LIBOCHOVICE—Jews settled in this little town near Terezin, in the 15th century. The Jewish cemetery, founded in 1583, occupies a low hilltop just outside town, past the railway tracks and next to a brick factory. Garden allotments back up against the slope, and a path lined with fruit trees leads up from the road to the entrance. There are many examples of fine baroque and Renaissance carving on the tombstones. When first visited, I found it one of the most utterly devastated Jewish cemeteries I had seen, with stones toppled, broken, chipped, or even smashed. Over the past few years, however, there has been a concerted effort to clean, restore, and preserve the cemetery. Vegetation has been cleared away, and shards of broken stones have been heaped into piles. Some larger fragments of broken stones have been embedded in a new wall to form a memorial.

MLADA BOLESLAV (MLADÁ BOLESLAV) (GERMAN: JUNG-BUNZLAU)–An industrial town northeast of Prague, Mlada Boleslav retains a charming old center with some fine Renaissance and baroque buildings, including a monumental 16th-century castle. Jews settled here in the 15th century and developed into one of the most important historic communities in Bohemia and a noted center of learning. Near the town hall, a Star of David set in the pavement marks the spot where a baroque synagogue stood until its demolition in the 1960s.

A fascinating Jewish cemetery sprawls up a steep hill directly opposite the castle, which today houses the town museum. The cemetery—the key can be obtained at the museum desk—includes about 2,000 tombstones, ranging from the 16th century almost to the present day. There are beautiful examples of symbolic and folk-style carving, including one stone with the unusual carving of a woman's figure. But acid rain and other pollution have taken a heavy toll; many older gravestones are literally crumbling away, and even many newer tombstones have begun to erode.

Among the prominent personalities buried here is Jacob Bashevi (1580–1634), one of the most notable Jewish figures of his age. A financier, leader of the Prague Jewish community, philanthropist, and adviser to the Hapsburg rulers, he was named to the rank of Court Jew by King Matthias of Bohemia. In 1622 he was knighted by Emperor Ferdinand II, becoming the first Jew in the Hapsburg monarchy to be raised to the nobility. His tomb proudly bears his coat of arms above the epitaph.

In the upper part of the cemetery, the octagonal ceremonial hall, built in 1889, now houses an exhibition on local Jewish history and traditions. Though the cemetery is well maintained, there is also evidence of apparent vandalism. Years ago, for example, I had been charmed by a double tomb from the early

The old Jewish cemetery in Mlada Boleslav affords a striking view of the town and castle.

20th century that featured a lifelike portrait of the elderly husband and wife interred there, Salomon and Peppie Strenitz. Salomon, who sported mutton-chop whiskers, had died at the age of 94, and Peppie, portrayed with a bow in her hair, lived to be 88. On my latest visit, I easily found the black marble tomb, but the place where their portrait plaque had been was an empty blank.

RAKOVNIK (RAKOVNÍK) (GERMAN: RAKONITZ)–In this industrial town west of Prague, the ornate synagogue built in 1764 has been painstakingly restored as a concert hall. It retains its full Jewish character and synagogue decor, including a fantastic rococo Aron ha Kodesh, stained-glass windows, decorative stuccoed dome with raised cupola and other rich ornamentation. The rabbi's house next door is now an art gallery. On the road heading out of town toward Beroun, a walled Jewish cemetery dating from the 17th century straggles up a hill. The ceremonial hall preserves some original interior decoration, and there is a small Jewish exhibition in the former gravedigger's house.

ROUDNICE NAD LABEM (GERMAN: RAUDNITZ)–Situated on the Elbe (Czech: Labe) River north of Prague, Roudnice is famous for its impressive castle, originally built in the 13th century and rebuilt in the baroque style in the 17th century. Jews settled here in the 16th century. The town has two Jewish cemeteries, both of which were rescued from utter oblivion in recent years. The old cemetery on Trebizskeho street was established in 1613 and used until the end of the 19th century. Its more than 1,500 stones are spread out on a steep, tree-shaded slope. The older part—including many extremely fine baroque and Renaissance stones—is at the top, where a grandiose new entry way from Farskeho street affords a striking panorama.

The New Jewish Cemetery, opened in about 1890, is at the end of the road leading past the town's main cemetery. It was devastated during and after World War II; almost all the tombstones were stolen or smashed. The huge, Moorish-style ceremonial hall burned out in a fire in 1985 and was left a crumbling hulk in the midst of an overgrown jungle. (The ravaged building so impressed a visitor from San Diego, California, that a replica of the facade was included in the design of his congregation's new synagogue.) Today, a stout new wall encloses the area and the mass of undergrowth has been cleared. The ceremonial hall has not been reconstructed, though; it stands bare and almost defiant in its ruined condition, its ravaged pink stone a striking memorial.

TEREZIN (TEREZÍN) (GERMAN: THERESIENSTADT)–Terezin, about 30 miles northeast of Prague, was built as a fortress at the end of the 18th century and named after the Hapsburg empress Maria Theresa. During World War II, the Nazis turned it into a major concentration camp complex. The camp had two components. One was a concentration camp and prison located in the so-called Small Fortress, just outside of town, which mostly served as a transit camp for political prisoners. The other was the entire town of Terezin itself, which was turned into a Jewish ghetto from which Jews were deported to Auschwitz and other death camps.

About 150,000 Jews from Czech lands, Austria, Germany, The Netherlands, Denmark, and elsewhere passed through Terezin between 1941 and 1945. At least 34,000 perished under the cruel conditions of the ghetto itself. Of the 87,000 deported from Terezin to death camps, only 3,000 survived. Whole families were interned, including many children. Despite the hardships, the internees maintained a rich cultural life. There were clandestine schools for the children, whose writings and drawings form a poignant exhibit at the Prague Jewish Museum. More than half a dozen secret prayer houses were set up, too. One of them, found in the 1990s at Dlouha 1, can now can be visited.

With calculated cynicism, the Nazis tried to pass Terezin off as an "exemplary Jewish settlement." At the beginning, many Jews believed (or hoped) that they would be able to sit the war out in the ghetto there and escape deportation to the death camps in the east. In July 1944, the Nazis created an entire false-front charade of Jewish life there in order to fool a visiting Red Cross commission investigating the Nazi treatment of the Jews.

Today, the former concentration camp and sites of the ghetto form part of a national monument and memorial. The main sights include:

• **A museum and memorial to the Jewish ghetto,** opened in 1991, after the fall of communism. There is also an exhibition in the Magdeburg barracks that shows how internees lived.

• **The National Cemetery** for thousands of Nazi victims, laid out in a rose garden at the entrance to the Small Fortress.

• **The Small Fortress**, outside the town proper, where many prisoners were tortured to death or executed. This site is maintained as a concentration camp museum, with the infamous Nazi slogan *"Arbeit Macht Frei*—Work Makes You Free" painted over the arched gateway.

• **The Ghetto Cemetery**, where more than 10,000 prisoners were buried, mainly in mass graves, between December 1941 and October 1942. After that, bodies were burned, and here, too, is the crematorium, which houses a small exhibition. Dominating the area is a huge, modernistic sculpture of a menorah, surrounded by symbolic nameless graves. Next door, a few prewar Jewish tombstones remain in a small section of the municipal cemetery.

• **A memorial on the bank of the Ohre River** at the spot where the Nazis threw the ashes of about 22,000 victims in 1944. *(Additional information: www.pamatnik-terezin.cz)*

USTEK (ÚŠTĚK) (GERMAN: AUSCHA)–In the early 1990s, the synagogue in this quaint town north of Prague was little more than a roofless pile of rubble. Today, beautifully restored, it serves as a Jewish museum and cultural venue. Jews settled here in the early 16th century, but the community never reached 200 people and only a few dozen Jews lived here in the 1930s. The synagogue, built in 1794, stands on the rim of a rocky outcrop above the steep valley that forms one edge of town; its tall, narrow shape makes it look like a defensive tower. Restoration work got under way in the 1990s, with financing from a variety of public, private, Jewish, and international sources, and the building was rededicated with gala ceremonies in 2003. Painted tomato red with cream-colored detail, it is a jewel. The little sanctuary, glowing with wooden paneling and dazzling fresco ornamentation, is used for exhibitions and concerts and has a permanent display on local Jewish history. Among other things, it documents the firm of Benjamin Schwartz and Sons, hop merchants who had branches in Ustek, in the northern Bohemian town of Zatec—and on Broadway in New York City. Schwartz's great-granddaughter, one of the last Ustek Jews, was killed in Terezin. The basement area, where the Jewish school once functioned, has been transformed into a museum installation re-creating the classroom and the apartment of the teacher.

The Jewish cemetery lies deep in a forest on a slope beyond the southern edge of the village, off the road to Lhota. The oldest legible tombstone dates from 1650. The cemetery was devastated after World War II; many tombstones were toppled, smashed, or stolen for use as building material. In recent years, however, local volunteers have begun trying to clean up and restore the area. *(Additional information: www.synagoga-ustek.org)*

BRNO

(German: Brünn)

THE ANCIENT CAPITAL OF MORAVIA, BRNO IS A BIG INDUSTRIAL AND TRADE FAIR center that preserves a charming historic Old Town with many medieval and baroque buildings. The city makes an excellent hub for nearby sites of Jewish heritage. Jews lived in Brno in the 13th century, and a few Jewish tombstones from this period are found in the Brno City Museum. The Jews were expelled in 1454, however, and were not allowed back until 1848—although a few (generally very wealthy) Jews did manage to obtain residency permits from time to time, and a small Jewish community developed in a suburb. After 1848 though, Brno—as a leading center of the industrial revolution in the Austro-Hungarian Empire—became a magnet for Jews from small towns and villages. The Jewish population soared from a little over 200 in 1860 to more than 8,300 in 1900. In the decade or so after World War I, Jewish refugees boosted the Jewish population to 12,000.

The Nazis destroyed the 19th-century Great Synagogue, and the large New Synagogue was demolished under the communist regime in the

1980s—a memorial plaque at Ponavka 8 now marks the spot. Another 19th-century synagogue was demolished in 2006. Only one synagogue remains standing, a small, spare, functionalist building designed by the architect Otto Eisler and built in the 1930s. It is located at Skorepka 13 and is still in use by today's small but active Jewish community. The Prague Jewish Museum operates a branch of its Educational and Cultural Center in the Jewish community building at Kpt. Jarose 3. There is a large Jewish cemetery in the Zidenice District, at Nezamyslova 27. Established in the 1850s, it has a grand, neo-Romanesque ceremonial hall and impressive tombs of wealthy 19th-century industrialists and businessmen. Here, too, is a memorial commemorating the 11,000 local Jews deported to their deaths by the Nazis. *(Jewish community: ul. Kpt. Jarose 3. Tel: +420/545-244-710, fax: +420/545-213-803. E-mail: zob@zob.cz. www.zob.cz)*

Near Brno

BOSKOVICE–This postcard-picturesque little town north of Brno has one of the most extensive old Jewish ghetto areas in Central Europe. Its narrow lanes, low houses, and little squares lie just off the main market square, below the church. Jews lived in Boskovice as early as the 14th century. One street, Plackova, still retains the arched gate that once closed the ghetto off from the rest of the town. The area became derelict after World War II, and in 1990 the abandoned synagogue, originally built in the 17th century, was little more than an empty shell. By now, many of the houses have been renovated and painted soothing mint and ochre, and some of them have been converted into boutiques and upscale cafés. Most importantly, the synagogue has been fully restored and now houses a Jewish museum. It has gorgeous interior frescoes, including intricate floral motifs and Hebrew wall texts painted in the first years of the 18th century by Jeshajah Maler, the son of Jehudah Leib—the Cracow-based artist who painted the interior decoration of the synagogue in Pinczow, Poland. A mikvah brought to light in 2003 at U Templu 5 is also open to visitors.

The large Jewish cemetery is located just outside of town on Potocni street. Founded in the 16th century, it includes more than 2,000 tombstones; the oldest legible dates from 1670. Many of the tombstones feature exceptionally elaborate carved epitaphs and decorative sculptural relief. There is also a large memorial to Jewish soldiers killed in World War I.

Detail of the ornate interior frescoes in the synagogue in Boskovice, which now serves as a Jewish museum

BRECLAV (BŘECLAV) (GERMAN: LUNDENBURG)–Jews lived in this trade-and-transport hub south of Brno as early as the 15th century. The late 19th-century synagogue stood forlornly empty for years, right in the middle of town. Fully restored now, it forms part of the town museum and houses an exhibition on local Jewish history. The museum and its main collection are in the building next to the synagogue, at U Trziste 10, which used to be a Jewish school. The Jewish cemetery, founded in the 17th century, is located on Jana Cerneho street and has a very striking, neo-Gothic ceremonial hall. Local authorities attempted to demolish the cemetery in the 1980s, but some of the tombstones were reerected in the 1990s.

DOLNI KOUNICE (DOLNÍ KOUNICE) (GERMAN: KANITZ)–Jews settled in this small town south of Brno in the 14th century. Originally built in the 1650s and expanded in 1851, the synagogue stands on U Synagogy street. Large and barnlike, with thick walls and round-arched windows, it was used as a warehouse for decades. A slow restoration process, begun in 1988, was completed in 2004, and the building now serves as a museum and culture center that includes an exhibit on local Jewish history and traditions *(open only in summer)*. Striking plant-motif carving decorates the stone portal above the arched entrance, and the interior features a beautifully proportioned arched gallery and some lovely baroque frescoes and wall texts.

The synagogue is in the heart of the old Jewish quarter, and an information placard with a map and old photographs helps visitors get their bearings. The house at U Synagogy 581 was a Jewish school, and above the door of the building at No. 577, which once housed a wine press, there is a carved relief, dating to 1818, showing palm trees and men carrying a huge bunch of grapes. The Jewish cemetery, whose oldest tombstones date to the late 17th century, lies high on a grassy hilltop overlooking the pastoral landscape and red-roofed town below. It is located on Trbousanska street, across a lane from the Christian cemetery. There are well over a thousand tombstones, many with lovely baroque carving.

IVANCICE (IVANČICE) (GERMAN: EIBENSCHÜTZ)–The Jewish cemetery in this small town south of Brno is one of the oldest in the Czech Republic, and one of the most beautiful. The ancient tombstones, sunken into the turf or jammed together in tight rows, are shaded by trees and spread out over a steep slope on Mrenkova street, behind a large but somewhat dilapidated, neo-baroque ceremonial hall built in 1902. Jews settled here in the 15th century or earlier, and the earliest legible tombstone dates from 1552. The first time I visited, in 1990, an elderly man who lived across the street opened the gate and guided me around, throwing in bits of (sometimes erroneous) information as we peered at the vividly carved inscriptions. On my latest visit, I got the key from the same house—No. 36—but this time it was from a younger man, who seemed rather surly. It was late winter and the cemetery was covered by snow; he clearly thought I was crazy to want to visit it under such conditions. The snow, in fact, lay shin deep; my boots made the only tracks besides those of birds or what appeared to be a hare. The first time I had visited, I had come across one tombstone whose carving I had found particularly lovely—it marked the grave of a Cohen, and the traditional two hands, symbolizing the priestly blessing, looked as if they were wearing fancy gloves. I wanted to see it again and tromped through the snow, slipping in places, looking and looking—but I couldn't find it.

The Ivancice synagogue still stands on Josefa Vavry street, in the heart of the old Jewish quarter. It is a plain-looking, oblong building, built in 1853, with arched windows and a large Hebrew inscription running across the facade. Long used as a warehouse, it has stood empty for years, though I was told that there are plans to turn it into a library.

LOMNICE—Lomnice is little more than a big village whose main square is dominated by a picturesque, twin-towered church. One of my favorite places in the Czech Republic, it retains the soothingly sleepy aspect of a place out of time—and somehow was largely spared any ugly industry or communist-era "modernization." The former Jewish quarter occupies Zidovske namesti (Jewish square), a quiet area shaded by leafy horse chestnut and linden trees, and spills over into Josefa Uhra street. Most of the buildings here are still rather run-down, but the 18th-century synagogue, with its elegant, white, baroque facade, has been restored as a gallery and culture center. Other Jewish buildings on the square include the rabbi's house and school (No. 212), a tavern (No. 208), and an infirmary and bathhouse (No. 216). The Jewish cemetery is a two-minute walk away, down a narrow street leading out of the square, diagonally across from the synagogue. It straddles a hill and affords beautiful vistas of the town. Jews established a permanent community in Lomnice in the early 18th century, and the earliest known tombstones date from that period. Many bear intricate carving showing the influence of local folk motifs.

MIKULOV (GERMAN: NIKOLSBURG)—Picturesquely situated on the Austrian border and dominated by a medieval castle, this beautiful and ancient town was for centuries the center of Moravian Jewry. Jews settled here in the 15th century or earlier and became active in the wine trade, transport, and commerce. Mikulov was the seat of the powerful chief rabbi (Landesrabbiner) of Moravia, who had the right of jurisdiction over Jews in both religious and secular affairs and headed two councils of delegates from Moravian Jewish communities that functioned into the 18th century. Many famous rabbis held the post, including Rabbi Judah Loew ben Bezalel, who served from 1553 to 1573 and was the legendary creator of Prague's Golem, and the famous mystic and cabalist Rabbi Shmuel Shmelke Horowitz, a Hasidic master who served from 1772 to 1778. Menachem Mendel Krochmal, who was Landesrabbiner from 1648 to 1661, collected and published the acts passed by the councils. A century later, the Hapsburg rulers had these translated into German as an official guide to the regulation of Jewish life in Moravia.

Today's Husova street includes much of what is left of the old Jewish quarter, including the Old (or Upper) Synagogue, which now serves as a Jewish museum. Believed to have been built around 1550, the synagogue was totally reconstructed in 1719 to 1723 after fire destroyed much of the ghetto. It has a high-peaked roof and an elegant four-pillared central bimah, integrated as central support for the decorated vaulted ceiling. The house at Husova 52 served as a Jewish old-age home, and Husova 4 and 48 were once Jewish schools. Husova 8—now the Krokodyl Hotel—was the rabbi's house, and part of a mikvah was found in its cellar; ask at the desk for the keys. (A second mikvah was discovered in 2004 and may eventually be opened to the public.) Husova 50, once a private synagogue, was recently turned into a hotel—called the Templ—that evokes the Jewish history of Mikulov in its design and decoration. It also hosts Jewish-themed cultural programs *(Hotel Templ, ul. Husova 50. Tel: +420/519-323-095, fax: +420/519-323-096. www.templ.cz)*

The sprawling Jewish cemetery, a couple hundred yards from the top of Husova, is one of the most impressive and historically important in the Czech Republic. Founded in the 15th century, it has some 4,000 tombstones, the oldest legible example that of Shmuel ben Leb Ashkenazi, dating from 1605. The late baroque tombstones in particular feature fine script and rich floral and folk motifs whose style and design had a powerful influence on tomb sculpture throughout southern and central Moravia. Grouped in a special section—the so-called rabbi's hill—are the tombs of famous sages, including Menachem Mendel Krochmal (who died in 1661), Mordechai Benet (who died in 1829), and Shmuel Shmelke Horowitz (who died in 1778). There are also memorials to Holocaust victims and a poignant, partially ruined monument to 25 Jewish soldiers killed in World War I. "Oh, how the heroes have been cut down!" the memorial to Moriz Jung, Max Feldsberger, Heinrich Deutsch, Hans Kohn, and their comrades reads, in German. The ornate ceremonial hall at the cemetery entrance, designed by the architect Max Fleischer and built in 1898, houses a small exhibition on the cemetery.

PODIVIN (PODIVÍN)–Just off the motorway near Brno, Podivin has the oldest recorded evidence of Jewish presence in Moravia, dating from the 11th century. A permanent community was only established in the 17th century. Today, the elegant domed ceremonial hall at the Jewish cemetery on Palackeho street houses an exhibition on local Jewish history. The oldest stones in the cemetery date from the late 17th century.

SLAVKOV U BRNA (GERMAN: AUSTERLITZ)–This small town near Brno is famed as the scene of Napoleon's crushing defeat of Russian and Austrian Armies in the 1805 Battle of Austerlitz. A neo-

Romanesque synagogue, built in the 1850s, now serves as the district archives and has a Holocaust memorial plaque on the facade. Next door, the former Jewish school houses a Jewish museum opened in 2005. The Jewish cemetery, founded in 1744, lies on a forested slope above the road to Rousinov. The museum and other Jewish projects were sparked by the interest of the Progressive Synagogue in Nottingham, England, whose Torah scroll came from Slavkov, one of 1,500 Torahs found in the basement of a Prague synagogue in the 1960s and sent out on permanent loan to congregations worldwide by the Memorial Scrolls Trust. *(Additional information: www.czechtorah.org)*

TREBIC (TŘEBÍČ)–Located on the Jihlava River in the southern Moravian highlands, this historic town contains an extraordinary Jewish cemetery and the most extensive and best preserved old Jewish quarter in the Czech Republic. Its importance was recognized in 2003, when the entire Jewish district, along with the magnificent St. Procopius Basilica, was listed by UNESCO on its roster of World Heritage sites. Jews settled in Trebic in the 1400s, but the community dwindled sharply in the late 19th century. The Jewish quarter, stretched out along the opposite bank of the river from the main market square, is known as Zamosti, meaning "across the bridge." It includes a wide range of houses and other buildings dating from the Renaissance to the 19th century. There is a fascinating juxtaposition of narrow alleys and broad thoroughfares, little courtyards and arched passageways, sagging low houses and the quasi mansions of the well-to-do. Two former synagogues stand here. One, the so-called Front Synagogue, originally dates from 1639 to 1642. It was rebuilt in the 19th century in neo-Gothic style and now serves as a church. It has a plaque inside memorializing the Trebic Jewish community annihilated in the Holocaust. The buttressed Rear Synagogue, long abandoned, was reopened to the public in 1997 after a lengthy restoration process. Originally built around 1700 and enlarged and renovated in the 19th century, it functioned as a house or worship only until World War I. After that, it was turned into a warehouse and was a ruined shell when restoration work began in the early 1990s. Today it is used for cultural purposes and has an exhibition on local Jewish history and traditions. Walls and ceiling are covered with baroque stucco decoration and colorful paintings that include Hebrew texts, floral motifs, and painted lions.

The Jewish cemetery, one of the most striking and interesting in the Czech Republic, is on a hill above the ghetto area. Established in the 15th century, it includes a pretty ceremonial hall built in 1903 and more than 2,500 tombstones dating from the 16th to the 20th century, all spread out on rolling terrain under shady trees.

VELKE MEZIRICI (VELKÉ MEZIŘÍČÍ) (GERMAN: GROSS-MESERITSCH)–An industrial town that retains a quaint center, Velke Mezirici is an exit on Prague-Brno highway, and its Jewish relics are worth a stop. Much of the old Jewish quarter, along Novobranska street, is still visible, including a few narrow lanes and arched passageways. Two fascinating former synagogues stand almost right next to each other on Novobranska. One, set back from the street in a little yard, was probably built in the 16th century and is one of the oldest synagogues in the country. It is a massive masonry structure with a high-peaked roof, decorative stone portal, big iron doors and Hebrew inscriptions on the facade. Almost next door stands a striking, redbrick, neo-Gothic synagogue that was built in 1867 to a design by the architect August Prokop. Both buildings were long used as warehouses, and almost all Jewish interior elements were destroyed. In the 1990s the old synagogue was transformed into an art gallery and cultural space, with a small exhibition on local Jewish history and traditions mounted in the women's gallery. The exhibition, one of several in small Moravian towns designed by the Brno-based researcher Jaroslav Klenovsky, includes ritual objects, photographs, and descriptive wall panels. The newer synagogue, meanwhile, was turned into a discount department store, but some decorative work on its ceiling is still visible. The Jewish cemetery, on a hillside outside town on Bezdekov street, has about a thousand gravestones dating back to about 1680, many of which feature the finely carved floral and folk motifs typical of Moravia.

ELSEWHERE IN THE CZECH REPUBLIC

BATELOV–Jews settled in this small town southwest of Brno in the 15th century. The little ghetto area, off Trestska street, has a charming baroque synagogue, built in 1794, with distinctive red-ochre trim, and a Holocaust memorial on the site of the demolished rabbi's house. There is a walled cemetery with 18th-century tombstones on a hill above town off Polni street.

BREZNICE (BŘEZNICE)–In the center of this town about 50 miles southwest of Prague is an evocative old Jewish quarter, centered around two small squares. In the middle of the larger one stands a fine, 18th- to 19th-century synagogue with a peaked roof. It has been under restoration for some time; the aim is to turn it into a regional Jewish museum. The small, walled Jewish cemetery, dating back to the 17th century, has beautiful carved tombstones and is easily reached, about a mile outside town on the road to Rozmital.

CASLAV (ČÁSLAV)–An ornate, Moorish-style synagogue with a huge horseshoe arch stands at Masarykova 111, near the center of this town near Kutna Hora. It was designed by the architect Wilhelm Stiassny and built in 1899–1900. After World War II it was used as a warehouse and then an art gallery. Disused for a decade, it looks very dilapidated, although plans for a full-scale restoration have been drawn up. It preserves a beautiful painted wooden ceiling.

DECIN (DĚČÍN) (GERMAN: TETSCHEN BODENBACH)–Decin is home to one of the few synagogues in German-occupied northern Bohemia that was left standing after Kristallnacht. The grand, domed temple on Zizkova street was built in 1907, and combines elements of Moorish and art nouveau styles. It is now used not only to serve the town's revitalized Jewish community, but also as a center for exhibitions, concerts, and educational programs for the general public. *(Jewish community: ul. Zizkova 4. Tel: +420/412-531-095. E-mail: zidovska.obec.decin@volny.cz. www.zidovskaobecdecin.wz.cz)*

DOBRUSKA (DOBRUŠKA)–The local museum in this town near the Polish border occupies the former rabbi's house, school, and Jewish community center. It has a small exhibition on local Jewish history that includes a mikvah in a windowless, barrel-vaulted chamber. Next door, the 19th-century synagogue has been converted into a functioning church. The Jewish cemetery, founded in 1675, is just outside town on Krovicka street. (The municipal information office keeps the very large key.) The fine carvings, particularly on the 18th-century tombstones, are typical examples of a local northern Bohemian style. Entry is through a simple ceremonial hall with a memorial listing the names of the 31 local Jews killed in the Holocaust. (See also Rychnov nad Kneznou, p. 175.)

The 19th-century synagogue looms over the former Jewish quarter in Golcuv Jenikov.

GOLCUV JENIKOV (GOLČŮV JENIKOV)–The old Jewish quarter in this little town about 55 miles southeast of Prague evokes the uncanny feel of a village from an earlier century. Situated in a hollow on and around Pod Vysehradem street, just southwest of the main square, it's like a village within a village, cut off from the rest of the town. There are dirt roads, grassy and weed-choked areas, narrow cobbled lanes, and a little bridge across a small stream. Though people live all around, it feels deserted, almost a ghost town.

Dominating the scene is the big neo-Romanesque synagogue, built around 1871. Used as a Protestant prayer hall after World War II, it has long served as storage space for the Prague Jewish Museum. Its exterior, which features a flat, three-part facade, arched windows, and little decorative turrets, has recently been restored, and the interior includes a fine, ornate Aron ha Kodesh. It may not be possible to gain entrance to the building, but just experiencing the physical layout and lingering spatial relationships of the area is worthwhile. The synagogue faces a big, white building that once served as the Jewish school and probably housed the mikvah. Other remaining buildings include the rabbi's house (at No. 159), the hospital (at No. 165), and the yeshivah (at Nos. 13/14).

The fascinating Jewish cemetery is on the outskirts of town, behind a wall on a narrow, unmarked lane off the main new bypass road around town. The earliest gravestones date from the late 17th century. Many of the older stones feature some delicate carving—trees, flowers, palms, decorative borders. On some, the forms of living vines and creepers eerily merge with those of the carving.

HARTMANICE–The simple little 19th-century synagogue in this remote town in the Sumava Mountains near the German border was opened in 2006 as a local Jewish history museum. The project was carried out by Prague publisher Michal Klima, son of the noted Czech Jewish novelist Ivan Klima, who purchased the building in 2003. In the nearby village of Dobra Voda, there is another private Jewish museum in a former Jewish house.

HERMANUV MESTEC (HEŘMANŮV MĚSTEC) (GERMAN: HERRMANNSTÄDTL)–Jews settled in this town about 60 miles east of Prague in the early 16th century. At its height, in the mid-19th century, the community numbered about 840 Jews, many of them active in the local shoe industry. By 1939, though, only about 60 Jews lived here.

The neo-Romanesque synagogue was designed by the architect Frantisek Schmoranz and built in 1870 on the site of an earlier synagogue. It stands in the remains of the old Jewish quarter on Havlickova street, near St. Bartholomew's church. (Schmoranz had planned a larger and more ornate building with a tower, but that design was quashed over fears by the local Catholic clergy that it would overshadow the church.) After World War II the synagogue was used as a church and then as a warehouse—piles of huge industrial spindles filled the sanctuary. It has been beautifully restored and now, along with the Jewish school and rabbi's house next door, forms part of an art gallery complex. The walls glow with intricate geometric and floral patterns; stained-glass windows gleam again in the windows, and the Ark, topped by the Ten Commandments, is resplendent with gilding.

The Jewish cemetery, whose oldest legible gravestone dates from 1647, is about 200 yards away, off Havlickova. It has more than a thousand tombs and like the synagogue has been declared a national cultural monument. Some of the crowded old tombstones feature extremely delicate carving and asymmetric shapes; others have an almost clumsy, primitive look. The ceremonial hall still bears an inscription, dated 1838, which reads, "Founded and finished is the House of Eternity. Charity will save us from death."

HOLESOV (HOLEŠOV)–A signpost reading "*Zidovske pamatky*—Jewish monuments" points the way from the main square of this central Moravian town to one of the most precious sites of Jewish heritage in the Czech Republic, the so-called Schach Synagogue. Originally built in 1560, it was later named for Rabbi Shabtai ben Meir Kohen, known as Schach, a noted scholar who served as rabbi here from 1648 to 1663. Opened to the public in the 1960s, this was one of the few synagogues fully restored in the communist period and the only Jewish museum outside of Prague. It still serves as a city-run museum on Moravian Jewry, with an informative exhibit that was extensively revamped and expanded in the 1990s. Located on Pricni street, the synagogue is so understated that you may walk right by it, though its compact solidity is in high contrast to the drab new apartment block development around it. Inside, the walls glow with 18th-century wall paintings incorporating flowers, folk themes, and Hebrew inscriptions. Time-darkened wooden wall hangings bear Hebrew inscriptions from the psalms and other sources, and an elaborate wrought-iron grille surrounds the central bimah.

Nearby, directly across the housing development, is the fascinating cemetery, established in the 15th century. Many of the stones feature unusual shapes and fine carving, but erosion has also taken a serious toll, and the faces of many stones have flaked away. Schach's tomb, located toward the back of the cemetery at the end of the concrete path, is a place of pilgrimage.

HRANICE—Designed by the architect Franz Macher and built in the 1860s, the lovely neo-Romanesque synagogue in this town in the eastern part of the country has long been used as the town museum. It was fully restored in the mid 1990s, and a plaque commemorating Holocaust victims was placed on its facade in 1998. There is a beautiful, tree-shaded cemetery dating to the 17th century on Zborovska street.

HROZNETIN (HROZNĚTIN) (GERMAN: LICHTENSTADT)—The Jewish cemetery is hidden deep in the woods on a hillside about half a mile outside of this town near Karlovy Vary. It may have been established as early as the 15th century, but the oldest tombstones date from the late 17th century. Devastated during World War II, it has recently been restored and cleaned up. The surviving tombstones include extremely fine examples of local carving.

HUMPOLEC (GERMAN: GUMPOLDS)—A small town in the central Czech Republic, Humpolec has a Jewish cemetery dating to the early 18th century, located outside town on Hradska street. The oldest of the thousand or so tombstones is from 1719, and the grandparents of the composer Gustav Mahler are buried here. The former synagogue, originally built in the 18th century, dominates the former Jewish quarter on U Vinopalny Square. It was converted into a church in the 1950s, and inside some of the original decorative elements can still be seen.

JICIN (JIČÍN)–A district center at the edge of stunning hill country northeast of Prague, Jicin was founded around the year 1300 and has a Renaissance-baroque castle and exquisite, arcaded town square. Jews first settled here in the 14th century. The town was the birthplace of the caustic Jewish writer Karl Kraus (1874–1936), who made his name in Vienna and founded and published the influential magazine, *Die Fackel (The Torch)*. The old Jewish street, Zidovska ulice, is located just outside the main square. Several former Jewish buildings remain, including the former school and rabbi's house (No. 100) and the synagogue, which was originally built in the late 18th century and was rebuilt after a fire in 1840. It was used as a warehouse after World War II, though some interior decoration, including a fine Aron ha Kodesh, survives. Restoration work got under way in 2006 to turn it into a cultural venue that will also house a Jewish exhibition.

Jicin has a very interesting Jewish cemetery, with finely carved gravestones dating back to the 17th century. The ancestors of the socialist leader Rosa Luxemburg are buried here. The cemetery is kept locked and can only be visited by contacting the custodian. (Ask at the town information office.) It is located about a mile out of town, at the edge of a dense, dark forest, looking out over rolling fields of alfalfa. Surrounded by a high wall, it is an extraordinary sight—even if you can't find the custodian to let you in.

KARLOVY VARY (GERMAN: KARLSBAD)–There is a small, active Jewish community in this famous spa town in western Bohemia. The Jewish cemetery, founded in 1869 near the municipal cemetery on Mozartova street, has many impressive tombs and also the graves of people from various countries who died while staying at the spa. There are big monuments to Holocaust victims and Jewish soldiers killed in both World Wars. *(Jewish community: ul. Bezrucova 8. Tel/Fax: (+420-353) 230-658. E-mail: jewishkv@volny.cz)*

KASEJOVICE–The charming, 18th-century baroque synagogue in this small town southwest of Prague stands amid the remains of the former Jewish quarter. Distinctive for its bell-shaped windows, scalloped gables, and lavish decoration, it has been turned into a museum that includes exhibitions on local Jewish history and Jewish and local folk art. There is a Jewish cemetery on a hill above town with beautiful 18th-century baroque-style tombstones.

KRNOV (GERMAN: JÄGERNDORF)–A stately neo-Romanesque synagogue with two domed towers stands on Soukenicka street in this town on the Polish border. It was designed by Ernst Latzel and built in 1871–72. It retains important interior decoration and has undergone extensive renovation for cultural use. New stained-glass windows incorporate the Ten Commandments. There is a small, partially ruined cemetery outside town on V Osade street.

LEDEC NAD SAZAVOU (LEDEČ NAD SÁZAVOU)–The synagogue in this town southeast of Prague was built in the 1730s and used as a warehouse and garage after World War II. Located on Na Potoce street, it was restored to its original state in the 1990s and now serves as a cultural center. During the restoration process, fragments of the lovely original decoration on the vaulted ceiling, as well as the painted background to the Ark and painted wall inscriptions, were revealed. The Jewish cemetery, on a hill next to the Christian cemetery, was founded in the early 17th century.

LIPNIK NAD BECVOU (LIPNÍK NAD BEČVOU) (GERMAN: LEIPNIK)–The synagogue in this town near Olomouc was originally built in the early 16th century and is believed to be the oldest synagogue building in Moravia. Located on Pernstejnska street, it was converted into a church after World War II but retains its Gothic vaulting. There are two Jewish cemeteries next to each other off Zahradni street. The old cemetery, founded in the 16th century, was destroyed during and after World War II but restored to some extent in the 1990s. The new cemetery, established in 1883, was partly demolished in the 1980s but also restored in the 1990s.

LUZE (LUŽE)–A picturesque little town in eastern Bohemia, Luze has a well-preserved Jewish ghetto area at the foot of stairs leading to the main square. The nicely restored baroque synagogue, built in 1780, preserves fine interior decoration, including the Ark. Used as a leather workshop after World War II, it now serves as a venue for cultural events. The lovely, walled Jewish cemetery, established in the 17th century, stands, partially overgrown, deep in a forest, reached via a rutted dirt road near an agricultural complex, off the main road about half a mile northeast of town.

MILEVSKO (GERMAN: MÜHLHAUSEN)–There is a very interesting synagogue in this town south of Prague. Built between 1914 and 1918, its design combines neoclassic and cubist elements, including a big portico decorated with geometric forms. Located on Sokolovska street, it now serves as a church. The Jewish cemetery, dating to the late 17th or early 18th century, is located outside town in a wooded area about a mile east of the synagogue. It has a ceremonial hall that also features cubist elements.

MIROSLAV (GERMAN: MISSLITZ)–The walled Jewish cemetery is on the main road south just outside this small town near the border with Austria. Its tombstones date from the 17th century. Some have vivid carving incorporating grape motifs. The cemetery, like the town, suffered bomb damage during World War II. More than 200 tombstones were re-erected during major restoration in 1999, and now members of a local church volunteer to keep it maintained, clearing brush and cleaning stones. (They keep the key, but you can obtain it through the town information office or Town Hall.) A former synagogue, now converted into a community center, stands in a park-like area amid a few remaining houses of the onetime Jewish quarter.

NOVA CEREKEV (NOVÁ CEREKEV)–A very striking, neo-Romanesque synagogue with two fortress-like towers looms over the outskirts of this little town southeast of Prague. Designed by Stepan Walser, it was built in the mid-19th century. Jews settled here in the 16th century, but only a score lived in the town by the 1930s and the synagogue fell out of use. It served as a warehouse until the 1990s, when the Czech Jewish community reacquired ownership and a slow process of reconstruction began. Nearby, on the road to Stanovice, there is a Jewish cemetery founded in the 17th century.

OSOBLAHA (GERMAN: HOTZENPLOTZ)–This remote little town in the Czech part of Silesia is well off the beaten track near the Polish border north of Krnov, but if you manage to get here, you will find the remains of an artistically important cemetery, unique in the Czech Republic because of the strong influence of Polish-Silesian–style gravestone art.

Osoblaha was an important Jewish community in the Middle Ages, but the Jewish population declined sharply in the 19th century and had virtually ceased to exist by the 1930s. The cemetery dates from the 1570s, and the remaining tombstones contain some of the most vivid carving I have seen in the Czech Republic. The Polish-Silesian influence is seen in the exaggerated semicircular top part of the stones, where there is a rich concentration of ornamental relief based on plant motifs combined with lively renditions of Jewish symbols and inscriptions. There are identical gravestones in cemeteries just across the border in Poland (see Biala, Poland, p. 50).

PILSEN (PLZEŇ)–Jews lived in Pilsen in the Middle Ages but were expelled in the 16th century and barred from residing in the city proper until 1848. During this period, Jewish communities developed in nearby villages, and Jews continued to take part in the important Pilsen fairs and markets. Today, famed as the home of Pilsner beer, Pilsen is a bustling center of commerce and industry. Less than an hour's drive southwest of Prague, it has a small but active Jewish community.

The huge, neo-Gothic–Moorish Great Synagogue with two domed towers is a city landmark, at Sady Petatricatniku 11. Built in 1890–92 and seating 2,000 people, it was one of the biggest synagogues in Europe. It was seriously damaged during the war and later used as a warehouse. The remnant postwar Jewish community took it over again in the 1950s and used it for religious purposes into the 1970s, when lack of funds forced them to abandon the building. Long empty, it was partially restored in the 1990s and reopened as a concert hall whose corridors house an exhibit on local Jewish history. An older, neo-Romanesque synagogue, built in the 1850s, stands in the courtyard of the building at Smetanovy sady 5 where the Jewish community has its offices and prayer room. A third, smaller synagogue, built in 1875, serves as a Holocaust memorial: Preserved as a ruin, its roofless walls enclose a monument shaped like a Star of David formed by thousands of stones bearing the names of local Jews killed by the Nazis. The New Jewish Cemetery is located on Rokycanska namesti, across the street from the main municipal cemetery. Established in 1898, it encompasses about 2,000 tombs and also has a Holocaust monument. A small, surviving remnant of an earlier cemetery is located in the Bolevec district. *(Jewish community: ul. Smetanovy sady 5. Tel/fax: +420/377-235-749)*

POLNA (POLNÁ)–A pleasant little town on the border between Bohemia and Moravia near Jihlava, Polna is infamous in Czech and Jewish history as the scene of the so-called Hilsner affair, an ugly blood libel in 1899 that sparked a wave of anti-Semitic violence and is sometimes compared to the Dreyfus Affair in France. Police arrested Leopold Hilsner, a 22-year-old Jewish shoemaker, after a young seamstress, Anezka Hruzova, was found dead outside the village just before Easter. He was accused of murdering her with the complicity of the Polna Jewish community in order to drain the girl's blood and use it to make Passover matzos. After a trial rife with anti-Semitic rhetoric, Hilsner was convicted of killing the girl and sentenced to death. During the affair, Tomas G. Masaryk, the future first president of Czechoslovakia, spoke out strongly against the superstition and backwardness that underlay the ritual-murder accusation. Hilsner's sentence was eventually commuted to life imprisonment, and he was amnestied in 1916.

Jews settled in Polna in the early 16th century, and its ghetto, established in 1681, has survived almost entirely intact. It consists of two areas, triangular-shaped Karlovo namesti, with an old-fashioned cast-iron water pump in the middle, and a smaller, oblong square known as Rabbi's Place, noted for an imposing baroque mansion. The heavy-walled synagogue, originally built in 1684 (but reconstructed several times), stands more or less at the intersection of the two areas. During the war, the Nazis used the synagogue as a warehouse for furniture seized from local Jews. After standing derelict for decades, it underwent full-scale renovation in 1998 to 2000 and now serves as a regional Jewish museum that focuses in part on the Hilsner case.

Polna has an extremely beautiful Jewish cemetery in a low-lying, sometimes marshy area across a small stream just outside town. The oldest tombstones date from the late 17th century. I love to visit there in the autumn, when the play of afternoon light hitting the carved gravestones and reflecting off fallen leaves can be breathtaking.

PROSTEJOV (PROSTĚJOV) (GERMAN: PROSSNITZ)–There is a large, 19th-century Jewish cemetery with a big ceremonial hall and many fine tombs of the wealthy bourgeoisie in the this former textile center near Olomouc. The philosopher Edmund Husserl was born here in 1859, and the noted scholar Chatam Sofer headed the yeshivah in the late 18th century. Two synagogues remain, one, off Husserlovo namesti, was modernized and is used as a church. The other, built nearby in 1836, was long used as a gallery.

ROUSINOV (GERMAN: NEU-RAUSSNITZ)–The remains of an extensive Jewish quarter exist near the market square of this little town near Brno, where Jews settled in the 15th or 16th century. A prominent, freestanding synagogue (now a church) that was probably originally built in the 16th century stands on V Ulickach street. There is a fine cemetery, dating to the 17th century or earlier, on Travniky street just outside of town. It includes about 1,500 tombstones, many of them with beautiful decorative carvings.

RYCHNOV NAD KNEZNOU (RYCHNOV NAD KNĚŽNOU) (GERMAN: REICHENAU)–The 18th-century synagogue in this pleasant town in the foothills of western Bohemia's Orlicke (Eagle) Mountains is the site of a regional Jewish museum. Jews settled in the area in the mid-16th century, establishing communities on the estates of local noblemen after being expelled from Bohemian royal towns. Rychnov was the earliest and most important of these settlements. The Jewish community here was never large: At its peak in 1836 it numbered about 260 people, and only a few dozen Jews lived here in the 1930s.

The synagogue, built in 1782, was used as a warehouse after World War II. It was restored and reopened in 1995 as a complex comprising the museum and a memorial to the local Jewish writer and journalist Karel Polacek, who was killed during the Holocaust. A large, rectangular building with a tall peaked roof topped by two Stars of David, it stands in a plaza on Palackeho street—the former Jewish street. There is a Holocaust memorial on an outer wall. The airy, elegant sanctuary displays photographs, information panels, documents, and other material about Jewish life, history, and traditions in Rychnov and other towns in the Eagle Mountains area, including Dobruska (see p. 166), Skalka-Podbrezi, Doudleby, Vamberk, and Zamberk, all of which have Jewish cemeteries and/or synagogues worth visiting.

The beautifully maintained cemetery spreads out on a slope on U Zidovskeho Hrbitova (Jewish Cemetery) street. It includes about 400 tombstones, the earliest dating from the late 17th century. There are wonderful examples of ornate baroque carving, including tombstones with flamboyantly scalloped edges and intricate, raised calligraphy.

STRAZNICE (STRÁŽNICE) (GERMAN: STRASSNITZ)–A small town on the border of Moravia and Slovakia, Straznice has a remarkable synagogue, cemetery, and ghetto complex, reached down a narrow lane off Bzenecka street. The Jewish quarter developed here from the 15th century, and almost all its buildings survive, forming an evocative, unified whole. No. 1211 was a Jewish hospital and has a mikvah in the basement. The large, early 19th-century synagogue is one of the few synagogues that actually sits on the edge of a cemetery. It has a rare example of a sundial in the upper portion of its flat facade, and a Hebrew inscription runs over the projecting entrance. Long used for storage, it underwent restoration between 1994 and 2001 and is now used for cultural events. There is rich decorative painting on its vaulted ceiling. The synagogue is surrounded on three sides by the cemetery, which was founded in the mid-17th century. Ivy trails amid the graves, and the effect is reminiscent of a church surrounded by an old village churchyard. Some of the 19th-century tombstones bear laminated photographs of the deceased. I wondered at the fate of Josef and Georg Reiss, apparently brothers, who died within months of each other in 1899, both of them only in their 40s.

TREST (TŘEŠT) (GERMAN: TRIESCH)–The elegant, striking-looking synagogue in this town in southern Moravia near Telc was probably built in the 17th century. It features a unique overhanging arcade and stands amid the remains of the Jewish quarter. The synagogue was turned into a church and now is also the site of a Franz Kafka exhibition. Just off the main road outside town and clearly signposted, there is a large, well-maintained, and very interesting Jewish cemetery, probably founded in the 17th century.

TURNOV–In this small town about 50 miles northeast of Prague, there is an easily visited Jewish cemetery dating to the 17th century. It is located on Sobotecka street, partially (and rather disconcertingly) underneath a roadway overpass, and has beautifully carved stones. There is a Holocaust memorial and small exhibition on local Jewish history in the ceremonial hall. In town, on and around Krajirova street, are the remnants of the Jewish quarter, including an 18th-century synagogue, now used as a warehouse, in the courtyard of No. 479.

UHERSKE HRADISTE (UHERSKÉ HRADIŠTĚ) (GERMAN: UNGARISCH HRADISCH)–Driving into this southern Moravian town on the main road from the north, you can't miss the imposing, 19th-century synagogue, now used as the town library. Built in 1875, it was ravaged

The Jewish cemetery in Trest was probably founded as early as the 17th century, when the town's synagogue was also believed to have been built.

during World War II. None of the interior decoration remains, but a display in the lobby documents the reconstruction of the building.

USOV (ÚSOV) (GERMAN: MÄRISCH AUSEE)—Walking through the former Jewish quarter of this little town in north-central Moravia is like stepping back in time. Jews settled here in the 15th century. A self-contained Jewish quarter developed around what today are U Synagogy, Skolni, Nerudova, and 5-Kvetna streets. Straggling up a rise, it still feels cut off from the rest of the town. Dominating the area is a synagogue built in 1784, a large, peak-roofed building whose simple facade is highlighted by an unusual central window with scalloped sides. Damaged by the Nazis, it was turned into a church in the 1950s. In recent years it has undergone restoration and is now used for concerts and other cultural events. During the restoration process, wall inscriptions and the foundations of the destroyed central bimah were revealed. The lovely Jewish cemetery, entered through a large ceremonial hall at the end of U Synagogy street, has about a thousand tombstones, the oldest dating from the end of the 17th century.

This broken tombstone in the Jewish cemetery outside Velka Bukovina bears a carving of the two hands of the Cohen raised in a blessing.

VELKA BUKOVINA (VELKÁ BUKOVINA)–This village in eastern Bohemia near Ceska Skalice is so small that it doesn't appear on most maps. The Jewish population disappeared in the early 20th century as Jews moved out to bigger cities. Here, however, are the rare remains of an 18th-century rural Jewish quarter—a few sagging wooden houses, clustered on a lane near the village pond. There is also a wonderful little walled Jewish cemetery, located in the middle of fields—there's no road, and I had to hike half a mile through waist-high weeds and hay to reach it. The hike was worth it. The cemetery is an oasis, and surprisingly well maintained; there is even a park bench set up outside the gate. The oldest tombstones date from the mid-18th century, and many are decorated with rustic lettering and floral motifs.

VOLYNE (VOLYNĚ)–Volyne has one of the most artistically important Jewish cemeteries in southern Bohemia. Located on U Vodojemu, it has tombstones dating from the late 17th century. Many are gleaming white and characterized by richly ornamental lettering and floral and plant motifs. The synagogue, built in 1838–40, stands on Zizkova street. It was long used as a movie theater and then turned into a shop and disco. Above the entrance there is still a Hebrew inscription and bold stuccowork of lions supporting a crown, apparently once a clock.

ZATEC (ŽATEC) (GERMAN: SAAZ)–Located northwest of Prague near the border with Germany, Zatec has a Moorish-style synagogue with two towers, designed by the architect Johann Staniek and built in 1872. Turned into a warehouse after World War II, it was used in Barbra Streisand's movie *Yentl*.

RESOURCES ON THE CZECH REPUBLIC

Numerous English-language publications on Czech Jewry and Czech Jewish heritage are available in Prague and elsewhere. They range from lavishly illustrated coffee-table books to pamphlets and brochures on individual sites. Especially noteworthy are two encyclopedic guidebooks that provide detailed descriptions and photographs of virtually all Jewish heritage sites in the country. Both come equipped with handy maps. I recommend them highly.

- Jakubec, Pavel, and Blanka Rozkosna. *Zidovske Pamatky Cech/Jewish Monuments in Bohemia.* Brno: Era, 2004
- Klenovsky, Jaroslav. *Zidovske Pamatky Moravy a Slezska/Jewish Monuments of Moravia and Silesia.* Brno: Era, 2001. Klenovsky is one of the pioneers of Jewish heritage documentation in the Czech Republic. He has written many booklets and monographs on Jewish heritage in individual towns in Moravia.

An extremely useful map of Jewish heritage in the Czech Republic can also be found. If you are traveling by car, however, make sure you take another map—the largest-scale map you can find, as Czech road signs can be confusing.

Websites:

- www.chaiworks.org — Jewish heritage sites in the Czech Republic
- www.czechtorah.org — Memorial Scrolls Trust

- www.fzo.cz — Federation of Jewish Communities in the Czech Republic
- www.heritageabroad.gov/reports/index.html — Survey of Jewish heritage sites in the Czech Republic, carried out by the U.S. Commission for the Preservation of America's Heritage Abroad
- www.jewishgen.org/cemetery/e-europe/czech.html — Jewish cemeteries in the Czech Republic
- www.jewishmuseum.cz — Prague Jewish Museum

ADDITIONAL PUBLICATIONS:

- Berger, Natalia, ed. *Where Cultures Meet: The Story of the Jews of Czechoslovakia.* Tel Aviv: Beth Hatefutsoth, 1990
- Fiedler, Jiri. *Jewish Sights of Bohemia and Moravia.* Prague: Sefer, 1991. A pioneering work
- Iggers, Wilma Abeles, ed. *The Jews of Bohemia and Moravia: A Historical Reader.* Detroit: Wayne State University Press, 1992. A valuable sourcebook
- Pawel, Ernst. *The Nightmare of Reason.* London: Collins Harvill, 1988

CURRENT POPULATION: 5.4 MILLION
JEWISH POPULATION BEFORE WORLD WAR II: APPROX. 137,000
JEWISH POPULATION TODAY: APPROX. 3,000

A LITTLE HISTORY

SLOVAKIA BECAME AN INDEPENDENT COUNTRY ON JANUARY 1, 1993, WHEN, THREE years after the Velvet Revolution brought on the fall of communism, Czechoslovakia split peacefully into two independent states. Czechoslovakia had come into existence in 1918, following the breakup of the Austro-Hungarian Empire after World War I. Before that, Slovakia for centuries had formed part of Hungary, and the history of Jews here parallels that of Jews in Hungary proper.

Archaeological finds indicate that there were Jews in what today is Slovakia in ancient Roman times, but the first documentation of organized Jewish communities dates to the early Middle Ages. Anti-Jewish edicts were issued already in the 11th century, and in 1096, Crusaders en route to the Holy Land killed a number of Jews in Bratislava. By 1400, there were flourishing Jewish communities in more than half a dozen towns, including Bratislava, Trnava, Komarno, Topolcany, Trencin, Banska Stiavnica, Devin, and Holic. Jews in this period were barred from many professions and compelled to work as moneylenders or other financial operators. Subject to many restrictions, they lived in their own delineated town quarters, and ran communal institutions with a degree of autonomy.

Invading armies of the Ottoman Empire crushed Hungarian forces at the Battle of Mohacs, in southern Hungary in 1526, killing the king on the battlefield and forcing his widow to seek refuge in Bratislava. In the wake of this defeat, Jews were expelled from many towns. In 1529, a blood libel accusation was raised against Jews in Pezinok, and Jews there were burned at the stake. (Some 16 Jews had been executed after a similar blood libel accusation in Trnava in 1494.) The Ottomans occupied the southern part of Hungary, but the northern part—that is, Slovakia—remained under Hapsburg rule. The Jewish presence here dropped sharply. Barred from living in most towns, Jews only began to return to the region in the mid-18th century, when, for economic reasons, the Hungarian nobility invited them back to settle on their estates.

The Jewish population was bolstered by two main waves of immigration. One comprised Jews from Polish Galicia and Ukraine, who settled mainly in eastern Slovakia. The other came from the West, after the Hapsburg emperor Charles VI issued the so-called Familiants Laws in 1726 and 1727. These laws, which remained in force until 1849, strictly limited the number of Jewish families allowed to live in Bohemia and Moravia and also stipulated that only one son from any Jewish household in those regions could legally marry and start a family. As many as 30,000 Jews are estimated to have crossed the border into Slovakia from neighboring Moravia during this period. Between the late 1730s and the 1830s, for example, the Jewish population of Bratislava more than tripled, from under 800 to more than 2,800. Similar expansion took place in many other towns.

Change came to the Jewish communal experience throughout the Hapsburg domain after the Emperor Joseph II took the throne in 1780 and issued his Edicts of Tolerance, which removed most restrictions on Jewish economic activity and included reforms that actively encouraged Jewish assimilation. The Jewish Enlightenment, or Haskalah, emerged in this period and began spreading its message of reform to the east, triggering religious conflicts between reformers and proponents of strict Orthodoxy; in eastern Slovakia, conflicts also emerged between mainstream Orthodox Jews and followers of Hasidism. In the early part of the 19th century, Bratislava remained a bastion of Orthodoxy, under the leadership of its influential chief rabbi Moshe Schreiber, known as Chatam Sofer, who was one of the most adamant opponents of the Haskalah.

The Hungarian Parliament lifted almost all residency restrictions on Jews in 1840. Soon, Jewish communities were established in all parts of the region. By 1910, there were more than 750 towns and villages in Slovakia where more than 50 Jews lived—and 95 that had more than 200 Jewish residents. Following Hungarian Jewry's formal schism in 1869, Slovak Jewry split into separate Orthodox, Neolog (moderate Reform), and Status Quo Ante streams.

A 1920s view of the Kertesz shoe store, one of the Jewish-owned businesses in the city of Kosice

The end of World War I and defeat of the Austro-Hungarian Empire saw the redrawing of European borders. Slovakia became part of the new Czechoslovak Republic, founded on October 28, 1918. (Other components of Czechoslovakia included Bohemia, Moravia, part of Silesia, and sub-Carpathian Ruthenia, which became part of Ukraine after World War II.) Jews contributed greatly to the economic and cultural development of the new state. Nonetheless, anti-Semitism bubbled under the surface, and Zionism was a popular movement among Jews. On the eve of World War II, almost 137,000 Jews lived in Slovakia, composing about 4 percent of the total population. While there was a substantial, acculturated urban Jewish population, many Jews lived in small towns and villages. Most led highly traditional lives and, particularly in eastern Slovakia, Hasidic rebbes had large followings.

In 1938, with the Munich Pact and subsequent Vienna Arbitrage, Czechoslovakia was forced to cede its western border regions to Nazi Germany and the southern part of Slovakia to Hungary. This area was home to 46,000 Jews, and they suffered the fate of Jews in the rest of Hungary—deportation to Auschwitz after the Nazi occupation in 1944. On March 14, 1939, the remaining part of Slovakia declared itself an independent state, ruled by the Catholic priest Father Jozef Tiso. Hungary occupied the easternmost region of Czechoslovakia, sub-Carpathian

Ruthenia, and the following day Nazi troops occupied the rest of the country, declaring it the Protectorate of Bohemia and Moravia. Tiso ruled Slovakia as a Nazi-allied puppet state during World War II. Until independence in 1993, this was the only time Slovakia existed as a nominally sovereign entity. (Tiso was executed as a war criminal in 1947.)

Some 89,000 Jews lived in the Slovak fascist state. In 1942, after a series of escalating measures that stripped Jews of their possessions and legal rights, the government deported nearly 58,000 Slovak Jews to labor camps and Nazi death camps; the Slovak state paid 500 reichsmarks to the Nazis for each Jew deported, drawing this payment from the looted assets of the Jewish deportees themselves. Other Jews were killed outright. Thousands of others still were deported after the German Army and its Slovak fascist allies crushed the anti-fascist Slovak National Uprising in 1944. After the war, the survivors tried to rebuild their communities, but the communist takeover in 1948 stifled Jewish life. Jewish property was neglected, sold, confiscated, abandoned, converted for secular use, or destroyed. Abandoned cemeteries were vandalized and left to the elements. Some were bulldozed to make way for new construction, and tombstones were stolen for reuse.

The fall of communism and a new independence ushered in religious freedom and enabled efforts to revive Jewish life in Slovakia. Today, about 3,000 Jews live in the country. There are ten organized Jewish communities, linked under the umbrella of the Central Union of Jewish Religious Communities in Slovakia. The biggest communities are in Bratislava and Kosice. The union maintains an old-age home in Bratislava, and there are social welfare services and educational and cultural programs. A number of Jewish organizations—from the B'nai B'rith lodge to the Pressburger Klezmer Band—flourish. Slovakia has a resident, full-time rabbi, but most Slovak Jews are secular, non-observant or non-Orthodox.

JEWISH HERITAGE IN SLOVAKIA

Nearly 700 Jewish cemeteries and about 105 synagogues are scattered throughout Slovakia, though only about half a dozen synagogues are still used as houses of worship. Some synagogues were destroyed during World War II, but, as in the Czech Republic, many more were demolished during the more than 40 years of postwar communist rule.

A number of important restoration and repair projects have been carried out since the early 1990s, with funding from private individuals or families as well as from Slovak Jewish and public sources. Nonetheless, many Jewish heritage sites—including the overwhelming majority of Jewish cemeteries—are in badly neglected, dilapidated, or ruinous condition. Vandalism remains a threat. The Slovak government has listed more than a hundred Jewish sites as national cultural monuments, but even sites so recognized can be found in poor shape. The Slovak National Museum in Bratislava maintains a Museum of Jewish Culture, with a main seat in Bratislava and smaller branches located in synagogues in Presov, Trnava, Zilina, and Nitra. (A new branch is to open in Spisske Podhradie in 2007.)

TIPS ON VISITING

From Bratislava you can easily visit Malacky, Stupava, Trnava, Beckov, Trencin, and Nitra. In eastern Slovakia, Kosice, Presov, and Bardejov are near each other and should not be missed. Six sites in Slovakia have been selected to form a "Route of Slovak Jewish Heritage" as part of a new European Route of Jewish Heritage: the Chatam Sofer Mausoleum, Museum of Jewish Culture, and Heydukova Street Synagogue in Bratislava; the Status Quo Ante Synagogue in Trnava; and the Orthodox Jewish communal compounds in Presov and in Kosice.

BRATISLAVA

(Hungarian: Pozsony, German: Pressburg)

Situated on the Danube River just 40 miles downstream from Vienna, the Slovak capital is a vivid contrast between rococo splendor and communist concrete. Its historic Old Town is a charming, pedestrian-only warren of cobbled streets lined by pastel-colored baroque and Renaissance palaces housing cafés, boutiques, and restaurants. At its heart is Hlavne namestie (Main Square), a lovely plaza dominated by the peak-roofed Old Town Hall, whose tall tower has a cannonball fired by Napoleon's forces in 1809 lodged in its wall. The communist authorities, however, demolished one-third of the Old Town—including most of the Jewish quarter—when it built the soaring Novy Most (New Bridge) and crosstown highway in the late 1960s and early 1970s. On the other side of the bridge is Petrzalka, a vast suburb of anonymous, communist-era prefabricated apartment blocks.

For centuries Bratislava was part of the Hungarian kingdom; it served as the capital of Hungary for about 250 years when Budapest was occupied by the Ottoman Turks. Jews probably lived in here in Roman times. They established a permanent settlement in the early Middle Ages, forming one of the oldest Jewish communities in the area. A pointed arch from a medieval synagogue, bearing the remnants of a Hebrew inscription, can still be seen in a courtyard at Panska 11 in the heart of the Old Town. Eventually, Bratislava developed into one of the most important Jewish centers in the region. As elsewhere in what was then Hungary, the 19th century saw the Jewish community torn by deep internal conflicts between Orthodox Jews and reformers. The influential scholar and educator Chatam Sofer, born Moshe Schreiber in Frankfurt in 1762, was rabbi in Bratislava in the early 19th century. An authoritative exponent of strict Orthodoxy, he bluntly reiterated his position in his ethical will: "Be warned not to change your Jewish names, speech, and clothing—God forbid," he wrote. "Never say, 'Times have changed!' We have an old Father—praised be his name—who has never changed and never will change . . . the order of prayer and synagogue shall remain forever as it has been up to now, and no one may presume to change anything of its structure."

Eventually, Bratislava Jews split into separate Orthodox and Neolog (moderate Reform) streams, each with its own synagogues, cemeteries, and other institutions. Well over 15,000 Jews lived in the city before World War II.

Today, Bratislava has a small but active Jewish community of 600 to 800 people. American-born Chabad rabbi Baruch Myers took up the post of rabbi here in 1993 and leads a number of religious and educational programs. He oversees the community's kosher lunchroom, where visitors may obtain kosher midday meals. In addition to the Orthodox congregation, a liberal Chavurah group is active, and there are many Jewish cultural events and initiatives throughout the year.

Main Sites of Jewish Interest in Bratislava

Site of Old Jewish Quarter: Bratislava's Jewish quarter was located under the looming castle, an ancient fortress that was rebuilt by the communist regime in the 1960s. A partly ruined street called Zidovska (Jewish street) runs right alongside the communist-era crosstown highway and is all that is left of this historic Jewish neighborhood.

Jewish Museum: ul. Zidovska 17—Founded in 1993, the Museum of Jewish Culture is a branch of the Slovak National Museum. It displays its collection in the Zsigray mansion, one of the few remaining buildings from the destroyed old Jewish quarter. Exhibits in the museum include Jewish ritual objects as well as material relating to Jewish culture, history, and traditions. In addition to its main premises in Bratislava, the museum maintains smaller permanent exhibitions in synagogue buildings in four other cities—Zilina, Presov, Trnava, and Nitra. (There are plans to mount a similar exhibition in the restored synagogue in Spisske Podhradie in 2007.)

Synagogue: ul. Heydukova 11/13—Out of more than a score of synagogues that functioned before World War II, only one still stands in Bratislava today: the Orthodox synagogue, designed by Artur Szalatnai-Slatinsky and built in 1923–26. A striking, if austere, building made of reinforced concrete, the synagogue is located outside the historic area of the old Jewish quarter. When it was built, Jews were already well integrated into society at large and had moved to other neighborhoods. The exterior is defined by seven big columns that face the street; interior decoration includes modern fixtures and trim in artificial stone. The sanctuary is still used regularly for services, but the complex also includes an upstairs prayer room used by the small congregation in the winter.

Holocaust Memorial: The twin-towered Moorish-style synagogue used by the Neolog community, once a city landmark, was destroyed when the new bridge and highway were built, leaving an empty plaza next to the cathedral across from the Hotel Danube. After the ouster of the communists in 1989, young people painted a big picture of the synagogue on the pavement, just where it had stood, with the indignant words, "Here there stood a synagogue!" Today, the spot has been turned into a memorial for Slovak Jews killed in the Holocaust. It includes a picture of the destroyed synagogue etched into a big slab of black marble.

Chatam Sofer Mausoleum: On the Danube Embankment near the tram tunnel. The underground mausoleum of the rabbi and sage Chatam Sofer (1762–1839) is the most remarkable Jewish monument in Bratislava. Chatam Sofer was buried in a Jewish cemetery on the bank of the Danube that was founded in the 17th century and used until 1847. The cemetery was almost totally destroyed during World War II in an urban renewal project. The only section that survived was a small plot around Chatam Sofer's tomb. This area, including 22 other graves, was encased in concrete and preserved underground, covered by a busy roadway near a tramway tunnel. It was a dank, eerie place but even in communist times drew a steady stream of Orthodox pilgrims. In 2002, the mausoleum was rededicated after a full-scale reconstruction. It now forms a memorial and monument that protects the tombs and also allows easy access to visitors. A raised bridge and separate prayer room enable Cohens, or descendants of the priestly tribe of Aaron (who are forbidden by Jewish ritual to set foot in a cemetery), to visit the tombs and pray there. *(For access, contact the Bratislava Jewish community: Fax: +421-2/5441-8041. E-mail: znoba@znoba.sk)*

Jewish cemeteries: The vast Orthodox cemetery is located on Zizkova street, on the hilltop above the Chatam Sofer Mausoleum. Still in use by the local Jewish community, it spreads out over the slope and into the distance. Ketav Sofer, the son of Chatam Sofer, is buried here. The extensive Neolog cemetery is located nearby. In the cemetery of the huge high-rise Petrzalka suburb across the Danube River stands a monument to 500 Hungarian Jews massacred at a concentration camp there on Good Friday, 1945.

ADDRESSES OF NOTE IN BRATISLAVA

- Central Union of Jewish Religious Communities in Slovakia: ul. Kozia 21. Tel: +421-2/5441-2167. E-mail: uzzno@netax.sk
- Jewish community and kosher canteen: ul. Kozia 18. Tel: +421-2/5441-6949. E-mail: znoba@znoba.sk. The canteen serves only lunch. Arrangements to eat here can be made through the Jewish community office, at least a day in advance.
- Synagogue: ul. Heydukova 13/15
- Museum of Jewish Culture: ul. Zidovska 17. Tel: +421-2/5934-9142. www.snm.sk
- www.chatamsofer.com — Bratislava Jewish Web portal
- Chez David, ul. Zamocka 13. Tel: +421-2/5441-3824, fax: +421-2/5441-2642. www.chezdavid.sk. A pension, with a kosher-style restaurant, near the Jewish community offices.

NEAR BRATISLAVA

MALACKY–Malacky is located just off the highway about 20 miles north of Bratislava. One of the first buildings you see when you drive in to town is

The Moorish-style synagogue in Malacky was designed by the architect Wilhelm Stiassny.

the lovely, ornate little synagogue, built for the Neolog community in 1886 to 1887 and designed in the Moorish style by Bratislava-born Wilhelm Stiassny, one of Central Europe's most prominent 19th-century synagogue architects. With its cream and orange striped exterior, two bulbous side domes topped with Stars of David, horseshoe arches, and bright blue-and-yellow decorative detail, the building looks wonderfully cheery but totally out of place: an exotic holdover from some prior life amid a concrete urban setting of parking lots, a supermarket, apartment blocks, and other modern development.

The synagogue is now used as an art school, and the sanctuary was cut in half horizontally to create two floors. Still, most of the lush interior decor has been preserved in fine condition and almost intact. The upper floor, used as a concert hall, features a wonderful, ornately carved and painted wooden ceiling. The lower floor preserves the elaborate Ark, with a decorative motif featuring clusters of grapes.

PEZINOK—A wine-producing center at the foot of the Little Carpathian Mountains, just 12 miles northeast of Bratislava, Pezinok is a popular destination for day trips—and is rapidly becoming a bedroom suburb of the capital.

Though the modern Jewish community originated only in the mid-19th century, Pezinok was a major Jewish center in medieval times and was the scene of an infamous trumped-up blood libel case. In 1529, a local nobleman who was in debt to Jewish creditors faked the abduction of a child and charged local Jews (including his creditors) with having killed him to use his blood for rituals. Some 30 Jews were burned at the stake after confessing to the crime under torture; others were expelled from the town. The child eventually turned up alive.

The Jewish cemetery here represents a success story of recovery and preservation. The cemetery had been privatized after World War II, and on my first visit I found it a very disturbing sight. Most stones had been uprooted and piled up. A remaining few formed part of the backyard of a suburban home; they poked up amid fruit trees and garden sheds as if taking the place of more customary garden ornaments, like plaster gnomes or reflecting balls on pedestals. One was used as a bench.

Thanks to the efforts of the Brooklyn-based Heritage Foundation for the Preservation of Jewish Cemeteries, the cemetery has been restored to some extent and now forms a meditative enclave, a secret Jewish space surrounded by suburbia. With the cooperation of the owner of the property, the stones were patched together and reerected in one part of the grounds. It was impossible to place them in their original positions, but, even in a symbolic form, the reconstructed cemetery now preserves the memory of the destroyed community. Access is through a low wooden gate into a cement driveway at Slnecna 4 (a turnoff from the main road to Modra, opposite the Christian cemetery). At the end of the driveway, another gate opens into the cemetery.

The project apparently had an impact on neighbors. When I asked people two streets away how to find the cemetery, they gave me detailed directions, and when I still couldn't find it, a smartly dressed woman, walking down the street, rang doorbells to help. She came with me into the graveyard and wandered among the *mazzevot.* Meanwhile, on the other side of the fence, a man—the owner of the plot, I imagine—was mowing the lawn next to his swimming pool.

ROHOZNIK (ROHOŽNÍK)–With its arched windows, compact form, and decorative vertical lines, the charming little synagogue in this picturesque village at the edge of the Little Carpathian Mountains is a fine example of Slovak rural synagogue architecture. Built in the 19th century, it was the private property of a local Jewish businessman. After World War II, it was taken over by the local municipality and for years was used as a storage place for coffins. In 2005 the building was fully restored, inside and out. The work was conducted by the village, in cooperation with the Slovak Jewish community. Fero Alexander, the head of the Central Union of Slovak Jewish Communities, described it to me as "a bonbon, just lovely." Now painted mint green and pale buttercup—the same colors that appear on the fading walls of other nearby buildings—it stands resplendent on the main village square, a long, tree-shaded space bisected by a rushing stream. A plaque on the outside wall commemorates the destroyed Jewish community.

SAMORIN (ŠAMORÍN)–The lovely little synagogue in this town on the Danube River near Bratislava now anchors the At Home Gallery, a trendsetting center for the contemporary arts. The complex, which also includes the former Jewish school and an open-air stage, hosts exhibitions, concerts, workshops, performances, and other events and also provides temporary living and working space to visiting international artists and writers. "Our idea was not just to save the synagogue, but to do something positive," said Csaba Kiss, who with his Canadian-born wife Suzanne—neither of whom is Jewish—founded the center in 1995. "We have a multicultural place here," he told me. Indeed, prominent guests have included the Tibetan Dalai Lama, who planted a tree in the complex garden when four visiting Tibetan artists created a mandala display inside the synagogue. (Due to lack of heating, the center is closed December through March, but if Kiss is at home, he will let you in to see it.)

Some 700 Jews lived in Samorin before World War II. Fewer than three dozen survived, and no Jews live there today. The synagogue was used as a warehouse after the war and stood derelict for decades, until Csaba and Suzanne took it over. They rent it from the Central Union of Slovak Jewish

Communities, and, like the synagogues in Trnava, Slovakia (see below), and Cluj-Napoca, Romania (see pp. 262–63), which also serve as contemporary art galleries (and with which the At Home Gallery formed a "synagogue chain" arts association in the late 1990s), the transformation of the synagogue into a cultural center retained evidence of wartime and postwar desecration. Geometric patterns still decorate the ceiling of the sanctuary, and there are traces of frescoes on the walls and around the Ark, but they have been left as fragments and shadows, not repainted or "prettied up"; you can still see the scars. "Our idea was not to touch the walls," said Kiss. "They have memories. We can see them."

Samorin's Jewish cemetery is a couple of hundred yards away, behind a wall near the Catholic cemetery. *(At Home Gallery: ul. Mliecnanska 5. Tel: +421-31/562-7999)*

STUPAVA—Jews settled in Stupava, just north of Bratislava, in the 17th century. The synagogue, dating from 1803, is an extremely important building. Along with the synagogue in Bardejov (see pp. 196–97), it is one of only two synagogues in Slovakia built in the Polish style, around a four-pillared central bimah. Long a ruin, it stands just off the main street and is now under reconstruction. (An Ark curtain, or parochet, from this synagogue is on display at the Yad Vashem Museum in Jerusalem.) There is a large and very interesting Jewish cemetery a short walk down the road.

SVATY JUR (SVÄTÝ JUR)—Originally built in 1790 and reconstructed in 1876, the synagogue in this winemaking village has been used for decades as a barn and storage area. In ruinous condition, it anchors a Jewish complex on Pezinska street that also includes a courtyard, rabbi's house (where the family that owns the complex now lives), and ghetto street.

TRNAVA—The back of a Slovak 200-crown note bears a panorama of Trnava, adapted from a 17th-century engraving, showing nearly a dozen of the spires that still bristle over this historic center of religion, education, and industry 30 miles northeast of Bratislava.

Jews settled here in the 14th century, forming one of the earliest Jewish settlements of what was then Hungary. In 1494, 16 Jews were killed in the aftermath of a blood libel accusation, and soon after the entire Jewish community was expelled. Jews were not allowed to set foot in the town again for more than two hundred years and did not return to live here until the 18th century.

Two former synagogues form part of Trnava's architectural fabric, both of them built in the late 19th century. The Orthodox synagogue, a small, rather plain building erected in 1892, is privately owned and remains abandoned and almost hidden by shrubbery behind a tall wall on narrow Havlikova street. The synagogue for the main Status Quo Ante community, however, designed by the Viennese architect Jakub Gartner and built in 1897 just across the way on Halenarska street, has undergone a remarkable transformation into a contemporary art center and concert hall.

The first time I saw it, in the early 1990s, the twin-towered brick structure was a ruined shell, a portrait of utter desolation and despair. In converting the building, restorers (as in Samorin) chose to retain and incorporate evidence of the devastation. The synagogue thus also serves as a striking memorial to the more than 2,000 local Jews who were murdered in the Holocaust. (There is also a large Holocaust memorial outside the synagogue, designed by Artur Szalatnai-Slatinsky.) From the outside, the synagogue still looks like a ruin, and inside, rather than replaster and repaint, the architects conserved damaged frescoes and half-obliterated Hebrew inscriptions. The atmosphere is unique and lends a special touch to performances and exhibitions. The women's gallery houses an exhibition of Judaica that forms a branch of the Slovak National Museum's Museum of Jewish Culture.

Trnava has a well-maintained Jewish cemetery, located on the main road leading in to town from the superhighway. The tombstones are crowded together edge to edge in closely laid-out rows. The ceremonial hall was restored in the 1990s to pristine condition.

KOSICE (KOŠICE)

(Hungarian: Kassa, German: Kaschau)

KOSICE IS A LIVELY CENTER OF TRADE, INDUSTRY, CULTURE, AND COMMUNICATIONS in the far eastern tip of the country. It centers around an elongated main square that stretches for more than half a mile through the heart of the city.

Jews were not allowed to settle in Kosice until 1841, but by the eve of World War II the community numbered around 11,500. Today, Kosice's Jewish community, with more than 500 members, is the second largest in Slovakia, after Bratislava. The Jewish community offices and facilities are centered in two courtyards surrounding a big Orthodox synagogue at Zvonarska 7, just off the main square. Designed by the architect Janos Balogh and built

In 2001, the first traditional Jewish wedding in decades was celebrated in the Jewish communal compound in Kosice.

in 1899, the synagogue anchored the city's Orthodox communal compound. Communist authorities turned it into a book repository. After the fall of communism, it was returned to Jewish communal ownership. The books were removed, but the synagogue stands empty and bare, and in shabby condition; there is no money to restore it. Lovely, Moorish-style decorative painting still covers the inner walls.

The surrounding courtyards—with their balconied buildings housing community offices, a lunchroom, a new mikvah, a renovated prayer house, meeting rooms, and other facilities—form a rare, unified Jewish complex that is highly reminiscent of prewar Jewish life. Sometimes the complex still comes alive in ways that vividly merge past, present, and future. In August 2001 the main courtyard was filled with guests attending the first traditional Jewish wedding to be held in Kosice for decades. The groom was a young American scholar, his bride the daughter of a local Jewish family. Both dressed in white, the couple stood under a velvet chuppah, or wedding canopy, that had been set up in the courtyard. Friends and relatives clustered as close as possible, and some of us stood on the balconies to get a better view. A group of Hasidim visiting from New York bolstered the congregation.

The wedding was conducted by Rabbi Hershel Gluck, a London-based Orthodox rabbi who was a friend of the couple. He was assisted by the

British scholar Jonathan Webber. The two made the ceremony a sort of teaching experience for the congregation, many of whom had little knowledge of traditional Jewish ritual. Webber carefully explained each step of the ceremony—from the bride's ritual circling of the groom to the breaking of the wine glass. "We are celebrating a marriage in the way marriages were celebrated in this part of the world for hundreds of years," said Rabbi Gluck. "Thank God we are here again, celebrating a marriage like this in Slovakia! The message is that they've broken the ice. In a place where for decades people have been battered—by the Holocaust, by communism, by the difficulties of the postcommunist period—it says that positive and constructive things can happen here, too."

Away from the Jewish compound, there are several other important Jewish sites in Kosice. These include:

(New) Orthodox Synagogue: ul. Puskinova 3—This monumental synagogue was designed by the local architects Ludovit Oelschlager and Gejza Zoltan Bosko and built in 1926–27. The building resembles a mythical fortress, and its design, which incorporates stylized battlements, has a medieval as well as a slightly Middle Eastern feel. The splendid interior decoration includes a red marble Ark and brilliant stained-glass windows.

Former Neolog Synagogue: ul. Moyzesova 66—Designed by the Budapest-based architect Lajos Kozma and built in 1927, the synagogue for the Neolog community was an immense structure with a massive dome 121 feet tall. Today, it serves as a concert hall, and much of the original decoration has been removed. A metal harp now tops the dome; the big Star of David that used to be there now stands as a monument to Holocaust victims in the Neolog cemetery.

Jewish Cemeteries: The Old Jewish Cemetery on Tatranska street in the southern part of town was established in about 1844 and functioned until a Jewish section of the new municipal cemetery was opened in 1889. (The old cemetery was officially closed in 1904.) Only a few tombstones remain standing in a plot almost surrounded by new apartment construction, and there is evidence of vandalism. The vast New Jewish Cemetery, part of the big municipal cemetery on Rastislavova street, spreads out over a grassy expanse surrounded by trees. One of the biggest Jewish cemeteries in Slovakia, it is still used by the Jewish community and includes both an

Orthodox and a Neolog section (site of the Holocaust memorial formed by the Star of David that once topped the Neolog synagogue). There are ohels of Hasidic rebbes in the Orthodox section. *(Jewish community: ul. Zvonarska 5. Tel: +421-55/622-1272)*

Near Kosice

BARDEJOV—The center of this beautiful little town in the mountainous far northeast corner of Slovakia is the best preserved medieval town complex in the country. Its large, oblong market square, edged by Gothic and Renaissance houses, is at the heart of an architecturally protected pedestrian zone surrounded by the remnants of the ancient town walls, bastions, and moat. The entire area, including its important former Jewish quarter, have been included on UNESCO's list of World Heritage sites.

Bardejov is on the main historic trade route between Hungary and Poland, and Jews, mainly from Polish Galicia, began settling here in the 18th century. By 1869 they represented about one-fifth of the local population. Many were active in exporting wine to Poland, and the town was an important center of Hebrew publishing. Bardejov was also a center of Hasidism; Jews here had strong ties with the Jews in the southern Polish town of Nowy Sacz (see pp. 36–37) and were followers of the Nowy Sacz rebbe, Chaim Halberstamm, whose grandson Moshe became rabbi in Bardejov in the late 19th century.

All but a few of the more than 4,000 Jews who lived here before World War II were murdered in the Holocaust; only 30 survivors returned after the war. Much of the so-called Jewish suburb neighborhood was razed and replaced by new construction, including the town theater. The surviving buildings are among the most important and impressive Jewish heritage sites in Slovakia—as well as among the most poignant. Located on Mlynska street, not far from the main square, they include the large Great Synagogue built in the first part of the 19th century, a Bet ha Midrash, or study house, dating from the latter part of the 19th century, and an imposing ritual bathhouse. Though still owned by the Slovak Jewish community, they have long been rented out to a plumbing supply company. (Plans to renovate the complex for cultural use were announced in 2006.) Holocaust memorial plaques were placed on the synagogue and the bathhouse in 1992.

The Great Synagogue is one of only two surviving synagogues in Slovakia built in the Polish style around a central four-pillared bimah. Ravaged during the war, it has been used for years as a warehouse for pipes, sinks, and bathroom fixtures, but traces of beautiful red- and blue-colored frescoes featuring stars and floral designs still decorate its arched, domed, and vaulted ceiling. A Hebrew inscription reading "*Keter torah*—Crown of the Torah" remains above the niche that once held the Aron ha Kodesh, and another Hebrew inscription includes a verse from Psalm 113: "From the rising of the sun until the setting thereof, the Lord's name is to be praised." A dedication tablet with decorative raised letters remains over the main entrance, bearing poetically phrased information about the date of the synagogue's construction and the names of the donors who financed it—a certain Joseph Guttman and his son-in-law, Isaac.

When I first visited, an elderly local (non-Jewish) man guided me through the complex. "This was a beautiful church," he sighed. He mourned the vanished Jewish community. "They were—how do you say it?—they were killed here. Men, women, and children. Young and old."

Maximilian (Meyer) Spira, the last surviving Jewish man in town, died in 2005. A retired kosher butcher, Mr. Spira had made it his mission to conserve what he could of other traces of Jewish history in Bardejov. These include a small synagogue established in 1929 by a Jewish charitable organization, Chevra Bikur Cholim. Located in a converted older building on Klastorska street, a few steps away from the market square, it has tall, pointed Gothic-style windows and the Hebrew inscription of its name on its outer wall. Inside, the little sanctuary is fully intact, just as it was decades ago. It has recently been cleaned and opened to visitors; information on the current caretaker is posted on the door. Until his death, Mr. Spira prayed there every day, a lone and lonely figure whose solitary prayers were the legacy of generations.

In the northern part of town, on Ludovit Stur street, there is a large and very interesting Jewish cemetery, whose oldest tombstones date back to the 18th century. There is also an ohel housing the tombs of Moshe Halberstamm and several other rabbis from the Halberstamm dynasty.

CERHOV (ČERHOV)–A newly cleaned up Jewish cemetery stands just at the side of the main road outside this village southeast of Kosice on the Hungarian border; I came on it quite by chance and had to stop: a few tilted stones surrounded by a low, broken wall.

HUMENNE (HUMENNÉ)–This town east of Kosice was home to one of the largest Jewish communities in the region. Jews settled here in the 18th century, and two synagogues, including one built in the 1790s, were demolished under the communist regime in the 1970s. Today, there is little left to recall the Jewish past but a lonely, meditative cemetery with a spectacular view, located on a hilltop outside town.

PRESOV (PREŠOV)–An ancient town north of Kosice, Presov is an industrial and educational center and also has a pleasant Gothic and Renaissance Old Town around its elongated main market square.

Jews first settled here in the early 19th century. Some 6,000 Jews were deported to their deaths from Presov and neighboring villages during the Shoah. Today only few dozen Jews still live here, but Presov's sites of Jewish heritage comprise some of the most important and impressive in Slovakia. Most are centered on and around a traditional Jewish courtyard located on Svermova street, just outside the old town walls. The centerpiece is a magnificent synagogue with sumptuous interior decoration, built for the town's Orthodox Jewish community in 1898. Though still used on occasion for prayers, it also houses a branch of the Slovak National Museum's Museum of Jewish Culture, which includes an important collection of ritual objects and other Judaica from eastern Slovakia assembled before World War II by Eugen Barkany, an architect who founded the first Jewish museum in Presov in 1928.

The offices of the Jewish community are in a building along one side of the courtyard. Other structures that form part of the complex, including the onetime Jewish school and rabbi's residence, have been modernized and now house various businesses. A monument to the 6,000 victims of the Nazi deportations stands in a lawn in the middle of the courtyard: a black obelisk leaning inside an iron cage. Just outside the courtyard, a small, 20th-century Hasidic synagogue still retains a round window decorated with menorah grillework and a brightly painted Hebrew inscription denoting it as a Bet ha Midrash, or prayer and study house. But today the boxy building serves as a private "relax center" with a bar and lounge.

Presov's Neolog (Reform) Synagogue is located on the other side of the main square, at Konstantinova 7. Dating from 1887, it was once a striking building with a slim central tower, little side turrets, and a red and yellow striped facade. Today, a plaque denotes it as a former synagogue, but none of its former spritely appearance remains. It serves as a housewares store. Inside, dishes, pots and pans, and other domestic supplies crowd beneath the arches and vaulting of the erstwhile sanctuary.

Presov has an Orthodox and a Neolog Jewish cemetery, both large and both located on the outskirts of town near the Catholic cemetery. Despite care by the local community, both have suffered vandalism and the theft of precious black marble gravestones over the years. *(Jewish community: ul. Svermova 32. Tel: +421-51/773-1271)*

PRIBENIK (PRIBENÍK)–Pribenik is the end of the road in Slovakia—literally. The little village lies on the Hungarian border in the far eastern tip of the country. I was told that a derelict former synagogue—the easternmost synagogue in Slovakia—stood here, and that's what I looked for. What I found was a pleasant surprise. The synagogue, a simple, rectangular building at the crossroads of Pribenik's two main streets, had just undergone a full-scale restoration. The brickwork gleamed; the Stars of David decorating the simple facade were clearly visible; there was still scaffolding in the interior. "It's beautiful, isn't it?" a man walking by, wheeling a bicycle, called out in a burst of local pride when he saw me taking pictures. He said the building, owned by the municipality, would be used as a museum. "It looks now like it did a hundred years ago," he said. Including the synagogue, he told me, there were "four churches" in Pribenik—Roman Catholic, Protestant, Greek Catholic, and Jewish. "The restoration has brought back what was here," he said. Of course, no Jews live in Pribenik anymore. But I found the Jewish section of the municipal cemetery (just down the road from the synagogue) beautifully maintained, with a multifaith monument to local victims of World War II.

A few doors down the street from the synagogue, I came across one of the more remarkable sights I've seen in Central Europe—a house whose elderly and almost toothless owner, Jozsef Balogh, had spent 25 years decorating with all sorts of trash and found objects. He had positioned them all over the exterior of the house to create a huge, exhilarating collage-sculpture. When I met them in 2006, Balogh was 86 and his wife 85. They, too, expressed pride at the synagogue's restoration. "It's like it used to be, beautiful," Mrs. Balogh said. She phased out for a moment, eyes blank. "The Jews are all gone," she said. "There are none here left." Pribenik's mayor, she added, had wanted to restore the synagogue as a kind of memorial.

SLOVENSKE NOVE MESTO (SLOVENSKÉ NOVÉ MESTO)–Before the present Hungarian-Slovak border was drawn after World War I, Slovenske Nove Mesto was a suburb of the Hungarian town of Satoraljaujhely (see pp. 229–30), a leading center of Hasidism. The compact, 19th-century synagogue at Hlavna 87, with columns in front and a high-peaked metal roof, is now a Catholic church, the only example in Slovakia of a synagogue turned into a Catholic church.

SPISSKE PODHRADIE (SPIŠSKÉ PODHRADIE)–This quaint little town is located under the mighty ruins of majestic Spis castle west of Kosice. The entire town and castle have been recognized by UNESCO as a World Heritage site. Built in 1905, the simple, pale-painted synagogue on Stefanikova street has been undergoing renovation for use as a branch of the Museum of Jewish Culture (it is due to open in September 2007). Much of the interior decoration remains, including the women's gallery, some wall and ceiling paintings, and the structure of the Ark. There is a Jewish cemetery on a country lane outside town—the town information office can provide directions.

ELSEWHERE IN SLOVAKIA

BANSKA STIAVNICA (BANSKÁ ŠTIAVNICA)–The synagogue, built in 1893, towers over the center of this historic mining town in central Slovakia. It has a tall, flat facade dominated by a peaked gable and three grand, arched windows. A Hebrew quotation from the Psalms runs across the facade. The beautiful Jewish cemetery, a two-minute walk from the parking lot under the New Castle fortress, is located on a slope with a lovely view of the valley. It has a Moorish-style ceremonial hall that, like the synagogue, is under restoration.

BECKOV–A ruined Gothic castle atop a craggy hill looms over this quaint little village in western Slovakia, just off the highway south of Trencin. On the slopes just below are two of the most picturesquely situated of Slovakia's Jewish cemeteries. The scene is unforgettable.

Both cemeteries, dating from the 19th century, were abandoned to the elements for decades and suffered considerable vandalism. Now both have been cleared of undergrowth, and some of the toppled stones have been re-erected or repaired. The lower, older, cemetery is right under the castle walls, just off the road, and includes some beautifully carved epitaphs. The upper cemetery is located on a grassy knoll, separated from the castle by a sunken lane. A path leads upward from it and affords a stunning view of the cemetery, the castle, and the village church beyond.

A ruined Gothic castle looms over the two Jewish cemeteries in Beckov.

BOJNA (BOJNÁ)–The two most prominent buildings in this rundown village in west-central Slovakia are the church and the 19th-century former synagogue. Located on the main square, the synagogue has been turned into a pub—from one side all you see is the brash new orange facade. The other part of the building, used as a wine store, still looks like a synagogue, with stubby decorative turrets. The remnants of the Jewish cemetery still exist, on a hill above town, a few hundred yards from the synagogue: a few standing tombstones submerged in high weeds and undergrowth.

BREZNO–The former Neolog synagogue in this small town in central Slovakia has an unusual and rather grand tower topped by a bulbous dome above the facade. It was designed by Peter Payerberger and built in 1901–02. Today, located on Sturova street, it has been nicely converted into a cultural center and exhibition hall. Much of the interior decoration remains, including the women's gallery and the Aron ha Kodesh, which is set back in a deep enclosure resembling the apse of a church.

KOKAVA NAD RIMAVICOU–A sweet little synagogue stands on Sturova street, in the center of this small town in central Slovakia. It has a flat, peaked facade that seems almost disproportionately large compared to the size of the building. The sanctuary has been fully restored for use as a concert hall and exhibition center. The pale blue ceiling with its decorative white stuccowork is especially pretty.

KOMARNO (KOMÁRNO) (HUNGARIAN: KOMÁROM)–There is a small, very active Jewish community in this riverside town on the Danube River between Bratislava and Budapest. A charming little prayer house with a big rose window was built in 1896 as part of the Jewish old-age home on Sturova (Eotvos) street. The complex now serves as a Jewish community center. An Orthodox synagogue, built in 1904, was incorporated into a newly built old-age home on Biskupa Kiralya street. The Neolog synagogue, built in 1863 on Sturova street, has been totally reconstructed and is used as a fitness and sports center. There is a well-maintained Jewish cemetery. *(Jewish community: Eotvos [Sturova]. Tel/fax: +421-35/773-1224. E-mail: kile@menhaz.sk. www.menhaz.sk)*

LIPTOVSKY MIKULAS (LIPTOVSKÝ MIKULÁŠ)–A stately neoclassic synagogue, built in 1846, looms over Holleho street in the heart of this northern Slovak town near the Tatra Mountains. Surrounded by parking lots, modern construction, and a few lingering old houses, it is a magnificent building that was restored in the 1990s for use as an exhibition hall. Four tall pillars support the porch. Inside, the sumptuous decoration, including an elaborate Ark, was designed by the prolific Hungarian synagogue architect Lipot Baumhorn, who renovated the building in 1904–06 after it was gutted by fire. Liptovsky Mikulas was the first city in then Hungary to elect a Jewish mayor; Isaac Diner, elected in 1865, was the first of several Jews to serve in the post.

LUCENEC (LUČENEC) (HUNGARIAN: LOSONC)–The majestic, ruined synagogue in this textile town in southern Slovakia near the border with Hungary stands as a monument to the destruction of a community.

Jews settled here in the late 18th and early 19th centuries and on the eve of World War II numbered 2,200—about 15 percent of the town. The community was destroyed in the Holocaust, and the houses where the people had lived were torn down. Only a handful of elderly Jews live here today.

Completed in 1926, the synagogue—the only surviving synagogue out of the five that once stood in Lucenec—was designed by the prolific Hungarian synagogue architect Lipot Baumhorn and is a typical example of Baumhorn's grand, eclectic style. An immense domed structure, it stands in a sort of wasteland of ugly, communist-era construction. The communist authorities nationalized the building in 1948 and for more than 30 years it was used as a warehouse for artificial fertilizers. Abandoned in 1980, it has stood empty since then, a tragic looming wreck; squatters caused further damage by setting a fire there in the 1990s. The sheer size of the building emphasizes everything: the gutted fixtures, sagging and broken planks, crumbling walls. When I first saw it, in the failing light of dusk, I had an almost physical reaction. It struck me as an unquiet ghost whose agony was accentuated when I compared it to the Baumhorn Great Synagogue in Szeged, Hungary (see pp. 243–45), which has been restored.

The synagogue is owned by the municipality, and local officials say they want to preserve it and turn it into an education center. It received a new roof in the 1990s, but little has been done since then; there is no funding for further reconstruction.

NITRA–This ancient town east of Bratislava is rich in history. Jews lived here in medieval times but were expelled in the 16th century. Immigrants from Moravia settled here around 1650 and established a Jewish community that rapidly grew into one of the most important in Slovakia. Some 4,200 Jews lived in Nitra in 1910, making up nearly a quarter of the local population.

The Orthodox synagogue was demolished after World War II, but the Neolog synagogue, designed by Lipot Baumhorn, still stands and remains a local landmark. Built in 1908–11, it is located in a little fenced yard on pedestrian-only Pri Synagoge street, a narrow, sloping lane in the town center. The yellow-brick building embodies many of Baumhorn's trademark design features, such as the two towers flanking the facade, the ribbed outer decoration, the arched doors and windows, and the domed sanctuary.

After more than a decade of restoration work, the synagogue was inaugurated on September 8, 2005 (the eve of Slovakia's annual Holocaust Remembrance Day), as Slovakia's main Holocaust memorial museum and exhibit. A branch of the Slovak National Museum's Museum of Jewish Culture, the collection here is displayed as an artistic memorial exhibition rather than a didactic, explanatory museum. Called "The Fate of Slovak Jews," it is housed in the women's gallery. The names of all the more than

4,000 deportees from Nitra are written on transparent cases that contain personal possessions or items relating to local Jewish history or the Holocaust experience. The sanctuary itself is used as a concert hall. The walls have been painted white, but one can still admire many of the original decorative elements, including the tall dome and intricate carving on the Ark and on the ribs of the vaulting.

NOVE ZAMKY (NOVÉ ZÁMKY)–Jews settled here in the early 19th century and prospered as Nove Zamky, in southwest Slovakia near the Hungarian border, became a commercial center. The majority of the Jews in the town were Neolog and built an ornate, twin-towered Moorish-style synagogue in the 1860s. This building was destroyed in 1945 by World War II bombing.

The Orthodox minority built their own synagogue in 1880, just off the main square on what historically was part of the hexagonal city bastions. The building survived the war and is still used by the local Jewish community; it was declared a protected historic monument in 1991. A simple, two-story building, it is set in a small, fenced yard. Its facade features decorative ribbing, four oval upper windows, and a main arched entryway flanked by two other arched doors. Miniature turrets decorate the roofline, and the peak of the roof is surmounted by the Ten Commandments. A plaque commemorates the 4,843 Holocaust victims from Nove Zamky and surrounding villages. The synagogue anchors a traditional Jewish courtyard, where there is a small prayer room used for regular services and a memorial to Raoul Wallenberg, the Swedish diplomat who saved thousands of Jews in Budapest. *(Jewish community: ul. Ceska basta 5. E-mail: kehilanz@novotrade.sk)*

SAHY (ŠAHY) (HUNGARIAN: IPOLYSÁG)–Today a sleepy town on the border between Slovakia and Hungary, Sahy was once a regional market center and retains a strong Hungarian minority. Jews were only permitted to settle here in 1840, and the community flourished until the Holocaust—a big memorial plaque erected in the mid-1990s on an outer wall of the town's history museum lists more than 900 Jews deported from here to their deaths.

Two synagogues remain standing amid the remnants of the former Jewish quarter. One, built in 1852, served the main Status Quo Ante community. Located on a square named for the Hungarian composer Bela Bartok, it was recently restored after decades of neglect and now serves as a contemporary arts center, called Menora. Menora was the brainchild of a Sahy-born psychologist and philanthropist, Peter Huncik, who conceived it as a "European Atrium" where regional and minority cultures could meet, mix, and interact. The synagogue is used now as gallery space for exhibitions and events, anchoring a permanent outdoor display of artwork whose themes are heavy with symbolism. An abstract bronze figure, representing the local citizenry, stands in front of the gleaming white facade. Bearded figures top two lattice-like structures resembling gates, which lead into a large courtyard dominated by a fanciful "Tree of Life" sculpture and an outdoor stage. Arched niches along the courtyard walls frame a series of paintings by a Roma (Gypsy) artist, Fero Guldan, that represent the progress of civilization, from Genesis and ancient Greece to Auschwitz, communism, and modern art.

The former Orthodox synagogue, built in 1929, stands a few dozen yards away on Ruzova street. When I saw it, it was empty and derelict, but Huncik has plans to restore it, too, for cultural use.

Sahy has two Jewish cemeteries. The grassy, tree-shaded Neolog cemetery is nicely maintained, with neat rows of 19th- and 20th-century tombstones in a variety of styles. Less care appears to be taken of the much smaller Orthodox cemetery, which languishes, overgrown by weeds, behind a chain-link fence in an industrial area on the other side of town.

SASTIN-STRAZE (ŠAŠTÍN-STRÁŽE)—Jews had an organized community in this small town north of Bratislava in the 16th century, making it one of the earliest sites of Jewish settlement in Slovakia. More than 500 Jews lived here when the imposing, neoclassic synagogue was built in 1852. The building still stands, in lonely disrepair, looming over small houses and the remnants of a typical Jewish complex that once comprised the rabbi's house and a Jewish school. Used for storage after World War II, the building is ravaged, but some traces of the original decoration still remain. These include outer stuccowork and traces of the brightly painted ceiling inside—I was able to peer in through the gaping windows and a gap in a wooden door.

I visited on a freezing day in late winter. Next to the synagogue stands a small pub, painted bright green and called "At the Temple." I wanted to go in and warm myself, but a local woman walking by wheeling her bicycle dissuaded me and instead invited me to have a coffee at the home of her friend Helena, who lives behind the synagogue in what used to be the Jewish school. We sat in the snug kitchen, sipping our coffee and chatting, while the wind whistled outside. Helena, a plumpish women in her late 40s, told me that four owls lived in the synagogue, two adults and two young ones. "They make noise when they sleep," she told me, imitating a person snoring. "When I first heard them, I thought they were ghosts."

After coffee, the women pointed me in the direction of the ruined Jewish cemetery, a few hundred yards down the street from the synagogue, on the other side of railroad tracks just opposite some big industrial silos. The cemetery is fenced by a concrete wall and has a locked gate, but parts of the wall were low enough to look over at the scene: amid leafless trees and briars, scattered tombstones, some toppled and some broken, poked through an untouched bed of recent snow.

SENEC—Topped by an iron Star of David, the sadly dilapidated synagogue, built in 1904, stands empty and abandoned on Mierove namestie, just a couple of doors down from the municipal hall in this small town east of Bratislava. Its facade features Moorish-style horseshoe arches around its windows. Local authorities hope to restore the building and use it for cultural purposes—if they can find the funding.

SENICA—Next to the soccer stadium in this northwest Slovak town is a rare and precious Jewish cemetery. Surrounded by a wall, it is circular in shape with a mound in the middle. The tombstones, dating from the 18th to the 20th centuries, are arranged in circles, climbing the mound, on which noted local rabbis are buried. The cemetery is closed, but it is possible to get a fairly good view over the wall near the ceremonial hall. (On the Internet, it also shows up clearly on Google Earth!)

SKALICA—A peak-roofed fragment of the former synagogue, built in 1760, forms part of the wall surrounding the center of this charming town on the Czech border north of Bratislava. It faces a parking lot that occupies the site of a Jewish cemetery. Just above, surviving tombstones spill down a steep slope below the 12th- or 13th-century St. George's Rotunda tower. The site forms part of an interesting cultural area maintained as a park. Opposite, on another hill, is a representation of Calvary, where Jesus was crucified. A path zigzags up past a series of chapels to a large crucifixion at the summit.

SURANY (ŠURANY)—A large synagogue, built in the early 20th century, stands near the center of this drab town in south-central Slovakia, just off Hrdinov Square. The building has been converted into a culture center,

The huge, domed synagogue, consecrated in 1913, is one of the landmarks of Trencin.

and the modernized sanctuary is used for concerts and exhibitions. The exterior has a fascinating wealth of ornate eclectic stucco decoration.

TRENCIN (TRENČÍN)–Located in the hill country of western Slovakia along the Vah River north of Bratislava, Trencin dates back to ancient Roman times, when it was the site of the Roman military outpost Laugaritio, the northernmost in Central Europe. Jews, many of them merchants and traders, lived here in the Middle Ages but then were banned from the town proper in the early 16th century. In the 17th and 18th centuries, many refugees fleeing the restrictive laws in Moravia found a home here.

A grandiose, domed synagogue, designed by the Berlin-based architects Richard Scheibner and Hugo Pal and consecrated in 1913, dominates bustling Sturovo Square, in the heart of the city's quaint Old Town. (Lipot Baumhorn submitted a design in the architectural competition for the synagogue, but it was not chosen.) Designated a historic monument, it is a marvelous building, a vivid and vigorous mix of art nouveau and Byzantine styles. The large green dome is surrounded by squat towers topped by smaller domes. The spacious sanctuary is used as an art gallery, and only some of the once lavish interior ornamentation remains intact. This includes colorful stained-glass windows and the richly decorated interior of the dome, painted in various shades of blue. In a courtyard outside there is a memorial plaque to the 1,573 local Jews deported to their deaths during the Holocaust. The synagogue complex also includes a snug little prayer room, still used on occasion by Trencin's few remaining Jews.

Trencin itself is dominated by a breathtaking Gothic castle that crouches atop a hill above town. From certain angles, the view of the castle looming up behind the synagogue is like a telescopic vision of past and present.

There is a large, well-maintained Jewish cemetery at the intersection of Partizanska and nad Tehelnou streets. It has thousands of tombstones dating from the 19th and 20th century as well as monuments to victims of the Holocaust.

TVRDOSIN (TVRDOŠÍN)–Built in 1885, the solid, cream-colored synagogue in this town in northern Slovakia near the Polish border retains its original look on the outside, including a Hebrew inscription at the top of its peaked facade that indicates the date of its construction—1885. Today, however, the building is used as a café and restaurant. It is located at the edge of the town center on the Oravske Embankment.

VRBOVE (VRBOVÉ)–A sadly crumbling, Moorish-style synagogue, built in 1883, stands on Benovskeho, the main street of this drab town in west-central Slovakia near Piestany. The distinctive building with slim turrets and orange and red stripes underwent partial restoration in the late 1980s and early 1990s, but ownership questions halted work a decade ago, and the building has been left to deteriorate.

ZILINA (ŽILINA)–Until the 19th century, Jews were barred from establishing a permanent settlement in Zilina, a trade, transport, and industrial center on the Vah River in northern Slovakia. A Jewish community was organized in 1852, and Jews soon became driving forces in the expansion of local business and industry. About 3,500 Jews lived in Zilina before World War II. During the war the town was the site of a major transit concentration camp set up by the Slovak fascist government; as many as 25,000 Jews passed through here on their way to death camps in Poland.

Most Jews in Zilina were Neolog, and the former Neolog synagogue, built in 1929–31, is one of the most significant surviving examples of modern synagogue architecture in Europe. Located at Kuzmanyho 1, it was designed by the noted Berlin architect Peter Behrens, whose plan won an international competition that had attracted a number of prominent architects (including Lipot Baumhorn). Behrens's spare, functionalist design is quite different from traditional synagogue forms. The building has a horizontal facade, pierced by slim windows, below a low dome. Today it is used as a cinema, and only the outer appearance remains intact, but a memorial plaque testifies to the original function.

Orthodox Jews broke away and established their own congregation in the 1920s, and a small Orthodox synagogue, built in 1927 at Dlabacova 15, still serves the tiny local Jewish community. It also houses an exhibition on local Jewish traditions and history that forms a branch of the Slovak National Museum's Museum of Jewish Culture.

RESOURCES ON SLOVAKIA

Pamphlets and brief publications are available for some specific Jewish heritage sites in Slovakia. The most detailed and comprehensive material, particularly for synagogues, can be found in the printed and online publications by the Bratislava-based scholar Maros Borsky of the Slovak Jewish Heritage Center, the leading expert on Slovak Jewish heritage. These sources include an online database at www.slovak-jewish-heritage.org and a very useful map-guide, *Jewish Monuments in Slovakia,* published in 2003 and available at the Bratislava Jewish Museum. (Borsky's book *Synagogue Architecture in Slovakia: Towards Creating a Memorial Landscape of Lost Community* is due to be published in Bratislava in September 2007.)

Websites:

- www.cemeteries.wz.cz — Jewish cemeteries in eastern Slovakia.
- www.haruth.com/JewsSlovakia.html — Information and links on Slovak Jewry
- www.jewishgen.org/cemetery/e-europe/slovakia.html — Jewish cemeteries in Slovakia
- www.slovak-jewish-heritage.org — Searchable database of all known synagogue buildings in Slovakia. Cemeteries and other Jewish sites are being added.

HUNGARY

CURRENT POPULATION: 10 MILLION
JEWISH POPULATION BEFORE WORLD WAR II: APPROX. 650,000
(IN GREAT HUNGARY, APPROX. 800,000)
JEWISH POPULATION TODAY: APPROX. 100,000

A LITTLE HISTORY

Flat, fertile Hungary, cut north to south by the Danube and the Tisza Rivers, has been a crossroads of competing tribes and empires for millennia. Jews lived here in ancient Roman times, well before the arrival of the conquering Magyar (Hungarian) tribes who came from the east in the ninth century, but more modern Jewish history began here with the immigration of Jews from Bohemia, Moravia, and Germany in the 11th century. Several major communities existed in the Middle Ages. The following centuries were marked by pendulum swings from persecution to prosperity, from expulsions to acceptance. A relatively long period of stability for Hungary's Jews began when Muslim Turkish forces defeated Hapsburg armies in the early 16th century and incorporated most of Hungary into the Ottoman Empire, which had long been a refuge for Jews expelled and persecuted in Western Christian countries. Anti-Jewish terror and mass expulsions of Jews from cities accompanied the recapture of Hungary by the Hapsburgs in the late 17th century. Many Hungarian Jews fled south and east with the retreating Ottoman forces, and by the early 18th century only a few strongholds of Jewish life still remained. The Jewish population was bolstered later in the century by Jews from Moravia and Poland, who settled in provincial towns and villages and formed most of the Jewish communities that thrived until the Holocaust.

The Edicts of Tolerance issued in the 1780s by the Emperor Joseph II eased many restrictions on where Jews could live and granted them other civil rights. By 1850, Hungary's Jewish population reached 340,000. Jews played vital roles in Hungarian industry, agriculture, business, and finance, even before achieving full, formal emancipation in 1867. They were active, too, in culture, the arts, and the professions. Before World War I, 42 percent of Hungarian journalists and 49 percent of Hungarian doctors were Jewish, and powerful Jewish capitalists ran great shipping, textile, lumber, railway, grain, flour-milling, sugar-refining, cement, petroleum, and many other commercial empires. From mid-century until World War I, the Hapsburg rulers raised 346 Jewish (or formerly Jewish) families to the nobility.

But anti-Semitism was on the rise, particularly from the latter part of the 19th century. In 1882 a blood libel case rocked the village of Tiszaeszlar, in northeast Hungary near Tokaj; a local Jew was accused of having carried out a murder in order to drain the victim's blood for ritual purposes. The Jew was acquitted, and Christian leaders condemned the superstition behind the accusation, but the affair sparked off anti-Jewish riots in several towns. Meanwhile, Hungarian Jews faced bitter internal conflicts that ultimately led to a religious schism in 1869. Jews formally split into three distinct communities: Orthodox, strictly adhering to traditional observance; Neolog, the Hungarian version of European Reform Judaism; and Status Quo Ante communities, affiliated with neither but generally following Orthodox practice. Northeastern Hungary became a center of Hasidism, where several rebbes had their courts. Neology became the dominant Jewish stream in Budapest and larger cities. Many Jews "Magyarized" and assimilated into mainstream life; many changed their names to more Hungarian-sounding ones: Cohen became "Kovacs," for example, or Klein—"small" in German—became Kis—"small" in Hungarian. Mixed marriages were common, and tens of thousands of Jews converted to Christianity.

In the breakup of the Austro-Hungarian Empire after World War I, Hungary lost two-thirds of its territory. Anti-Semitism grew stronger. Anti-Jewish pogroms following the overthrow of a short-lived communist revolutionary government in 1919 left as many as 3,000 dead. That government was led by a Jew, Bela Kun, and many other Jews held senior positions. In 1920, Hungary reintroduced anti-Jewish legislation with the "numerus clausus" law restricting the number of Jewish students in universities.

At the outset of World War II, Budapest allied itself with the Axis powers and was rewarded with parts of Slovakia, Transylvania, Yugoslavia, and sub-Carpathian Ruthenia that had belonged to Hungary before World War I. More than 800,000 Jews lived in this "Great Hungary" in 1941. Hungary's ruler,

Four young female employees of the Goldberger Textile Factory in 1930s Budapest

Adm. Miklos Horthy, initially staved off the deportation of Hungary's Jews. But after the Germans occupied the country in March 1944, the full-scale annihilation of Hungarian Jewry began. Between April and June, aided by what one Nazi chief called the "zealous and full participation" of Hungarian police, the Germans rounded up more than 430,000 Jews in provincial towns and villages and deported them to Auschwitz. Meanwhile, tens of thousands of other Hungarian Jews died in forced labor battalions, on ghetto streets, or in mass executions. In Budapest, home to more than 200,000 Jews, squads from the homegrown fascist Arrow Cross movement, which eventually seized power in October 1944, let loose a reign of anti-Jewish terror. In all, out of more than 800,000 Jews in Great Hungary before the war, at least 550,000 perished, and most Jewish communities in the provinces were wiped out. The 1999 film *Sunshine* by director Istvan Szabo vividly recounts the multigenerational saga of a Hungarian Jewish family in the 19th and 20th centuries.

Estimates of the number of Jews in Hungary today range from 54,000 to 130,000—or even thousands more, depending on the definition of "Jew." All but a few thousand live in Budapest, and the vast majority are secular or unaffiliated with Jewish institutions. Still, as in other postcommunist countries,

Hungary has seen a dramatic revival of Jewish communal activities and individual assertion of Jewish identity since the fall of communism. Budapest today boasts a full infrastructure for Jewish life: synagogues, schools, a Jewish community center, kosher shops, and cultural programs and institutions including a Jewish university incorporating a teacher-training college and rabbinical seminary.

JEWISH HERITAGE IN HUNGARY

HUNGARY IS A SMALL COUNTRY—YOU CAN DRIVE FROM ONE END TO THE OTHER in a few hours. Still, it has a tremendous wealth of Jewish heritage sites, including more than a hundred remaining synagogue buildings and at least 1,300 Jewish cemeteries. Most Hungarian synagogues date from the 19th and early 20th centuries, and some were designed by leading architects. Most have been transformed for other use, and some are in ruins, but a good number are still used as houses of worship. The Jewish cemeteries range from village graveyards to huge urban cemeteries with thousands of tombs and imposing mausoleums. Though there have been important efforts to fence, maintain, and repair cemeteries in recent years, most Jewish cemeteries in Hungary lie neglected and overgrown. Many cemeteries and many synagogue buildings, even when put to secular use, feature prominent memorials to local Jews killed in the Holocaust. Often these consist of plaques or inscriptions listing the names of all the deported.

Special Itineraries: Hungary's Jewish heritage lends itself to two meaningful itineraries—the so-called Pilgrimage Route, taking in former Hasidic centers in northeastern Hungary, and a trip based on synagogues designed by Lipot Baumhorn, modern Europe's most prolific synagogue architect.

• **Pilgrimage Route:** Northeastern Hungary was the heartland of Hungarian Hasidism and home to several Hasidic rebbes who attracted a wide following. Their tombs can be found in a number of Jewish cemeteries, some of them in picturesque winemaking villages, and pilgrims still visit them to pay homage, particularly on the anniversaries (or yahrzeits) of their death. Synagogue buildings still stand in several towns in the region. The main localities are Satoraljaujhely, Tokaj, Olaszliszka, Mad, Tarcal, Bodrogkeresztur, and Nagykallo. In addition, there are fascinating Jewish cemeteries in the villages of Abaujszanto, Erdobenye, Gonc, Goncruszka, Tallya, Tolcsva, and Zsujta. *(English-language website devoted to this route: www.haverim.hu/indexuk.html)*

• **Synagogues of Lipot Baumhorn:** Lipot Baumhorn (1860–1932) designed or remodeled about two dozen synagogues. Most were highly ornate, and about half still stand, in one form or another. Baumhorn was forgotten after World War II; in the early 1990s, I found his tombstone in Budapest's enormous main Jewish cemetery almost totally hidden by a wild growth of ivy. The stone bears a long list of Baumhorn's synagogues and a bas relief of his masterpiece, the Great Synagogue in the southeastern Hungarian town of Szeged. Synagogues designed or remodeled by Baumhorn can also be found in Budapest, Szolnok, Esztergom, Kecskemet, Cegled, Gyongyos, and Nyiregyhaza. His synagogues also still stand in Novi Sad (Serbia); Nitra, Lucenec, and Liptovsky Mikulas (Slovakia); and Brasov and Timisoara (Romania). Visiting them is a good way to get a feel for the vitality of the Jewish world that was destroyed in the Holocaust—and also to see some astonishing architecture.

BUDAPEST

HUNGARY'S CAPITAL SPREADS OUT ON BOTH BANKS OF THE DANUBE RIVER. THE CITY was formed officially in 1873 when what were then three separate towns—hilly Buda, on the western side of the Danube, flat Pest on the eastern bank, and Obuda, to the north—were joined together. Today, its more than two million people make up about one fifth of Hungary's population. It is figuratively and literally the hub of the nation. Just take a look at a map: all roads lead to Budapest.

With 80,000 or more Jews, Budapest is the biggest Jewish city in East-Central Europe outside the former Soviet Union, but only a small minority have any active Jewish affiliation. Pre–World War II assimilation, followed by the physical devastation of the Holocaust and the systematic stifling of Jewish life under communism have left lingering scars that shadow the dramatic revival of Jewish life since the fall of communism.

Jews lived in the Budapest region in ancient times, but their earliest documented presence is from the 12th century, when they settled in Buda. There they flourished, particularly after the Ottoman Turkish conquest of the city in the mid-1500s. Jews suffered greatly after the Hapsburgs recaptured the city in 1686. Expelled from both Buda and Pest, many Jews settled in Obuda, which was located on the private estate of Count Peter Zichy. Jews were only allowed to return to Buda and Pest after the reforms introduced

The ornate Dohany street synagogue is a landmark in downtown Budapest and a symbol of Jewish life in the city. The arched wing houses the Jewish Museum.

by the Emperor Joseph II in the 1780s. After emancipation in the mid-19th century, Hungary's Jews rapidly embarked on a process of acculturation and assimilation. Following the formal religious schism in 1869, Neology, the Hungarian version of Reform Judaism, became—and remains—the dominant religious stream in the city.

About 220,000 Jews lived in Budapest before World War II. In June 1944 they were ordered into 2,000 houses, each marked with a yellow star, scattered around the city. Tens of thousands of Budapest Jews were forced on a death march toward the Austrian border in November, and the Nazis forced tens of thousands of remaining Jews into a closed ghetto. About 30,000 Jews who had been granted false papers by Raoul Wallenberg and other neutral diplomats were saved in protected houses. Meanwhile, Arrow Cross squads in the city continued bloody attacks; they shot dead thousands of Jews on the bank of the Danube and tumbled the bodies into the river. The Soviet conquest of the city in January 1945 prevented mass deportations, enabling about half of Budapest's Jews to survive the war.

Today, about two dozen synagogues function in Budapest. There are Jewish schools, a Jewish university, kosher facilities, a Jewish hospital, and old-age homes, a Jewish community center, and a wide variety of social and cultural offerings. These range from an annual Jewish culture festival at the end of August, to a variety of publications, to a regular public lecture series sponsored by the Jewish Studies program of Central European University.

MAIN SITES OF JEWISH INTEREST IN BUDAPEST

Seventh District: The old Jewish section in and around Pest's downtown Seventh District remains the center of contemporary Jewish life in Budapest. The offices of the Federation of Hungarian Jewish Communities and other institutions are found here, as are the main synagogues, an Orthodox mikvah (at Kazinczy utca 16), the Jewish Museum, Holocaust memorials, Judaica shops, kosher restaurants and grocery stores, and other facilities.

The Seventh District was the first and most important Jewish quarter in Pest. The big redbrick Madach apartment complex on Deak Square occupies the site of Orczy House, a vast structure built in the 1700s that formed a focus of Jewish life until it was torn down in the 1930s. Within its walls were synagogues, study houses, apartments, baths, restaurants, cafés, shops, warehouses, and workshops. Kiraly street was the Jewish district's major commercial avenue, and the back streets branching off it composed a network of shops, artisans' workshops, and tenements. One series of interconnecting buildings and courtyards cuts all the way through from Kiraly street to Dob street. Called Gozsdu Udvar (Gozsdu Court), it is now being converted into upscale apartments, luxury shops, and restaurants. At the heart of the district is Klauzal Square, an open space fronting one of the city's district market halls that became the center of the World War II ghetto.

The inner part of the Seventh District is sometimes referred to as a Jewish Triangle, because it is anchored by three grand synagogues: the monumental Neolog Dohany street synagogue, the main Orthodox synagogue on Kazinczy street, and the Moorish-style synagogue on Rumbach street, built for the Neolog community but used by a congregation close to Status Quo Ante practices.

• **Dohany Street Synagogue and Jewish Museum:** Designed by Vienna architect Ludwig von Forster and inaugurated in 1859, the twin-towered, richly ornate synagogue on Dohany street is major city landmark and a symbol of Jewish life in the capital. The largest active synagogue in Europe today (and the second largest in the world), the Moorish-style building seats about 3,000 people, and on the High Holidays every seat is filled—mainly by Jews who never go near the synagogue at any other time during the year. This practice held true even under communism, when the sanctuary was dilapidated, with a sagging ceiling held up somehow by plastic sheeting. Today, after a full-scale restoration in the 1990s mainly funded by the state, the sanctuary is breathtaking in its opulence. The women's galleries rise majestically to the vaulted ceiling, and the Aron ha Kodesh and bimah—as big as a small chapel—stand backed by the pipes of a mighty organ.

During the war, Jews were massed in the synagogue and its grounds before being deported; the arcaded courtyard encloses a Holocaust cemetery where thousands of people who died in the wartime Budapest Ghetto were buried. A granite-and-steel Holocaust memorial shaped like a weeping willow tree stands in a plaza behind the synagogue. Designed by the sculptor Imre Varga, it was erected in 1990. The domed Heroes Synagogue, next door, was built in 1929–31 as a memorial to the thousands of Jewish soldiers who died in World War I.

The Dohany street synagogue can be visited during a tour of the Jewish Museum, which is located in a new wing of the synagogue that was built between 1921 and 1931 on the site where Zionist leader Theodore Herzl was born. Security is tight—be prepared to open your bags and pass through a metal detector to get into the complex. The museum grew out of a small exhibit prepared for the great Millennium Celebration staged by Hungary in 1896 to celebrate a thousand years of the Hungarian state. Today its collections include priceless silver ritual objects, ceramics, richly embroidered textiles, photographs, documents, illustrated manuscripts, and paintings and sculptures by Jewish artists. *(Hungarian Jewish Museum and Archives: Dohany utca 2. www.bpjewmus.hu)*

• **Main Orthodox Synagogue:** Kazinczy utca 27—Built in 1913 by the architects Sandor and Lajos Loeffler, the synagogue anchors a self-contained Jewish courtyard, the seat of the city's small Orthodox community. Its design foreshadows art deco, with a flat facade set at an angle to the narrow, crooked street. The interior is stunning, with almost Byzantine decoration around the Ark. In the courtyard behind the synagogue is an outdoor chuppah, or wedding canopy, and the building to the rear houses a kosher restaurant, Hanna, where you can rub shoulders with everyone from trendy young students to Hasidic rabbis in traditional fur hats.

• **Rumbach Street Synagogue:** Rumbach Sebestyen utca 11/13—Completed in 1872, this synagogue was one of the first major projects by the influential Viennese architect Otto Wagner. It has an unusual, octagonal sanctuary, and its striped, Moorish-style facade is broken by tall, arched windows and topped by two slim turrets resembling minarets. Severely damaged during World War II, it was sold to the state by the Jewish community in the 1980s and partially restored in the early 1990s. Work was halted, however, when money ran out. It was returned to Jewish ownership in 2005 and opened to visitors while awaiting further restoration.

• **Jewish Theological Seminary–University of Jewish Studies:** Berkocsis utca 2—Throughout the communist period, Budapest was the only city in the Soviet Bloc to have a rabbinical seminary. Neolog in orientation, it was founded in 1877. The rabbinical school now forms part of a much broader theological seminary, university, and teacher-training center that occupies the old seminary building as well as the new premises nearby. The seminary complex at Jozsef korut 27 includes a small, homey synagogue, which is often overcrowded for services on Friday nights and holidays. *(Additional information: www.or-zse.hu)*

ELSEWHERE IN BUDAPEST

Medieval Synagogue: Tancsics Mihaly utca 26—In the 1960s, archaeologists uncovered the ruins of two 15th-century Gothic synagogues in the castle district, near the site of the first Jewish settlement in Buda. Surrounded by an apartment building, the synagogue at Tancsics Mihaly utca 26 was restored in 1966 to reveal its vaulting and frescoes and opened to the public. Medieval tombstones from Jewish cemeteries that no longer exist are displayed here *(open only in summer)*. No. 23 of the same street was the site of the Great Synagogue, the main Jewish house of worship from the mid-15th century until 1686, when it was burned down during the Austrian reconquest of the city. Archaeologists found shot, cannonballs, and other evidence of the fiery battle that destroyed the building, including the skeletons of Jews who had apparently sought refuge there. The synagogue has never been fully excavated or restored and cannot be seen.

Obuda: A handsome, neoclassic synagogue stands in the northern Obuda section of town, on the riverbank near the Hotel Aquincum. It was designed by Andras Landherr and built in 1820–21. Today it is owned by Hungarian television and only the elegant exterior, with its six Corinthian columns and Hebrew inscription on the portico, remain intact. There is a picturesque cemetery at Kulso Becsi utca 369. The Textile Museum, at Lajos utca 138, is housed in the 18th-century building where the Jewish-owned Goldberger Textile Factory was founded in 1784. This remained a family business for nearly 200 years and by the mid-20th century accounted for 40 percent of Hungary's textile exports. The communists nationalized the operation in 1948 and the factory shut down in the early 1990s.

Kobanya Synagogue: Cserkesz utca 7/9—This striking synagogue in the outlying southeast district of Kobanya is owned today by a Christian organization. Designed by Richard Schontheil and built in 1909–12, it is a fine example of art nouveau architecture, featuring a low, wide dome and decorative cupolas.

Jewish Cemeteries: Budapest's Jewish cemeteries are well worth visiting, both for the architectural and sculptural importance of their tombs as well as for their powerful evocation of the size, prestige, and prosperity of the prewar Jewish community. Here you can see the enormous mausoleums of barons, politicians, and the industrial and commercial elite, as well as the graves of ordinary citizens. There are also some impressive monuments to Jewish athletes.

• **Rakoskeresztur Cemetery:** Main Jewish cemetery, Kozma utca 6—The vast main Jewish cemetery is the final resting place of hundreds of thousands of Budapest Jews. Many of the tombstones are fine examples of 19th- and early 20th-century cemetery art; many are very sentimental, with somber sculptural detail, mournfully drooping floral motifs, sad portraits, and epitaphs incorporating pet names and loving farewells. Along the walls and near the huge ceremonial hall, there are numerous sumptuous family tombs, many of them designed by leading architects. Odon Lechner, the father of Hungary's distinctive art nouveau style, and his disciple, Bela Lajta, employed sinuous lines, turquoise tile, gilding, and brilliant mosaics in their design for the Schmidl family mausoleum erected in 1903. In the 1990s, the list of who is buried here was computerized, so, if you know the name and date of death, the cemetery office should be able to pinpoint the location of anyone whose grave you wish to visit.

One section of the cemetery serves as a large Holocaust memorial. Thousands of names are inscribed on walls surrounding a symbolic tomb. Poignantly, friends and relatives have written in by hand in pencil and ink the names of others whose names were somehow left out of the stone inscriptions.

• **Kerepesi Cemetery:** Salgotarjani utca—Opened in 1874, this is the Jewish part of Budapest's monumental Kerepesi Cemetery, where many national heroes and cultural icons are buried. Some tombs bear proud epitaphs identifying the deceased as a pioneer in the "Magyarization" of

The sumptuous Schmidl family tomb (left) in Budapest's main Jewish cemetery is a fine example of Hungarian art nouveau design.

Hungarian Jewry. Others bear the coat of arms of Jewish families who were raised to the nobility. Many of the elaborate mausoleums are crumbling or totally overgrown with brush. The gateway and ceremonial hall, now partly ruined, were designed by Bela Lajta, one of the most important of Hungary's turn-of-the-20th-century architects. Lajta also designed several magnificent tombs here, some of them large sculptural monuments in black marble. The cemetery was long left totally neglected, but there have been (and still are) periodic attempts to clear the undergrowth. In the rear, almost buried in weeds and brush, are the simple graves of people who died in the wartime Budapest Ghetto.

• **Cemetery at Csorsz utca 55**—Founded in the mid-19th century and used until 1961, this small, walled, and very picturesque cemetery is the oldest Orthodox Jewish cemetery in Budapest preserved in its original state.

Holocaust Memorials and Sites:

• **Holocaust Museum and Memorial Center:** Pava utca 39—Hungary's Holocaust Memorial Center opened in April 2004, during ceremonies marking the 60th anniversary of the deportation of Hungarian Jews to Auschwitz. Funded by the state, the striking complex centers on an ornate synagogue (designed by Lipot Baumhorn and built in 1924) that was used as an internment camp in 1944 and 1945 and stood derelict for many years. Its classic style provides a contrast to surrounding new structures, whose broken contours, slanted walls, and narrowing corridors are aimed at evoking a nightmare world. The complex includes a permanent exhibit, archives, temporary exhibition space, and a memorial wall bearing the names of tens of thousands of Holocaust victims. *(Additional information: www.hdke.hu)*

• **Danube-side Holocaust Monument:** A striking memorial was dedicated in 2005 to the thousands of Budapest Jews shot dead on the banks of the Danube River and tossed into the water by thugs allied to wartime Hungary's fascist Arrow Cross regime. Designed by the sculptor Gyula Pauer, it is located on the Pest side of the river, south of the Parliament building. The monument comprises 60 pairs of iron shoes, lined up, empty, on the edge of the embankment.

• **Monuments to Rescuers:** As many as 30,000 Budapest Jews survived in the protected houses of an "International Ghetto" thanks to foreign diplomats from neutral countries who issued them false documents. The most famous was Raoul Wallenberg, who was sent to Budapest by the Swedish Foreign Ministry in July 1944 and issued thousands of Swedish identity documents, dubbed "Wallenberg passports." Wallenberg worked closely with Swiss consul Charles Lutz and representatives of Portuguese and Spanish missions. Wallenberg was last seen just after the Soviet Army liberated the city on January 17, 1945; he was being driven under escort toward the Soviet border. No one knows for sure his fate. The Soviets claimed he died soon after the war ended; other reports said he was seen alive in a Soviet prison camp long afterward. Monuments to several rescuers are found around the city:

Raoul Wallenberg Monument: Szilagyi Erszebet Fasor. Erected in 1987 in a little park, the monument portrays Wallenberg between two massive stone walls. A street named after Wallenberg, with a plaque, is in Budapest's 13th District, near where most of the protected houses were located. The former Swedish Embassy on Kelenhegy street also bears a plaque.

Charles Lutz Monument: corner of Dob utca and Rumbach utca. Erected in 1991, the memorial is in a little plaza near the Dohany street synagogue.

Giorgio Perlasca Memorial Plaque: Szt. Istvan Park. A plaque here honors Perlasca, an Italian businessman who masqueraded as a Spanish diplomat and handed out thousands of false papers to Jews.

Monsignor Angelo Rotta Memorial Plaque: Uri utca 6. Rotta was the Papal Nuncio in Budapest and also helped save Jews.

Lipot Baumhorn Trail: There are four Lipot Baumhorn synagogues in Budapest, as well as a huge family mausoleum that he designed in the Kozma utca cemetery.

• **Pava utca 39:** The most easily accessible of Baumhorn's Budapest synagogues now forms the core of Budapest's Holocaust Museum and Memorial Center.

• **Dosza Gyorgy ut 55:** Built in 1908 on a busy traffic artery, this large synagogue features typical Baumhorn touches, such as rose windows and sweeping decorative ribbing around the gables and windows. It is used as a sports hall but retains elaborate decoration on the inside of its dome.

• **Hegedus Gyula utca 55:** Built in 1926–27 in a downtown courtyard and still used as a house of worship, this was Baumhorn's first collaborative work with his son-in-law, Gyorgy Somogyi.

• **Istvan utca 17 (Bethlen ter):** This small prayer hall, located inside a big school building and built in 1932, was Baumhorn's last synagogue (designed in partnership with Somogyi). It is still used for worship.

• **Ujhely family tomb (Kozma utca Jewish cemetery):** Bigger than some houses, this grandly domed tomb resembles some of Baumhorn's synagogues.

Addresses of Note in Budapest

- Federation of Jewish Communities: Sip utca 12. Tel: +36-1/322-6478
- Budapest Jewish community (Neolog): Sip utca 12. Tel: +36-1/342-1335
- Orthodox Jewish community: Kazinczy utca 27. Tel: +36-1/351-0525
- Chabad: Karoly korut 20. Tel: +36-1/268-0183. www.zsido.com. The Chabad synagogue is at Vasvari Pal utca 5.
- Pesti Shul (modern Orthodox): Visegradi utca 3. www.pestisul.hu
- Sim Shalom (Reform): Csalogany utca 5. Tel/fax: +36-1/201-7648. www.szimsalom.hu
- Balint Haz Jewish Community Center: Revay utca 16

Kosher restaurants:

- Cari Mama Kosher Pizzeria, Kazinczy utca 28. Tel: +36-1/342-0231
- Hanna, Dob utca 35. Tel: +36-1/342-1072
- Kinor David, Dohany utca 10. Tel: +36-1/413-7304
- Salamon, Nagydiofa utca 27. Tel: +36-1/413-6969. Glatt kosher restaurant next to the Jewish-run King's Hotel (Tel: +36-1/352-7675).

Near Budapest

ESZTERGOM—Built in 1888, the synagogue in this town on the Danube River north of Budapest was Lipot Baumhorn's first. He designed it in the Moorish style, with bright orange stripes, a central dome, fretted Oriental-style horseshoe arches, and bulbous cupolas at the top edges of the rectangular facade—quite different from his later synagogues. Located on Galamb street, it is used today as the offices of a technical institute. A Holocaust memorial, a stark sculpture of an anguished human figure, stands in front of the building.

LOVASBERENY (LOVASBERÉNY)—The picturesque and beautifully maintained old Jewish cemetery sprawls up a slope on the road to Bickse, just outside this village between Budapest and Lake Balaton. Jews from Moravia settled here in the early 18th century, under the protection of the local Count Cziraky (whose run-down palace forms the centerpiece of the village). Lovasbereny became a market center in 1765, and the Jewish community prospered. Restoration work on the Jewish cemetery, listed as a cultural monument since the 1980s, began in 2001 thanks to the efforts of a local foundation and a Catholic parish in Germany.

SZENTENDRE—Just north of Budapest on the Danube River, Szentendre has long been an artists' colony and magnet for tourists. The narrow streets of its quaint old center are lined with boutiques, art galleries, and craft shops—and generally filled with tour groups and day-trippers from the capital.

Jews settled here in the 18th century. The Szanto Memorial and Prayer House, a small Jewish museum-cum-synagogue, was founded in 1998 in the heart of the old town to serve as a memorial for the Jewish community. Located at Alkotmany utca 3, it stands in the courtyard of the former home of Laszlo Szanto and his wife, who were among the 250 Jews from Szentendre and surrounding areas deported to their deaths in June 1944. Szanto's surviving descendents created the center, which includes a tiny prayer room, an exhibition on local Jewish history, and a Holocaust memorial. Since the memorial opened, Szentendre's long-derelict Jewish cemetery, located off Mehesz street, has been cleared of a jungle of undergrowth.

Several of the artists who had studios in Szentendre before World War II were Jewish. A museum at the corner of Kigyo and Hunyadi streets is dedicated to Lajos Vajda, who was killed in the Holocaust. Another museum, at Bogdanyi utca 12, houses the work of the Jewish husband and wife artists Imre Amos and Margit Anna. Amos, a noted surrealist, died during the Holocaust in 1944. He was deported to work in a forced labor brigade and secretly sketched what he saw; many of the works in the museum depict the horrors of those years. Margit Anna survived the war and was known for her colorful works employing puppet figures.

TOKAJ

With its winding, narrow streets, pastel baroque architecture and numerous wine cellars, Tokaj is the capital of Hungary's most renowned wine region and gave its name to the semisweet amber vintage described as "the king of wines and the wine of kings." Wine production in the Tokaj region dates back nearly a thousand years. Jews began settling here in the 18th century. With wine an important part of Jewish ritual, Jews soon became involved in the wine trade, and Jewish vintners and wine merchants in Tokaj and nearby villages once bought, sold, produced, and transported wine to much of Central and Eastern Europe. The municipal museum displays all sorts of tools and material depicting how wine is made, and it also has a corner devoted to Jewish traditions and ritual objects. About 800 Jews lived here before World War II. "I remember Friday nights," an elderly woman once told me. "It was very quiet in the town. Before the Sabbath came, women would make *solet* (cholent). Everything was made ready on Friday evening; in every home candles were lit."

Tokaj's first synagogue, built in the mid-1700s, was destroyed in a fire in 1890. It was replaced by the grand edifice that still stands—it could seat a thousand people in its heyday and was so ornately decorated that it was considered the "jewel box" of the town. The synagogue was wrecked during World War II, and in the 1960s it was used as a warehouse. An abortive attempt to restore it left it an almost total ruin, without a roof, for years. Today, the building stands proud again, after a restoration completed in 2006 that transformed it into a conference and culture center.

Only two or three Jews now live in Tokaj. But, thanks to a chance encounter between two childhood friends, Tokaj now has a new spiritual infrastructure. Lajos Lowy, a local shopkeeper, and Tokaj-born Morton Berkovits, who runs a kosher food business in Brooklyn, were friends as boys, when

Berkovits's father served as the rabbi for the survivor Jewish community after World War II. But the Berkovits family emigrated to the United States, and most other surviving Jews also moved away. The Lowys remained in Tokaj; until his death in 1981, Lowy's own father, an Auschwitz survivor, conducted services in a little prayer house next to the then derelict Great Synagogue.

Over the years, Lowy dedicated his spare time to preserving the memory of local Jews. He documented Jewish cemeteries in the area, collected photographs and archival material, and tried to help Jewish visitors. He and Berkovits met again several years ago. The two kept in touch, and step by step Berkovits helped Lowy reconnect with the religious life he had lived in his youth. He then financed the complete restoration of the Tokaj prayer house, refurbishing the prayer room and adding a kosher kitchen, a dining and study room, and a library. The renovated building, a simple, one-story structure built in 1928, reopened in 2002, primarily to serve groups of Hasidim visiting the tombs of the local rabbis. In 2004, Lowy, Berkovits, and several others formed an association to organize these pilgrimages and monitor and raise money to restore Jewish cemeteries in the region.

Tokaj's tree-shaded old cemetery, founded in the mid-18th century, is situated on the triangle of land at the confluence of the Bodrog and Tisza Rivers. To reach it, you must take a ferry. This was the original burying place for Tokaj Jews, and the oldest decipherable tombstone dates from 1825; the last burial was in 1878. It is a beautiful place, quiet and hushed, shaded by plum trees whose fruit hangs like purple jewels in the early autumn. The new cemetery, with several hundred tombstones dating back to the 19th century, climbs the slope of Mount Kopasz, along the river just outside town on the road to Bodrogkeresztur. *(Contact: Lajos Lowy, Rakoczi utca 41. Tel: +36-47/352-737)*

Near Tokaj

BODROGKERESZTUR (BODROGKERESZTÚR)–The Hasidic rebbe Saje Steiner (1851–1925) had his court in this winemaking village, and pilgrims still come in great numbers to pay their respects at his tomb in the Jewish cemetery, high on a vineyard-covered hill overlooking the village. The first time I tried to get up there, the road was a river of mud; I got hopelessly stuck and never reached the cemetery. Today there is a paved road. Follow the sign marked "Reb Sajele" and keep going up. The cemetery is surrounded by a fence made of concrete slabs that look like tombstones and affords a beautiful view of the lush surrounding landscape. A yellow, barnlike former synagogue, built in 1906, stands behind the house at Kossuth utca 30. Steiner's home, at Kossuth utca 65, is maintained as a memorial and can also be visited. (The key is kept at house No. 48, across the street.)

KISVARDA (KISVÁRDA)–Jews settled in this town about 45 miles northeast of Tokaj in the 18th century, with the permission of the local landlords, the Esterhazy family. In 1941, the nearly 3,800 Jews made up a quarter of the local population. About 800 survived the Holocaust, but few live in Kisvarda today. The imposing brick synagogue, designed by Ferenc Grosz and built in 1901, now houses the regional museum and includes a small Judaica exhibition, as well as a large Holocaust memorial listing all the deportees. The large, recently restored and well-maintained Jewish cemetery, with many tall gravestones in pink marble, is located near the Christian cemetery.

MAD (MÁD)–The baroque synagogue in this winemaking village is my architectural amour. I fell in love with it from photographs before I ever saw it. Built in the 1790s, it rises on a hill above the red-tiled roofs of the village, forming an interfaith triangle with the Roman Catholic and Protestant churches nearby.

Jews from Poland settled here in the early 18th century and became active in the wine trade. At its height, the Jewish community numbered about 800; all were deported to Auschwitz. When I first saw the synagogue, in 1990, it had long stood empty. The two arched windows in its elegant, scalloped facade gaped open, like eyes, and the interior bore sad, shadowy traces of once sumptuous decoration. Today, fully restored, it is one of Hungary's cultural treasures and, along with the L-shaped, arcaded rabbi's house and yeshivah standing next to it, forms one of Hungary's most important complexes of Jewish buildings. The restoration, completed in 2004, won a European Prize for Cultural Heritage from Europa Nostra, the pan-European Federation for Heritage. The work was carried out by the Budapest-based architects Peter Wirth and his wife, Agnes Benko. (Wirth had won a Europa Nostra award in 1988 for his restoration of the synagogue in Apostag; see pp. 231–32). Most of the surviving decoration dated from the 19th century and was restored as accurately as possible. The walls now glow with intricate designs in blue, pink, tan, and cream. At the same time, the Ark was restored to how it looked in the baroque period. Trompe l'oeil draperies flank it, and gilded carvings of lions and griffins rear above amid pink flowers, silver ornaments, and a blue gilded crown. The four simple columns of the raised bimah support the central vaulting. Plaques list the names of Holocaust victims, and in a side room, a small exhibit recounts local Jewish history.

Mad also has a wonderful Jewish cemetery, on a hillside just outside the town center. The gravestones feature some exceptionally fine carving, and some still bear traces of polychrome painting.

MISKOLC–Miskolc, about 30 miles west of Tokaj, is an important hub of commerce and transport and the country's main center of industry. Jews settled here in the 18th century on the estates of local noblemen and eventually made up 20 percent of the local population. Hungary's first Jewish commercial school was founded here in 1848. As many as 15,000 Jews lived here on the eve of World War II. Only 105 survived the Holocaust, but the community swelled to more than 2,000 people after the war's end when Miskolc became a center for Jews returning from concentration camps. Today a few hundred Jews live here. The grand Orthodox synagogue, which has been undergoing fitful renovation, dominates a Jewish compound on Kazinczy street that includes a kosher lunchroom, a small guesthouse, and a Holocaust memorial. (The community has a mikvah at a different site—ask at the Jewish community office.) Built between 1856 and 1863, the synagogue was designed by Ludwig von Forster, the same architect who designed the Dohany street synagogue in Budapest. The opulent interior includes graceful columns supporting lovely vaulting, completely covered by elaborate Moorish-style geometric designs. The Jewish cemetery, founded in 1759, sprawls over Avas hill, at the end of Mendikas street. It has Holocaust memorials and some beautifully carved 19th-century gravestones, and the hilltop site affords an extraordinary view of the city. *(Jewish community: Kazinczy utca 7. Tel: +36-46/344-884)*

NAGYKALLO (NAGYKÁLLÓ)–Nagykallo was the seat of the first Hasidic rebbe to live permanently in Hungary, Isaac Taub (also known as Isaac Yitzhak Kallo), whose tomb is here in the Jewish cemetery. Born in 1851, Taub was rabbi in Nagykallo from 1781 until his death in 1821. He was a disciple of Shmuel Shmelke Horowitz of Nikolsburg (today Mikulov, Czech Republic) and Elimelekh of Lizhensk (today Lezajsk, Poland). Reb Isaac was famous for his mystical interpretation of dreams and, especially, his songs. His most famous song, "*Szol a Kakas Mar*—The Cock Is Always Crowing," is a standard among Hungarian Jews and non-Jews alike.

NYIREGYHAZA (NYIREGYHÁZA)—The synagogue on busy Martyrs Square (Martirok tere) was designed by Lipot Baumhorn and built in 1924–32 and is still used by the local Jewish community. The interior decoration is sumptuous; colors are bright and big golden lions rear on the eastern wall flanking the Ark. The congregation's offices and other facilities, including a prayer room and a small exhibition on Jewish traditions, are in the building next door. The well-maintained Jewish cemetery on Kotaji street, on the way to Debrecen, was established in 1840 and includes an Orthodox and a Status Quo Ante section. There is a large Holocaust memorial. *(Jewish community: Martirok tere 6. Tel: +36-42/417-939)*

OLASZLISZKA—Olasz in Hungarian means "Italy," and the story goes that this quaint winemaking village near Tokaj got its name from Italian winemakers brought here in the Middle Ages. In the 19th century, it was the seat of the Hasidic rebbe Zvi Hirsch Friedmann (1808–1874), a disciple of Moses Teitelbaum of nearby Satoraljaujhely, the major Hasidic figure in Hungary. Pilgrims still visit his tomb in the Jewish cemetery, a fascinating graveyard now protected by a fortresslike wall. Many of the carved tombstones bear traces of painted decoration. Many were shattered by war and vandalism, but considerable restoration work has been carried out.

Like many tzaddikim, Friedmann incorporated symbolic actions in everyday life. When the synagogue was built here in the mid-19th century, the last stone was never laid; this was to recall the destruction of the Temple in Jerusalem. Today, all that is left of the building is its half-destroyed eastern wall at one end of a fenced-off vacant lot in the middle of town. The niche for the Ark is clearly visible, but each time I visit, I find that more of the wall has crumbled away; it is, people say, a "wailing wall" for Hungarian Jewry.

SATORALJAUJHELY (SÁTORALJAÚJHELY)—Today a sleepy town on the Slovak border, Satoraljaujhely was a cradle of Hasidism in Hungary, most notably the seat of the 19th-century tzaddik Moses Teitelbaum. Jews settled here in the early 18th century, and more than 4,000 Jews lived here before World War II. Satoraljaujhely was divided between Hungary and Czechoslovakia after World War I, with most of the urban center remaining in Hungary. The big 19th-century synagogue used by the Status Quo Ante congregation, now transformed out of recognition, still stands at Dozsa Gyorgy utca 13. Another old synagogue remains across the border, in what is now the Slovak town of Slovenske Nove Mesto (see pp. 199–200).

Moses Teitelbaum headed the Jewish community here for more than 30 years and founded an influential Hasidic dynasty. Believed to have been born in 1759 in Przemysl, Poland, he studied with the charismatic Hasidic master known as the Seer of Lublin and was said to be a descendant of the great 16th-century rabbi of Cracow, Moses Isserles, or Remuh. Teitelbaum settled in Satoraljaujhely in 1808. Revered as a mystical healer, he inspired many legends and drew a huge following. (One legend has it that Lajos Kossuth, the great Hungarian national leader, visited Teitelbaum as a boy and received his blessing.) Teitelbaum died in 1841, and each year, on the anniversary of his death—the 28th of Tammuz in the Jewish calendar—Jews from all over eastern Europe flocked to his tomb. In the 1920s, the nearby border would be open so that pilgrims could cross without transit documents, and the scene at the tomb resembled a fair, with crowded stalls selling prayer books and other religious items. Teitelbaum's tomb in the Old Jewish Cemetery is still a major focus for religious pilgrims. The cemetery is right on the main road, Route 37, just south of the town center, and a wall and fence enclose the weathered gravestones. Teitelbaum's tomb is at the center of an elaborate domed ohel complex, which includes a new ritual bath and hospitality center for pilgrims.

There is another Jewish cemetery at the opposite end of town, on the main road leading to the border crossing. This is the New Jewish Cemetery; with 19th- and 20th-century graves spread out on a hillside. One of the people buried here is Rozsika Roth, the woman who introduced me to Satoraljaujhely, a Holocaust survivor who lost all her family to the Nazis. Every doorpost of her rambling, ground-floor apartment bore a mezuzah, and she kissed the one on the outer door repeatedly whenever she entered the house. Pictures of famous tzaddikim were lined up on her dressing table; candlesticks stood on shelves; her refrigerator was stocked with kosher meat brought by a ritual butcher who made his rounds twice a month. When I visited her once, unannounced, on a Friday afternoon, four round, braided loaves of challah were rising on a baking tray, ready for the oven. When a prayer book got knocked off the table, she quickly picked it up and kissed it. "Are you married?" was the first thing she asked me, in Yiddish, when we met. "Do you maintain *Yiddishkeit?*"

Mrs. Roth died early one Saturday morning, on August 26, 1995; she was murdered. Robbers broke into her home, tied her up, gagged her, and ransacked the apartment. Apparently she choked to death. If you visit the New Jewish Cemetery in Satoraljaujhely, look for her grave and spare her a thought, and a thought for her lost world.

TARCAL—The little baroque village synagogue here, the "sister" to the synagogue in nearby Mad (see pp. 227–28), has been remodeled for use as a gallery and artists' residence. Almost all the Jewish ornamentation has been removed, but still conserved above the entrance is a weathered Hebrew inscription from Psalm 118: "This is the gate of the Lord, let the righteous enter thereby." There is also a newly placed memorial plaque to the destroyed Jewish community. Two fenced Jewish cemeteries with weathered stones stand just outside the town limits.

ELSEWHERE IN HUNGARY

ABONY—The synagogue in this quiet little town some 50 miles southeast of Budapest has always struck me as one of the most evocative Jewish relics in the country. It is not the most ruined synagogue building in Hungary, nor the most beautiful or the most ravaged. Somehow, though, it reminds me of a living creature. It seems to feel and actually to mourn, as if it were alive.

Located on Deak Ferenc street, the synagogue dominates its immediate neighborhood. Designed by the architect Andras Landherr and built in 1825, it is a beautifully pure, serenely classical structure with four Corinthian columns supporting the portico over the main entrance. Long used as a warehouse, it is listed now as a protected cultural monument but still stands empty, awaiting repair. The mustard-and-orange stucco is falling away, and flimsy looking wooden scaffolding somehow supports the front portico. Torn green mosquito netting flaps from the side windows. Several other former Jewish buildings, including the former Jewish school, still stand in the synagogue compound.

Jews settled in Abony in the mid-18th century, and about 500 lived here before World War II. The tree-shaded Jewish cemetery is located behind a chain-link fence on Route 4, on the way to Szolnok. It was early spring when I last visited. Ivy trailed from some of the tombstones, and the bright green grass was ablaze with blue and purple wildflowers.

APOSTAG—Jews lived in Apostag, an out-of-the-way village on the Danube, about 45 miles south of Budapest, in the 17th century—there is a tombstone dating from 1650 in the Jewish cemetery, but the major wave of Jewish settlement came around 1760. The Jewish population dwindled sharply in the late 19th century, and by the outbreak of World War II, only 150 Jews still lived here.

The synagogue, built in 1822, is a large, rectangular structure with a peaked roof, whose simple exterior hides colorful interior decoration. Looted and ransacked during and after World War II, it was listed as a historic monument but long used as a warehouse. By the early 1980s it was in such bad shape that local authorities wanted to pull it down. Peter Wirth, an architect and monuments preservation expert, was called to the scene from Budapest and became convinced that the building must be saved. He still recalls an elderly local peasant telling him how he remembered from his childhood the "mysterious building with an ornamented ceiling, beautiful like the starry sky."

In what was then, under communism, a rare example of such cooperation, local and county officials, joined by ordinary citizens, pitched in on the total restoration of the building as a local library and culture center. The classical and late baroque ornamentation was restored, including wall paintings, decorative stucco reliefs, the elegant, four-pillar central bimah, and the ornate Aron ha Kodesh, which is surrounded by a beautiful fresco of pulled-back curtains. The restoration won an international award, the Europa Nostra Prize in 1988—an award granted both to Wirth himself as well as to the entire village of Apostag. (Wirth has since worked on a number of other synagogue restorations and in 2005 won a second Europa Nostra Prize for his restoration of the synagogue in Mad; see pp. 227–28.)

The care with which the synagogue was restored contrasts sharply with the state of the Jewish cemetery, which lies, abandoned and devastatingly overgrown, a couple of hundred yards away across a grassy park. There are some fine tombstones here, and I tried to pick my way into the thicket to see them, following narrow trails made, I guess, by animals. It was early spring, and even though new vegetation had only begun to sprout, I could scarcely penetrate the dense brush and saplings grown up around the stones.

BAJA—With its beautiful, big central plaza right on the Danube River, about 70 miles south of Budapest, Baja was long a vital commercial center. Jews settled here around 1725. The community grew rapidly and by 1910 made up nearly a fifth of the local population.

The graceful neoclassic synagogue on Munkacsy street, built in 1845, was restored in 1986 to virtually its original appearance. Stars of David top the peaked roof, and a Hebrew inscription runs across the facade over the pillared entryway. Inside, the vaulted ceiling exhibits beautiful geometric painting, and the ornate Aron ha Kodesh, painted red, green, blue, and gold, is framed by a frescoed curtain held in place by gilded eagles and topped by gilded lions supporting a crown. The synagogue is now used as the town library, and the sensitive reconstruction won the Hungarian Architects' Prize for Restoration.

A large Holocaust memorial occupies part of the surrounding walled garden. An arched arcade protects inscriptions listing the names of each of the approximately 3,000 Jews from Baja and the surrounding communities who were deported to their deaths in Auschwitz in 1944. There is also a large Jewish cemetery, dating to about 1750, outside of town on the road to Szeged.

BALASSAGYARMAT—The tree-shaded Jewish cemetery in this ancient trading center on the Slovak border north of Budapest is located on Temeto street near the town's Christian cemeteries. With about 3,000 tombstones, it is one of the best maintained Jewish cemeteries in Hungary and has been declared a national historic monument. The sole surviving synagogue stands at Hunyadi utca 24. Built in the 1920s, it has a simple, red-and-white facade and since 2000 has housed the Ipoly Region Jewish Collection and Exhibition. Notices at the synagogue and the cemetery provide contact information for people who keep the keys and can help with visits.

BONYHAD (BONYHÁD)–In the mid-18th century, Jews, mainly from Germany, were invited to settle in this small town in southern Hungary by the local landowners, who granted them protection. The Jewish community grew quickly, and by 1828 more than 1,600 Jews lived here. Before World War II, the town's more than 1,100 Jews represented about 15 percent of the local population.

The massive Old Synagogue was built in 1795. Now very dilapidated, it serves as a warehouse; a faded Star of David and Hebrew inscription can still be seen above the arched main portal. The building has a simple exterior with a peaked roof, and is one the few Hungarian synagogues—like those in Mad and Apostag—to have been built around a four-pillared central bimah. The synagogue stands amid the remains of the former Jewish quarter at the edge of a grassy open space called Maritrok tere, or Martyrs Square. Long rundown, the area is changing, with new shops and commercial buildings. The former yeshivah, a yellow building next to the synagogue, is now a dwelling. A few steps away, on a side street on the other side of Rakoczi street, stands

A young woman walks past the old synagogue in Bonyhad, which stands in a plaza off the main street.

another synagogue, built in 1924. It has been totally reconstructed and serves as a used furniture store.

Bonyhad has two well-kept Jewish cemeteries. The Orthodox cemetery is at Kossuth utca 8, next to a big school. I find it a rather amazing and somewhat uncomfortable place. The caretakers who live in a cottage at the edge of the cemetery take their job so seriously that the ground between the tombstones looks shaven. Many of the mazzevot are of bright pink marble, their inscriptions emphasized with black paint. To me, this house of the living seems sterile and rather dehumanized (but then again I also feel uncomfortable in the homes of people who keep everything squeaky clean and rigorously in place). My latest visit was in early spring, and I think this timing emphasized my feeling of discomfort. Life was burgeoning around me. Trees were in blossom; birds were twittering; two cats were rolling in the grass; and, right there, with great fanfare, a rooster was mounting a hen.

The larger Neolog cemetery has a different feel altogether. Located right across the main street from the Old Synagogue, next to the Christian cemetery on Vorosmarty Square, it occupies an undulating grassy expanse. The tombstones tilt a bit; they seem to talk to each other and do not stand at rigid attention. Its large Holocaust memorial resembles an open Torah scroll, with the names of local Holocaust victims inscribed on black marble plaques. (If the cemetery gate is locked, the keys can be obtained at the Orthodox cemetery.)

CEGLED (CEGLÉD)–Jews settled in this town southeast of Budapest in the middle of the 19th century. In 1904, they commissioned Lipot Baumhorn to build a new synagogue. Dedicated in 1905, it stands on Damjanich street, a rather boxy building with pale yellow brick outer walls and lovely art nouveau detailing. It was converted into a sports hall after being sold to the city under communism.

DEBRECEN–Founded in the 14th century, Debrecen is an economic, cultural and university center in eastern Hungary as well as the centuries-old stronghold of Hungarian Protestantism. Jews were only allowed to settle here after 1840, but from the mid-19th century on Debrecen became a major center of Jewish life. More than 10,000 Jews lived here before World War II. There were several big synagogues as well as numerous tiny Hasidic study houses scattered through the Jewish quarter of town, which was located near central Calvin Square and its imposing Calvinist church.

Today, several hundred Jews live in Debrecen, and the community is the largest and most active outside Budapest. Facilities include a mikvah and a kosher lunchroom, bakery, and butcher shop. The Debrecen community serves as a reference point for Jews living in smaller communities nearby, and each spring it hosts a regional gathering of Hungarian-speaking Jews from neighboring countries—Romania, Slovakia, Serbia, and Ukraine. Debrecen's magnificent Great Synagogue was destroyed by bombing in World War II, but two synagogues remain standing. Both have been beautifully restored and are open to visitors. The main Status Quo Ante synagogue is located in a peaceful, shady garden on Kapolnas street. Built in 1909, it is a low, stone building with two decorative arches over three central doors. The small Orthodox synagogue, built in 1913, stands half a block away on Pasti street. It has a simple interior and a bold brick-and-stucco facade marked by arched doorways and false arcades along the peak of the roof. The large Jewish cemetery is located on Monostorpalyi street. *(Jewish community: Bajcsy-Zsilinszky utca 26. Tel: +36-52/415-861)*

GYONGYOS (GYÖNGYÖS)–An enormous domed synagogue stands in this pretty town between Budapest and Miskolc. Built in 1931, it was Lipot Baumhorn's last major work (his son-in-law, Gyorgy Somogyi, collaborated on it). It has always reminded me of the Taj Mahal. Today, painted dull pea-green, it is a furniture store, but it retains a surprising amount of its original decoration, including Moorish archways and carving, and brilliant stained glass inside the dome. Next door stands a simple, neo-classic synagogue, designed by Karoly Rabl and built around 1816. It is listed as a historic monument but used today as a TV studio. The large, partially overgrown Jewish cemetery has a big Holocaust memorial and a poignant monument to World War I soldiers.

GYOR (GYŐR)—A monumental synagogue with a great segmented dome and intricate exterior stonework is a landmark in this pretty city halfway between Budapest and Vienna. Designed by Karoly Benko, it was built in the late 1860s and stands on Kossuth street. Abandoned and in poor condition for decades, the synagogue was reopened in 2006 after a restoration process that took nearly ten years. Its ornate octagonal sanctuary will be used as a concert hall, and the city's tiny Jewish community will have space in the complex. There is a well-maintained Jewish cemetery, with a monumental ceremonial hall and a large Holocaust memorial, at Temeto utca 33.

HODMEZOVASARHELY (HÓDMEZŐVÁSÁRHELY)—The synagogue on Szeremlei street in this town in southeast Hungary was built in 1857 and then remodeled in 1906. An enormous, deep, central arch frames a huge rose window, flanked by small, domed towers. The synagogue was beautifully restored and reconsecrated in 2004 and serves as a house of worship for the little local Jewish community. The former Jewish school building next door houses an exhibition on the Holocaust.

JANOSHALMA (JÁNOSHALMA)—The small synagogue in this village 70 miles south of Budapest once struck me as a time capsule of the past, as if, when the Jews were deported, everything was simply left in place to decay. Located on Petofi street, it has been restored now and is used again as a house of worship. Its outer wall bears a Holocaust memorial that lists the names of the 300 or so local Jews killed at Auschwitz. There is a small Jewish cemetery off Jozsef Attila street, outside town.

KECSKEMET (KECSKEMÉT)—A sprawling agricultural and market city about 50 miles southeast of Budapest, Kecskemet has a town center full

Designed by Lipot Baumhorn, the enormous domed synagogue in Gyongyos is now used as a furniture store but retains some of its original decoration.

of wonderful examples of art nouveau architecture. One of the landmarks on the tree-shaded main square is a Moorish-Romantic-style former synagogue topped by a lotus-bud-shaped dome on its soaring central tower. Designed by architect Janos Zitterbarth and consecrated in 1871, it was damaged in an earthquake in 1911. Among other things, the quake dislodged the tower's original onion dome. Lipot Baumhorn was called in from Budapest to carry out the restoration work, and it was he who added the lotus-bud dome and other features. The synagogue was transformed into the national headquarters of the Union of Technical and National Science Associations in 1974 and today is called the House of Science and Technology. Almost nothing is left of the once sumptuous interior. Instead, there are lecture halls, a conference center, a bar-café, and a gallery housing copies of sculptures by Michelangelo.

Jews were barred from living in Kecskemet until the end of the 18th century. The town's first synagogue dates from 1818—it still stands in a courtyard directly behind the main synagogue, a run-down neoclassic building now used as a food-processing center. A third synagogue, an Orthodox synagogue dating from the early 20th century, now houses a photography museum on Katona Jozsef street, just off the main square. From the outside, you can see the Star of David embedded in one of its windows, and inside, charming ceiling paintings show a tiger, an eagle, a stag, and a lion.

Kecskemet has a large, well-maintained Jewish cemetery, located on the main road (Route 5) leading north toward Budapest. Dominated by an ornate, Moorish-style ceremonial hall, it contains memorials to Holocaust victims and to Jewish World War I soldiers. *(Jewish community: Nagykorosi utca 5. Tel: +36-76/484-541)*

KESZTHELY–Keszthely is a popular resort town at the western tip of Lake Balaton. The neoclassic synagogue, built in 1852, is at the end of a tree-shaded courtyard on Kossuth street, lined with arcaded baroque buildings. It underwent full restoration and was reconsecrated in 1995. The small local Jewish congregation planted a Bible garden, with plants mentioned in scriptures, in a plot next door. There is also a monument to the 829 local Jews killed in the Holocaust. Above the courtyard entrance is a plaque to the Jewish composer Karoly Goldmark, who was born here in 1830. *(Jewish community: Fodor utca 20. Tel: +36-83/312-458)*

KISKUNHALAS–The synagogue on Petofi street, built in 1858, is still used by the tiny Jewish community in this town in southern Hungary. It is a stately white building with a charming fresco of a curtain around the Ark. Other surviving Jewish buildings—including a small prayer house, rabbi's house, school, and kosher butcher shop—still stand, forming a traditional Jewish courtyard. The synagogue has a Holocaust memorial listing the names of hundreds of people deported and killed in 1944. *(Jewish community: Kazai J. utca. Tel: +36-77/422-058)*

KOSZEG (KŐSZEG)–Nestled in hill country on the Austrian border, Koszeg has one of the best preserved complexes of medieval and baroque buildings in Hungary. And, to my mind, the sadly abandoned, 19th-century synagogue here is one of the most beautiful synagogues in central Europe.

King Sigismund granted Jews permission to live in Koszeg in 1395, but they were banished in the 16th century and did not return until the late 18th century. The Jewish population never amounted to more than 300 people, and fewer than 120 Jews lived here on the eve of World War II. During the war, Hungary's fascist Arrow Cross regime set up a forced labor camp outside town, where 5,000 Jews from elsewhere were held. Some 3,000 died there; in March 1945 the survivors were force marched to camps at Mauthausen and Wels, in Austria.

The synagogue was built in 1859. Located at Varkor utca 38, it is a charming, beautifully proportioned building that remains an evocative monument both to the annihilated Jewish community and to the optimistic future that seemed so open to Hungarian Jews in the 19th century. Constructed of red brick, with twin crenellated towers protecting a low, flat dome, it is set back from the street in a long, narrow yard, flanked by buildings that formed a harmonious Jewish complex. On one side was the Jewish school, and on the other, the home of the shammas, or sexton.

Construction of the compound was financed by Philip Schey, a Jewish philanthropist born here in 1798, who grew rich as a textile merchant and later became a banker for the Hapsburgs. In 1859, Emperor Franz Joseph raised Schey to the Hungarian nobility. He took the title Philip Schey van Koromla. Before his death in 1881, Schey carried out many good works, particularly in the field of education. (In the Romanian city of Satu Mare, formerly part of Hungarian Transylvania, Jewish community leaders years ago presented me with a Hebrew-teaching book that had been printed in Vienna in 1886. A full page in the front of the book noted that it had been published in Schey's memory.)

The synagogue in Koszeg has stood empty for decades. I find both the exterior and the interior very haunting and ghostly. Inside, the recessed Ark is surmounted by a huge, filigree-like wrought-iron Star of David; the bimah is set off by a delicate wrought-iron grille; and the graceful women's gallery, set on slim iron pillars, encircles three-quarters of the sanctuary. Walls and ceiling bear traces of delicate frescoes. On the inside of the cupola, a legend is written in fading fancy script: "*Zur Ehre Gottes erbaut von Philip Schey von Koromla*—For the honor of God, this was built by Philip Schey von Koromla."

The small, walled Jewish cemetery in Koszeg is on Temeto street, near the Catholic cemetery. Near the entrance there is a memorial to 2,000 Jews from Koszeg and nearby villages deported by the Nazis.

KOVAGOORS (KŐVAGÓÖRS)–A charming village near the north shore of Lake Balaton, Kovagoors has a number of quaint, thatch-roof houses that are being done up now as vacation homes. In the middle of town, on Dozsa Gyorgy street, stands a rare example of a surviving village synagogue, a simple structure like a big barn, that was built in 1822. Today it is a ruin, surrounded by houses and chicken coops and fenced-in gardens. A woman in a red dress who was preparing seed beds in the plot next to the synagogue told me that there was a Jewish cemetery here, on Temeto—Cemetery—

street, near where the Christian burial grounds are located. I found Temeto street easily, but not the Jewish cemetery; the dirt road I followed past the Christian cemetery seemed to lead nowhere. A man across the street gave me directions, gesturing that I should park and walk—over there, over there; it was close. But there seemed to be no "there," just bushes, trees, forest, and wasteland. I tried another way, walking through the Christian cemetery to its rear. Here I found a poorly maintained dry-stone wall that appeared to be enclosing a young forest. This, of course, was the Jewish cemetery. An absolutely impenetrable thicket, with one huge tree rearing up from within, spreading its branches. The wall was broken in a few places, and I clomped up and peered over. I could make out a few tilting tombstones near the wall, but nothing more. In one corner, a single red tulip bloomed incongruously amid the utter abandon. Like a drop of blood? I thought, giving myself over to melodrama. Or a ray of light?

KUNSZENTMARTON (KUNSZENTMÁRTON)–The art nouveau synagogue on Deak Ferenc street in this town in southeast Hungary was designed by Jozsef Dobovszky and built in 1911–12. It has two distinctively shaped towers and many decorative elements drawn from Hungarian folk art. It is now used as a concert hall.

MAKO (MAKÓ)–The charming synagogue on Eotvos street in this town in the southeast corner of Hungary was built in the 1870s for the Orthodox congregation. Restored by Peter Wirth and Agnes Benko and reconsecrated in 2002, it has a flat orange and cream facade with a tall central section flanked by lower side elements. A grand synagogue designed by Lipot Baumhorn and built here in 1914 was demolished after World War II.

MATESZALKA (MÁTÉSZALKA)–Jews were invited to settle in this town in northeast Hungary by the local landowners in the 18th century. By the early 1900s, about a thousand Jews lived here; the numbers swelled in the 1930s with refugees from Poland. The neoclassic synagogue on Kossuth street was built in 1857 and has fine ceiling frescoes and other decoration. There is a walled and well-maintained Jewish cemetery with beautiful old tombstones on Fellegvar street.

NAGYKANIZSA–Jews were invited to settle in this southwest town by the noble Batthyany family in about 1700. The early 19th-century neoclassic synagogue is in a Jewish courtyard off Fo street, near the offices and prayer room of today's Jewish community. The Reform rabbi Lipot Loew served here between 1841 and 1846, and when the synagogue was remodeled in 1845, it became the first in Hungary to get an organ. The sanctuary has a deep blue arched-and-domed ceiling studded with golden stars. At the door stands an obelisk to the 2,700 local Jews killed at Auschwitz. There is a large Jewish cemetery, with a Holocaust memorial and many sentimental 19th-century tombs. *(Jewish community: Szabadsag utca 8. Tel: +36-93/311-425)*

OROSHAZA (OROSHÁZA)–Jews settled in this town in southeastern Hungary in the 18th century and prospered as merchants. The synagogue on Bajcsy-Zsinlinszky street, built in 1890, has a simple facade surmounted by two slender towers topped by bulbous metal cupolas. When I first saw it, it was used as a warehouse for kitchen appliances. It was recently renovated and enlarged for use as a culture center and conference hall, with a small Jewish exhibit.

PAPA (PÁPA)–The grand but shabby 18th-century palace of the noble Esterhazy family dominates the somewhat run-down baroque center of this industrial and commercial town in northwest Hungary. A few hundred yards away, on Petofi Sandor street, an enormous ruined synagogue with a huge rose window dominates the former Jewish quarter.

Papa was a Protestant stronghold and known for its religious tolerance. Jews first settled here in the late 17th century. Half a century later, the Esterhazy count granted 15 Jewish families the formal right to establish a congregation, sell kosher wine, set up kosher butcher shops, and construct an eruv, or symbolic Sabbath enclosure. The town soon became an important Jewish center and the site of one of Hungary's most noted yeshivahs. From the 1840s, Jews averaged about 20 percent of the population; about 2,500 Jews lived here on the eve of World War II.

The Reform Jewish pioneer Rabbi Lipot (or Leopold) Loew served here from 1846 to 1850 (see Szeged pp. 243–45). The synagogue was consecrated in 1846—Count Pal Esterhazy donated 100,000 bricks for its construction—and its design reflects Reform practice. The bimah was situated in front of the Ark, rather than in the middle of the sanctuary as in Orthodox synagogues. Also, space was left for an organ, although none was ever installed. Rabbi Loew, who was one of the first Hungarian rabbis to deliver his sermons in Hungarian, spoke in that language at the dedication ceremony in 1846. "Speak to the

Magyars in their own tongue," he said, "and your beautiful words will find a kind reception in their hearts."

Today, the building looms like a mournful admonition over old, low houses. Birds fly in and out of its gaping windows, and a sapling obscures what was once an entrance. A number of nearby buildings have recently been restored and done up in pastel colors. The contrast is disconcerting, but the gentrification offers hope that the synagogue may also be restored. There are two Jewish cemeteries (an older one and new cemetery, which has a Holocaust monument) on the road leading out of town toward Varoslod.

PECS (PÉCS)–An ancient and important city in southern Hungary, Pecs has Hungary's most important relics of the Ottoman occupation in the 16th and 17th century, including two historic mosques. Jews first settled here in the early 17th century, but in 1692, after the Ottomans withdrew, they were expelled, and the citizens of Pecs ceremoniously swore that no non-Catholics would ever be permitted to live within the walls of the town. This prevented Jewish settlement for a century. The community prospered and grew quickly after most restrictions on Jewish life were lifted in the mid-19th century. Nearly 3,500 Jews lived in Pecs on the eve of World War II. Today only about 100 Jews live here.

The grand synagogue, built between 1866 and 1869 and designed by the architects Karoly Gerster and Lajos Frey, dominates downtown Kossuth Square. Its pale orange facade features tall arched windows and a high, arched central section framing a big clock and topped by the Tablets of Moses. Inside, the two tiers of the women's galleries, supported by cast-iron columns, have beautifully decorated ceilings, and there is a choir loft and organ.

The Jewish community compound includes a small courtyard prayer house, where regular services are held, as well as offices and apartments for the rabbi and cantor. Other Jewish buildings stand in the neighborhood, including a former school at Fürdo utca 3. There is a large Jewish cemetery on Sziv street, not far from the town center, that has a number of monumental tombs as well as memorials to Auschwitz victims. *(Jewish community: Furdo utca 11. Tel: +36-72/315-881)*

SOPRON–Centuries of Jewish experience have left their traces in Sopron, a beautiful town on the Austrian border whose bustling modern district encircles an ancient core of medieval and baroque buildings. Jews lived here from early medieval times until they were expelled in 1526. They returned in the 19th century, and nearly 2,000 Jews lived in the town on the eve of World War II. A few elderly Jews live here today.

Uj utca (New street), in the heart of the horseshoe-shaped Old Town, was called Jewish street until the 15th century, and it is here, facing each other, that the two oldest synagogues in Hungary still stand. Both were transformed into dwellings centuries ago. They were rediscovered, excavated by archaeologists, and restored to their original appearance between the 1950s and 1970s. Both synagogues have simple interiors, thick walls, ribbed Gothic vaulted ceilings, and an Aron ha Kodesh formed by a deep niche in the wall.

No. 22, the Old Synagogue, was Sopron's first synagogue. Built between 1300 and 1320 and set back in a courtyard, it is a splendid Gothic building that now houses a Jewish museum. The Ark is framed by lovely carved grapevine motifs, and the six-sided foundations of the central bimah still exist. A medieval mikvah forms an important part of the complex. Across the street, the "New" Synagogue at No. 11 was built around 1370 as the private prayer house of a Jewish banker.

The synagogue used by the Sopron Jewish community before World War II still stands, too, empty and dilapidated, on sycamore-shaded Papret Square. Designed by the architect Janos Schiller and built in the late 19th century, it is a redbrick structure with a central dome and flaking facade, its arched windows now bricked or boarded up. In 2004, on the 60th anniversary of the deportation of local Jews to Auschwitz, a small but striking Holocaust memorial was erected in the square. Bronze casts of shoes and toys form a heap under bronze casts of clothing bearing Stars of David, hung on numbered hooks as if in a locker room—the locker room, clearly, that led to the gas chamber. On a cold, damp day in early March, big black crows flew back and forth, back and forth, high up in the leafless sycamores; their constant cawing provided a haunting backdrop to the scene.

Sopron has a large Jewish cemetery dating to the 19th century located on Tomalom street near St. Mihaly's Church. Here there is also a large Holocaust memorial listing the names of all the local Jews deported and killed during the war. *(Jewish community: Kiss Janos utca 3. Tel: +36-99/313-558)*

SZEGED—Located on the Tisza River in southern Hungary near the Serbian and Romanian borders, Szeged was devastated by a flood on March 12, 1879, and rebuilt in grand style, copying Vienna and Budapest by girdling the city center along the river with broad ring boulevards. The monumental Great Synagogue—Lipot Baumhorn's masterpiece—is one of the city's standout attractions.

Jews settled here toward the end of the 18th century, and by the end of the 19th century, when Hungary's borders still stretched far to the south and east, about 6,000 Jews lived here. Szeged was a booming commercial center, a home of the paprika industry, and many of its leading businessmen were Jewish. About 5,000 Jews lived here on the eve of World War II. About half of them survived, but few remained here after the war.

From the mid-19th century until the Holocaust, Jewish life in Szeged was dominated by Lipot (Leopold) Loew, the pioneering Reform rabbi, and his son, Immanuel. Lipot Loew served as rabbi in Szeged from 1850 until his death in 1875. Born in 1811 in Moravia, he was descended from the famous Rabbi Judah Loew ben Bezalel of Prague and had previously been rabbi in Nagykanisza and Papa. A terra-cotta bust in the Budapest Jewish Museum shows him resembling a long-haired, full-bearded biblical prophet. Loew was a Hungarian patriot as well as a Jewish activist. His fiery sermons when he served as a chaplain to Hungarian revolutionaries during their abortive insurrection against Austria in 1848–49 landed him in jail for three months.

Immanuel Loew took over as chief rabbi a couple years after his father died and led the Szeged community for nearly six decades. In 1944, at the age of 90, he was deported by the Nazis and died in the Budapest Ghetto. Loew was a scholar who spent years researching the plants and flowers mentioned in the Bible and other religious texts. He was a keen proponent of Neology and a patriotic Hungarian, a leading figure among Jews who considered themselves "Hungarians of the Mosaic faith."

Szeged's Great Synagogue, one of the most magnificent in Europe even today, was built between 1900 and 1903. Rabbi Loew worked closely with Baumhorn on the decoration, having him incorporate intricate floral and plant motifs and other symbolism. Every panel, every inscription, and every carving was imbued with a meaning that Loew explained in published accounts. Set in a large garden on Gutenberg street, the building has a forest of pale brick domes and turreted towers. Inside, it shimmers with marble, mosaics, gold fittings, chandeliers, and stained glass. Tall bronze menorahs, gilded and decorated with semiprecious stones, flank the Ark, and the enormous dome is supported by 24 columns, representing the 24 hours of the day. The dome's stained-glass interior was designed by Miksa Roth, the most famous stained-glass artist of the day, and depicts the heavens, with the sun's rays spreading out from a Star of David. An ornate interior facade frames the Ark and bimah with Moorish-style arches; the pipes of a mighty organ form a dramatic backdrop.

Used for concerts now as well as for occasional religious services, the Great Synagogue overshadows the much smaller, much simpler Old Synagogue on Hajnoczy street, an austere, neoclassic building built in 1842–43 by Henryk and Joszef Lipovszky. Plaques on an outer wall, written in Hebrew and Hungarian, show how high the floodwaters came in 1879.

Several hundred Jews live in Szeged today, and regular services are held in the ornate prayer hall of the community center at the corner of Gutenberg and Josika streets—this, too, was designed by Lipot Baumhorn, as was the domed ceremonial hall in the large Jewish cemetery on the road to Dorozsma, near the main municipal cemetery. Lipot Loew is buried here, in an impressive tomb shaped like a Greek temple. His son Immanuel's simple gravestone is a few feet away. *(Jewish community: Gutenberg utca 20. Tel: +36-62/423-849)*

SZEKSZARD (SZEKSZÁRD)–A red-and-yellow-striped brick synagogue stands on Szent Istvan Square in this town in southern Hungary. It was designed by the Austrian Johann Petschnik and built in 1896. The broad, tripartite facade, with a raised central portion and tall arched windows edged with decorative terra-cotta tiles recalls that of the destroyed Tempelgasse Synagogue in Vienna. The building was turned into a concert and exhibition hall in the 1980s. Outside stands a very striking sculptural Holocaust memorial.

SZOLNOK–An important industrial center and railway junction, Szolnok lies on the Tisza River about 60 miles southeast of Budapest. Jews settled here around 1830, and about 2,500 Jews lived in the city by the outbreak of World War II. A few Jews still live here today.

One of Szolnok's most striking landmarks is its former Great Synagogue, a grand structure with a soaring central dome, beautifully situated in a park on the riverbank near the heart of town. The building was designed for the Neolog community by Lipot Baumhorn and dedicated on August 29, 1899. Used after World War II to store the furniture of the town's murdered Jews, it was bought by the city in the 1960s and restored as an exhibition hall and gallery. Today, the outside gleams in shades of white and palest rose, and there is a Holocaust memorial plaque on the facade. The interior has been painted white throughout, but it is still possible to admire architectural details, including the inner cupola, rose windows, and grand arch that once surmounted the Ark. Across the little square in front of the triple-arched entrance is the former study house, built in the 1930s, which has been turned into a cinema but still has the Ten Commandments embedded in its outer wall.

To my delight, a new monument to Lipot Baumhorn—possibly the only one in existence—now stands in the plaza between the two buildings. It is a larger-than-life-size bust set on a black marble plinth. With a proud but quizzical look above his upturned waxed moustache, Baumhorn gazes at the facade of the synagogue. On the day I was there, a military band was preparing for a concert in the synagogue's main hall. Over and over again, they rehearsed one piece of music—the theme from *Star Wars*—as teenagers skateboarded in the plaza outside, circling Baumhorn's statue and clattering over the cobbles. *(Jewish community: Maria utca 33. Tel: +36-56/373-886)*

SZOMBATHELY—Located in western Hungary near the Austrian border, Szombathely was founded as Savaria by the Roman emperor Claudius in 43 C.E., and many Roman ruins still remain. Jews lived in Szombathely from the late 17th century but were only permitted to settle here permanently in 1840. The community developed rapidly; more than 4,200 Jews lived in Szombathely and its surroundings on the eve of World War II. A small Jewish community carries on today.

The former synagogue is one of the town's most imposing buildings—and, to my mind, one of the most extraordinary-looking synagogues in Hungary. Now used as a concert hall (sounds of symphony rehearsals waft out into the parking lot next door), it stands on Rakoczi street opposite the remains of a Roman temple to Isis. Only the exterior remains as it once was. Designed in 1880 by Ludwig Schone, it is a Moorish-Romantic building, horizontally striped in red and yellow and lavishly decorated with fancy brickwork, ceramics, and bulblike cupolas. It is dominated by two huge, cupola-topped towers whose grandeur seems out of proportion to the rest of the building. Just next to the synagogue is a large memorial to local Jews killed in the Holocaust.

The building just next door houses the offices, culture hall, and pleasant little prayer room of the small local Jewish community. Szombathely has two well-kept, adjoining Jewish cemeteries, one each for the Orthodox and Neolog communities, about a mile or so from the synagogue—ask at the Jewish community office in order to visit them. *(Jewish community: Batthyanyi ter 9. Tel: +36-94/312-500)*

The beautiful former synagogue in Szombathely is now used as a concert hall.

TATA—The synagogue on Hosok Square in this town west of Budapest was designed by Ignac Wechselmann and built in 1861. It now serves as a rather odd museum housing copies of ancient Greek and Roman statues. The building is rather plain, but outside stands an impressive sculptural Holocaust memorial, dedicated in 2004 on the 60th anniversary of the deportation of Tata's 650 Jews to Auschwitz. It shows a human figure being engulfed, little by little, piece by piece, by blackness.

VARPALOTA (VÁRPALOTA)—A stately neoclassic synagogue, built in 1834–39 with a columned facade, stands on Szt. Istvan street in the center of this town between Budapest and Lake Balaton. Since 1986 it has been used as a museum, exhibition, and concert hall.

ZALAEGERSZEG—The imposing synagogue on Ady Endre street, with red walls and two squat, domed towers, was designed by Jozsef Stern and built in this town in western Hungary in 1903. Today it is used as a concert and exhibition hall. There is also a Jewish cemetery.

RESOURCES ON HUNGARY

A NUMBER OF LOCALLY PUBLISHED ENGLISH-LANGUAGE BOOKS AND PAMPHLETS on Hungarian Jewish heritage are available. In Budapest, the Bestsellers bookshop, at Oktober 6 utca 11, has a wide selection of English language books dealing with Hungary and Central Europe. I have found the following local publications very useful:

- *Budapest: Walks in the Jewish Quarter*. Budapest: Vince Kiado, 2006
- Gazda, Aniko et al. *Magyarorszagi Zsinagogak*. Budapest: Muszaki Konyvkiado, 1989
- Komoroczy, Geza, ed. *Jewish Budapest: Monuments, Rites, History*. Budapest: Central European University Press, 1999
- Kormos, Peter, Andras Villanyi, and Tamas Raj. *The Synagogues of Budapest*. Budapest: Villanyi Kiado, 2005
- Orban, Frenc. *Guide to Jewish Hungary*. Budapest: Makkabi, 2004. The most comprehensive local guidebook in English
- Podonyi, Hedvig. *Zsinagogak Magyarorszagon/Synagogues in Hungary*. Budapest: Viva, n.d.
- Wirth, Peter. *Itt Van Elrejtve*. Budapest: Europa Konyvkiado, 1985. Photo documentation of Jewish cemeteries in northeastern Hungary

WEBSITES:

- www.haverim.hu/indexuk.html
- www.jewishgen.org/cemetery/e-europe/hungary.html — Jewish cemeteries in Hungary
- www.mazsihisz.com — Hungarian Jewish Federation
- www.zsido.hu — Hungarian Jewish Web portal in English and Hungarian

ADDITIONAL PUBLICATIONS:

- Fenyvesi, Charles. *When the World Was Whole: Three Generations of Memories*. New York: Viking, 1990
- McCagg Jr., William O. *Jewish Nobles and Geniuses in Modern Hungary*. New York: Columbia University Press, 1972
- Sas, Meir. *Vanished Communities in Hungary: The History and Tragic Fate of the Jews in Ujhely and Zemplen County*. Toronto: Memorial Book Committee, 1986
- Suleiman, Susan Rubin. *Budapest Diary: In Search of the Motherbook*. Lincoln: University of Nebraska Press, 1997

ROMANIA

CURRENT POPULATION: 22 MILLION
JEWISH POPULATION BEFORE WORLD WAR II: APPROX. 800,000
JEWISH POPULATION TODAY: APPROX. 6,000–10,000

A LITTLE HISTORY

Straddling the Carpathian Mountains and stretching to the Black Sea, Romania is a country where two great Jewish worlds come together. Here, Central Europe meets Eastern Europe. The Reform-influenced Austro-Hungarian Jewish tradition, as found in Transylvanian cities, meets antiquity: the old-fashioned Jewish shtetl, as found in Moldavia.

Romania as we know it was established after World War I, when Transylvania (which for centuries had come under Hungarian rule) was joined with the Romanian principalities of Walachia and Moldavia, which had combined in the 19th century as the independent Romanian Kingdom. Jews lived in the region in ancient times, when Roman legions were stationed here in the second century, but permanent Jewish settlement began in the Middle Ages, when Jews fleeing Poland and Hungary found refuge. Jews expelled from Spain and Portugal in the 1490s also found a home here. Moldavia and Walachia, which came largely under Ottoman rule in the 15th and 16th centuries, were on the main trade route between Poland and Turkey, and Polish Jewish merchants set up storehouses, trading posts, and eventually permanent settlements. Several towns in northern Moldavia had thriving Jewish communities by the early 16th century. Their numbers were swelled by waves of Jews fleeing south after the devastation wrought by Bogdan Chmielnicki's Cossack uprising in Poland and Ukraine in 1648 and 1649 and the subsequent decades of war and upheavals.

Fears of commercial competition led to anti-Jewish legislation and sparked sporadic anti-Jewish violence from the 16th century onward. The

19th century spelled particular hardship and persecution. It was a century that saw the emergence of Romanian nationalism as the Romanians struggled to win independence from the Ottoman Turks and the Russians, who fought over the region for more than a century. When Moldavia and Walachia united in 1859 as an independent kingdom, an estimated 130,000 Jews made up about 3 percent of the total population. A viciously anti-Semitic regime took power in 1866 and instigated a large-scale and often violent campaign against the Jews. Among other things, Jews were expelled from villages and confronted by a series of restrictions on economic, social, and religious life. The constitution was changed to allow Romanian citizenship only to Christians. The dire situation triggered repeated protests and condemnation from several Western governments. At the Congress of Berlin in 1878, which set the seal on the independence of several Balkan states after the final Russian victory over the Ottomans, the great powers made independence conditional on the new states guaranteeing full civil rights to their Jewish populations. Romanian rulers paid this provision little heed. In the decades leading up to World War I, anti-Semitic persecution only intensified. Jews were barred from a long list of trades and professions; Jewish children were barred from state schools. Meanwhile, anti-Semitic political parties became active, and violent episodes erupted. A peasants' revolt in Moldavia in 1907 looted Jewish homes and shops and forced Jews out of many villages. Tens of thousands of Jews decided to pick up and leave; many of them trekked hundreds of miles on foot to western European ports on their way to America.

After World War I, Romania annexed the former Austro-Hungarian provinces of Transylvania and Bucovina, as well as Russian Bessarabia. As a result, Romania's Jewish population went from under 240,000 to about 750,000, virtually overnight. But the Jews in these new territories had a different history than did those of old Romania. In Bessarabia, the Jews had suffered even harsher persecution. In the Austro-Hungarian lands, however, Jews were full citizens who had achieved civil rights and emancipation in the early to mid-19th century. Many Jewish communities in Transylvania were heavily influenced by Reform Judaism and had large Neolog congregations. A large proportion of Jews from Transylvanian cities such as Oradea, Cluj, Arad, and Targu Mures were well inserted into mainstream, upper-middle-class life and followed professions barred to Romanian Jews. Most used the Hungarian language, and some Jewish families in Transylvania had even been raised to the Hungarian nobility.

The Jewish community in the Transylvanian town of Sighet congregates in front of its wooden synagogue sometime in the 1930s.

These diverse Jewish groups never really merged, but the anti-Semitism and "Romanization" that continued to grow throughout the 1920s and 1930s affected them all. Discrimination against Jews grew harsher, particularly after the formation of the paramilitary Iron Guard, a right-wing anti-Semitic movement headed by the ultranationalist student leader Corneliu Zelea Codreanu. Iron Guard thugs carried out anti-Semitic violence, and the movement also wielded political clout.

At the outbreak of World War II, Romania's King Carol II at first attempted to keep the country neutral. He was forced by Germany to cede Bessarabia and part of Bucovina to the Soviet Union, northern Transylvania to Hungary, and part of the Dobrudja region, near the Black Sea, to Bulgaria. On September 6, 1940, Marshal Ion Antonescu, allied with the Iron Guard, deposed Carol and took power as the head of a Nazi-style government and soon after formally joined the Nazi Axis. The regime promptly introduced harsh anti-Jewish legislation, accompanied by anti-Jewish violence. On January 21, 1941, the Iron Guard revolted against Antonescu in a bid to gain complete power. This sparked a brief civil war between the Iron Guard and the Romanian Army loyal to Antonescu—and also unleashed a horrific pogrom against Bucharest Jews. Antonescu clung to power, but only with the support of Adolf Hitler.

Antonescu's policy toward the Jews was somewhat ambiguous. He imposed harsh anti-Jewish measures, and Romanian troops murdered, plundered, and displaced thousands—they massacred 30,000 Jews in Romanian-occupied Odessa. But he refused to allow the mass deportation of Romanian Jews to Nazi death camps. The Romanian port of Constanta was one of the only ports open for Jewish emigration, much of it illegal. Still, in August 1941, the Romanians began the mass deportation of Jews from Bucovina, Moldavia, and Bessarabia to ghettos and labor camps in Transnistria, a part of Ukraine occupied by German and Romanian troops. Of the 150,000 or so deported, only 60,000 survived. When the Germans invaded Hungary in 1944, they dealt with the Jews of northern Transylvania as they did with all the Jews of provincial Hungary: they herded them into ghettos and then deported them en masse to Auschwitz. About 160,000 Jews from Transylvania suffered this fate.

About half of the approximately 800,000 Jews who lived in prewar Romania survived the Holocaust. Of these, well over 300,000 had emigrated, mostly to Israel, by the late 1960s. Under the communist dictator Nicolae Ceausescu, who ruled Romania from 1965 until he was overthrown and executed in December 1989, Romania suffered under one of the most oppressive communist governments in Eastern Europe. But Ceausescu was the only communist leader who did not break diplomatic relations with Israel after the Six Day War in 1967. He permitted the steady emigration of Romanian Jews to Israel, although eventually he extorted large financial payments for each Jew who left the country. He also allowed foreign Jewish charitable organizations, notably the American Jewish Joint Distribution Committee (JDC), to help the Jews who stayed behind. With JDC aid, the Federation of Jewish Communities in Romania, or FedRom, was able to organize Romanian Jews into active communities that ran Talmud Torah classes, youth choirs, welfare services, and kosher canteens. Cemeteries and many synagogues were maintained in decent repair (although the overwhelming majority of synagogues were destroyed), and old-age homes were set up.

Ceausescu's policy toward Jews and Israel was clearly aimed at winning support—and money—from the West. A key player in all this was Rabbi Moses Rosen, who served as Romania's chief rabbi from 1948 until his death in 1994. Rosen was a larger-than-life figure—and also a controversial one, because of his relationship with the Ceausescu regime and his policy of trading public support for the authorities for religious and communal rights for Jews, including the right to emigrate. Rosen himself repeatedly maintained that the only way he could help Jews emigrate and obtain better conditions in Romania was by working with Ceausescu. "My only sin is to have helped my people," he told me, a bit more than a year after Ceausescu's execution.

Today, fewer than 10,000 Jews live in Romania, which entered the European Union in January 2007. Half live in Bucharest. Scattered around the country are 32 other Jewish communities with more than 30 members and 22 with 8 to 30 members. In addition, individuals or small groups of Jews live in 90 other localities.

JEWISH HERITAGE IN ROMANIA

MOST SITES OF JEWISH HERITAGE IN ROMANIA LIE ABANDONED OR WERE DESTROYED during World War II or—most frequently—during the communist era. Nearly 100 synagogues are known to stand, about half still used for worship; 34 are listed as historic monuments. In Transylvania, the architectural styles are similar to those found in Hungary and other parts of the old Austro-Hungarian Empire. They include large, elaborately decorated synagogues dating mainly from the late 19th and early 20th centuries. In Moldavia, there remain a number of folk-style synagogues, plain on the exterior but highly decorated on the inside with naïve paintings and lavish wood carving. Until mass urban-renewal schemes in the 1980s and earlier, such synagogues in Dorohoi, Botosani, Falticeni, and other towns stood amid wooden houses and shops that perfectly preserved the old atmosphere of traditional shtetls. Now most stand surrounded by shabby modern apartment blocks.

More than 800 Jewish cemeteries are scattered around the country, including more than 650 in places where no Jews live anymore. Each active Jewish community is responsible for the upkeep of Jewish cemeteries in surrounding areas. For example, the Jewish community in Satu Mare, in northwest Romania, is responsible for 120 cemeteries in villages where there are no longer any Jews. Many Jewish communities, however, do not have the resources to visit and check their status during the year. In many cases, non-Jewish peasant families living on or near the cemetery grounds care for the graveyards in return either for token payment or for the right to use the grass grown there to feed their animals or to cultivate parts of the cemetery grounds where there are no burials. Caring for the cemeteries, however, is an uphill battle. Many are overgrown and abandoned to the elements, and even well-maintained cemeteries get choked with tall grass and weeds in the late spring and summer.

It will be essential to meet with Jewish community leaders in order to gain access to synagogues and some cemeteries. Contact information is noted within each community's individual entry. People there should be able help with visits to smaller communities and localities where no Jews live.

TIPS ON VISITING

THE MOST INTERESTING JEWISH HERITAGE SITES ARE IN NORTHERN MOLDAVIA, where there are historic painted synagogues in towns such as Botosani, Piatra Neamt, and Suceava, and dozens of cemeteries whose tombstones exhibit extraordinarily vivid carving, similar to that found in Ukraine and parts of Poland. Don't miss the cemeteries in Siret! This region is where Romania's famous painted monasteries are located, so the tourist infrastructure is better than in some other regions.

BUCHAREST

(Romanian: Bucureşti)

BETWEEN THE TWO WORLD WARS, THE ROMANIAN CAPITAL WAS KNOWN AS THE Little Paris of the East. I find it today a chaotic city, whose remaining picturesque corners and gracious 19th- and early 20th-century architecture are overwhelmed by the late dictator Nicolae Ceausescu's grandiose urban-renewal schemes. Some people, however, love Bucharest's raw energy and surging street life, and you may, too. There is a rich nightlife, and new buildings, shops, restaurants, and other infrastructure have begun to change the streetscape and dispel the overall air of grim dilapidation.

Bucharest was founded in the early 1400s and over the centuries attracted Jewish settlers from Russia and Constantinople in the east, from Balkan regions south of the Danube River, and from Germany, Austria, Hungary, and elsewhere in Central and Western Europe, creating a diverse mixture of varied Jewish life and traditions that included both Sephardic and Ashkenazic Jews. There are believed to have been about 1,000 Jews in Bucharest in 1800; six decades later there were about 6,000, worshipping in more than 30 synagogues.

From the latter part of the 18th century on, the fast-growing Jewish community was the target of anti-Jewish legislation, violence, and occasional blood libel accusations. More than a hundred Jews were killed during anti-Jewish riots in 1801. Mounting anti-Semitism formed a backdrop for ugly internal conflicts within the Jewish community itself. These conflicts mainly pitted western-oriented Progressive or Reform Jews against traditionalist Orthodox factions. They culminated in the 1860s in a clash between Iuliu Barasch, a radical writer and prominent physician who led the "enlightened" faction, and the traditionalist scholar Meir Loeb ben Yechiel Michael (called the MaLBiM), who had become the Orthodox chief rabbi in Bucharest in 1858. In 1864, the year after Barasch's death, radicals engineered the MaLBiM's arrest, imprisonment, and expulsion from Romania.

Mounting anti-Semitism throughout the 19th century prompted thousands of Jews to leave Bucharest. During this period, one of the most important Jewish personalities in the city was, in fact, an American—Benjamin Franklin Peixotto, who arrived in town in 1870 as the first U.S. consul. Peixotto viewed the situation for Jews in Romania as so bleak that he counseled emigration. Nonetheless, on the eve of World War II, Bucharest had a Jewish population of 95,000—nearly twice the entire Jewish population of neighboring Bulgaria.

During the war, the fascist Iron Guard carried out vicious anti-Semitic attacks that culminated in the horrifying pogrom in Bucharest in January 1941. Synagogues, Jewish homes, and Jewish businesses were ransacked or razed to the ground; Jews were hauled from their homes, arrested, and taken out to the snowy forests beyond the city limits and brutally murdered. At least 170 were killed. Some of their bodies were hung in the local slaughterhouse with signs proclaiming "Kosher meat." Photographs show what at the time was regarded as a wartime miracle: a single Torah scroll salvaged from the carnage. The fascists had torn the Torahs from the Aron ha Kodesh of the Great Synagogue and hurled them everywhere; the streets of the Jewish quarter were covered with shredded parchment. In the Great Synagogue, though, one Torah was found undamaged, caught in a chandelier and suspended high in the air. One of the looters apparently had thrown it upward, expecting it to smash when it hit the ground. Instead, it was saved.

Today, Bucharest's Jewish community numbers about 4,000, including about 1,000 people who are family members of Jews in mixed marriages. Thanks to the infrastructure kept alive under communism, the community (and the Jewish federation) operate a range of medical and social welfare services, facilities for the elderly, and educational programs. There is a kosher canteen, a Jewish culture center and library, and a branch of the Jewish youth organization, OTER. In addition, Bucharest has an academic center for the study of Romanian Jews and a new center for the study of the Holocaust in Romania. The Hasefer publishing house issues a selection of books each year. There is a Chabad House, a Jewish school supported by the Ronald S. Lauder Foundation, and also a Jewish theater that performs modern plays as well as Yiddish classics.

Main Sites of Jewish Interest in Bucharest

Choral Synagogue: Str. Sf. Vineri 9/11—The Choral Temple, so called because it incorporates a choir loft and organ, is set back behind iron gates and dominates the courtyard containing the offices of the Jewish community and federation. In front of it stands a Holocaust memorial, erected in 1991, incorporating a huge menorah. Designed by the architects Enderle and Frewald, the Choral Temple was built for the wealthy Reform community in 1866–67; it was meant to be a "living monument to the emancipation of Romanian Jews." The magnificent interior and flat facade, with Moorish turrets and two lower side elements flanking a higher central section, are reminiscent of Ludwig von Forster's influential design for the Tempelgasse Synagogue in Vienna, which was built in the 1850s and destroyed in the so-called Kristallnacht pogrom in November 1938.

Until a few decades ago, the Choral Synagogue towered over Bucharest's old Jewish quarter, Vacaresti. But the neighborhood was almost completely razed to the ground, much of it destroyed in the 1980s to make way for the gargantuan palace built by communist dictator Ceausescu—today used as the Palace of Parliament—that looms up above a district of new apartments and ministry buildings.

Great Synagogue: Str. Vasile Adamache 11—Built in the 1840s and remodeled several times in subsequent years, the Great Synagogue (Sinagoga Mare) is almost totally hemmed in by apartment houses built in the late 1980s and early 1990s. (Jewish community members have told me that the new construction was a deliberate attempt by the communist authorities to cut the synagogue off from the surrounding city.) The building looks soot-scarred and seedy, but its interior features lush Moorish-style detail work on the walls and barrel-vaulted ceiling and an elaborate Aron ha Kodesh decorated with gilding and carved lions. It now houses a Holocaust Museum. Unfortunately, because of the hemmed-in location, it is hard to find. And though theoretically the museum is open every morning, it is best to check with the Jewish community or with the Jewish museum to make an appointment if you wish to visit.

Jewish Museum: Str. Mamoulari 3—Opened in 1978, the Rabbi Moses Rosen Jewish Museum is housed in the former Akhdut Kodesh (Holy

The Choral Synagogue in Bucharest dominates a courtyard surrounded by new buildings.

Union) Synagogue, also called the Tailors' Synagogue, as it was built and used by the Tailors' Guild. Originally consecrated in 1850, the synagogue was totally remodeled in the early 20th century. Its exterior boasts horizontal striped brickwork. The museum exhibition, displayed in the sanctuary, was revamped in the 1990s, and the collection includes ritual objects, the works of Jewish artists, and numerous documents relating to local Jewish history and the Holocaust.

Cemeteries: Bucharest has several large Jewish cemeteries. The most easily visited is the so-called Philanthropic Cemetery, at Blvd. 1-Mai 91 in the northern part of town. It was founded in the mid-19th century and has a large preburial house and many interesting monuments, including the elaborate tombs of leading families and a poignant memorial to Jewish soldiers killed in World War I. Other cemeteries in Bucharest include a large Sephardic cemetery in the southern part of the city at Soseau Giurgiului 2, near the major municipal cemeteries. Farther south, there is another, vast Jewish cemetery, still in use by the local community, at Soseau Giurgiului 162.

Addresses of Note in Bucharest

- Jewish Community of Bucharest: Str. Sf. Vineri 9/11. Tel: +40-21/315-5090
- Jewish Cultural and Communal Center: Str. Popa Soare 18. Includes a kosher lunchroom
- Chabad: Str. Sfanta Ana 7, Sector 2. Tel: +40-21/210-6160
- Jewish Theater: Str. Dr. Iuliu Barasch 15

ELSEWHERE IN ROMANIA

ALBA IULIA—Alba Iulia, in central Transylvania, has been a trade, cultural, and defensive center since ancient Roman times and still has important historic monuments in and around its vast, 18th-century fortress.

Jews were living here by the 16th century. In 1623 Prince Gabor Bethlen granted liberal residency rights to Jews. After this, Alba Iulia became the main Jewish center in Transylvania. Between the two World Wars, the city was a stronghold of the fascist Iron Guard; a synagogue was bombed in 1938, and there were many other anti-Semitic incidents. Only a few dozen Jews live in Alba Iulia today. One synagogue—the Old Synagogue—remains and is still in use. Built in 1840, it stands flush on Tudor Vladimirescu street. Its recently restored facade, with arched windows and a curved baroque gable, includes a Hebrew inscription over the door. Inside, the richly ornamented bimah and Ark stand out against the otherwise plain decoration.

The extensive walled Jewish cemetery on Vasile Alecsandri street includes numerous gravestones dating to the early 19th century or earlier spaced out over grassy slopes, shaded by fruit trees. Though many stones are eroded, some still bear interesting carving. At the entrance is a monument, similar to those in several other Romanian Jewish cemeteries, where soap reputedly made out of Jewish bodies during the Holocaust is buried. The cemetery is beautifully maintained by a family who lives on its edge. When I visited, men were forking freshly cut hay from around the tombstones into a horse-drawn wagon. Entry is through the door to the family's home and garden, at No. 51. The teenaged son, Mircea, speaks excellent, slangy English; he learned it, he said, at school—and from cartoons, movies, and songs. "Sweet!" was his response when I complimented him on his family's care for the cemetery. *(Jewish community: Str. Tudor Vladimirescu 4. Tel: +40-258/817-840)*

In the Jewish cemetery in Alba Iulia, a worker takes a break while cutting the grass.

ARAD—Located in western Transylvania near the Hungarian border, downtown Arad still preserves some of its considerable Austro-Hungarian charm. Jews settled here in the early 18th century, and in the first half of the 19th century the town became a center of Reform Judaism under the dynamic leadership of Rabbi Aaron Chorin. Born in Moravia in 1766, Chorin became rabbi in Arad in 1789 and served here until his death in 1844. A pioneer in the Reform movement, he advocated changes in the synagogue ritual, including the use of the German language and organ music during services, and also urged changes in other practices, including the dietary laws and Sabbath travel restrictions.

About 10,000 Jews lived in Arad before World War II; the community survived the Holocaust, and most moved to Israel. Today, there are fewer than 300 Jews in the city. The community has an old-age home and a youth club, and it publishes a lively magazine, *Shalom*. Its kosher canteen became famous in 1999 as "Aunt Rosie's Kitchen" when its then director, a woman in her 90s known as Aunt Rosie, was featured on ABC television's *Nightline* program.

The magnificent Neolog synagogue at which Aaron Chorin officiated forms part of the Jewish communal complex on Tribunal Dobra street.

Built in 1828–34, it stands hidden within what looks like a normal, neoclassic town block. Entry is from the courtyard; a grand arched portal leads into a majestic sanctuary featuring stately, almost somber furnishings under a high, richly decorated dome. Today, the synagogue is used for worship and also as a venue for classical and other concerts; in June 2006, the heavy wooden pews were packed for a concert by a klezmer group from Budapest. "It was fantastic, like a rock concert!" said Jewish community president, Ionel Schlesinger.

Arad has several Jewish cemeteries. The biggest, and most easily visited, is the huge Neolog cemetery on Visinului street, where Aaron Chorin is buried in a big mausoleum. *(Jewish community and kosher canteen: Str. Tribunal Dobra 10. Tel: +40-257/281-346)*

BACAU (BĂCAU)–At one time, there were 30 synagogues in this city near Iasi in northern Romania, and Jews made up 30 percent of the local population. Today, only one synagogue, built in 1850 and beautifully decorated, is in use, but the community has a kosher canteen, a youth club, and a small museum. There is also a historic Jewish cemetery and a memorial to the Holocaust. *(Jewish community and kosher canteen: Str. Gh Apostu 11. Tel: +40-234/534-714)*

BOTOSANI (BOTOŞANI)–A historic market town in the northeast corner of Romania, Botosani is one of many Moldavian cities where all but a few old streets were razed under the Ceausescu regime and replaced by characterless concrete blocks. Jews probably settled here in the 17th century, and in the 19th century the community grew to be one of the largest in Moldavia, making up more than half of the local population. Some 11,000 Jews lived here before World War II. Thousands of Jewish refugees poured into Botosani during the war, swelling the Jewish population to as many as 20,000 people.

Most of the Jews here at the war's end emigrated to Israel, and only a few dozen remain here today. "There used to be 72 synagogues in Botosani," one local Jew told me, shaking his head sadly. "Now there is only one." The one that remains is the Great Synagogue, built in 1834 and one of the oldest and most richly decorated in Moldavia. Hemmed in now by shabby new apartment blocks, it appears plain from the outside. Its interior, though, is a revelation. Intricate chandeliers hang from a lofty ceiling decorated with exquisite naïve representations of scenes of Jerusalem, zodiac signs, biblical

Detail of the elaborately painted ceiling in the synagogue in Botosani.

animals, and symbols representing the tribes of Israel. The central bimah, enclosed by a wrought-iron trellis, stands in the middle of the sanctuary, in front of an extravagantly carved and brightly painted Aron ha Kodesh that overhangs into the sanctuary, topped by gilded griffins and a gilded two-headed eagle, wearing a crown.

Botosani has a large and fascinating Jewish cemetery, located at Str. Mihai Eminescu 403. The entrance is just off the road, and the caretaker can let you in. There are actually two cemeteries here—a newer section, still in use, which has tombstones dating back to the 19th century, and an older cemetery, entered through an arched stone gate. The older cemetery includes marvelously carved tombstones, but—at least in late spring and early summer—it is so choked with vegetation that it may be hard to penetrate. At the rear of the the newer section, at the end of an asphalt path, you step into a magic world of fanciful animal carvings rising up through the weeds and undergrowth as if in a jungle: wonderful lions, snakes, stags, and other beasts, some of the most vigorous folk carving I have encountered. *(Jewish community: Str. 1 Decembrie 54. Tel: +40-231/514-659)*

BRASOV (BRAŞOV) (HUNGARIAN: BRASSÓ)–The prolific Budapest-based synagogue architect Lipot Baumhorn designed the magnificent Great Synagogue in this historic and bustling Transylvanian city. Built in 1901, it is an outstanding example of Baumhorn's work, featuring his trademark dome, arches, and lavish ornamentation, and it is still used by the local Jewish community. Celebrations were held to mark the synagogue's centenary in 2001. *(Jewish community, synagogue, and kosher canteen: Str. Poarta Schei 27)*

CAMARASU DEAL–SARMASU (CĂMĂRAŞU DEAL–SĂRMAŞU)–On an isolated, treeless hillside above the village of Camarasu Deal, east of Cluj, is a lonely cemetery containing the graves of 126 Jews from the village of Sarmas who were massacred by Hungarian soldiers retreating from Transylvania in September 1944. The cemetery constitutes a dramatic and very moving Holocaust memorial and is well worth the winding drive from Cluj to see it.

CLUJ-NAPOCA (HUNGARIAN: KOLOSVÁR, GERMAN: KLAUSENBURG)–The historic capital of Transylvania, Cluj-Napoca is located about 280 miles northwest of Bucharest. A bustling cultural, education, and industrial center, it has a downtown area that still exudes an Austro-Hungarian flavor with elegant 18th- and 19th-century buildings and several important earlier monuments.

Jews were not permitted to settle legally in Cluj until 1848. In 1944, about 16,700 Jews from Cluj and nearby towns and villages were deported to Auschwitz. A few hundred Jews live here today. Sabbath prayers are held in a small prayer room at Str. David Francisc 16, in a courtyard complex that also houses the community's medical center and youth club.

Several synagogue buildings still stand. The Moorish-style main synagogue on Horea street, a main artery leading from the town center to the train station, is now called the Synagogue of the Deportees and serves as a memorial to victims of the Holocaust. Built in 1887 by the Neolog community, it has a flat, cream-colored facade topped by four bulbous silvery domes.

The former Poalei Tzedek Synagogue, entered through a courtyard at Str. Baritiu 16A, now houses a contemporary art and culture center called Tranzit House. A simple structure, built between the two World Wars, it was used for worship until 1974 and then was turned into a warehouse; striking frescoes of the classic biblical animals remain on the ceiling. Since taking it over in 1997, Tranzit House has been attempting a gradual restoration of the building, while at the same time using it as a venue for experimental art exhibits, performances, and concerts. Before and after 2000, it formed part of a "synagogue chain" of former synagogues in several countries now used as similar art centers—those, for example, in Samorin (see pp. 191–92) and Trnava (see pp. 192–93), Slovakia. A number of Tranzit House projects have Jewish content, and its directors have carried out research on Jewish heritage in Romania. *(Additional information: www.tranzithouse.ro/index.htm)*

The former Sas Chevra Synagogue, built in 1922 and located on Croitorilor street, has undergone a remarkable transformation since I first saw in 1991. At that time, it was used for worship and displayed a large plaque commemorating victims of the Holocaust. By the late 1990s, it had been closed and rented out for use as a furniture store; all vestiges of its original identity were removed. The building now serves as the premises of the Moshe Carmilly Institute for Hebrew and Jewish History, a department of Babes-Bolyai University that was founded in the early 1990s and runs courses in Jewish history, the Hebrew language, and other Jewish subjects. One room houses a permanent exhibition by Egon Marc Lovith, a local artist and Holocaust survivor, born in 1923, who uses Jewish and Holocaust themes in his work.

Cluj has several Jewish cemeteries, located on Badescu, Turzii, and Soimului streets, near the main municipal cemetery. *(Jewish community: Str. Tipografiei 25. Tel: +40-264/596-600. Kosher canteen: Str. Parisu 5/7)*

DOROHOI—Until the late 1980s, visiting Dorohoi was like taking a step back in time. The little town, set in rolling hills in the northeast corner of Romania, retained the look of an old shtetl. Low wooden shops and houses, jammed tightly together on cobbled squares and narrow streets, perfectly preserved the atmosphere of bygone days when Jews made up the majority of the population.

Today, all is changed. As in most Moldavian towns, most of Dorohoi's old buildings were razed during the Ceausescu regime and replaced by new apartment blocks. Granted, these have running water (unlike many of the old homes they replaced), but they transformed a town full of wonderful historic character into a charmless replica of every other town in the region. And the passing years have only made the new cityscape look worse. Dorohoi's two remaining synagogues, which I remember surrounded by a peaceful, cobbled plaza, are now isolated in the middle of ugly concrete.

Jews from Poland settled here in the 17th century, becoming shopkeepers, artisans, and merchants. Hasidism became a major force, and ohels of local rabbis stand in the Jewish cemetery on a hill just outside town on the way to Suceava. About 5,300 Jews lived in Dorohoi on the eve of World War II. Most were transported to labor camps in Transnistria on November 11, 1941. A monument in the cemetery commemorates victims of the deportations and other casualties of the Holocaust, including those killed on July 1, 1940, when Romanian soldiers massacred scores of Jews attending a funeral.

Today, fewer than 40 Jews live in Dorohoi. Only one of the two surviving synagogues is still in use. Its small Aron ha Kodesh is topped by a gilded, double-headed eagle and the hands of a Cohen outstretched in blessing, and distinctive memorial lamps bear the names of the deceased. Community president Todor Iancu showed me around and then was insistent that I see something else. "One street has been left as it was," he told me. "No one lives in the houses, but it is kept as a reminder of how it was, to remind how Jews lived." In fact, one old street in town has somehow evaded the wrecker's ball, but who knows for how long. The row of shops and houses stands largely empty, almost totally derelict, left to crumble, a sad and eerie sight, full of ghosts. I walked its length, taking photos, and wondering when this, too, would be wiped from the map and from memory. *(Jewish community: Str. Spiru Haret 95. Tel: +40-231/611-797)*

FALTICENI (FĂLTICENI)–A small industrial city founded in 1780, Falticeni today is another anonymous Moldavian town whose heart was cut out and replaced by shabby concrete blocks in the Ceausescu era. Jews lived in the area even before the town was officially established, and the community built its first synagogue in 1792. Eventually there were 13 Jewish houses of worship here, most of them catering to members of specific craft guilds. Before World War II, about 4,000 Jews made up one-third of the local population. Falticeni was the hometown of Romania's postwar chief rabbi, Moses Rosen, whose own father served here as rabbi. Today, the Jewish community numbers only about 30 people, and only the Great Synagogue, built in the mid-19th century on the site of the town's first synagogue, still exists. It is a dusty, pale yellow building with arched windows, but its plain exterior hides a splendidly ornamented sanctuary with a spectacular carved, painted, and gilded Aron ha Kodesh, supported by two pillars and surmounted by a gilded, two-headed eagle.

Falticeni has two Jewish cemeteries. The newer of them, dating back to the 19th century, is easily visited. It is located at the end of Brosteni street, a semipaved residential street not far from the town center. I parked my car by the cemetery wall and followed a woman in a denim pantsuit as she entered through the former ceremonial hall—now the residence of the peasant caretaker. Chickens fluttered about in the hallway, and outside, brightly colored laundry was flapping amid the tombstones. Older parts of the cemetery were quite overgrown, but it was still possible to wander about and see many stones with elaborate carving. The woman I followed was on her way to visit the grave of her husband in the newer part of the cemetery. He is buried in a large tomb, bordered by flowers—with a place for her waiting beside him. His picture is incorporated in the tomb decoration, a youngish man wearing glasses. We stood there together, looking on; she mourning, and I paying respects to someone I had never met, but whose life and death were part of the dwindling Jewish continuity of the town.

Falticeni's older Jewish cemetery, on nearby Victoriei street, was established in the 18th century and already closed in the mid-19th century. Today, the stones are toppled, overgrown, and sunken into the earth. *(Jewish community: Str. Dr. Bobulescu 5. Tel: +40-230/540-090)*

GURA HUMORULUI—This pleasant little town in southern Bucovina is a center for visiting the region's painted monasteries. It has a wonderful and easily visited Jewish cemetery, whose tombstones feature especially vivid folk carvings of lions and other symbols. *(A detailed map of the cemetery can be found online at http://humora.tripod.com.)* The cemetery is about a mile from the town center, on the road to Humor Monastery. The entrance is up a dirt driveway on the right side of the road; entry is through an unlocked gate. In town, a simple, abandoned synagogue stands on Daniel Catargiu street. Through the broken windows I could see dusty pews and a menorah, and what looked like a lulav—the palm frond used at Sukkoth—lying on the bimah.

IASI (IAŞI)—The capital of Moldavia from 1565 to 1862, Iasi grew up at the crossroads of important ancient trade routes and today is a lively cultural, university, and commercial center in the northeast corner of Romania. Despite much modern construction and a mushrooming population of nearly 350,000, many historical monuments remain, and the city—the second largest in Romania—is a lot more livable than other Moldavian towns.

Iasi was a great center of Jewish life and learning in East-Central Europe, famous for its rabbis and intellectuals, skilled craftsmen, and acute businessmen, as well as for its Jewish schools, hospitals, publications, and other civic, social, and cultural institutions. The world's first professional Yiddish theater opened in Iasi in 1876, founded by the Polish director, composer, and playwright Abraham Goldfaden (1840–1908), an avid exponent of the Haskalah and the father of the Yiddish stage. When he died in New York, 75,000 people attended his funeral; his obituary in the *New York Times* described him as the "Yiddish Shakespeare." A monument to Goldfaden stands now next to Iasi's ornate National Theater, and, nearby, another small monument marks the so-called Green Fruit-Tree Garden, the spot where the first public performance of Goldfaden's Yiddish songs took place.

In the 1920s, the nearly 45,000 Jews in Iasi made up more than half the local population, and more than 110 synagogues were in operation. Elderly residents recall that one street, still called Synagogue street, once had 17 synagogues on it. The city's one remaining functioning synagogue still stands here: the Great Synagogue, built in 1671 and the oldest surviving synagogue in Romania. An unusual-looking building with simple lines and a metal-roofed dome, it is set in a small garden, almost totally surrounded by new construction. Inside, a huge, elaborate Ark, surrounded by frescoes, fills one end of the hall. The floor of the sanctuary is below ground level, either because of a ban on synagogues being built taller than Christian churches or as a reference to Psalm 130, which begins, "Out of the depths I call to you."

The former women's gallery houses a small, dusty museum of local Jewish history, organized in the 1980s, which can be visited by appointment. The pictures are faded and peeling, and some material is long out of date, but touring the exhibit can be a compelling experience; it reeks of memories that are fast fading into oblivion. Behind the synagogue, two weathered tombstones stand side by side: Legend has it that they memorialize a bride and a groom who somehow were killed as they stood under the wedding canopy; no one seems to know the full story.

A memorial to the more than 13,000 Jews killed by Romanian soldiers in a brutal pogrom at the end of June 1941 stands in the garden facing the synagogue. Most of the pogrom victims are buried in huge concrete bunkers that form a Holocaust memorial in the Jewish cemetery on the eastern edge of the city, up a hill through a big ornamental gate on Pacurari street. "They were butchered like sheep brought to slaughter, and the sun and moon gazed in shame upon the murders in the streets of the city, which had become a 'Killing

City,'" reads a plaque. Monuments there also mark the mass graves of victims of other wartime pogroms, at the towns of Targu Frumos and Podul Iloaiei. The cemetery contains tens of thousands of other tombstones and also a large memorial section for Jewish soldiers who died in World War I.

The Jewish community offices are in a building with a colonnaded porch, across the street from the synagogue. The building next door is a former synagogue, once used by the apple carriers' guild, but which now serves as storage space. *(Jewish community and kosher canteen: Str. Elena Doamna 15. Tel: +40-232/313-711)*

ORADEA (HUNGARIAN: NAGYVÁRAD)–Oradea was one of the oldest and most important Jewish communities in Transylvania. Jews may have lived here as early as the 15th century, and there was an organized community by the early 18th century. By the 1940s, Oradea had 27 synagogues, and its 30,000 Jews made up about one-third of the local population. Located in northwest Romania on the Hungarian border, the city was very prosperous, and, following the post-emancipation Hungarian pattern, Jews were among the social, business, commercial, and professional elite. During World War II, Oradea was annexed by Hungary and was the site of the largest Jewish ghetto in Hungary outside that in Budapest. Between May 23 and June 27, 1944, as many as 38,000 Jews were deported from Oradea to Auschwitz.

Today, Oradea's turn-of-the-20th-century center is a striking collection of art nouveau buildings, many of them once owned by Jewish firms and families, that are slowly being restored to their original splendor. One of the most remarkable is the Black Eagle (Vulturul Negru), a shopping, entertainment, and hotel complex built in 1908 and designed by the Jewish architects Marcell Komor and Dezso Jakab (who designed the synagogue in Subotica, Serbia) that includes a winding, glass-roofed arcade with gorgeous stained-glass windows.

Oradea was a major center of the Jewish reform movement, and another city landmark is the monumental Zion Synagogue, a grandiose Neolog temple whose soaring dome towers over the Cris River. Designed by David Busch, at the time the town's chief municipal architect, it was built in 1878 and has long been out of use. Its stunning interior—run-down now, and in serious need of repair—features elegant columns, delicate arches, and vaulting decorated by geometric designs. The Ark is framed by an elaborate arch and surmounted by a pipe organ.

The Jewish community today numbers about 500 and is probably the most active outside Bucharest. It has a kosher canteen, a youth club and computer center, and a choir and dance troupe. The communal complex includes the Orthodox Great Synagogue, built in 1890, whose Moorish-style redbrick-and-stucco design is almost identical to that of synagogues in Satu Mare (see pp. 272–73) and Dej. It has a splendid Ark and a vaulted interior covered with intricate geometric frescoes. A large Holocaust memorial stands next to it, in a parklike plaza.

The smaller Chevra Sas Synagogue, built in 1882 and also part of the communal complex, is currently in regular use; Oradea is one of the few communities in Romania that can muster a daily minyan. Nearby, the so-called Teleki Synagogue, built in the 1920s (the last synagogue to be built in Oradea), is on Primariei street and is used today as a vegetable warehouse. The private, U.S.-based Lempert Family Foundation hopes to raise funds to transform the Moorish-style building into a Holocaust memorial and learning center. (Another synagogue, once a court of the Hasidic Vizhnitzer rabbi, is used today as a wood-working shop.) Oradea has large Neolog and Orthodox Jewish cemeteries, located near the municipal cemeteries. *(Jewish community and kosher canteen: Str. Mihai Viteazul 4. Tel: +40-259/434-843. Additional information: www.oradeajc.com)*

PIATRA NEAMT (PIATRA NEAMŢ)–Beautifully situated in the forested foothills of the Carpathians about 220 miles north of Bucharest, Piatra Neamt is another historic Moldavian town that has lost much of its city center to the wrecker's ball. A few historic pockets remain, however. One is the little street where the old Jewish courtyard is located. Two synagogues stand here. One—the so-called Ba'al Shem Tov Synagogue—is one of the most fascinating and precious synagogues in Romania, both for its architecture and for the legend that surrounds it.

Jewish merchants from Poland settled in Piatra Neamt centuries ago, but the major wave of settlement came in the 17th century, after the Chmielnicki Uprising forced thousands of Jews to flee Poland and the Ukraine. More than 8,000 Jews lived in Piatra Neamt before World War II, making up one-quarter of the local population. Through the 1930s they suffered serious episodes of anti-Semitism; Corneliu Codreanu, the founder of the Iron Guard, was elected to Parliament from Piatra Neamt in 1931. The Jewish community survived the war largely intact, but most left for Israel. Today, the community numbers fewer than 150 people—including several families who have returned from Israel on either a permanent or part-time basis.

The Ba'al Shem Tov Synagogue, also called the Cathedral Synagogue, was built of wood in 1766, on the foundations of an earlier masonry synagogue. The present building is halfway underground, probably to conform to regulations that forbade synagogues from being higher than surrounding Christian buildings. The sanctuary is entered down stairs leading from a little outer prayer room, where regular services are held. Chandeliers hang from the ribbed wooden dome arching over the dull, brown-green walls decorated by pale stenciled flowers. Carved and gilded lions, griffins, bunches of grapes, and other decorations ornament the compact but elaborate Aron ha Kodesh, built in 1835 by Saraga Yitzhak ben Moshe. The Ba'al Shem Tov, the legendary and mysterious founder of the Hasidic movement, is said to have worshipped here (in the earlier synagogue on the same spot). One legend says that he lived for a time in a small, lonely village in a place known as "Jews' Valley," high in the nearby mountains. From time to time, the story goes, he came down to Piatra Neamt to pray. (See Medzhybizh, Ukraine pp. 128–29.)

The Great (or Leipziger) Synagogue next door, originally built in 1839 and reconstructed after a fire in 1904, is very similar to other folk-style Moldavian synagogues. Maintained beautifully, it has a small, raised bimah with a trellised frame and a highly elaborate Aron ha Kodesh with trompe l'oeil draperies. The walls are decorated with bright frescoes representing Holy Land themes. Frescoes of biblical animals—the stag, the lion, the tiger, and the eagle—are painted on the ceiling. "The eyes of the lion are looking right at you wherever you are in the sanctuary," Hari Solomon, the president of the Jewish community, told me, "and the book that lies open seems to be open in your direction." He was right.

Piatra Neamt has two Jewish cemeteries. The marvelously evocative old cemetery, at Str. Orhei 10, has tombstones dating back to the 17th century and was closed down in 1860. Massive, richly carved tombstones straggle up a steep slope at the foot of a dramatic wooded hill above the town, but many of the stones have tumbled down now, and it is not always possible to gain entrance. The newer cemetery, founded in 1860 when the old one was closed, is located at Str. Petru Movila 4, and has a caretaker who can let you in. Wonderful old tombstones with sumptuous carving stand here on a hill above town. Part of the cemetery is overgrown, but most of the vegetation is seasonal; the grass and weeds were waist high when I visited in early summer, but the caretaker had cut paths into some of the sections and the tombstones stood amid bright, waving wildflowers. A chorus of birdsong filled the air, and at ground level, among the stones, a carpet of wild strawberry plants bore sweet red fruit. *(Jewish community: Str. Petru Rares 7. Tel: +40-233/223-815)*

RADAUTI (RĂDĂUŢI)–Mainstream guidebooks use the terms "dusty" and "sleepy" to describe Radauti, a market town in the far north of Romania near the Ukrainian border. Its claim to fame for most visitors is its position as a base for touring the beautiful painted monasteries scattered amid the lovely rolling countryside nearby. For me, Radauti holds another significance—it is the town my paternal grandparents came from. My great-grandmother, Ettel Gruber, is buried here. She died in 1947, and I was given my middle name, Ellen, in her honor.

My grandparents left Radauti before World War I, when about 5,000 Jews made up nearly one-third of the local population. My grandmother was just a child, and my grandfather—Ettel's son—was the only one of his family to emigrate to America. The others stayed in Radauti; a picture from the 1920s shows Ettel, rather grim-faced, sitting there amid a big family gathering of bearded men and stylishly dressed women. Like the rest of the Jews of Radauti, they were deported to ghettos and labor camps in Transnistria. Almost all the family survived the war. All of them emigrated to Israel except for my grandfather's brother Pinkas, whom I met in Bucharest. He died in 1980 at the ripe old age of 98.

I first visited Radauti in 1978, when I traveled around Romania with Chief Rabbi Moses Rosen during Hanukkah. In 1991, I returned to celebrate Passover with the few dozen, mainly elderly, people who then made up the community. The seder was held in the small prayer room of the big, twin-towered synagogue that still stands, a local landmark, in the center of town. It was a curious, moving evening. Only one old man, the grizzled patriarch who led the seder, had any recollection of my family—and about all he could remember was that my great-grandfather, Anschel, had not come from Radauti itself but from a nearby village, Vicovo de Sus. The old man was sick and went through the service in a quavering voice. I, the honored guest, was seated next to him at the head table. Tall candlesticks guttered. The one child—the son of the then community president—raced through the Four Questions at top speed, and everyone applauded. We ate matzo kugel and hard-boiled eggs, brisket and potatoes; we drank sweet Carmel wine from Israel.

At the end of the evening, a few of us sat singing Passover songs. We stalled on "Had Gadyah"—the song about buying a baby goat. I knew one tune. The friend from Bucharest with whom I was traveling knew another.

And the old man, the leader of the seder? He sat silent for a moment. I could almost feel time dropping away as he reached back across half a century. He took a breath, smiled a little, and started singing. It was a tune I had never heard before, a wavering, almost Oriental melody, sung in a strange, twangy Yiddish accent—the way my great-grandparents and their parents before them probably sang it.

I didn't return to Radauti for 15 years. When I did, I found that almost all the people I had met on previous trips had passed on, or passed away, and few were there to take their places. I sat and drank tea with the community manager, Tania Grinberg, and Alexandra Losneanu, a teenager who was one of the few young people left. We got in my car and drove to the Jewish cemetery. It is a vast walled expanse at the outskirts of town, with hundreds of gorgeously decorated old tombstones. On them, hands of God break off branches from Trees of Life; hands of women bless candlesticks; lions rear; and griffins flap their wings. I had forgotten where Ettel's grave was located, so we fanned out through the stones to look. "Here! Over here!" Tania called. There it was, near the wall, tilting to the left, bearing the image of candles. And just as I had done on my previous two visits, I posed at its side, trying to appear unmoved as Alexandra took my picture. *(Jewish community: Al. Primaverii 11. Tel/fax: +40-230/561-333. Additional information: www.shtetlinks .jewishgen.org/Radauti/radautz.html or http://radautz-jewisheritage.org)*

ROMAN—Some 17 synagogues once stood in this town near Iasi in northern Romania. Only one remains, located on the square of the big open-air produce market. Called the Leipziger shul because of the commercial contacts between its congregants and the German city of Leipzig, the site of an important trade fair, it has a lovely folk-style baroque Aron ha Kodesh. Many of the tombs in the big Jewish cemetery on Bogdan Dragos street bear laminated photographs of the deceased, providing a highly personalized glimpse of the changing face of the local Jewish community. The cemetery has an ornate ceremonial hall and a dramatic monument to Jewish soldiers killed in World War I. *(Jewish community: Str. Sucedava 131. Tel: +40-233/726-621)*

SAPANTA (SĂPÂNŢA)—Located just west of Sighetu Marmatiei in northern Romania near the border with Ukraine, Sapanta is famous for its so-called Merry Cemetery—a Christian cemetery whose grave markers boast carved and brightly painted crosses. In the center of the village, right on the main road, there is also a well-maintained and easily visited Jewish cemetery;

you can see most of it fairly clearly from the road if the gate is locked. Sapanta is one of the few places in Romania that regards its Jewish cemetery is an attraction—it is listed on the tourist information billboard at the edge of town.

SATU MARE (HUNGARIAN: SZATMÁR)–Located on the Hungarian border in northern Transylvania, at the edge of Maramures county, Satu Mare was long part of Hungary, and much of the local population is ethnic Hungarian. Jews settled here around 1700, but the main growth of the community took place in the 19th and early 20th centuries. About 13,000 Jews lived here before World War II, making up nearly a quarter of the local population; there were at least eight synagogues, a yeshivah, and a Hebrew printing house. In the last two weeks of May 1944, the Nazis deported the Jewish population to Auschwitz.

In the late 19th and early 20th centuries, Satu Mare was a seat of the Teitelbaum and Gruenwald Hasidic dynasties and gave its name to the Satmar Hasidic group, most of whose members now live in Brooklyn. To this day, pilgrims come to pay their respects at the tombs of rabbis in the sprawling, tree-shaded Orthodox Jewish cemetery, located on 9-Mai street. Windows are cut into the masonry wall to allow Cohens (who are not allowed by Jewish law to visit cemeteries) to look in from outside, and there is also a large Holocaust memorial in the form of a chapel with the names of the thousands of local victims. (Nearby, there is also a Neolog cemetery. Tombstones in both cemeteries still show bullet holes and other damage from World War II combat.)

Today, only a few dozen Jews live in town, but they maintain links with the Jewish community in Debrecen, Hungary, not far across the border, and a rabbi comes from Budapest each month to hold classes and conduct services. Local Jews, however, have almost no contact with the stream of Hasidic pilgrims. "We in the community today are not traditional, Orthodox Jews," community president Dezideriu Decei told me. "We are modern, and the pilgrims don't recognize our community. They come only to pray, to visit the cemetery, and then go back."

Two synagogues remain standing, right next to each other, in the complex that also contains the community offices. The Great Synagogue, built in the 1890s, is almost identical to that of synagogues in Oradea and Dej, with two little onion domes atop a grand facade with a decorative main arch and long, narrow windows. It had remained closed for decades until the community cleaned it up and reopened it not long ago for use as a concert hall and cultural venue. "The dust inside was as thick as my finger!" Decei exclaimed. Little has been done to restore the building, however, and there is no electricity; concerts are lit by natural light, and if microphones or other equipment is needed, power is brought in from outside on long extension cords. Right next door, the flat-fronted Saar HaTorah Synagogue, built in the 1920s, is still used by the community. It has some interesting ornamentation and furnishings that show an art deco influence. It also has a small prayer room where regular services are held.

Between the two synagogues stands a jagged, eight-ton block of stone mounted on a pedestal, erected in 2004 as a memorial to the 18,000 Jews from Satu Mare and surrounding villages murdered in the Holocaust. *(Jewish community: Str. Decebal 4A. Tel: +40-261/713-703)*

SIGHETU MARMATIEI (SIGHETU MARMAŢIEI) (HUNGARIAN: SIGHET)–Set amid beautiful mountains and farmland on the Ukrainian border in northern Transylvania, Sighetu Marmatiei—also known as Sighet—is one of the main towns in Maramures County, an area noted for its rich folkloric traditions. Beautifully carved wooden gates can be seen in many nearby villages, and on feast days and market days, both men and women from the countryside wear colorful peasant costumes.

Jews lived in Sighet by the 17th century, and the town eventually became a center of both Hasidism and the bizarre Frankist sect (see Poland p. 17). In 1920, the town's more than 11,000 Jews made up nearly half of the local population. Today the Jewish community numbers about 100. Once there were eight synagogues in Sighet; today there is just one, a simply decorated building with vertical red striping on its facade that was erected in 1885. There is monument to the Holocaust on Gheorghe Doja street, on the site of the Great Synagogue, which was destroyed during the war.

In the late 19th and early 20th centuries, Sighet was home to a court of the Teitelbaum Hasidic dynasty, which originated in the Hungarian town of Satoraljaujhely in Hungary (see pp. 229–30). Pilgrims from all over still come to visit the tombs of the tzaddikim in the Old Jewish Cemetery on Szilagyi Istvan street. "This is still the biggest cemetery in town," a member of the Jewish community told me as we strolled amid the graves. The peasant caretakers had just mown the grass, and there was a heady, sweet smell of hay in the air.

For the non-Hasidic world, Sighet is better known as the birthplace of the author and Holocaust survivor Elie Wiesel, who won the Nobel Peace Prize in 1986. Born in 1928, Wiesel has written movingly of his childhood in Sighet, eloquently describing the warm, familial Jewish life in the town, where his parents—like so many other Jews—were shopkeepers, and where he himself lived for his prayers and his studies. He has also written how, virtually until the moment of their ghettoization and deportation to Auschwitz in 1944, Sighet's Jews were not aware of their impending doom; they could not even conceive of the destruction of their people and way of life, despite the occasional report that filtered in from Poland and elsewhere.

Wiesel's childhood home stands at the corner of Dragos Voda and Tudor Vladmirescu streets, around the corner from the synagogue. It is now a museum that commemorates the Holocaust and also pays homage to the Jewish way of life that was annihilated in the Shoah. It includes rooms furnished the way a Jewish family would have lived before World War II, as well as memorabilia, documents, photographs, and other material. Wiesel himself—along with Romania's then president Ion Iliescu—took part in the opening in 2002. Wiesel urged local people to face the past and query the older generation about the life—and death—of the Jews in Sighet. "Ask them what happened when Sighet, which used to have a vibrant Jewish community, all of sudden became empty of Jews," he told them. "Ask them if they shed a tear, if they cried, if they slept well. And then, you children, when you grow up, tell your children that you have seen a Jew in Sighet telling his story."

Sighet's open-air Village Museum, located just outside of town on Dobaies street, is a collection of traditional wooden houses and other buildings brought from around Maramures and includes two houses once owned and lived in by Jews. *(Jewish community: Str. Basarabia 8. Tel: +40-262/311-652)*

SIMLEU SILVANIEI (ŞIMLEU SILVANIEI)–New signboards bearing the silhouette of a synagogue guide you in to this little town in northern Transylvania. They lead the way to the Northern Transylvanian Holocaust Memorial Museum, a unique institution that opened September 11, 2005, in the 19th-century synagogue. The museum, privately run, was organized by Alex Hecht, a New York dentist who was born near Simleu Silvaniei and attended services in the synagogue. The building has been partially restored, but the sanctuary still looks ravaged and provides an atmospheric setting for the exhibition, a collection of photographs, documents, memorabilia, and other material. The complex also includes a small prayer room and a computer center. English-speaking students from the local high school serve as volunteer guides. "It is very interesting to me, this history," 17-year-old Tomi told me. "I can learn about what I see here, what I learn here." The high school curriculum, he said, now includes lessons on the Holocaust; the students visit the museum and then discuss what they find in the exhibition. Tomi also led me to Simleu Silvaniei's Jewish cemetery, a peaceful collection of tombstones, shaded by fruit trees on a grassy slope, that affords a lovely view of the town nestled at the foot of forested hills. *(Museum website: www.jahf.org)*

SIRET—A pleasant little town in the rolling Bucovina hills on the Ukrainian border, Siret has my favorite of all Romanian Jewish cemeteries. Recognized as historic monuments, the three distinct graveyards are easily found near the center of town, a few dozen yards from each other. There is something particularly mystical about them, lonely and spectacular stone reminders where no Jews live today.

Like other towns in the region, Siret was a staging point on medieval trade routes. Jewish merchants lived here from the 16th century. By 1880, Jews made up more than 43 percent of the local population. Jews from Siret were deported to camps in Transnistria in 1941. Most died there, and most survivors moved to Israel. The last Jew to have lived in Siret is believed to have died in 2000. The town's synagogue still stands (I was able to visit it through the Jewish community in Radauti). Though locked and empty, it bears majestic paintings on its walls and ceiling, including lifelike images of biblical animals against a bird-filled sky and a representation of the entire wheel of the zodiac. There is a sumptuous Aron ha Kodesh and memorials listing the names of local Holocaust victims.

The breathtaking Old Jewish Cemetery dates from the 18th century or earlier and is one of the oldest in Moldavia. Its richly carved tombstones are scattered over a small, but extremely hilly, enclosure surrounded by a stout wall. (Enter through a gate just off Cimitirul Vechi—Old Cemetery—street.) Though many of the stones are weathered, the cemetery is very well maintained. It underwent extensive restoration work in the 1990s, and the Romanian scholar Silviu Sanie has carried out detailed research on the tombstones, their symbolic decoration, and their epitaphs. "Here lies the honest righteous man, the Torah scholar, the wonderful master of the Law, Avraham, son of Simeon, master of the Law," reads the epitaph on a tomb from 1795, whose decoration includes birds, flowers, and columns.

The newer cemeteries are across the main road, down a narrow lane—a caretaker will let you in. The adjoining graveyards form an unforgettable sight: a vast expanse of richly carved tombstones set in regular rows on two

A group of wonderfully carved tombstones in the "middle" Jewish cemetery in Siret

levels, the older section high above the other, on and on and on—a real tribe of stones, where lions and griffins are poised to leap, and hand after hand reaches out to place money in charity boxes, bless the Sabbath candles, or extend the peace of a priestly benediction.

SUCEAVA—An ancient city whose history dates back two millennia, Suceava, about 270 miles north of Bucharest, served as the capital of Moldavia at one point during the Middle Ages. Today the medieval fortress, churches and other important historic monuments that remain are surrounded by characterless concrete.

Suceava was one of the earliest sites of Jewish settlement in the region. A community was already established by the beginning of the 16th century. Before World War II, some 18 synagogues and small Hasidic prayer rooms served Suceava's thousands of Jews. Today, fewer than 90 Jews live in the town, and only one synagogue remains standing: all the others were torn down during the "systemization"—urban renewal—that began in the 1950s. The synagogue that still serves the community, the so-called Gah Synagogue, was built in 1870 and is beautifully maintained. Like other Moldavian synagogues, it is unprepossessing on the outside, but its simple, boxlike interior is richly decorated with biblical and symbolic scenes and imaginary landscapes. The ceiling is painted deep sky blue, and at its corners are splendid representations of scriptural beasts: the lion, the eagle, the tiger, and the stag. On the walls are zodiac symbols representing the months of the year, as well as symbolic representations of the Tribes of Israel and dreamlike views of Jerusalem. Little windows of pebble glass enclose the women's gallery. The central bimah faces a small but elaborately carved Aron ha Kodesh.

Suceava has two Jewish cemeteries. The newer one is located at Str. Parcului 6, and the young caretaker can let you in. There are some impressive tombs, mainly from the late 19th and early 20th centuries, including Holocaust memorials and a big monument to Jewish soldiers killed in World War I. The Old Jewish Cemetery, on Stefan Tomsa street, may date to the 16th century and is one of the oldest in Moldavia. As in the Old Jewish Cemetery in Prague, hundreds of exceptionally fine and elaborately carved tombstones are crowded into a relatively small, walled enclosure. There is an elderly caretaker, but on my last visit, in 2006, I found the cemetery extremely overgrown, parts of it impenetrable. Still, it is well worth a visit (particularly at times of year when grass and weeds are not high). The massive tombstones bear intricate and extraordinary designs of biblical animals, mythical beasts, braided candlesticks, blessing hands, and other traditional Jewish symbols. They deserve to be seen—just as the artists who created them and the people who are commemorated by them deserve to be remembered and appreciated. *(Jewish community: Str. Armeneasca 8. Tel: 1 40-230/213-084)*

TARGU MURES (TÂRGU MUREȘ) (HUNGARIAN: MAROSVÁSÁRHELY)–Overlooking the Mures River in eastern Transylvania, 200 miles or so northwest of Bucharest, Targu Mures preserves a charming downtown district that is an important complex of Hungarian art nouveau architecture. Jews settled within the city in the 19th century, though Jewish communities existed much earlier in nearby villages.

The wealth and importance of the prewar Jewish community can be seen by the magnificence of the Great Synagogue, a large, domed, highly ornate building on Aurel Filimon street, built for the Status Quo Ante community in 1899–1900 and designed by the Viennese architect Jakub Gartner, the same architect who designed the Status Quo Ante synagogue in Trnava, Slovakia. Seating more than 550 people, it is lavishly decorated with stained glass, frescoes, and intricate carved detail. The carving and stuccowork—inside and out—are so fanciful they almost look like stone lace. It is all brought to earth by rather pompous plaques that honor the community leaders who financed the construction of the synagogue—and by a prominent memorial in front of the Ark to the 7,500 local Jews deported to their deaths during the Shoah.

Around the corner, in a small park on Calarasi street, stands an impressive Holocaust memorial, a wrenching bronze sculpture by the local artist Iszak Martin that shows a Jewish family facing destruction. The sculpture formed the centerpiece of a Holocaust memorial in the Jewish cemetery for years, until it was moved to its present location in 2003. "The mayor wanted to place it in the center of the city," a Jewish community leader told me, "but we wanted it here, because this was the Jewish neighborhood. All the houses around it were lived in by Jews."

The oldest Jewish cemeteries in the Targu Mures area are the two small cemeteries in the hamlet of Nazna, about three miles away. The older one, a very small, fenced enclosure with a couple of dozen gravestones, dates back to the 18th century. Entry is through the back garden of house No. 92A on the Nazna main street; in the summer, the path takes you through neat rows of corn and beans and potatoes and flowers. The tombstones here are very weathered, but they display a beautiful, living quality—the carved hands representing the priestly blessing on one stone look almost as if they are alive, and some of the Hebrew calligraphy is fantastically delicate and ornate. Fruit trees planted by the caretaker family drop petals from their blossoms among the graves in the spring; in the summer, green apples and deep red cherries hang from the branches like living ornaments. In the center, in a sort of clearing, stands one stone shaped almost like a human being; its back is even curved like the back of a living person. The man buried here was named Moses, son of Israel. His epitaph tells us that he was a man of integrity; the carved decoration represents a crown and an upside-down heart pierced by an arrow. The second cemetery in Nazna is located over the hill, at Str. Liliaclui 35. *(Jewish community: Str. Aurel Filimon 23. Tel: +40-265/261-810)*

TIMISOARA (TIMIŞOARA) (HUNGARIAN: TEMESVAR)–
Set amid the vast fertile plains of the Banat region of Transylvania near the Serbian and Hungarian borders, Timisoara is the city where the 1989 revolution that toppled Nicolae Ceausescu was sparked off during antigovernment riots. Timisoara was ruled by the Ottoman Turks from 1552 to 1716 and then became part of Hungary until 1918. Long a center of both

Hungarian and German ethnic groups, it has charming art nouveau and 19th-century Hapsburg architecture.

There was a Jewish presence in Timisoara before the Ottoman conquest, but permanent settlement dates from the mid-16th century. The oldest tombstone in the historic Jewish cemetery is that of a rabbi and surgeon named Azriel Asael, who died in 1636. In 1715, some 155 Jews lived in Timisoara. In 1858, there were 2,200, and by 1940 the Jewish community numbered 11,000, at least 10 percent of the local population. The city was an important center of Zionism, but in the 1930s it also became a hotbed of the anti-Semitic Iron Guard. In 1936, the Iron Guard bombed a Jewish theater, killing two and injuring many others. The majority of Timisoara's Jews survived World War II—in 1947, some 11,400 Jews lived there—but by the 1970s, most had moved to Israel. Today, fewer than 500 Jews live here.

Timisoara's three remaining synagogues represent a rich architectural heritage. The imposing, Moorish-style Citadel Synagogue, designed by the Viennese architect Karl Schuman, was built in 1864. The Austro-Hungarian emperor Franz Joseph attended a formal dedication ceremony in 1867. Its monumental facade, with small side steeples and a rose window over the horseshoe-arched entry, stands flush on Marasesti street. There have been long-term plans to transform the building, which has a richly decorated sanctuary, into a concert hall. The prolific Budapest synagogue architect Lipot Baumhorn designed the so-called Fabrik Synagogue, which was built for the Neolog community in 1899 on Coloniei street. The building was one of Baumhorn's most ornate synagogues, with fanciful domes and carving and a gorgeous interior featuring a huge pipe organ beneath scalloped double arches surmounting the lavishly decorated Ark and bimah. Today it stands empty and sadly dilapidated. Still in use by the Jewish community is the Josefin Temple at Str. Resitei 55, a smaller and less ornate building constructed in 1910. Its restrained ornamentation lends the compact sanctuary an intimate atmosphere. *(Jewish community and kosher canteen: Str. Gh. Lazar 5. Tel: +40-256/201-698. http://cet.rdstm.ro/. Jewish Youth Club website: http://otertimisoara.jewish.ro/home.htm)*

VATRA DORNEI—A derelict, Moorish-style synagogue, built in 1902, looms over the main street of this once-grand spa town, located at the foot of dramatic mountains in southern Bucovina on the border with Transylvania. It is a sad, but monumental, reminder of the past. Years ago, I attended a Hanukkah celebration here; the sanctuary was brightly lit and crowded with people in winter coats and fur hats. A Jewish children's choir performed. One little girl had an especially powerful voice, and she sang with a serious intensity that was very endearing. Vatra Dornei was once home to the "summer court" of the Hasidic Vizhnitzer rebbe. Today, fewer than 20 Jews live in the town. They worship in a simple, small synagogue, built in the 1920s at Str. Luceafarului 16. The town also has a picturesque Old Jewish Cemetery.

RESOURCES ON ROMANIA

THE INSTITUTE FOR HEBREW AND JEWISH HISTORY IN CLUJ PUBLISHES SOME material in English. A few books and pamphlets issued by the Jewish publishing house Hasefer are available at some Jewish community offices. They include:

- Sanie, Silviu. *Dainuire prin Piatra: Monumentele Cimitirului Medieval Evreiesc de la Siret.* Bucharest: Hasefer, 2000. This Romanian book on Siret's medieval Jewish cemetery has photographs and a useful English summary on the symbolism of tomb carvings.
- Streja, Aristide and Lucian Schwarz. *Synagogues of Romania.* Bucharest: Hasefer, 1997

WEBSITES:

- www.romanianjewish.org — Portal to today's Romanian Jewish community
- www.haruth.com/JewsRomania.html — English-language portal to material on Romanian Jews
- www.jewishgen.org/cemetery/e-europe/romania.html — Jewish cemeteries in Romania and links to other Romania-interest websites
- www.jewishgen.org/Yizkor/pinkas_romania/pinkas_romania1.html — Translations of the Yizkor books of several Romanian Jewish communities
- www.shtetlinks.jewishgen.org/sadgura/ReischToronto.html — Links to resources on the Bucovina region in northern Romania and western Ukraine

ADDITIONAL PUBLICATIONS:

- Dicker, Herman. *Piety and Perseverance: Jews from the Carpathian Mountains.* New York: Sepher-Hermon Press, 1981
- Ioanid, Radu. *The Holocaust in Romania: The Destruction of Jews and Gypsies under the Antonescu Regime, 1940–1944.* Chicago: Ivan R. Dee, 2000
- ———. *The Ransom of the Jews: The Story of the Extraordinary Secret Bargain Between Romania and Israel.* Chicago: Ivan R. Dee, 2005
- Jagendorf, Siegfried. *Jagendorf's Foundry: A Memoir of the Romanian Holocaust, 1941–1944.* New York: Harper Collins, 1991
- Salzmann, Laurence, and Ayse Gursan-Salzmann. *The Last Jews of Radauti.* Garden City, NY: Dial Press, 1983
- Weggemann, Thomas, Christian Meyer, and John Montigel. *Die Sprechenden Steine von Siret.* Bludenz, 2001

WESTERN BALKANS

FROM 1918 UNTIL THE BLOODY BALKAN WARS STARTING IN 1991, TODAY'S INDEPENDENT countries of Slovenia, Croatia, Bosnia and Herzegovina, Serbia, Macedonia, and Montenegro formed one state, Yugoslavia. Yugoslavia (meaning "land of the South Slavs") had been created after World War I by joining ethnically different territories long ruled by different powers, mainly the Austro-Hungarian and Ottoman Empires. The people were ethnically diverse; they spoke different languages, had different histories, and even used different alphabets.

The Nazis stormed into Yugoslavia in April 1941, and most of the country was divided up among its various German-allied neighbors. Croatia became a Nazi-allied puppet state headed by Ante Pavelic, leader of the extreme nationalist terror movement called the Ustasha. As the war against the Nazis raged on, civil war within Yugoslavia also broke out, pitting three main groups against each other: the Croatian Nazi-allied Ustasha, the communist partisans led by Josip Broz Tito, and the Serbian Chetniks, promonarchy guerrilla groups that also eventually collaborated with the Germans and Italians.

The communists emerged the victors, and Tito ruled the country from the end of the war until his death in 1980. Communist Yugoslavia was not part of the Soviet Bloc or allied with Moscow, but it broke relations with Israel in 1967 along with most other communist states. The country was a federation of six republics and two autonomous provinces. Ethnic tensions and nationalist ambitions simmered but were kept in check during Tito's regime. The wars that erupted in 1991 after Slovenia and then Croatia declared independence raged for months in Croatia, then centered on Bosnia and Herzegovina and soon became the bloodiest conflict in Europe since World War II, leaving hundreds of thousands dead and millions displaced from their homes. The Dayton Accord in 1995 put an end to the fighting, but tensions persisted. In 1999, NATO forces bombed Serbia to force an end to Serbian aggression against ethic Albanians in Kosovo province. Today, the region is nominally at peace, but in some of the newly independent states deep-seated scars still linger and tensions still smolder close to the surface.

Jews lived in the western Balkans in ancient Roman times, but, because of the subsequent historic variation, Jewish history also differed from region to region. Much of the southern, eastern, and coastal areas, particularly the parts under Ottoman occupation, were havens for Sephardic Jews fleeing the expulsion from Spain and Portugal after 1492. Conditions were much rougher for Jews in the areas ruled by Austria. During World War II, Jews were persecuted everywhere. They were sent to local forced labor and death camps and were also deported to Auschwitz and other death camps. By mid-1942, the Nazis boasted that Serbia was *Judenrein*—cleansed of Jews. Altogether, only about 12,000 of the 80,000 Jews who lived in prewar Yugoslavia survived.

Hundreds of Jews joined the anti-Nazi communist partisans and after the war were declared national heroes. Foremost among them was Moshe Pijade, a bespectacled Marxist intellectual and one of Tito's closest aides. In communist times, streets, businesses, and organizations all over the country were named for him.

About 6,000 Jews lived in Yugoslavia before its breakup in the 1990s. They belonged to local communities linked in autonomous organizations in each Yugoslav republic, which in turn were members of a nationwide Federation of Yugoslav Jewish Communities, based in Belgrade, the capital of both Serbia and the federal state. Most Jews lived in Belgrade, the Croatian capital Zagreb, and Sarajevo, the capital of Bosnia-Herzegovina. Only one rabbi served the entire country. Jews were not persecuted or isolated as they were in other communist states, but they assimilated into society and lost contact with religious life: They were "Yugoslavs" first, and "Jews" second. It has been said, in fact, that the Jews in former Yugoslavia were the quintessential "Yugoslavs," neutral in the historic tensions between Serbs, Croats, Muslims, and other ethnic groups.

The violent breakup of Yugoslavia was paralleled by a forced disintegration of pan-Yugoslav Jewish institutional links. In societies where ethnic identification became bound up with war, Jews had to reconsider their own identity. Meanwhile, as the former Yugoslav republics became independent, local Jewish communities also became fully autonomous. Politically, Jews were pressured to take sides with the warring ethnic groups of the new nation states. And, to some extent, the authorities of all the warring factions courted Jewish interests as a means of winning support from the West and from what they perceived as a powerful, international Jewish lobby.

Aided in large part by the American Jewish Joint Distribution Committee, Jews in the various new states maintained fragile links during the years of war, sometimes traveling to meet in Austria or Hungary. From the mid-1990s, when travel and other restrictions eased, regular contact and cooperation resumed. A major event each year is Bejachad, a social, educational, and cultural gathering on Croatia's Adriatic coast that draws Jews from all over the former Yugoslavia, as well as Jews who have emigrated.

SLOVENIA

CURRENT POPULATION: 2 MILLION
JEWISH POPULATION BEFORE WORLD WAR II: APPROX. 500–800
JEWISH POPULATION TODAY: 200–600

A LITTLE HISTORY

SLOVENIA ENCOMPASSES ALPINE MOUNTAINS, UPLAND VALLEYS, AND A SMALL BUT lovely slice of Adriatic seacoast. The first region of the former Yugoslavia to break away from the federal state, it won independence during a ten-day war in 1991. In 2004 it became a member of the European Union.

What is today Slovenia comprises parts of the historic regions of Carniola, Styria, and Hungary. Jews lived here during ancient Roman times, but major settlement came around the 12th century, with immigrations to the region from Italy and Central Europe—some Jews arrived here seeking refuge from the Crusades. In medieval times, there were Jewish communities in at least ten towns. Until Yugoslavia was formed after World War I, most of today's Slovenia was ruled by Austria; under the Hapsburg monarchy all Jews were expelled from the region between the late 15th and early 18th centuries. In the late 18th century a small number of Jews moved to what is now the region of Prekmurje, the far eastern corner of the country, which was then part of Hungary. This region became the main Jewish center of what is today

Slovenia. Restrictions remained on Jewish settlement and business activity until 1861; only a few Jews moved back in the 19th and 20th centuries,

Nowadays, several hundred Jews are believed to live in Slovenia. Communal life was weak until the mid-1990s, when there was a revival of activity. In 2003, the Jewish community inaugurated a small synagogue in the capital, Ljubljana—the first synagogue to function in the city in nearly 500 years—and installed Rabbi Ariel Haddad, the director of the Jewish museum in nearby Trieste, Italy, as the country's rabbi.

JEWISH HERITAGE IN SLOVENIA

Since Jews did not return after the wave of expulsions that began in 1496, few physical traces of Jewish heritage remain. Still, there are several interesting sights to see, including the cemetery at Nova Gorica, the synagogue in Maribor, the synagogue and Jewish cemetery in Lendava, and a few medieval tombstones in local museums.

TIPS ON VISITING

Visit the Jewish cemetery in Nova Gorica, but make sure to cross the border into Italy and visit the synagogue and ghetto area in Gorizia. Maribor, with its medieval synagogue, is less than two hours from Ljubljana.

MAIN SITES OF JEWISH INTEREST IN SLOVENIA

LENDAVA—Lendava is situated amid undulating farmland in Slovenia's Prekmurje region, the northeast corner of the country. Prekmurje formed part of Hungary until the collapse of the Austro-Hungarian Empire in 1918, and the Jews who settled here in the late 18th century came mainly from around the Hungarian town of Zalaegerszeg. Prekmurje was occupied by the Hungarians in World War II, and more than 460 Jews, most of them from the town of Murska Sobota, were deported to Auschwitz in 1944.

Lendava's peak-roofed synagogue, built in the late 1860s, stands today in the heart of town, just across a parking lot from a huge new local culture center designed by the prominent Hungarian architect Imre Makovecz in a rather bombastic style utilizing Hungarian national motifs. The synagogue was heavily damaged during World War II, and the Federation of Yugoslav

Jewish Communities sold it to the town. It was long used as a warehouse. Reconstruction work began in 1994, and today it is an art gallery and exhibition hall. Little of the original decor remains, other than the iron pillars that support the women's gallery, which have been painted white and gold. On the staircase and in the women's gallery is a permanent, and rather poignant, exhibition on local Jewish history.

The evocative, tree-shaded Jewish cemetery, established in the mid-19th century, stands near the suburb of Dolga Vas, just outside town and only a few hundred yards from the Hungarian border. The tombstones are from the late 19th and early 20th centuries, and they surround a simple Holocaust memorial erected in 1947. Entry is through a pale yellow ceremonial hall with a big arched central door. Inside it, a plaque commemorates the Jewish cemetery in the nearby town of Beltinci, which ceased operation around 1900.

LJUBLJANA–The Slovene capital is a charming complex of baroque, medieval, and art nouveau architecture that straddles the Ljubljanica River. Jews were expelled from here in 1515, and the only reminders of historic Jewish presence are Zidovska ulica (Jewish street) and Zidovska steza (Jewish Path), two narrow, intersecting streets in the picturesque Old Town that mark the site of the medieval Jewish quarter. Nothing is left of the original appearance except the placement of the streets, but the building at Zidovska steza 4 is believed to stand on the site of a synagogue. There is a small, modern, Jewish section in the municipal cemetery, which also has a simple Holocaust memorial. Most of Slovenia's Jews today live in Ljubljana, and the new little synagogue—a simple prayer room set up in an office block as part of the Jewish community administrative suite—is the only functioning synagogue in the country. *(Jewish community: Trzaska 2. Tel: +386-1/426-9150, fax: +386-1/252-1836. E-mail: jss@siol.net)*

MARIBOR (GERMAN: MARBURG)–Dramatically situated on the Drava River near the border with Austria, Maribor grew up around a fortress built nearly a thousand years ago. Today, it is a lively university town whose Old Town is a picturesque mix of medieval and baroque architecture. Its recently restored medieval synagogue is one of the few surviving synagogues from that era in Central Europe and is one of Slovenia's most important Jewish relics.

Maribor was a medieval stronghold of Jewish life. A Jewish community was first mentioned in the late 13th century, but Jews probably settled here even earlier. Maribor's Regional Museum displays the tombstone of the town's first known rabbi, who died in 1379. Rabbi Israel Isserlein (1390–1460), a noted scholar and expert in Jewish law and one of the foremost rabbis in Germany of the time, lived in Maribor for about 20 years.

Jews prospered in Maribor as artisans, bankers, moneylenders, and merchants whose commercial interests extended to Italy, Hungary, and Moravia. They were also involved in the wine trade. This flourishing life came to an abrupt end when the Emperor Maximilian I ordered all the Jews of Styria, including Maribor, expelled as of January 6, 1497. Few Jews have lived in the town since then; nonetheless, the medieval Jewish quarter, located near the southwest corner of the town walls, is still known as Zidovska ulica (Jewish street) and an old defensive tower nearby is known as the Jewish Tower.

Maribor's synagogue stands here. It is believed to date from the 13th century, but the exact date and original appearance of the building are unknown. In 1501, it was converted into a church dedicated to All Saints (it was fairly common for synagogues to be converted into churches with this name and for Jewish streets to be renamed All Saints streets). It functioned as a church until the late 18th century, and in the early 19th century it was sold and turned into a warehouse and, later, a dwelling. Long-empty, the building was renovated in the 1990s and reopened in 2001 as a cultural center, administered by the Regional Museum. The only physical evidence that the building was once a synagogue is the large niche in the eastern wall, presumably for the Ark. Also, numerous stone fragments with carved Hebrew inscriptions were found during excavations for the renovation. An initial geo-radar survey in 2004 revealed the existence of what may have been a medieval Jewish cemetery and a mikvah, about five yards beneath the surface of the plaza extending from the synagogue to the Jewish Tower.

MURSKA SOBOTA—Located in Prekmurje, near the Hungarian border, Murska Sobota was the home of Slovenia's biggest Jewish community between the two World Wars. Lipot Baumhorn, the Budapest-based architect who was Europe's most prolific synagogue designer, built a synagogue here in 1907–08, but it was demolished in 1954. Prekmurje was occupied by Hungary in World War II, and Jews from Murska Sobota made up most of the more than 460 Jews from the region who were deported to Auschwitz in 1944. The 19th-century Jewish cemetery, located at the corner of Malanova and Panonska streets, was demolished in the 1980s and turned into a park. Town authorities chose eight of the more elaborate tombstones and used them to create a Holocaust memorial there, erecting seven of them in a semicircle facing benches. At the street, under a big weeping willow, they placed the black marble tombstone of Edmund Furst, a president of the Murska Sobota Jewish community who died in 1929. On the back of the tombstone is written that this is a Jewish cemetery and memorial park to the victims of fascism and Nazism.

In 1997 a small permanent exhibit on local Jews, including portions of Torah scrolls from the Baumhorn synagogue as well as a few ritual objects, was opened in the local provincial museum.

NOVA GORICA (ROZNA DOLINA)–When new borders were drawn after World War II, the town of Gorizia, north of Trieste, was awarded to Italy, but its suburbs went to Yugoslavia and became the site of a new town called Nova Gorica. Most Jewish sites, including the former ghetto area on today's via Ascoli and a synagogue built in 1699, remained in the Italian section. The centuries-old Jewish cemetery, however, lies in Slovenia—just off the road on the Slovenia side of the main Casa Rossa border crossing.

Jews lived in Gorizia from medieval times. Though expelled in 1534, Jews were deemed so vital to the economic life of the town that local officials pressured the imperial authorities to lift the ban. A ghetto was established in 1698, and local Jews developed a flourishing silk industry. Few Jews, however, remained in Gorizia on the eve of World War II. Those in the town, mainly elderly people, were deported to Auschwitz on November 23, 1943.

A handful of Jews returned to Gorizia after the war, and the synagogue was in use until 1969, when the Jewish community formally dissolved for lack of numbers. Presented to the municipality in 1978, the building was restored by regional and municipal authorities and reopened in 1984. It houses a little Jewish museum that combines exhibits of Judaica with multimedia displays. It also features a separate room devoted to Gorizia's most famous Jewish native, Carlo Michelstaedter, a poet, painter, and philosopher who was born in 1887 and committed suicide in 1910. His posthumously published works are considered important precursors to existentialism.

Gorizia's Jewish cemetery, on the Slovenian side of the border, is in an area called Rozna Dolina. Its ceremonial hall has been turned into a casino—the Fortuna—and is heralded by banners, signs, and (on my last visit) a tall, inflated advertisement that looked something like a totem pole. The cemetery is in a walled enclosure just behind this building. Most of the 900 or so tombstones date from the 19th century, but some were brought here from an earlier, now destroyed cemetery. The oldest stone is believed be one from 1371, honoring

Detail of tombstone decoration in the Jewish cemetery in Nova Gorica

"Regina, daughter of Zerach, wife of Benedetto," that was brought to Gorizia from Maribor in 1831. Most of the stones are low, gray markers with flat rectangular or square faces and rounded tops. Many are so weathered that they are scarcely legible. There are also a number of stones from the early 20th century. The tombs of several members of the important Morpurgo family (originating in Maribor, called Marburg in German) show the Morpurgo family emblem of Jonah in the mouth of the whale. Carlo Michelstaedter's grave is marked by a low, upright stone simply bearing his name and dates.

ELSEWHERE IN SLOVENIA

THERE ARE TRACES OF MEDIEVAL JEWISH GHETTOS IN THE LOVELY PORTS OF **Koper** (known in Italian as Capodistria), where the former Zidovska ulica (Jewish street) is now called Triglavska ulica, and **Piran,** where the medieval ghetto square—Zidovski trg—is entered through a low archway and surrounded by multistory buildings, similar to the ghetto architecture in Venice. There are also traces of the ghetto in the picturesque town of **Ptuj,** where fragments of early medieval Jewish tombstones are displayed in the regional museum. In the valley below the village of **Stanjel,** renowned for its castle and formal gardens, are the haunting remains of an Austro-Hungarian World War I military cemetery. All that is left are the massive stone pillars of the gates, a huge temple-like monument, and a few scattered grave markers. Two of these are of Jewish soldiers, each bearing a Star of David.

CROATIA

CURRENT POPULATION: 4.5 MILLION
JEWISH POPULATION BEFORE WORLD WAR II: APPROX. 25,000
JEWISH POPULATION TODAY: APPROX. 2,500–3,000

A LITTLE HISTORY

CROATIA IS SHAPED LIKE A PAIR OF JAWS OPENING WIDE FROM THE SLOVENIAN border around a big, triangular chunk of Bosnia-Herzegovina. The upper "jaw" borders Hungary to the north and Serbia to the east. The lower stretches south between the Bosnian border and the Adriatic Sea to the frontier with Montenegro at its southern tip.

Jews lived on the Dalmatian coast in ancient Roman times and are known to have had ancient settlements inland, too. Along the coast, the Roman-era settlements, such as Salona near Split, persisted for centuries, and Jewish communities linked to seagoing commerce and trade developed in the Middle Ages. Refugees from Spain, Portugal, and parts of Italy settled on the coast in the late 15th and early 16th centuries. Much of the Dalmatian coast was ruled by Venice, but parts came under Ottoman domination until Austria annexed much of the region in 1814.

Most of inland Croatia came under Hapsburg rule in 1526. A few medieval Jewish communities had existed there, but the Hapsburg rulers ordered the wholesale expulsion of Jews from the territory, and few Jews lived in inland Croatia until after Emperor Joseph II issued his Edicts of Tolerance in the 1780s, which allowed Jews freedom of movement and other civil rights. Ashkenazic Jewish immigrants from Hungary, Bohemia, Moravia, and Austria soon moved south and founded most Jewish communities here, and by the end of the 19th century most Jews in this part of Croatia were prosperous, integrated, and upwardly mobile.

About 25,000 Jews lived in Croatia on the eve of World War II. In April 1941, Croatia was proclaimed an independent country. It was ruled as a Nazi puppet state by the fascist Ustasha movement under Ante Pavelic. The Ustasha implemented harsh anti-Semitic measures and carried out atrocities against Jews, Serbs, and Gypsies (Roma). Transit and concentration camps were set up, including the infamous Jasenovac death camp south of Zagreb. Most of the Dalmatian coast area, however, was occupied by the Italians, who were generally more lenient and refused to carry out mass deportations. Most Jews in the coastal area were interned on Rab Island (see p. 298). About 5,000 Croatian Jews survived the Shoah, most either in the Italian-occupied zone or as fighters in anti-fascist partisan units.

Croatia's secession from Yugoslavia in 1991 touched off vicious ethnic violence, as the Serb-led Yugoslav People's Army backed Serbian militias among the Serb minority in Croatia. During most of the 1990s, Croatia was ruled by a nationalist government headed by President Franjo Tudjman. Tudjman, who died in 1999, was accused throughout his tenure of trying to rehabilitate the Ustasha regime. As in other breakaway parts of Yugoslavia, the government tried to use support for Jews as a means of counterbalancing the negative image of nationalism. It funded the reconstruction of the Zagreb Jewish community building after a terrorist bomb exploded there in 1991, for example, and it provided financial assistance, fostered cooperative relationships with aid organizations, and awarded honors to Jews and Jewish causes.

About 2,000 Jews lived in Croatia on the eve of the 1990s wars. During the conflicts, the Jewish community tried to steer clear of ethnic politics and keep a low profile. Some Jews chose to emigrate; for those who remained, however, the crisis—and the emphasis on ethnicity—sparked a renewed sense of Jewish identity and bolstered a revival of Jewish communal life. Most Jews remained nonobservant and well integrated into mainstream society, but in 1998 a rabbi took up a regular position in Zagreb for the first time since World War II. Today, there is a full roster of Jewish religious, secular, cultural, and social activities, and contacts with Jews in other states of the former Yugoslavia once again flourish.

JEWISH HERITAGE IN CROATIA

At least 70 synagogues stood in Croatia before World War II. In northern and inland Croatia, many towns boasted large, ornate synagogues dating from the late 19th and early 20th centuries, some designed by leading architects. Almost all were destroyed by the fascist Ustasha regime, by the Nazis, by Allied bombing, by partisans, or by postwar communist authorities. The only three synagogues in Croatia that were not damaged, destroyed, or converted for other use are the centuries-old synagogues in Split and Dubrovnik and the modernist Orthodox synagogue in Rijeka. About 70 Jewish cemeteries remain in Croatia, most of them founded after the mid-19th century and most of them neglected and overgrown.

TIPS ON VISITING

Most visitors to Croatia head for the beautiful Dalmatian coast. The country's most fascinating and historically important sites of Jewish heritage are located in two of the coast's major tourism centers, Split and Dubrovnik.

MAIN SITES OF JEWISH INTEREST IN CROATIA

DUBROVNIK—Strikingly located on a rocky spur thrusting into the sea, the historic fortress city of Dubrovnik deserves its nickname, the Pearl of the Adriatic. An important port and trading center, Dubrovnik for centuries was an independent city-state republic, known as Ragusa.

A Jewish presence was recorded here in the 14th century—a Jewish doctor in 1326—but the community really began to flourish with the arrival of refugees from Spain and Portugal after 1492. Today, fewer than 40 Jews live in the city. From the mid-16th century on, a cramped Jewish ghetto was set up on a single street just off the Placa, or Stradun, the broad, pedestrian-only main street of the Old Town. This was—and still is—called Zudioska ulica (Jewish street), a narrow alleyway partly comprised of steeply rising steps. The ghetto comprised half a dozen or so houses and a synagogue, connected with each other by interior passageways. Gates, locked at night, were erected at either end, and Jews were forced to pay steep taxes for the "privilege" of living there. As late as the 18th century, Jews were barred from being out on the streets at night and from visiting Christian homes.

The synagogue is located on the upper floor of a narrow, two-story stone building at Zudioska 5. It is the oldest preserved synagogue in Croatia, probably established in the 15th century. From the outside, it looks like most other buildings on the street, except for its windows framed by pointed Saracen arches. Inside, the sanctuary was rebuilt in the baroque style in the mid-17th century and features a delicately carved wooden bimah and a small but highly ornate wooden Ark flanked by six Corinthian columns with twisted shafts.

The synagogue survived a major earthquake in 1667 and also World War II. When Serb forces attacked Dubrovnik in 1991 and 1992, two shells hit the roof, but the building underwent full restoration and was rededicated in 1997. On the floor beneath the sanctuary, two rooms serve as exhibition halls for a precious collection of ritual objects. These include valuable silver and textiles, as well as Torah scrolls written in the 13th and 14th centuries that were brought to Dubrovnik by Jews expelled from Spain. All were smuggled out of the synagogue and hidden from the Nazis during World War II by a local Jewish family, the Toletinos.

Dubrovnik has a fascinating Jewish cemetery in the Boninovo District just outside of town. It was founded in the late 19th century and has about 200 tombstones, including 30 or so centuries-old stones transferred there from an earlier cemetery. As a whole, the tombs provide a textbook illustration of different types of Jewish grave markers. Some are Sephardic-style horizontal slabs with Hebrew inscriptions and ornamental carving including the sun, moon, stars, and plant motifs. Others are horizontal tombs shaped like sarcophagi with peaked or gabled roofs and Hebrew inscriptions on their sides. Others still are the upright tombstones, including obelisks, typical of Ashkenazic Jews. In addition, fragments of old Jewish tombstones that were used as building materials can be found embedded in walls in several places around the city, including St. Jacob's Tower, the Sigurata Monastery, and a staircase in Za Kapelicom street. *(Jewish community: Zudioska 3. Tel/fax: +385-20/321-028)*

JASENOVAC—Sometimes referred to as the Auschwitz of the Balkans, Jasenovac was a notorious complex of death camps established by World War II Croatia's fascist Ustasha regime along the Sava River, about 70 miles southeast of Zagreb. From the summer of 1941 until April 1945, tens of thousands or more people were tortured and killed here. The great majority of victims were Serbs, but they also included Roma (Gypsies), antifascist Croats, and between 8,000 and 20,000 Jews. The exact number of victims is

People attend a commemorative ceremony at Jasenovac near the "flower of life" monument.

unknown—no systematic records were kept, and the camp and its records were destroyed at the end of the war.

In the late 1960s, a memorial area with a museum and national shrine was established here, dominated by a huge monument shaped like a "flower of life," designed by the Belgrade sculptor Bogdan Bogdanovic. During the wars of the 1990s, the area was occupied by Serbian forces, and the museum's archives, tapes, and other material documenting the camp were removed and taken into Serb-held territory. In 2000 parts of this material were sent to the Holocaust Memorial Museum in Washington, D.C., where they were catalogued and restored. This material was returned in December 2001. A new museum, curated with the help of the Holocaust Memorial Museum, opened in November 2006.

The fact that Jasenovac was not run by the Nazis but by Croatia's home-grown fascist regime made the camp, its history, and its symbolism take on particular significance in the postwar period, and particularly in light of the ethnic and nationalist passions fanned during the breakup of Yugoslavia. Scholars believe the number of those killed at Jasenovac was somewhere between 60,000 and 85,000, but there were claims in the 1980s that as many as 800,000 or more Serbs had been killed there by Croatian fascists. These claims were used to fuel ethnic hatred and justify Serb attacks in the 1990s. In the late 1990s,

Croatia's nationalist president Franjo Tudjman campaigned for what he termed a "reconciliation" between fascism and antifascism and proposed that Jasenovac be turned into a memorial to victims not just of fascism, but of communism and of the Serbo-Croatian War of the 1990s. Jewish and other critics accused him of equating victims and perpetrators, and the plan never came to pass.

SPLIT—The heart of this ancient Adriatic port is virtually an open-air museum, dominated by the remains of the enormous palace built by the Roman emperor Diocletian at the end of the third century. Much of the medieval Old Town was built within the palace walls.

In Roman times, Jews lived in Salona, once an important Roman port and now a suburb of Split called Solin. A Jewish tombstone and oil lamps and a fragment of a sarcophagus engraved with menorahs were found there during archaeological excavations. The Roman ruins at Solin can be visited, and various finds of Jewish interest can be found in the Archaeological Museum, at Zrinjsko-Frankopanska 25. Salona was destroyed by Avar invaders in the seventh century, and Jews, along with other survivors, presumably found refuge inside the walls of Diocletian's palace. This new settlement grew into the city of Split. Archaeologists have discovered ancient carvings of menorahs in an area believed to have been where Jews first lived. The first documentary evidence of a Jewish community in Split, however, dates from the late 14th century, when records mention a "synagogue" *(sdorium)* existing within the palace walls.

Jewish exiles from Spain and Portugal bolstered the community, and a number of Jews became prominent over the next centuries, when the city was ruled by Venice. One, Daniel Rodriguez, financed and built the Split harbor and customhouse in the 1570s and was elected a Split consul. Only in 1806, however, when Split came under French rule, were Jews granted full civil rights—rights that were rescinded eight years later when the Austrians took the town. It wasn't until 1867 that Jews in Split were fully emancipated. One of the town's leading citizens in the late 19th and early 20th centuries was a Jew—Vid Morpurgo, a banker, industrialist, and bookseller who was a leader in the Dalmatian nationalist movement. On the eve of World War II, about 280 Jews lived in Split. About 150 of them survived the war, and about 100 Jews live in the city today.

The synagogue and other remnants of the medieval Jewish quarter, still called the ghetto, are located in the northwestern part of Diocletian's palace. The synagogue, still in use, is on a narrow alley called Zidovski prolaz (Jewish Passage), and the northwestern tower of the palace is known as the

Jewish Tower. Believed to date from the early 16th century, the synagogue was installed in a simple residential building. In 1942, the tiny sanctuary was ransacked and badly damaged, and most of the ritual objects, Torah scrolls, books, and ancient archives were destroyed in a public bonfire in the main town square. Little was saved, but the synagogue itself was restored after the war. It underwent further renovation in the mid-1990s.

Split's Old Jewish Cemetery, with about 700 tombstones, spreads out above the city on a wooded slope of Mount Marjan. Jews obtained the site as a cemetery in 1573; it is one of the oldest Jewish cemeteries in the Balkans. There are two main types of tomb markers, both of them horizontal in the Sephardic fashion: One is in the shape of a sarcophagus roof, and the other is a flat slab. Both types have inscriptions in Hebrew, in often elaborate calligraphy, but only a few have other carving. There are two 17th-century tombstones brought to Split from the islands of Hvar and Brac. The one from Hvar shows a dove with an olive branch, and the one from Brac shows an angel climbing Jacob's ladder to the sky with the inscription, "This friend has mounted/Into angelic heights/To take a rest in the garden of Eden/In the Grove of Salvation." *(Jewish community: Zidovski prolaz 1. Tel/fax: +385-21/345-672. E-mail: zidovska-opcina-split@st.t-com.hr)*

ZAGREB—The Croatian capital is an attractive city with a quaint medieval section perched on a hilltop above the stately Austro-Hungarian Lower Town. Jews are believed to have settled here around 1355, but they were expelled a century later. The first formal Jewish community, comprising 20 Jewish families, was established in 1806—the Zagreb community celebrated its bicentennial in 2006. By 1940, nearly 12,000 Jews lived here, forming one of the biggest and most prosperous Jewish communities in Yugoslavia. Well-integrated into mainstream society, its members included businessmen, artists, writers, scholars, scientists, doctors, and other professionals and intellectuals. Zagreb was the seat of the Zionist Federation of Yugoslavia, and there were numerous Jewish clubs and social organizations. By 1943, most Zagreb Jews had either been killed outright or deported to the nearby Jasenovac concentration camp or Auschwitz.

The elegant Great Synagogue, once a city landmark, was blown up in 1941 on the orders of Ivan Werner, Zagreb's Ustasha Mayor. A parking lot now occupies the site at Praska ulica 7, and a plaque marks the spot. (The land was returned to the Zagreb Jewish community in 1999, and the community plans to erect a new Jewish complex there; the question of just what to build has sparked years of debate.)

Today, with at least 1,500 of Croatia's 2,500 to 3,000 Jews, Zagreb is the main center of Jewish life in Croatia. The Jewish communal building houses Jewish community offices, a synagogue, a kindergarten, an art gallery, function rooms, a Holocaust research and documentation center, and a collection of books, periodicals, and other material dating back to the 16th century that is the largest Jewish library in the Balkans. (A separate, independent congregation, Bet Israel, which broke away from the main Jewish community in 2006, also functions.) Elsewhere in the city, the Zagreb Arts and Crafts Museum, at Trg Marsala Tita 10, includes a Judaica collection including about a hundred ritual objects.

Zagreb's central Mirogoj Cemetery was established in 1876. Architect Herman Bollè designed it to be a park and an open-air art gallery, as well as a place of burial, and the tombs are located amid arcades, domes, greenery, and sculpture. Mirogoj was the city's first central cemetery serving all religions: Catholics, Orthodox, Protestants, Muslims, and Jews were (and are) all buried there. The Jewish section was established in 1878 to replace two earlier Jewish cemeteries. Prominent Zagreb Jews had family tombs located in one of the cemetery arcades. Under local law, graves that are not maintained for a certain period of time (20–25 years) may be sold as burial plots to others. Thus, a number of once Jewish graves are now occupied by gentiles. Some of the old tombstones have been replaced by new monuments, but in other cases, the name of the newly buried person, and often a cross or a communist five-pointed star, has been added to the old tombstone. An imposing statue of Moses by the sculptor Antun Augustincic stands in the cemetery as a Holocaust memorial. (Originally, it was intended to form part of a family tomb, but the family donated it after the war for use as a memorial.) *(Jewish community: Palmoticeva 16. Tel: +385-1/492-2692, fax: +385-1/492-2694. E-mail: jcz@zg.t-com.hr. www.zoz.hr; Bet Israel: Radiceva 26. Tel: +385-1/485-1008, fax: +385-1/485-1376. www.bet-israel.com.)*

ELSEWHERE IN CROATIA

BJELOVAR—The art nouveau synagogue, built in 1912–14, was seriously damaged during World War II but was reconstructed and is used now as a music school and concert hall. The Jewish cemetery, established in 1876 as part of the main municipal cemetery, has about 200 monuments and a ceremonial hall.

CAKOVEC (ČAKOVEC)—The Jewish section of the municipal cemetery in this town north of Zagreb is listed as a historical monument. Established in 1897, it includes tombstones from an older Jewish cemetery, as well as a few big family tombs dating from the turn of the 20th century. There is also a Holocaust monument. *(Jewish community: O. Kersovanija 4. Tel: +385-40/311-092. E-mail: andrej.pal@ck.t-com.hr)*

DANICA—This small town near Koprivnica was the site of the first concentration camp established by the Ustasha regime during World War II. A monument shaped like a giant gallows was erected there in 1981. About 600 Jews were interned in Danica in April 1941 before being transferred to other camps three months later, where most were killed.

DJAKOVO—A World War II transit camp for Jews operated in a local mill from December 1941 to the summer of 1942. More than 3,000 people, mainly women and children, were held here before being sent to Jasenovac. Nearly 570 people died during their detention and were buried in a Jewish part of the municipal cemetery, now designated a historical landmark.

KOPRIVNICA—The synagogue in this town near the Hungarian border was built in 1875–76. During World War II it was used as a prison and later as a warehouse and industrial site. In 1996 a plaque was put up to honor Holocaust victims. The Jewish cemetery dates from 1842 and has a Holocaust memorial and a monument to Jewish soldiers killed in World War I. The tombs bear bullet holes and other scars from the 1990s war. *(Jewish community: Kresimirov trg 5. Tel: +385-48/624-515)*

KRIZEVCI (KRIŽEVCI)—The once ornate synagogue built in 1895 by Bernard Hoenigsberg and Julius Deutsch now houses cultural offices and a radio station. The Old Jewish Cemetery, established in 1840, is listed as a national landmark and has about 70 tombs. The Jewish section of the municipal cemetery, established in 1899, has monumental arcades with tombs of prominent local Jews and also a monument to local Jews killed in World War I.

OSIJEK—The biggest town in the eastern region of Croatia known as Slavonia, Osijek lies on the Drava River near the border with Serbia. It has three sections: the Lower Town, the Upper Town, and the Fortress, which merged into one city in 1786. The Jewish community was formally established in 1849, and by the late 19th century, more Jews lived in Osijek than in any other Croatian city—even Zagreb. About a hundred Jews live in Osijek today. Headquarters of the community is in the former Jewish school. A sculptural Holocaust memorial by Oscar Nemon called "Mother and Child" stands in a park across the street.

Osijek's main synagogue, a 19th-century building that was once the grandest edifice in the Upper Town, was burned down in 1941, and its ruins were demolished after the war. A smaller synagogue, built in the Lower Town in 1903, still stands and is now used as a church. Its design combines Moorish and neo-Romanesque features, and a number of architectural elements remain, including Stars of David in the round windows of the former women's gallery. Outside, the Ten Commandments can still be seen—below a cross—at the peak of the facade.

The Jewish cemetery in the Upper Town, at Cepinska 11/13, was founded in 1867 and is still in use. It has a number of elaborate tombs denoting the prosperity of the prewar community. There is also a Jewish cemetery in the Lower Town. *(Jewish community: Radiceva 13. Tel/fax: +385-31/211-407. E-mail: zidovska-opcina-osijek@inet.hr)*

RAB ISLAND—During World War II, some 3,500 Jews were interned by the Italians on Rab Island. Jewish internees formed a Jewish Partisan Battalion here after Italy surrendered to the Allies in September 1943. A plaque honoring the battalion was erected in 1993.

RIJEKA—Under Austro-Hungarian rule, Rijeka was a major Adriatic seaport and attracted Jews from all over the Hapsburg Empire. When it became part of Italy after World War I, the city (known as Fiume in Italian—Fiume and Rijeka both mean "river") attracted many Jews from Italy. Jews lived here as far back as the 15th century, and a formal Jewish community was established in 1781. As many as 2,500 Jews lived in Rijeka between the two World Wars. The main congregation was Neolog, but there was a smaller Orthodox congregation mainly comprised of immigrants from Poland, Russia, and Galicia.

The prolific Hungarian synagogue architect Lipot Baumhorn designed an ornate, domed synagogue for the prosperous Neologs. Built in 1902–03, it was blown up and partially destroyed during World War II. The shell remained standing but was pulled down in 1948. The small Orthodox synagogue, built in 1928, survived the war and, listed as a historical landmark, is in use today by local Jews. Built in 1928 and designed by Gyozo Angyal and Pietro Fabbro, it is a striking, modernist building with a three-part facade featuring a brick tower and two entrances of different heights. Inside, the sanctuary is dominated by a beautiful Ark made of Carrara marble that was brought to Rijeka from Ancona, Italy.

The Jewish section in the Kozala Municipal Cemetery was laid out in 1875. Listed as a historical landmark, it has a ceremonial hall and about 550 monuments, plus a score of tombstones from an older Jewish cemetery incorporated in a commemorative wall. A Holocaust memorial erected in 1981 bears the names of the 278 Holocaust victims from Rijeka. *(Jewish community: Filipovica 9. Tel: +385-51/211-160. E-mail: vlado@abc-infoservis.hr. www.jcr.hr)*

VARAZDIN (VARAŽDIN)–Croatia's first Jewish school was founded in 1826 in this town northwest of Zagreb. The synagogue, built in 1862, was long used as a movie theater but is now empty, awaiting renovation into a museum. The Jewish cemetery, established in 1806, is just outside town on the road to Koprivnica. It has more than 500 tombstones, many with rich decoration, and a ceremonial hall built in 1900 that is listed as a historical landmark.

BOSNIA-HERZEGOVINA

CURRENT POPULATION: 4.5 MILLION
JEWISH POPULATION BEFORE WORLD WAR II: 14,000
JEWISH POPULATION TODAY: APPROX. 1,050

A LITTLE HISTORY

MOUNTAINOUS, ETHNICALLY MIXED BOSNIA-HERZEGOVINA WAS RULED BY THE Ottoman Empire from the mid-15th century until the Austrians annexed it in 1878, and today much of the population is still Muslim. Jews were welcome under the Ottoman rulers and many Jewish refugees from Spain settled here in the 16th century. Ladino (or Judeo-Spanish) became the local Jewish language, and Jews in the region wore distinctive clothing, similar to the Turkish style, but regulated by law. The men wore the Turkish-style fez, for example, but the Jewish fez could only be black; Jewish women wore beautifully embroidered dresses with a distinct Oriental air.

Before World War II, some 14,000 Jewish lived in Bosnia-Herzegovina, about 12,000 in Sarajevo and the rest scattered in a score of small communities. Between 1992 and 1995, the vicious ethnic war in Bosnia-Herzegovina left a quarter of a million people dead and as many as two million homeless.

Bosnian Serb ultranationalists, backed by the Yugoslav federal army, laid siege to Sarajevo and initiated a brutal campaign of "ethnic cleansing" against local Muslims. They set up concentration camps for Muslims and Croats and committed atrocities against civilians. Fighting erupted, too, between Muslims and Bosnian Croat nationalists. Croatian nationalists besieged and largely destroyed the Muslim quarter of Mostar, including the town's historic bridge, in 1993.

Amid the ethnic strife, Jews were perceived as neutral—not Serb, not Croat, not Muslim—and in Sarajevo and Mostar in particular, this enabled Jewish organizations and individual leaders to serve as key conduits of nonsectarian aid. Today, as mandated by the Dayton Peace Accord, Bosnia-Herzegovina comprises two ethnically separate sections, the Croatian-Muslim Federation of Bosnia-Herzegovina and the Serb Republic (Republika Srpska). Sarajevo remains the center of Jewish life, but small Jewish communities exist in several other towns, in both sectors of the country.

JEWISH HERITAGE IN BOSNIA-HERZEGOVINA

Bosnia-Herzegovina has a dozen surviving synagogues and more than two dozen Jewish cemeteries, but only a few outside Sarajevo are in good condition and worth a visit.

TIPS ON VISITING

The main sites of Jewish heritage are in Sarajevo and can easily be visited as part of a general tour of the city.

SARAJEVO

Cupped in the middle of mountains, the Bosnian capital is an extraordinary urban complex where the confrontation between East and West is apparent everywhere you look. Centuries-old mosques and a Turkish-style Old Town stand a few steps away from Austrian-style, late 19th-century buildings, and Sarajevo may be the only major city in Europe where you can find a synagogue, a mosque, and Catholic and Orthodox churches virtually on the same street. Burnt-out buildings still provide grim reminders of the 1990s war, but, more than a decade after the war's end, the city is once again a lively center of culture and commerce.

A 1920 studio portrait of two young Jewish men in Sarajevo. By law, Jews could only wear fezzes that were black.

Jews settled here in the 16th century, following the expulsion from Spain. They maintained generally good relations with local Christians and Muslims and prospered as merchants, artisans, physicians, and pharmacists. At one point in the 19th century, all the doctors in Sarajevo were reported to be Jewish. Still, a poor underclass also existed. Ashkenazic Jews from Central Europe arrived and founded their own congregation after the Austrian takeover in 1878. A monumental, domed Sephardic synagogue, built between 1927 and 1931 at Branilaca grada ulica 24, was one of the largest synagogues in the Balkans. Partially destroyed in World War II, it was totally rebuilt in 1966 as a modern municipal cultural center, with a menorah-shaped monument in its atrium to mark four centuries of Jewish presence in Bosnia and to commemorate the Holocaust and the destroyed synagogue itself.

Before World War II, the city's 12,000 Jews made up nearly one-fifth of the local population. About 85 percent of them were killed in the Holocaust. More than 1,300 Jews lived here in 1990. Hundreds fled the country during the Bosnian War, but hundreds also "came out" as Jews, prompted by the ethnic hatred to reclaim their identity, if only to avoid classification as a Serb, Croat, or Muslim.

Throughout the siege of Sarajevo, the Jewish community's social service organization, La Benevolencija, functioned as a key conduit for nonsectarian humanitarian aid to the city. Funded by international organizations such as the American Jewish Joint Distribution Committee and Britain's World Jewish Relief, it ran a soup kitchen, clinic, pharmacies, radio link, and other programs that served all citizens, regardless of ethnicity. During the war, too, Passover seders in Sarajevo became symbolic public events, attended by senior Christian, Muslim, and political leaders, as well as by diplomats and visiting foreigners. La Benevolencija and Bosnian Jewish leaders received numerous international awards for their role. Today, about 700 Jews live in the city.

Main Sites of Jewish Interest in Sarajevo

Ashkenazic Synagogue: Hamdije Kresevljakovica 59—Since the end of World War II, Jewish communal activities in Sarajevo have been centered in the Ashkenazic synagogue, a grand, Moorish-style edifice with four massive corner towers that was designed by Karl Parzik and built in 1902 on the bank of the Miljacka River. It underwent radical reconstruction in the 1960s to add community offices and function rooms. In the process, the grandiose sanctuary was divided horizontally into two levels, and today, the present prayer hall, still decorated with elaborate arabesques and colorful geometric patterns, occupies just the top half of the original space—it looks strange, but few people probably remember how it looked originally. *(Jewish community: Hamdije Kresevljakovica 59. Tel: +387-33/229-666. www.benevolencija.eu.org)*

Il Kal Vijezu (Old Synagogue): Velika Avlija 2—The historic Jewish quarter of Sarajevo lies in the Old Town area near the colorful Bas Carsija market, a sprawling complex of little stores, artisan workshops, cafés, and graceful mosques. In the late 16th century, the ruling Siavush-pasha built a special quarter for Jews here, called El Cortio. It included a synagogue, courtyard, and lodgings for the poor. The complex burned down in 1879, but Il Kal Vijezu, an austere stone building originally constructed in 1581, was rebuilt. In 1966 it was converted into a city-run Jewish museum. When the Bosnian War broke out in 1992, it was closed and became a storage place for collections from other museums in the city. In 2004 the synagogue was reopened as a Jewish museum that will also on occasion serve as a house of worship. A mezuzah was fixed to the door at Rosh Hashana that year, and services were held there for the first time in six decades. Among the museum's exhibits are historic local Jewish costumes, which clearly show Ottoman influence. There are also documents, ritual objects, and relics brought from Spain by early Sephardic settlers. Sections also recount Holocaust history and the Jewish experience during the 1990s war. Next door stands a second synagogue—Il Kal Nuevu, or the New Synagogue—built in 1746 and now used as an art gallery.

Jewish Cemetery: outside town at Kovacici on Mount Trebevic—Founded in 1630, the Sarajevo Jewish Cemetery is renowned for its distinctive tombstones: massive, slightly rounded blocks of stone with Hebrew inscriptions on their one flat face. They thrust out of the ground like miniature pillboxes, making an eerie, unforgettable sight. This type of tomb, in fact, resembles the big, blocky medieval Christian tombs called *stecaks,* which are particularly common in Bosnia-Herzegovina. Located high on a slope overlooking the city, the cemetery was on the frontline of fighting during the siege of Sarajevo in the 1990s. Bosnian Serbs used it as an artillery position to fire on the city. The ceremonial hall and many of the tombs suffered extensive damage, mainly from return fire from the city below, and the Serbs mined the area before they finally withdrew. After the end of the war, an international effort cleared the mines and repaired the war damage to the burial ground and to the graceful ceremonial hall at the entrance.

Sarajevo Haggadah: The most famous Jewish relic in Sarajevo is a 14th-century Haggadah—the story of the exodus of the Jews from Egypt, read at the Passover seder dinner—that was brought to Sarajevo by Jews fleeing Spain. Owned by the Sarajevo National Museum since 1894, the 109-page manuscript, lavishly illustrated with exquisite illuminated paintings, has long been the symbol of Jewish presence in the Balkans. During World War II, it was preserved hidden in a remote mountain village. During the 1992–95 Bosnian War, it was kept safe in an underground bank vault. Questions arose about its whereabouts and safety, and in 1995 Bosnian President Alija Izetbegovic brought it with him to the Passover seder to dispel rumors that it had been sold to purchase weapons. It is now displayed in a special room at the National Museum, along with other valuable religious texts from other faiths.

Vraca: In 1981 an old Austro-Hungarian fort at Vraca, on a hillside near the Jewish cemetery, became the centerpiece of a memorial park commemorating

The old Jewish cemetery in Sarajevo overlooks the city. During the siege of Sarajevo in the 1990s, Serb forces used it as an artillery position.

more than 9,000 local people, including more than 7,200 Jews, killed in World War II. The more than 2,000 fallen partisan fighters from Sarajevo, some 350 Jews among them, also were honored here. All the names were engraved on the complex's walls. The memorial site was heavily damaged during the 1990s war. Restoration is planned but has been postponed because of lack of funds.

ELSEWHERE IN BOSNIA-HERZEGOVINA

DOBOJ—The Jewish cemetery, founded in 1888, is situated together with cemeteries of other faiths outside of town. In 2003 a modern new Jewish community center, with a prayer room and other facilities, was opened for use by the tiny Jewish community, just outside the open produce market. *(Jewish community contact: Tel: +387-53/241-235)*

MOSTAR—Mostar's Old Town, including its famous bridge, was destroyed in the 1990s war, but the bridge and many other buildings have since been reconstructed thanks to international aid. The synagogue, built in 1902, was turned into a puppet theater after World War II. There is a restored and well-maintained Jewish cemetery with a Holocaust monument outside town in the Sutina District. *(Jewish community: Zalik 1. Tel: +387-36/580-027)*

STOLAC—The tomb of a 19th-century chief rabbi of Sarajevo, Moshe Danon, is preserved in this ancient village near Mostar. In 1820, the Turkish governor in Sarajevo, Ruzhdi-pasha, arrested Danon and ten other prominent Jews on trumped-up charges of having killed a Jewish convert to Islam, Moshe Havilio, who was known as the Dervish Ahmet. After an appeal for help by the Jewish community, local Muslims stormed the prison, freed the hostages and sent a petition to the sultan demanding that the pasha be dismissed—he was. Danon died in Stolac in 1830, shortly after setting out on a trip to the Holy Land. Before World War II, his tomb was a place of pilgrimage—and in recent years has become so again.

ZENICA—The Moorish-style synagogue in this town northeast of Sarajevo forms part of the municipal museum and has a small collection of Judaica. Though the exterior still looks like a synagogue, none of the original interior decoration remains. There is a small Jewish cemetery, founded in 1875, on a hillside in a district called Raspotocje at the edge of town. *(Jewish community: Doktora Aska Borica 41b. Tel: +387-32/410-309)*

SERBIA

CURRENT POPULATION: 9 MILLION
JEWISH POPULATION BEFORE WORLD WAR II: APPROX. 35,000
JEWISH POPULATION TODAY: APPROX. 3,000

A LITTLE HISTORY

Serbia, with its provinces Vojvodina and Kosovo, was the former Yugoslavia's largest republic. In medieval times, Serbia was an independent kingdom until it was conquered by the Ottoman Turks in the late 14th and early 15th centuries. Jews lived here in the Middle Ages, and their numbers were bolstered by waves of refugees following the expulsion from Spain and Portugal in the 1490s. During most of the nearly 500 years of

Ottoman occupation, Jews prospered as merchants and traders whose lives were relatively free from violent persecution or tight restrictions. For centuries, though, Serbia was on the front line during a series of wars between the Austrians and the Ottomans.

In the early 19th century, when Serbia gained a measure of autonomy, Jews flourished under Prince Milos, who had close contacts with the Jewish community. But Milos's successor, Prince Mihajlo, who came to power in 1839, expelled Jews from parts of Serbia and, under pressure from non-Jewish merchants, barred Jews from certain trades. Jews won emancipation only after 1878, when the Congress of Berlin, regulating the Ottoman defeat in the Balkans during the Russo-Turkish War, recognized the independence of Serbia and other Balkan countries only on the condition that Jews be granted full civil rights. In 1889, the Serbian Parliament formally declared all Serbian citizens, regardless of religion or ethnic origin, to be equal.

When Yugoslavia was founded following World War I, most Serbian Jews consolidated into a comfortable middle-class life. There was little organized or openly expressed anti-Semitism. That situation changed when the Germans occupied Belgrade and spread out through Serbia in April 1941, launching violent persecutions against the Jewish population. Shops and homes were ransacked, Jews were forced to wear a yellow star, and thousands were sent to forced labor brigades. Eventually, most Serbian Jews were massacred in concentration camps near Belgrade or deported to Auschwitz and other death camps in Poland and Germany.

Throughout the bloody 1990s, Serbia remained the heart of what was left of Yugoslavia, in federation with Montenegro. Ruled by nationalist strongman Slobodan Milosevic until his ouster in 2000, the country was little affected by direct warfare (until the NATO campaign in 1999 over Kosovo), but economic sanctions and dictatorial rule crippled it and turned it into a political pariah. About 2,000 to 3,000 Jews lived in Serbia on the eve of the 1990s wars. They were highly integrated into mainstream society and only a minority were religious. The Jewish community officially chose to steer clear of ethnic politics and keep a low profile. Hundreds of Jews left the country, but the community also took in several hundred Jewish refugees from Sarajevo. Many Jews in Serbia reclaimed affiliation with the Jewish world, though most remained religiously nonobservant. A young rabbi, Yitzhak Asiel, took up a position in Belgrade in 1994 and aided in the renewal of traditions.

JEWISH HERITAGE IN SERBIA

The vast majority of synagogues in Serbia were destroyed either during World War II or later, under the communists; about a score still stand today. By far the greatest number are in Vojvodina, the province that borders Hungary, where cemeteries and/or synagogues existed in as many as 80 localities before World War II. Dozens of Jewish cemeteries still exist in Serbia, but most are in poor condition.

TIPS ON VISITING

Outside Belgrade, three Jewish sites stand out: The synagogues in Subotica and Novi Sad can easily be visited on a day trip to the north; the newly cleaned-up Jewish cemetery in Nis can be visited on a day trip to the south.

BELGRADE

(Serbian: Beograd)

Thanks in part to its strategic location at the confluence of the Danube and Sava Rivers, the Serbian capital has been conquered and reconquered many times. For centuries, it was on the border between the Ottoman and Austrian Empires. It suffered particularly heavy damage during World War II. There was no fighting in Belgrade during the 1990s Bosnian wars, but NATO forces bombed the city in 1999.

Belgrade was a thriving Jewish center in the Middle Ages, settled first by Ashkenazic Jews and later by Sephardic refugees from Iberia. A large Sephardic community developed after the Ottoman Turks conquered Belgrade in 1521. The Jewish quarter was in and around the neighborhood called Dorcol, on the bank of the Danube. The main street, Jevrejksa ulica (Jewish street) still exists. Before World War II, more than 12,000 Jews lived in the city. The Nazis occupied Belgrade in April 1941, and by May 8, 1942, they boasted that Belgrade was the only large city in Europe totally cleared of Jews. An impressive monument by the sculptor Nandor Glid, a Holocaust survivor who fought as a partisan in World War II, stands on the bank of the Danube in Dorcol and depicts a menorah in flames. Another monument on the bank of the Sava marks the site of the Nazi concentration camp at the prewar Belgrade fairground where thousands of people, mainly women and children, were killed in specially made gas-chamber trucks. A memorial plaque in central Belgrade marks Topovske Supe, the first transit camp set up by the Nazis in Serbia, where at least 2,000 were killed. There is also a museum in a former building of the Banjica concentration camp at Veljka Luki a-Kurjaka 33.

During the 1990s wars, many Jews left Belgrade, but the city also took in at least 250 Jewish refugees from Bosnia. Today, the Jewish community numbers about 2,000 and remains one of the largest and most active in the Balkans. Jewish offices and organizations are concentrated in one large downtown building at Kralja Petra 71a. The Jewish community sponsors a wide range of activities, clubs, and events. The communal building also houses the Jewish Historical Museum, which has a rich collection of artifacts, ritual objects, documents, and photographs. *(Tel +381-11/622-634. www.jim-bg.org)*

Before World War II, Belgrade had three synagogues; only one remains. King Peter I laid the foundation stone of the Moorish-style Beth Israel synagogue in Dorcol, built in 1908. The Nazis destroyed it in 1941, and a museum of frescoes now stands on the site, at Cara Urosa 20. A memorial plaque commemorates the Jewish community.

The surviving synagogue is a simple but imposing building, designed by Milan Schlang and erected in 1925 for the Ashkenazic community. It stands behind a gated wall in a spacious yard at Marsala Birjuzova 19 . The Nazis used it as a military brothel. Today it is well maintained and a vibrant focus of religious life. It is used for regular services but also hosts cultural and educational events and has a kosher kitchen, supervised by Rabbi Yitzhak Asiel, the country's only rabbi.

Belgrade's two Jewish cemeteries are located across from each other on Mije Kovacevica street near the municipal cemetery. The large Sephardic cemetery is beautifully maintained and has many fine monuments, including one that marks a genizah, or cache of worn-out sacred books, erected in 1928. Inscriptions are in Serbian, German, Hebrew, Ladino, and Hungarian, recalling the mixed heritage of Jews here. There is an impressive monument to Jewish soldiers killed in the 1912–13 Balkan Wars and World War I and a massive monument to Holocaust victims, erected in 1952 and designed by Bogdan Bogdanovic (who also designed the monument at Jasenovac, Croatia). The Ashkenazic cemetery, on the other side of the street, is much smaller, with about 200 tombs, some of them by well-known local sculptors. *(Jewish communal building: Kralja Petra 71a. Federation of Jewish Communities: Tel: +381-11/624-359. Jewish community of Belgrade: Tel: +381-11/624-289. www.jobeograd.yu)*

NEAR BELGRADE

ZEMUN–Zemun today is little more than a suburb of Belgrade on the south side of the Danube River. Historically, however, it was the last outpost of the Austro-Hungarian Empire facing the Ottoman Turks. Jews settled here in the early 18th century. Zemun was the home of the 19th-century rabbi Jehudah ben Shlomo Haj Alcalaj, an early exponent of Zionism whose ideas may have been one of the earliest influences on Zionist pioneer Theodore Herzl, whose family came from Zemun; Herzl's ancestors are buried in the Jewish cemetery, which was founded in 1747. Built in 1850, the former Ashkenazic synagogue, a simple, rectangular building with arched windows, stands on Rabin Alcalaj street. The Jewish community is attempting to raise funds to buy it back from the city, which rented it out as a restaurant in 2005. *(Jewish community: Dubrovacka 21. Tel: +381-11/195-626. www.joz.org.yu)*

ELSEWHERE IN SERBIA

APATIN–The synagogue in this Vojvodina town, built in 1885, served as a church after World War II but is now empty and boarded up. A big fresco on its ceiling shows the Ten Commandments—with Hebrew writing that for some reason is a mirror image of the true text. The rabbi's house still exists, and there is a Jewish cemetery established in 1780.

CELAREVO (ČELAREVO)–Archaeological excavations at this town 20 miles west of Novi Sad uncovered a large graveyard dating to the eighth or ninth century, when the region was ruled by the Avar tribe. Hundreds of brick fragments unearthed here bear menorahs and other Jewish symbols. Research showed that the people buried here were apparently a Mongol tribe, but otherwise the origin of the apparently Jewish settlement remains a mystery.

NIS (NIŠ)–Since 2004, the historic Jewish cemetery in this town southeast of Belgrade has undergone a remarkable transformation. Dating back to the 17th century, it was expropriated by the communist authorities in 1948, and burials were barred in 1965. After that, Roma (Gypsy) families occupied part of the site, building homes among the tombstones and creating a makeshift village without proper plumbing or garbage disposal. Industry also encroached on the area, and the cemetery was long used as a dump for rubbish and human waste. Vandals over the years broke open tombs, scattering bones. Jasna Ciric, the president of the tiny Jewish community, and Ivan Ceresnjes, of the Center for Jewish Art in Jerusalem, raised the alarm. The cemetery "cannot be seen, examined, or photographed," Ms. Ciric wrote in an open letter at the end of 2003. "It is overgrown by grass and reeds and covered by tons of debris, excrement, and rubbish. The memorial stone tablets are overgrown by grass and weeds. The brush is some two meters high. The way it looks, the cemetery has become the sore spot of the town."

Since then a notable example of civic cooperation carried out an extensive operation to clean, clear up, and restore most of the cemetery. Organized and partly funded by the American Jewish Joint Distribution Committee and backed by the city, the operation involved Roma living at the site, as well as Serbian soldiers, who carted out tons of garbage and refuse to reveal the horizontal tombstones, many of which bear unusual carvings of human-like figures, snakes, and geometrical signs. Roma still live on part of the site, walled off now from the cleared area.

The former synagogue building in Nis stands on Rudjera Boskovica street. It has been partially renovated for eventual use as a cultural venue. Outside town, at Bubanj, a monument park centering on three huge sculptures shaped like defiant fists commemorates the site where more than 1,100 Jews from Nis and its surroundings were executed in World War II. *(Jewish community: Cairska 28/2)*

NOVI SAD (HUNGARIAN: ÚJVIDÉK)—The capital of Vojvodina province, about 70 miles north of Belgrade, Novi Sad was founded in 1694 as an Austrian fortress, Petrovaradin, built to guard a Danube River bridge from the Turks. Jewish presence here dates from 1699, when Jewish merchants supplied the fortress town. On the eve of World War II, more than 4,000 Jews lived in Novi Sad. About 1,200 survived. Today, with several hundred Jews, Novi Sad has Serbia's second largest Jewish community.

The magnificent synagogue here was designed by the Budapest architect Lipot Baumhorn and built in 1906–09 as part of a complex that includes private apartments and also the offices and function rooms of the Novi Sad Jewish community. Two fanciful towers flank the grandiose facade, which features a large rose window under an arch. The tall dome has a brilliantly colored stained-glass inner cupola. During World War II, Jews from Novi Sad were imprisoned in the synagogue before their deportation to Nazi death camps. The building was then used as a storehouse for furniture and other possessions left behind by the deportees. The synagogue underwent renovation in the 1990s and is currently used for concerts and performances and also for the celebration of major Jewish holidays.

Novi Sad has a large, walled Jewish cemetery founded in 1717. There is a ceremonial hall, built in 1905, with a Holocaust memorial next to it. A large monument to civilian victims of World War II stands on the bank of the Danube where more than 1,400 Jews and Serbs were lined up and shot at the edge of the frozen river, their bodies falling into the water through breaks in the ice. *(Jewish community: Jevrejska 11. Tel +381-21/423-882)*

SUBOTICA (HUNGARIAN: SZABADKA)–Built in 1902, the synagogue here is one of Europe's finest examples of art nouveau architecture. Designed by the Budapest Jewish architects Marcell Komor and Dezso Jakab, who also designed the Town Hall, it is an important component of the art nouveau architectural scheme that forms the town center. Komor and Jakab had submitted a virtually identical design in the competition for the Great Synagogue in the nearby Hungarian town of Szeged, which was won by Lipot Baumhorn.

The synagogue stands in a yard surrounded by a wrought-iron fence. Its tall, central, eight-sided dome, patterned in multicolored tiles, rises up from smaller, bulbous domes, sinuous gables, and ornamental buttresses. A Star of David tops each dome, and red bricks or terra-cotta tiles molded into floral or other decorative shapes edge the cream stucco outer walls. Colorful paintings inspired by Transylvanian folk art decorate the interior, recalling the embroidery on peasant blouses. Gorgeous stained-glass windows from the studio of Miksa Roth pick up these motifs.

The small, surviving Jewish community, unable to maintain the synagogue after World War II, presented it to the city under the condition that it be restored and used for cultural purposes. Restoration work has been going on, in fit and starts, since the mid-1970s. Between 1985 and 1992, the building was used as an avant-garde theater; performances included the use of animals and even performers urinating in front of the Ark. In 1996 and then again in 2000 the World Monuments Fund placed the synagogue on its Watch List of 100 Most Endangered Sites. A synagogue restoration foundation, SOS Synagogue, was established in September 2001, and slow restoration work continues. *(Additional information: www.sos-sinagoga.org.yu)*

The synagogue forms part of a complex of Jewish buildings that otherwise are still owned and used by the local Jewish community. These include

The synagogue in Subotica was designed by Marcell Komor and Dezso Jakab and is a standout example of Hungarian art nouveau architecture.

the Jewish community headquarters with function rooms, offices and a small, highly decorated prayer room, and a former ritual slaughterhouse. The Jewish cemetery, founded soon after the Jewish community was established in 1780, is large and well maintained and has an imposing Holocaust memorial to the 4,000 Subotica Jews deported to Auschwitz. A smaller Holocaust memorial stands in the synagogue yard. *(Jewish community: Dimitrija Tucovica 13/I. Tel: +381-24/28483)*

MACEDONIA

CURRENT POPULATION: 2 MILLION
JEWISH COMMUNITY BEFORE WORLD WAR II: APPROX. 8,000
JEWISH POPULATION TODAY: APPROX. 200

A LITTLE HISTORY

HISTORICALLY, THE REGION CALLED MACEDONIA EXTENDED OVER A SWATHE OF territory that encompasses today's independent Macedonian state as well as parts of Bulgaria and Greece. The region was partitioned among Serbia, Bulgaria, and Greece in 1913 after a series of Balkan wars. Today's Macedonia, once the poor, mainly mountainous southern republic of the former Yugoslavia, borders Albania, Bulgaria, Greece, and Serbia.

Jews lived here in ancient Roman times, and a few Jewish communities existed before and during the Middle Ages. Jewish refugees from Austria and Hungary settled here in medieval times. The largest influx of Jews came in the 16th century after their expulsion from Spain. They lived in three main communities—Monastir (today called Bitola), Stip, and Skopje—and had close links with communities now in northern Greece, notably Thessalonika (Salonika). Rabbis from the 16th and 17th centuries left behind fascinating records of everyday life, chronicling the rise of Jewish commerce, handicrafts, and industry, including mining, textiles, and leatherworks. These accounts also tell of poverty, housing shortages, unsafe roads, and crime—including murder and highway robbery. Bitola, in particular, was a lively center of Sephardic culture, although a poor Jewish underclass began to develop in the 19th century.

The 1912 and 1913 Balkan Wars, followed by World War I, devastated and further impoverished the region, forcing many people to emigrate. On the eve of World War II, the Jewish population in what today is Macedonia totaled about 8,000. Macedonia was annexed by Bulgaria, a Nazi ally, in 1941. On March 11, 1943, nearly all Jews, along with those in Bulgarian-annexed northern Greece, were rounded up and deported to the Treblinka death camp in Poland.

JEWISH HERITAGE IN MACEDONIA

TODAY, THE JEWISH COMMUNITY IN MACEDONIA CONSISTS OF ROUGHLY 200 people—all but one or two of whom live in Skopje. The community is tight-knit, and its leadership is very active in promoting various educational, cultural, and social projects. Only a few Jewish heritage sites remain.

MAIN SITES OF JEWISH INTEREST IN MACEDONIA

BITOLA—Located at the edge of wild mountain country near the Greek border, Bitola (formerly known as Monastir), was once a colorful—if impoverished—center of Sephardic Jewry, one of the major Jewish settlements in the Balkans. The Balkan Wars followed by World War I laid waste to much of the town. Jews remained very poor and lived in three ghettos, or *mahallas,* which have left few traces. About 3,350 Jews lived in Bitola on the eve of World War II; fewer than 100 survived deportation.

The Bitola Jewish cemetery, founded in 1497, is one of the oldest if not the oldest Jewish cemetery in the Balkans. It was abandoned and left to ruin after World War II. A civic campaign to restore it got under way in 1997, to coincide with the 500th anniversary of its foundation, and student groups have worked to clear vegetation and clean the stones. About a thousand tombstones—horizontal as in the Sephardic tradition—remain in place, but most are heavily eroded and illegible. Enclosed by a wall, they rise up a steep hillside in the northeast part of the town. Entry is at the bottom of the hill, through a big gate with an arched entrance flanked by two arched windows. Here there is a small, one-room Jewish museum and memorial to the annihilated community.

SKOPJE—Flattened by an earthquake in 1963, Skopje today is an almost totally modern city. The tiny Jewish community maintains a communal center, with a new little synagogue on its top floor. A commemorative marker stands on the spot of the former Jewish quarter, and in 2005 the cornerstone was laid there for an ambitious Holocaust museum and educational complex, which is being built thanks to a far-reaching property restitution agreement by the Macedonian government that also includes restitution of heirless property. The municipal cemetery has a small Jewish section, where there is also a Holocaust memorial. *(Jewish community: Borka Taleski 24. Tel: +389-2/321-4799, fax: +389-2/321-4880. E-mail: ezrm@telekabel.net.mk)*

STOBI—Stobi was an important ancient Roman commercial center near today's town of Gradsko. Archaeologists have found traces of two synagogues, one on top of the other; one dates from the second or third century and the other from the fourth century. The finds include a well-preserved floor mosaic with Jewish symbolism and a column from the third century bearing an inscription in Greek describing the construction of a synagogue here by one Claudius Tiberius Polycharmos. (The pillar is in the Ethnographic Museum in Belgrade, and a copy of it is in Belgrade's Jewish Historical Museum.)

MONTENEGRO

MONTENEGRO MEANS "BLACK MOUNTAIN"—AN APT DESCRIPTION. THIS SMALL, mountainous, and extremely rugged region became independent in 2006, after splitting off from Serbia. There is little Jewish heritage here. The two main sites are Duklja and Ulcinj.

DUKLJA–In 1960, archaeologists excavating this ancient Roman trade center near the Montenegrin capital, Podgorica, unearthed a Jewish grave dating to the late third or early fourth century. The tomb contained two skeletons and was decorated with Jewish symbols including a seven-branched menorah, birds, and floral motifs, traces of frescoed vines, a six-pointed star and the Sukkoth etrog fruit.

ULCINJ–This ancient seafront town near the Albanian border is the place where the false Messiah Shabbetai Zevi died in 1676. One of the most startling and, for better or worse, most influential Jewish figures of his age, Zevi was born in 1626 in Smyrna (now Izmir, Turkey). He became deeply involved in mysticism and the Kabbalah and in 1665 proclaimed that he was the Messiah. In the superstitious, war-ravaged times in which he lived, he obtained an immense, enthusiastic following all over Europe and the east. In the end, though, after a confrontation with the sultan at Constantinople, Zevi converted to Islam to save his life. Many of his followers also converted. Zevi took the name Mehamed Effendi, got the ceremonial title of Kapici-Baschi, or Royal Keeper of the Gate, and eventually was banished to Ulcinj, where he died after ten years of exile. What is believed to be his tomb is in the yard of an Albanian Muslim family, whose ancestors have kept guard over it for more than 300 years but bar access to outsiders. The room where Zevi is believed to have lived out his final years is still preserved in the Ulcinj fortress.

RESOURCES ON THE WESTERN BALKANS

Locally published books, pamphlets, and other material, some of it in English, can sometimes be found. They include:

- *Jews in Yugoslavia.* Zagreb: Muzejski Prostor, 1989
- Karac, Zlatko. *Synagogue Architecture in Croatia in the Age of Historicism.* Zagreb: Museum of Arts and Crafts, 2000
- Klein, Rudolf. *The Synagogue in Subotica.* Subotica: Grafoprodukt, 2003
- Sosberger, Pavle. *Sinagoge u Vojvodini: pomenica minulog vremena.* Novi Sad: Prometej, 1998

WEBSITES:

- www.heritageabroad.gov — Surveys of Jewish heritage sites in Slovenia and Croatia
- www.jewishgen.org/cemetery/e-europe/yugoslavia.html — Jewish cemeteries

ADDITIONAL PUBLICATIONS:

- Cohen, Mark. *Last Century of a Sephardic Community: The Jews of Monastir, 1839–1943.* New York: Foundation for the Advancement of Sephardic Studies and Culture, 2003
- Kis, Danilo. *Gardens, Ashes.* New York: Harcourt Brace Jovanovich, 1975
- Serotta, Edward. *Survival in Sarajevo: How a Jewish Community Came to the Aid of Its City.* Vienna: Brandstätter, 1994
- Schwartz, Stephen. *Sarajevo Rose: A Balkan Jewish Notebook.* London: Saqi Books, 2005
- West, Rebecca. *Black Lamb & Grey Falcon: A Journey through Yugoslavia.* New York: Macmillan, 1942; reprints 1977 and 2007

BULGARIA

CURRENT POPULATION: 7.4 MILLION
JEWISH POPULATION BEFORE WORLD WAR II: APPROX. 50,000
JEWISH POPULATION TODAY: APPROX. 5,000

A LITTLE HISTORY

A LAND OF TOWERING MOUNTAINS AND ROLLING HILLS SITUATED ON THE BLACK Sea along the main overland route between the Middle East and Europe, the Balkan territory now known as Bulgaria has been home to Jews since ancient times. Jewish merchants are believed to have arrived with the Phoenicians as early as the first and second centuries B.C.E., and later Jewish settlements are known to have developed in the second and third centuries C.E., when the region was under Roman domination.

Jewish settlement grew after the founding of the Bulgarian state in 681. Jews seem to have been welcome in Bulgarian lands in the early Middle Ages and were not harshly persecuted. Tsar Ivan Alexandar (1331–1371) even married a Jewish woman named Sarah, who took the name Theodora when she converted to Christianity and became queen. At the time of the Turkish conquest of Bulgaria in 1396, Jewish communities existed in Sofia, Plovdiv, Stara Zagora, Pleven, Jambol, Nikopol, Silistra, and Vidin.

Much of the medieval Jewish population in Bulgaria followed the Byzantine or Romaniote rite. Under Ottoman Turkish rule, Jews from elsewhere in Europe and the Ottoman Empire settled in Bulgaria and soon became driving forces in the local economy and international trade. The Ottoman rulers granted Jews special privileges in an effort to encourage commerce, allowing them to own land, build synagogues, and take up once barred professions. Several Jews are known to have held positions in government.

In the 14th and 15th centuries, Ashkenazic Jewish refugees arrived from Hungary, Germany, and France. Among them was Rabbi Sholom of Nitra (now Slovakia), who founded a noted yeshivah in the fortress town of Vidin on the Danube River. Following the expulsion of Jews from Spain in 1492, as many as 30,000 or more Sephardic Jewish refugees settled in Bulgaria. By the end of the 16th century, all but a small fraction of Bulgaria's Jews followed the Sephardic rite. Among the Spanish refugees was the great scholar and mystic Joseph Caro, who lived in Nikopol from 1523 to 1536. There he founded a yeshivah and worked on his influential treatise on the Talmud, *The House of Joseph.* Caro eventually moved to Palestine, where in 1567 he published an abbreviated version of his Talmudic commentaries and codification of Jewish law, called the *Shulchan Aruch.* A step-by-step guide to being a Jew, the book was widely circulated through the then new art of printing and became one of the most influential Jewish books ever published.

The Ottoman Turks ruled Bulgaria until their defeat in the Russo-Turkish War of 1877–78. Partly because the Jews were seen as pro-Turkish, anti-Jewish violence erupted in provincial towns after the Turks withdrew. The Treaty of Berlin in 1878, which paved the way to an independent Bulgaria, Serbia, and Romania, included a clause—insisted upon by Western powers—that guaranteed civil equality for the Jews. Nonetheless, anti-Semitism intensified over the following decades, and Jews were barred from various lines of work, including the civil service. Zionism became a highly influential movement within Bulgarian Jewry.

Before World War II, about 50,000 Jews lived in Bulgaria, more than half of them in the capital, Sofia. During the war, Bulgaria allied itself with the Nazis and enacted tough anti-Semitic legislation. Among other things, Jewish valuables were confiscated, and Jews were forced to wear a yellow badge; they were forbidden to use main roads, and they could not carry out trade or move from one town to another. In the early days of World War II, the Bulgarian port of Varna served as a major route of escape for Jewish refugees illegally fleeing Eastern Europe for Palestine via the Black Sea. This was virtually halted, however, when one ship, the *Salvador,* sank in the Sea of Marmora in December 1940, killing 204 people.

The planned deportation of Bulgarian Jews to Nazi death camps began in 1943. Between March 4 and March 11, Bulgarian soldiers rounded up more than 11,300 Jews from Yugoslav and Greek territories that had been annexed by Bulgaria, loaded them into boxcars, and shipped them to Treblinka (see pp. 26–27). More boxcars were already lined up to receive a first wave of 8,500 Jews

Members of a Zionist youth movement work the fields of their Bulgarian farm in 1938.

from Bulgaria proper. Word of the imminent deportations leaked out, however, and protests by some politicians and Orthodox Church figures, led by parliamentary vice president Dimitar Peshev, forced the government to halt the action at the last minute. King Boris III then told the Nazi leadership that he needed the Jews as road-construction workers. He moved Jewish men aged 18 to 65 into labor camps, but refused to deport Jews or hand them over to the Nazis.

Nearly 50,000 Bulgarian Jews survived the war. Between 1944 and 1951, all but a few thousand immigrated to Israel. Under the communist regime, religious Jewish life practically came to a halt. All but a handful of synagogues were demolished or converted for secular use; most Jewish cemeteries, too, were destroyed. Jews were not actively persecuted, but they were regarded strictly as an ethnic, not a religious, group. The rate of intermarriage was high. Bulgarian Jewry had formal, communist-dominated Jewish organizations, but these were culturally, not religiously, oriented, and there was no opportunity for Jewish education.

Since the fall of communism, Jewish life in Bulgaria has seen a dramatic revival on all fronts. Bulgaria and Israel resumed diplomatic relations that had been broken after the Six Day War in 1967, contacts and cooperation with international Jewish organizations and Jewish communities in neighboring countries have blossomed, and a wide range of educational, cultural, religious, and social service programs have been put in place. The communist-era Cultural and Educational Society of Jews in Bulgaria was replaced by the Shalom organization, founded in 1990, whose 19 branches serve as a coordinating network for Jewish activities throughout the country. Bulgaria is now served by a community rabbi, based in Sofia, and Chabad is also active. The restoration of synagogues in Sofia and Plovdiv, and the opening of a full-service Jewish community center in the capital, symbolize the Jewish renewal.

JEWISH HERITAGE IN BULGARIA

About a dozen synagogue buildings around the country are listed as historic monuments, but only two—in Sofia and Plovdiv—still function as houses of worship. Several have been restored for secular used, but others are empty or in ruins. A number of Jewish cemeteries also remain. Jewish communities attempt to maintain cemeteries in their districts, but most around the country are in neglected condition and subject to vandalism.

TIPS ON VISITING

Sofia has the most important sites, but Bulgaria is a small country, and most other places, including Plovdiv and Samokov, are within easy reach.

SOFIA

(Bulgarian: Sofiya)

An ancient city on a high plain ringed by mountains, the Bulgarian capital is a mixture of drab communist modernity, late 19th-century charm, and 21st-century glitz, studded throughout with historic churches and striking remnants of the 500-year Ottoman occupation.

The city lies almost in the geographical center of the Balkan Peninsula, and Jewish presence here dates back to the Byzantine period, long before the Turkish conquest in 1396. In the 17th century, many Jews in Sofia—as in the rest of Bulgaria—fell under the spell of the false Messiah Shabbetai Zevi. Two of Zevi's disciples, Samuel Primo and Nathan of Gaza were particularly active in the city.

Before World War II, about 27,700 Jews lived in Sofia—more than half of the country's Jewish population. Most were involved in trade; many owned their own shops or businesses, and there were also a few wealthy industrialists. Zionism was an influential movement, and the city boasted a rich Jewish cultural, intellectual, social, and religious life. Most of today's 5,000 or so Jews still live in the capital. The community is mainly Sephardic. Many older members still speak Ladino, and various cultural and other initiatives aim at preserving and enriching the Ladino and Sephardic heritage. The five-story Beit Ha-am building at Stambolijski 50 houses a Jewish community center, kosher facilities, function rooms and the offices of various Jewish organizations. (A second community center was opened in 2006 at Ekzarkh Jozef 50.) There is also a Jewish school and old-age home.

Sofia's magnificent Great Synagogue is the only surviving synagogue out of a dozen that stood in the city before World War II. It was designed by the architect Friedrich Gruenanger and built between 1905 and 1909, right in the heart of the capital, at the corner of George Washington and Ekzarkh Jozef streets near the 16th-century Banya Bashi Mosque. Believed to be the largest Sephardic synagogue in Europe, it seats 1,200 and was built in a lavish, Byzantine-Moorish style that fits right in with many of the other grand buildings in downtown Sofia. Small domes and cupola-topped towers surround a huge, rather flat central dome that soars above colorfully striped outer walls pierced by tall, thin windows topped by horseshoe arches. Inside, ornate designs in vivid shades of teal, blue, red, and gold cover the walls and highlight the interior arches of the octagonal sanctuary, and an enormous chandelier hangs from the inner dome.

The synagogue's dedication on September 9, 1909, was a lavish affair attended by Bulgaria's political elite. Tsar Ferdinand cut a ribbon in front of the Ark to formally inaugurate the building, and the prime minister, other government VIPs, and local bishops were in the crowd. As a choir sang, a procession of rabbis bore Torah scrolls into the sanctuary and placed them in the Ark. Community officials lit the eternal lamp, and the congregation recited the *shehechiyanu*, a prayer of thanksgiving. The chief rabbi then addressed the congregation with a sermon that stressed the Jewish community's sense of belonging in the city and the country:

> *This synagogue will connect us with the past generations and will tell of us to the future ones. Let us direct our prayers to the Almighty from our hearts and souls, so that there can be cooperation and tranquillity, brotherhood and peace. May God bless this land and*

The interior of the Great Synagogue in Sofia, the only synagogue in the city left standing after World War II

> *its sovereign, so that our country will grow from strength to strength. May God bless this land which we love dearly, for the good of all Bulgarians, in whose sufferings and joys we take an active part. Let this beautiful city blossom.*

The synagogue was damaged during World War II when the Allies bombed Sofia in 1944, and the community's priceless Judaica library was destroyed. After the war, the communist authorities tried to nationalize the building and turn it into a concert hall. This attempt failed, but the sanctuary stood filled with scaffolding for nearly 30 years. Finally, in the 1990s, large-scale restoration took place, financed by international foundations and individual donors, and the synagogue was rededicated with a gala ceremony in 1996. An upper floor of the complex houses Sofia's Jewish Museum, which was established in 1992. Its exhibits trace the history of Jews in Bulgaria and also tell the story of the Holocaust and the rescue of Bulgarian Jewry during World War II.

The Jewish cemetery occupies part of the main municipal cemetery in the Orlandovtzi District in the north of the city (at the end of the No. 2 tram line). Dating to the 19th century, it has many simple grave markers, some including laminated portraits of the deceased.

Addresses of Note in Sofia

- Shalom Organization of the Jews in Bulgaria: Stambolijski 50. Tel: +359-2/400-6301. www.shalom.bg. Kosher food is available.
- Great Synagogue and Jewish Museum: Ekzarkh Jozef 16. Tel: +359-2/983-1440. E-mail: jewishmuseum@shalom.bg or www.sofiasynagogue.com
- Chabad: Stara Planina 38. www.chabad-bulgaria.org. Kosher food is available.

ELSEWHERE IN BULGARIA

BURGAS—The synagogue in this Black Sea port and resort center has been well preserved and is currently being used as an art gallery. Designed in the Moorish style, perhaps by the same architect who designed the Great Synagogue in Sofia, it was built at the turn of the 20th century. It retains decorated horseshoe arches on its facade, and two short domed towers. The small local Jewish community uses the building next door as its community center.

KARNOBAT—One of the country's largest and best preserved Jewish cemeteries spreads out on a slope outside this town in southeast Bulgaria. Established as early as the 16th century, it was in use for about 300 years. Bulgarian and Israeli experts have carried out extensive research on the site in recent years. Thanks partly to international interest in the cemetery, the Shalom Organization was able to thwart plans to build a highway across it.

KJUSTENDIL—A museum honoring Dimitar Peshev, the Bulgarian politician who spearheaded the rescue of Bulgarian Jews during World War II, was opened in 2002 in the house in this town near the Macedonian border where Peshev was born in 1894. *(Dimitar Peshev House Museum: Tsar Simeon 11. Tel: +359-78/551-811)*

PASARDJIK—Jews settled here after their expulsion from Spain, and tombstones dating from the 17th century have been found in the Jewish cemetery. There are two beautiful mid-19th-century synagogues; the larger one, whose walls are covered with decorative paintings, is used as a warehouse, and the other as a coffee shop.

PLOVDIV—The picturesque Old Town of Bulgaria's second largest city is a treasure-house of Turkish and characteristic Balkan architecture: Medieval mosques thrust slim minarets into the sky alongside a labyrinth of cobbled streets shaded by charming overhanging buildings. There are also some important ancient Roman ruins—among them evidence documenting a Jewish settlement in Plovdiv nearly 2,000 years ago. These include a mosaic floor and panels depicting menorahs from a synagogue dating to 290 C.E.

Plovdiv was long one of the main trading centers on the overland route between Europe and the Middle East, and Jews maintained a continuous presence here as artisans and merchants, at least from Byzantine times. More than 5,000 Jews lived here on the eve of World War II. Today, with about 400 members, its Jewish community is the second largest in Bulgaria.

Plovdiv's beautiful synagogue, the so-called Zion Synagogue, is the only synagogue in the country besides that in Sofia that still functions as a house of worship. Built in the late 19th century, it underwent a full-scale restoration completed in 2003. Outwardly nondescript, the synagogue stands almost surrounded by new housing blocks at Tsar Kaloyan 13. The sanctuary is a glorious burst of color. All surfaces are covered in elaborate, oriental-style floral and geometric designs in rich shades of green, blue, cream, brown, and rose. Banks of fluffy, stylized clouds edge a starry sky painted on the ceiling, and bands of sinuous color outline the arched windows. An exquisite Venetian chandelier hangs from the small central dome. Slim columns flank the Aron ha Kodesh, which is topped by the Ten Commandments set within a complex gilded frame. *(Jewish community: Hristo G. Danov 20. Tel: +359-32/632–149)*

ROUSSE–This Danube River port in northeast Bulgaria was the home of Nobel Prize–winning author Elias Canetti. The Ashkenazic synagogue has been restored and is now a Jewish community center with a small prayer room. The local Jewish community sold the site of the Sephardic synagogue to raise money for the reconstruction. *(Jewish community: Pl. Ivan Vazoz 4. Tel: +359-82/270-540)*

SAMOKOV–This small, sleepy town in the forested foothills of the Rila Mountains 40 miles south of Sofia has a pleasant center whose most striking buildings are a mosque and a synagogue, both dating from the 19th century.

Jews settled here in the 17th century. By the mid-19th century, the community numbered more than 130 Jewish families. They owned quarries, leatherworks and other businesses, and many were very prosperous. The wealthy Jewish banking family, the Ariehs, financed the construction of the synagogue, one of the oldest remaining in Bulgaria, in the 1850s.

Today sadly derelict, its windows boarded up, the synagogue stands in a walled yard surrounded by the low houses of the former Jewish quarter. Considered a typical example of neobaroque Balkan Revival architecture, it is listed as a historic monument. The building was restored in the early 1970s to serve as a local museum, but it was gutted by fire in 1975. Nonetheless, some of the distinctive decoration still survives. On the main facade, a row of tall, arched ground-floor windows is topped by a row of elegant oval windows, once enclosed by wrought-iron grilles. Traces of sinuous red, black, and blue frescoes still wind like vines around the window frames. The Hebrew inscription above the entryway is also still visible, as are some flaking paintings on interior walls. There is no Jewish community in Samokov today, but the Sofia Jewish community, which owns the building, would like to restore it as a culture center and Jewish museum.

In a walled garden next door to the synagogue, the Museum of the Jewish Home has been established in the Sarafina House, the elegant residence of a prosperous 19th-century Jewish family.

SILISTRA—Rabbi Eliezer Papo, an influential expert on Jewish law and ethics who was born in Sarajevo in 1785, was buried in the Jewish cemetery here near the Danube River after his death in a cholera epidemic in the 1820s. His tomb is a place of pilgrimage, and a new monument, separated from the other graves by a fence, was erected to him in 1998. A mikvah (ritual bath) was also built there recently, for the use of pilgrims.

VARNA—Two synagogues survive in Bulgaria's third largest city, a major Black Sea port. Both have been returned to Jewish communal ownership, and both are listed as historic monuments. The small Ashkenazic synagogue, long used as a sports center, stood empty for some years but has been undergoing restoration. The larger Sephardic synagogue, built in an ornate Moorish-Gothic style in 1890 (it was the first synagogue built in Bulgaria after independence) was also used as a sports facility but has stood empty and abandoned now for more than a decade. Plans have been made to restore it, but so far they have proved unsuccessful. *(Jewish community: Musala 7. Tel: +359-52/612-653)*

VIDIN—The once magnificent synagogue here stands roofless and in ruinous condition; it suffered serious damage during an earthquake in 1976 and was then left to crumble. Some decorative elements remain, including arched windows, two small towers, and a big ornamental arch, supported by slim columns, on the projecting facade. The Jewish cemetery has suffered several incidents of vandalism. It has horizontal tombs with richly carved epitaphs. The oldest Jewish tombstone in Bulgaria, dating from the second century C.E., was found here.

RESOURCES ON BULGARIA

WEBSITES:

- www.shalom.bg — Website of the umbrella organization of Bulgarian Jewry
- www.heritage.hit.bg — Photos and information on sites of Jewish heritage in Bulgaria
- www.jewishgen.org/cemetery/e-europe/bulgaria.html — Jewish cemeteries in Bulgaria
- www.peshev.org — Website dedicated to Dimitar Peshev

BOOKS:

- Bar-Zohar, Michael. *Beyond Hitler's Grasp: The Heroic Rescue of Bulgaria's Jews.* Cincinnati, OH: Adams Media Corp., 1998
- Canetti, Elias. *The Memoirs of Elias Canetti: The Tongue Set Free, The Torch in My Ear, The Play of the Eyes.* New York: Farrar, Straus and Giroux, 1999

GLOSSARY

Aron ha Kodesh (Holy Ark)—The often highly decorated niche or cabinet at the eastern wall of the synagogue where the Torah scrolls are kept

Ashkenazic—Jews and their traditions originating in Germany and Eastern and Central Europe; from Ashkenaz, the medieval Hebrew name for Germany

Baroque—An artistic and architectural style in the 17th and 18th centuries characterized by curving lines, sculpture, niches, and other solid but lush ornamentation, all of whose diverse elements fit into a whole. The later, more fancifully decorative baroque style is called rococo.

Bet ha Midrash—Study house; a room or building where people gather to study the Torah and religious commentaries

Bet Hayyim—Literally, in Hebrew, "house of the living"; a Jewish cemetery (also, **Bet Olam**, or House of Eternity)

Bimah—The platform from which the Torah is read in the synagogue

Blood Libel—The slanderous accusation that Jews use human blood for ritual purposes, specifically in the preparation of matzo at Passover. Often used as a pretext for persecution

Ceremonial Hall—Also called mortuary or pre-burial hall; building often found at Jewish cemeteries where the dead are prepared for burial and (sometimes) funeral services held

Chabad Lubavitch—A Hasidic movement that stresses study and intellectualism as well as spiritual fulfillment. The Lubavitch rebbe Menachem Mendel Schneerson (1902–1994), who became Chabad leader in 1950, encouraged his followers to reach out to the Jewish world in general to bring Jews back to Orthodoxy. Chabad outreach programs have become highly organized and widespread.

Cohen—A descendant of the priestly house of Aaron, the brother of Moses

Genizah—Cache or depository of worn out prayer books and other documents, often hidden away

Ghetto—An enclosed area for Jews, separated from the rest of a town or city. The word comes from the Venetian dialect for "foundry," because the Jewish section of Venice was located on the site of an old foundry.

Glatt Kosher— Informal term for the very strictest standard of kosher observance

Halakhah—Jewish legal or ethical rules of behavior and life

Hasidism—A Jewish religious revival movement founded in the 18th century in western Ukraine that focused on prayer and spirituality rather than scholarship

Haskalah—The Jewish Enlightenment; the movement from the mid-18th to late 19th century that spread modern, Western European ideas among Jews who until then followed strict Orthodox traditions

Kippah—A yarmulke or skullcap

Klezmer—East European traditional Jewish music

Kosher—Ritually clean; generally refers to food prepared according to Jewish dietary laws

Kvittel—A small slip of paper left at the tomb of a great rabbi or sage on which a prayer or supplication is written

Ladino—The Jewish language derived from Spanish spoken by Sephardic Jews

Maggid—A popular preacher

Maskilim—Followers of the Jewish Enlightenment

Mazzevah—Gravestone in the form of an upright, usually rectangular slab

Menorah—The seven-branched candelabrum that, along with the six-pointed Star of David, is the most important, distinctly Jewish symbol

Mezuzah—A small parchment scroll containing two passages from the Book of Deuteronomy affixed to the right-hand doorposts of Jewish homes; often contained in a decorated case

Mikvah—The ritual bath, using flowing water

Minyan—The quorum of ten adult Jewish men required for a religious service

Mitnagdim—Traditional Orthodox Jews who opposed Hasidism

Moorish—Flamboyant architectural and decorative style popular with synagogue designers in the late 19th and early 20th centuries, incorporating Islamic and Middle Eastern elements such as horseshoe arches, spires resembling minarets, and complicated arabesques

Neoclassic—An art and architectural style of the late 18th and early 19th centuries in which simple lines replaced the frenzied ornamentation of the rococo

Neolog—The moderate Reform Judaism movement in Hungary that became strong in the 19th century

Ohel—Literally, "tent": A small building or protective shelter built around the tomb of a revered rabbi or sage

Orthodoxy—Strictly traditional Jewish observance

Rabbi—Today, the ordained leader of a Jewish congregation. Traditionally, a rabbi was a teacher or sage, a scholar who had completed studies at a yeshivah and was thus well versed in Jewish law and able to play a leading role in the Jewish community.

Rebbe—A Hasidic rabbi, often at the head of a devoted court of followers and disciples. Rebbes are often believed to be direct intermediaries with God and to be able to work miracles.

Reform Judaism—Judaism modified and modernized to fit the conditions of contemporary life. (It developed in the early 19th century, associated with the Jewish Enlightenment movement.) Innovations include the adaptation of clothing to modern styles, the use of local languages in services and for sermons and the use of an organ and choir in the synagogue.

Sephardic—Jews who trace their ancestry and traditions to Spain or Portugal; derived from Sepharad, the Hebrew word for Spain

Shoah—In Hebrew, "catastrophe"; the Holocaust

Shtetl—Means "little town" in Yiddish; an Eastern European Jewish small-town community

Talmud—Two great collections of Hebrew and Aramaic writings encompassing commentaries, debates, discussions, and explanations by numerous scholars and rabbis on the entire sphere of Jewish life, teaching, and belief

Tefillin—Small leather boxes containing scriptural verses that are strapped to a man's forehead and left arm during morning prayers

Torah—Literally, "law"; the handwritten parchment scroll containing the Pentateuch, or the first five books of Moses, regarded as the written Jewish law. Torah can also mean the entire corpus of traditional Jewish scriptures and teachings.

Tzaddik—An extremely pious, just man, revered for his saintliness and wisdom and believed to have a special relationship with God; often refers to a Hasidic rebbe

Yeshivah—An advanced Jewish religious school, particularly one dedicated to the study of the Talmud

Yiddish—The language traditionally spoken by Ashkenazic Jews, derived from German and written in Hebrew characters

Yiddishkeit—The world of Jewish (particularly Ashkenazic) traditions

Zionism—The movement that developed in the late 19th century, particularly through the writings of Theodore Herzl, advocating a Jewish return to the Holy Land

SELECTED RESOURCES

Hundreds of books, fiction and nonfiction—and hundreds if not thousands of websites—deal with Jewish history, culture, and heritage in Eastern and Central Europe. This small selection only skims the surface, but it includes many resources that were useful in preparing this book.

Websites

- www.aejm.org—Association of European Jewish Museums
- www.bh.org.il/communities/index.aspx—Portal of the Beth Hatefusoth Database of Jewish Communities
- www.bh.org.il/swj/index.php—Website accompanying the book *Synagogues without Jews* by Rivka and Ben-Zion Dorfman
- www.centropa.org—*Central Europe Center for Research and Documentation,* an online resource and database on Jewish life in Eastern and Central Europe
- www.haruth.com—Portal to numerous websites on Jewish history and heritage
- www.heritageabroad.gov—U.S. Commission for the Preservation of America's Heritage Abroad, includes extensive surveys of Jewish heritage sites in several countries
- www.isjm.org—International Survey of Jewish Monuments
- www.jewishgen.org—Jewish genealogy clearinghouse portal
- www.jewishgen.org/cemetery/e-europe/—Most comprehensive website on Jewish cemeteries in many countries
- www.jewish-heritage-europe.org—Clearinghouse for current information on Jewish heritage in Europe
- www.jewishvirtuallibrary.org—Portal to many articles and web resources
- www.jewishwebindex.com—Website with extensive information on Jewish genealogy around the world
- www.kosherdelight.com—Portal to numerous links on synagogues and kosher facilities
- www.shtetlinks.jewishgen.org—Extremely useful portal to websites dedicated to individual towns in a number of countries
- www.ushmm.org—U.S. Holocaust Memorial Museum website
- www.yadvashem.org—Holocaust memorial and museum center in Jerusalem

Books

- Buber, Martin. *Tales of the Hasidim,* 1947. (Reprint New York: Schocken, 1975.)
- Cohen, Israel. *Travels in Jewry*. New York: E.P. Dutton & Co., 1953.

- Davidowicz, Lucy S. *The War Against the Jews 1933–45*. London: Penguin, 1975.
- ———, ed. *The Golden Tradition: Jewish Life and Thought in Eastern Europe.* New York: Schocken Books, 1967.
- De Lange, Nicholas. *Atlas of the Jewish World.* Oxford: Phaidon, 1984.
- Dorfman, Rivka and Ben-Zion. *Synagogues without Jews.* Philadelphia: Jewish Publication Society, 2000.
- *Encyclopaedia Judaica.* Jerusalem: Keter, 1972.
- Frank, Ben G. *A Travel Guide to Jewish Europe,* 1992 (Reprint Gretna: Pelican, 1996.)
- Gruber, Ruth Ellen. *Upon the Doorposts of Thy House: Jewish Life in East-Central Europe, Yesterday and Today.* New York: John Wiley & Sons, 1994.
- ———. *Virtually Jewish: Reinventing Jewish Culture in Europe.* Berkeley: University of California Press, 2002.
- Gruber, Samuel D. *Synagogues.* New York: MetroBooks, 1999.
- Gusky, Jeffrey. *Silent Places: Landscapes of Jewish Life and Loss in Eastern Europe.* New York: Overlook Duckworth, 2003.
- Krinsky, Carol Herselle. *Synagogues of Europe.* Dover Publications, 1996.
- Lowenthal, Marvin, *A World Passed By: Scenes and Memories of Jewish Civilization in Europe and North Africa.* New York: Harper & Brothers, 1933.
- McCagg, William O., Jr. *A History of the Habsburg Jews 1670–1918.* Bloomington: Indiana University Press, 1989.
- Sack, Sallyann Amdur, and Gary Mokotoff. *Avotaynu Guide to Jewish Genealogy.* Bergenfield, NJ: Avotaynu, 2004.
- Schwartzman, Arnold. *Graven Images: Graphic Motifs of the Jewish Gravestones.* New York: Abrams, 1993.
- Semo, Marc et al. *The Cultural Guide to Jewish Europe (Le guide culturel des Juifs d'Europe).* San Francisco: Chronicle Books, 2004 (Paris: Editions du Seuill, 2004).
- Valley, Eli. *The Great Jewish Cities of Central and Eastern Europe.* Northvale, NJ: Jason Aronson, Inc., 1999.
- Wiesel, Elie. *Souls on Fire* and *Somewhere a Master.* London: Penguin, 1984.
- Young, James. *The Texture of Memory: Holocaust Memorials and Meaning.* New Haven: Yale University Press, 1993.
- Zborowski, Mark, and Elizabeth Herzog. *Life is with People.* New York: Schocken, 1952.

INDEX

Boldface indicates illustrations.